EMPIRICAL STUDIES
OF
PSYCHOANALYTICAL THEORIES

Volume 1

EMPIRICAL STUDIES
OF
PSYCHOANALYTICAL THEORIES

Volume 1

edited by

Joseph Masling
State University of New York at Buffalo

THE ANALYTIC PRESS
1983

Distributed by
LAWRENCE ERLBAUM ASSOCIATES, PUBLISHERS
Hillsdale, New Jersey   London

Distributed solely by
Lawrence Erlbaum Associates, Publishers, Inc.

The Analytic Press
365 Broadway
Hillsdale, N.J. 07642

Library of Congress Cataloging in Publication Data
Main entry under title:

Empirical studies of psychoanalytical theories.

  Bibliography: v. 1, p.
  Includes index.
  1. Psychoanalysis—Research.   I. Masling, Joseph M.
RC506.E46   1983   150.19'5   82-11536
ISBN 0-88163-000-4 (v. 1)

Printed in the United States of America
10 9 8 7 6 5 4 3 2

Contents

Preface

The purpose of these volumes is to present comprehensive, detailed descriptions of empirical testing of psychoanalytic hypotheses. It will be apparent to any reader that psychoanalytic theories have been extremely heuristic, although the misconception that they are inimical to experimental testing is still widely held. Despite a vast amount of experimental work, those who write about psychoanalysis present their material, almost without exception, *ex cathedra,* offering their views with no more substantial base than clinical evidence.

This exclusive reliance on clinical data to justify sweeping, generalized conclusions either ignores the experimental literature or dismisses it as irrelevant. Evidence secured from the clinical interaction clearly constitutes data of a particular sort, data which are the very foundation of psychoanalytic theories. But clinical data are always noticed, collected, integrated, and interpreted by one person who functions simultaneously as a participant in the therapy process and observer of it. This dual role both aids and hinders: it aids because the therapist observes the data in a natural setting and it hinders because the therapist may be rendered insensitive to some issues because of preconceived ideas or personal limitations.

Clinical data are scarcely self-evident or convincing. The mitotic splits in psychoanalytic approaches clearly demonstrate that evidence which is convincing to one school does not impress another. Each variation of psychoanalytic thought is somehow able to generate its own evidence.

One way out of the chaos created by each individual school of psychoanalysis generating its own clinical evidence as proof of its theoretical correctness is to do what each of the contributors of these volumes has done: subject clinical hypotheses to experimental test. Contrary to the expectations of some clinicians, experimental testing does not necessarily wrench and twist psychoanalytic thought into unrecognizable shape. Lloyd Silverman's description of his subliminal activation method demonstrates that a central theme of psychoanalytic thought can be experimentally investigated without doing violence to the concepts. Further, his results also show that experimental evidence can support and confirm clinical evidence. Greenberg and Fisher's chapter support one aspect of psychoanalytic thought but report no experimental confirmation of another aspect. All the chapters in this volume and in those to follow accept the richness and insights of psychoanalytic hypotheses as well as the necessity of putting them to meaningful, appropriate experimental test. Only in this way can we resolve the disputes between competing theories. Only in this way can we separate that which is useful in psychoanalytic thought from that which is unproductive and mistaken.

Contributors to

EMPIRICAL STUDIES
OF
PSYCHOANALYTICAL THEORIES

Volume 1

Edited by
JOSEPH MASLING

Sidney J. Blatt, *Yale University School of Medicine*

Hartvig Dahl, *Downstate Medical Center, State University of New York*

Morris Eagle, *Department of Psychology, York University*

Seymour Fisher, *Upstate Medical Center, State University of New York*

Roger P. Greenberg, *Upstate Medical Center, State University of New York*

Dianna E. Hartley, *Yale University School of Medicine*

Howard Lerner, *Psychology Department, Yale University*

Harold A. Sackeim, *Department of Psychology, New York University*

Lloyd H. Silverman, *Research Center for Mental Health,
New York University*

Hans H. Strupp, *Department of Psychology, Vanderbilt University*

EMPIRICAL STUDIES
OF
PSYCHOANALYTICAL THEORIES

Volume 1

1 The Therapeutic Alliance: Its Relationship to Outcome in Brief Psychotherapy

Dianna E. Hartley, Ph.D
Yale University School of Medicine
Department of Psychiatry

Hans H. Strupp
Vanderbilt University
Department of Psychology

In writing about the psychoanalytic relationship, Freud essentially focused his attention on transference and resistance. However, in his practice, and to a lesser extent in his writing, he paid great attention to the role of friendliness and affection as "the vehicle of success in psychoanalysis [Freud, 1912/1958, p. 105]." In 1913 he wrote:

> It remains the first aim of the treatment to attach (the patient) to it and to the person of the doctor. . . . If one exhibits a serious interest in him, carefully clears away the resistances that crop up at the beginning and avoids making certain mistakes, he will of himself form such an attachment. . . . It is certainly possible to forfeit this first success if from the start one takes any standpoint other than that of sympathetic understanding [pp. 139–140].

HISTORICAL DEVELOPMENT OF THE CONCEPT OF THERAPEUTIC ALLIANCE

Although the literature on transference has always been abundant, consideration of the relationship between therapist and patient other than the transferential one has come gradually to the fore, especially in the last decade. Sterba (1934) was among the first to write of an ego-level identification with and positive attitude toward the analyst that led the patient to work toward the accomplishment of the common therapeutic tasks. Sterba held that the analyst was able to form a bond by appealing to the observing "analyst" within the patient. Freud, in 1940, took a similar position when he described the analyst and patient as banding together against the patient's neurosis in a pact based on free exploration by the patient and discretion and competent understanding by the therapist.

1

Later conceptualizations of alliance were influenced by the concurrent development of object relations theory. Beginning with Zetzel (1956), increasing attention has been paid to the notion that the therapeutic alliance, which depends to a large degree on basic trust in relating to others and the mature functioning of some part of the patient's ego, as well as on the therapist's active participation and partnership, is an essential prerequisite for the effectiveness of any therapeutic intervention. She established the concept of therapeutic alliance as a stable, realistic, cooperative aspect of the analytic relationship that protects against excessive regression and mobilizes ego resources. Her work especially influenced that of Greenson (1965, 1967; Greenson & Wexler, 1969), who emerged as the leading proponent of the working alliance and the real relationship, carefully spelling out the theoretical and clinical implications of separating these aspects of the therapeutic interaction from those aspects that are more irrational or transferential.

The Primary Importance of the Therapeutic Alliance

Tarachow (1963) pointed out that therapy begins as a relationship between two persons, one seeking the help of the other who is professionally competent to offer such help. Both experience similar human needs for relatedness; but their roles, gratifications, frustrations, and anxieties in the therapy situation are quite different. This relationship may recede into the background as therapy proceeds or it may come strongly to the fore. Whether it becomes an asset in the exploration and resolution of the patient's problems or a disruptive obstacle to the achievement of the therapeutic aims, the relationship is among the most important realities of the treatment situation. Its maintenance is essential for the continuation and progress of therapy regardless of the therapist's theoretical orientation.

Among practitioners and theorists of psychotherapy, the full significance of the alliance is gaining recognition, with a few writers giving it primary importance. Greenson (1965, 1967) conceptualized the alliance not as a technical procedure nor as a therapeutic process but as essential to both. It is vital to the success of treatment, for it makes it possible for the patient to work in the therapy situation in cooperation with the therapist. Thus, the alliance and the techniques employed can be seen as complementary change agents. Chessick (1969) asserted that, in the absence of a proper therapeutic atmosphere, no changes occur in the mental health of the patient in any kind of therapy. In a similar vein, Menninger and Holzman (1973) spoke of the alliance as a necessary condition for the amelioration of problems, though it is not curative in itself. Langs (1973) repeatedly emphasized the value of monitoring the alliance as a significant measure of the stability of the therapy and the cooperation between patient and therapist.

The other side of the coin is the danger to therapy inherent in a poor or disrupted alliance. Wolberg (1967) called the lack of a sound working relationship the most common cause of ineffective psychotherapy. Expressing the same sentiment but elaborating upon it further, both Greenson (1967) and Langs (1973) proposed that disturbances in the alliance are responsible for premature terminations, stalemates, and other failures to benefit fully from therapy. Problems in the alliance take precedence over all others; the therapist must recognize them and intervene before further progress can be made.

Although the concept of therapeutic alliance is psychoanalytic, the real relationship between therapist and patient and the importance of the working "contract" have received attention in recent years from theorists of other schools of therapy. Perhaps Rogers (1957) took the most radical relationship-oriented stand when he advocated the idea that warmth, genuineness, and understanding were the necessary and sufficient conditions for psychotherapeutic benefit. Thus, if the therapist consistently conveyed sincere feelings of caring and understanding, even severely withdrawn and regressed psychotic patients could eventually be reached (Rogers, Gendlin, Kiesler, & Truax, 1967). Like analytic theorists, Rogerians speak of warmth, empathy, respect, and genuine concern; however, analytic therapists tend to maintain their role as expert healers, whereas client-centered therapists stress equality in the relationship. At the other, more work-oriented extreme, behavioral therapists have traditionally claimed that their techniques alone carried therapeutic impact. More recently, however, at least a few behavioral theorists (Goldfried & Davison, 1976; Lazarus, 1974; Wilson & Evans, 1976) are beginning to examine seriously the effects of interpersonal dynamics between therapists and patients, although the basic model remains one of an expert who directs the therapy and makes decisions to be carried out by the patient or client.

Definition of Therapeutic Alliance

In dynamic psychotherapy, the therapeutic alliance refers to the more reasonable, rational aspects of the therapeutic relationship in contrast to more transferential elements. Although the distinction is somewhat arbitrary and there is much overlap, it is clinically and heuristically valuable to consider them separately. Although most writers make only this two-part distinction, Greenson (1967) delineates three aspects: (1) the real relationship; (2) the working alliance; and (3) transference. Bordin (1975, 1976) spoke of three factors in addition to transference: (1) development of bonds and attachments between therapist and patient; (2) mutuality of goals; and (3) agreement regarding responsibilities and explication of the relationship of these responsibilities to the patient's goals. This scheme fits into the previous one when bonds and attachments are considered as components of the real relationship and the latter two factors are included in the working alliance. The following paragraphs present the definitions of these components and the contributions of the patient, the therapist, and the treatment situation to the alliance.

The Real Relationship.   A psychotherapy relationship, first of all, is a human relationship where many human sensitivities, hurts, gratifications, abilities, and inadequacies come into play. The real relationship concept refers to the appropriate and reasonable responses of the therapist and patient to each other, within the limits of a generally accepted social interaction. Greenson (1967) described this constituent of the relationship, a prerequisite for the working alliance, as realistic, undistorted, genuine, and authentic, founded on mutual liking, trust, and respect. However, inequities are inherent, because the primary basis for the existence of this particular dyad is recognition of the patient's problem and of the therapist's ability to be helpful (Langs, 1973). Variations in the real relationship can be expected across therapies and across time in therapy. Generally, the more intensive the therapy, the stronger must be the bonds between patient and therapist (Bordin, 1975, 1976). Also during early and late phases of therapy, according to some theorists, the real relationship is more important than in the middle phase when the "as if" barrier is imposed (Greenson, 1967; Tarachow, 1963; Weiner, 1975).

The Working Alliance.   According to Greenson (1967), the working alliance should be accorded equal status with the transference in dynamic therapy. Based on rational rapport, it both depends on and reflects the ability of the dyadic partners to work purposefully together in the treatment situation. In all therapies, the alliance begins with the decision of two people to work toward the alleviation of some problem or problems experienced by the patient and is essential to both the continuation of the therapy and the advancement of its goals. The aura of authoritarianism and mystery with which the therapy and the therapist are often initially endowed is to be replaced by a feeling that the two are collaborating adults, each with certain roles and responsibilities.

Ideally, in the initial sessions, the therapist explicitly and implicitly conveys to the patient how therapy works and establishes the ground rules and boundaries that make up the treatment contract. During the process of mutual agreement about the definition of problems, the goals of therapy, and the methods to be employed, the patient develops a more accurate perception of the treatment situation and an allegiance to the contract (Weiner, 1975). The need for consensus about goals and methods cannot be overemphasized. Bordin (1976) asserted that the effectiveness of any therapeutic technique depends on the vividness with which the therapist links the technical procedures to the patient's sense of his or her difficulties and ideas of how he or she wants to change.

Before patients can follow the basic rule of uncensored self-observation and reporting, they must acquire a sense of trust in the security of the therapeutic relationship. Because of inner resistances, this sense of trust is of course limited. Nonetheless, the patient must be given a clear understanding of what is expected and why. Such explanations are part of the foundation for a firm working alliance. As a result, the patient feels free to explore thoughts, feelings, and behavior; to communicate with the therapist; and to discard unproductive modes of behavior for newer and better ones that will diminish suffering.

The Contribution of the Patient to the Alliance. Probably the most important determinants of the patient's readiness to form a sound therapeutic alliance are previous experiences with important persons in life (Strupp, 1974). People come to therapy with varying abilities to trust others and to form close relationships, and this must be taken into account when planning their treatment. Bordin (1975) considered the demands made of patients entering a therapy relationship to vary along several dimensions: the type and degree of self-observation and self-disclosure, the range and complexity of cognitive processing, the extent of dependence on or compliance with the therapist, the degree of emphasis on nonverbalized material, and the amount of ambiguity inherent in the relationship.

The first step toward involvement in therapy is recognition of one's problems and the prospect of being helped by the therapist. Therapy requires motivation to overcome problems, combined with a certain sense of helplessness (Greenson, 1965). To engage in productive therapeutic work, the patient must feel some degree of trust, confidence, and attraction to the therapist as an expert healer and as a person. Beyond this, the ability and the willingness to follow instructions, to carry out recommended therapeutic procedures, and to work with the insights that emerge are essential. In short, a patient must be open to help from another person and consciously desire to cooperate with the ground rules of the particular form of therapy offered by the therapist. Additionally, the patient must assume the role of the prime communicator and tolerate a certain amount of deprivation and pain in the interest of achieving long-term goals (Langs, 1973).

The quality of the patient's self-exploration is perhaps the most important index of the status of the working alliance. When all is well, patients report thoughts and feelings relatively openly and vividly. They can begin to observe themselves, to abstract and generalize, to oscillate between their immediate experience and more cognitive processing, and (at least to some extent) to take initiatives in their own behalf. Specific signals of something amiss in the alliance are absences and cancellations, tardiness, threats of termination, or "forgetting" agreed-upon tasks. Others may take the form of attacks, criticism, mistrust, persistent disagreement, or obstinant silence directed at the therapist. At the opposite pole are seductiveness, dependency, sexualization of the relationship, and blind submission. More subtle cues, often missed by the therapist, include undue regression, rumination, distancing, denial of problems, denial of feelings for the therapist, and manueuvers aimed at abdicating the usual therapeutic roles.

The Therapist's Contribution to the Working Alliance.   The therapist, for his or her part, contributes to the alliance in terms of personal attitudes and professional therapeutic behavior. Ideally the therapist is sensitive, tolerant, warm, logical, and straightforward with the patient. He or she is also committed to respect the patient's integrity, dignity, and human rights. The therapist's personal qualities, professional competence, and genuine concern for the patient establish the ability to help and give the patient encouragement and hope. Working hard and seriously for the patient's benefit, the therapist consistently focuses on the therapeutic task, working in an orderly but flexible way. Although pain is an inevitable concommitant of growth, he or she makes interventions in a way that preserves the patient's self-esteem and dignity and allows reasonable gratification of needs. Personal reactions are restrained in the service of the therapeutic commitment and ideally should not color the therapist's communications.

This basic stance toward the patient and the therapy is conveyed largely by the general manner in which the therapist approaches the therapeutic task. Once a mutual agreement to work toward the resolution of particular problems is reached, the therapist conveys to the patient the role he or she is to play in therapy, thus bridging the gap between the taxing demands of the therapy situation and eventual improvement. Sterba (1934) proposed that the therapist ally with the patient against the problems by using "we" and "us" and explicitly calling on the patient to cooperate. The significance of the hour is recognized by setting and maintaining a regular schedule; accordingly, the therapist misses or rearranges sessions only for very important reasons. Realistic aspects of the patient's perceptions and feelings are affirmed, including reactions to personal qualities or errors of the therapist, a stance that reinforces the patient's capacities for accurate self-observation and independent action (Greenson, 1967).

Of particular consequence are those interventions made when a disruption of the alliance occurs. At such times it is important for the therapist to focus promptly on the events surrounding the occurrence, particularly identifying and analyzing the patient's anxieties and resistances as they manifest themselves in relation to the therapist (Langs, 1973). The terms of the working alliance should be reaffirmed when necessary, although the therapist should be willing to renegotiate when reasonable grounds for doing so exist (Weiner, 1975). Myerson (1973) recommended three steps in handling disruptions: The therapist presents himself as a helpful person, clarifies how and why the current behavior is unproductive, and relates the disruption to transference feelings if appropriate.

The Contribution of the Therapy Situation. The therapy relationship is unique in being established for the purpose of gaining a better understanding of one participant in order to change troublesome patterns of thinking, feeling, or acting. In very few interpersonal situations is the relationship itself subjected to such close scrutiny. Such formal and structural properties of the situation as confidentiality, regular appointment times, the frequency of visits, and the estimated duration of treatment contribute to the working alliance. In maximally effective therapy, the therapist and the patient develop a common framework in which to view the etiology and alleviation of the problems (Luborsky, 1976). The maintenance of the alliance implies that both participants experience the therapy as satisfying their expectations in a comprehensible and productive way and that they are making efforts to meet the demands of the situation.

The Therapeutic Alliance as a Common Factor in All Psychotherapies

In recent years many psychotherapy researchers have begun to question the traditional focus on patient, therapist, and technique variables. The results of major outcome studies (Auerbach, Luborsky, & Johnson, 1972; DiLoreto, 1971; Fiske, Cartwright, & Kirtner, 1964; Mitchell, Truax, Bozarth, & Krauft, 1973; Sloane, Staples, Cristol, Yorkston, & Whipple, 1975; Strupp & Hadley, 1979) have indicated that very little of the variance (usually less than 10%) in therapy outcomes can be accounted for by the effect of any of these predictor variables. Careful and thorough reviews (Luborsky, Singer, & Luborsky, 1975) further support the notion that little is to be gained by pursuing these lines of investigation in seeking the effective ingredients of psychotherapy. The reasoning seems clear: If a large variety of treatments produce similar benefits, there must exist some common elements that are responsible for these benefits.

Jerome Frank (1974), a leader in the search for common therapeutic factors, has delineated the ingredients hypothesized to underlie all approaches. These factors include a relationship with another person that serves to foster expectations of help and to facilitate the arousal of emotions. Once this relationship is established, certain rituals are carried out that furnish (1) a rationale for the suffering and for its relief; (2) new information about the individual and the world; and (3) experiences that lead to renewed sense of success, mastery, independence, and competence. Parallels with the components of the real and working relationships just described are obvious. Frank's idea that the rationale and rituals differ and that some are more effective than others with particular dyads parallels Bordin's view that therapies differ in terms of the demands they make of the working alliance. Strupp (1972, 1973, 1974) has written about "specific" or technique factors, and "nonspecific," or broad interpersonal factors, as two components of therapy whose relative importance is yet to be determined. Nonspecific factors operate to some degree in all therapies, which differ according to the specific methods they use to produce change in patients.

Discussion of the relative importance of relationship and technique will undoubtedly continue. However, it seems unproductive to conceptualize the two as separate dimensions—relationship *versus* technique or specific *versus* nonspecific factors. Rather, the two may best be viewed as interacting processes, with the concept of the therapeutic alliance capturing this interaction. Further, this concept offers the potential for integrating research on therapist and patient personality variables, since the contribution of each is taken into account. Bordin (1976) has suggested that the capacity and willingness of both therapist and patient to undertake particular therapeutic tasks with each other will be the most important predictor of therapy outcome. Thus, one of the most promising of the common elements for future investigation is the prominence in all forms of psychotherapy of a helping relationship or alliance.

Research Related to the Concept of Therapeutic Alliance

Paralleling the recent emphasis on the alliance in the clinical and theoretical literature, researchers are becoming more cognizant of the need to examine the central role of alliance in psychotherapy. Unfortunately, as is usually the case, research lags far behind clinical evidence and theoretical advances. Only one empirical study that directly examined the therapeutic alliance and its relationship to outcome has been published. Luborsky (1976) operationalized two kinds of helping relationships and found that improvers developed positive attitudes toward therapy early, whereas nonimprovers developed negative attitudes. Very few of the dyads in his sample actually achieved mutual, responsibility-sharing relationships. Additionally, Horwitz (1974) interpreted the results of the Menninger Foundation's longitudinal study of psychoanalysis and psychotherapy to indicate that the strength of the alliance is the major determinant of successful treatment. This association seemed especially to hold among patients whose therapy was more successful than had been predicted by the research team. Although alliance was not among the variables examined in the study itself, he built an impressive theoretical argument founded on the concept of internalization to support his ideas. In his view, the therapeutic alliance must be more than simply a positive human relationship. If the patient were able to take advantage of the healing powers of the friendship available in the everyday world, he would not need psychotherapy (Horwitz, 1976).

Despite the paucity of direct evidence, most psychotherapy process research has involved at least one component that can profitably be linked to the alliance concept and yields support for the notion of an alliance–outcome association (Orlinksy & Howard, 1978).

Soon after Rogers' (1957) seminal paper, Halkides (1958) found highly significant associations between so-called facilitative conditions and success in therapy across multiple outcome measures. Despite a great proliferation of studies since that time (reviewed by Parloff, Waskow, & Wolfe, 1978) the evidence for correlation between therapy outcome and such variables as warmth, respect, and understanding is generally modest, and other variables seem to account for most of the changes occurring in therapy. This interpretation is consistent with conceptions of the therapeutic alliance. Empathy, respect, and genuineness are essential therapist qualities and play a key role in establishing the alliance but are not themselves the most important ingredients of therapy. Thus, psychotherapy researchers now face the task of delineating more carefully other factors that may enhance or detract from the effect of these interpersonal skills and attitudes.

In addition to the therapist-offered conditions, research growing out of the client-centered tradition has included several measures of the patient's role in therapy. The concepts included in the Experiencing Scale (Gendlin, 1962; Klein, Mathieu, Gendlin, & Kiesler, 1970) are similar to analytic ideas of insight, lack of resistance, and working through. At the low end of the scale, discourse is impersonal and superficial, whereas at the high end feelings are explored and deeper experience of the self is a basic referent for problem solving and self-understanding. Research utilizing the scale generally supports the notion that level of experiencing is positively correlated with outcome measured in various ways. However, a change in level of experiencing associated with outcome has not been clearly established. Results of some studies employing the Depth of Self-Exploration Scale (Truax & Carkhuff, 1967) indicate that, regardless of orientation, degree of self-exploration has a significant impact on the outcome of psychotherapy. Although research in this area has tended to confirm clinical and theoretical writings, there is not a one-to-one relationship between self-exploration and outcome, indicating that successful therapy is mediated in part by other variables. The authors of a recent review (Strassberg, Roback, D'Antonio, & Gable, 1977) concluded that with populations other than psychotics and delinquents, self-disclosure on the part of the patient is positively associated with psychotherapy outcome. Rice and her associates (Butler, Rice, & Wagstaff, 1962; Rice, 1965; Rice & Wagstaff, 1967) developed a system to measure voice quality, connotation of language, and internal focus. This scale, applied to both therapists and patients, has been shown to predict differentially successful, unsuccessful, and attrition cases in therapy. Despite these preliminary results, the evidence is fragmentary and much work needs to be done to unravel the complexities of the statistical associations.

An important determinant of exploration and outcome is the patient's perception of the locus of his or her problem. Looking only at the first session, Kirtner and Cartwright (1958) were able to discriminate patients who would improve from those who would not from the style in which they stated their problem. Those who were successful were aware of their own responsibility for change and sought to explore how they might contribute to their own difficulties; those who intellectualized, externalized, or saw things as beyond their control failed to achieve substantial changes.

Unfortunately, none of these studies included measures of both therapist and patient participation in the exploratory process and of therapy outcome. Thus, there is a dearth of evidence to indicate how participants interacted to produce a deeper and clearer understanding of the patient's difficulties.

Two areas of patient expectations that have been investigated are relevant to the therapeutic alliance: (1) hope, the expectation of success, of receiving help; and (2) expectations about the process of therapy and the patient's role. Considering the rather self-evident importance of these variables, the lack of direct observation of their association with the process and outcome of psychotherapy is striking. Little work has been done to link expectations of outcome or process to what actually happens in therapy. The most reliable evidence suggests that expectations do affect the early development of the therapy relationship and the duration of therapy. Wilkins (1973), in a rigorous review of the literature, concluded that expectancy is thus far a poorly defined concept and that initial attitudes have not been shown to influence the eventual outcome of therapy. Thus far, there is apparently no research in which therapist or patient *in*-therapy behavior has been examined with the view of assessing how attitudes toward goals and roles change or how they influence the course of therapy.

Early attrition and poor outcome in therapy are frequently attributed to misinformation or incongruent expectations (Heitler, 1976; Strupp & Bloxom, 1973). People representing all socioeconomic status groups have been shown to share similar knowledge, expectations, and misconceptions about psychotherapy (Garfield & Wolpin, 1963; Lemkau & Crocetti, 1962; Nunnally, 1961). Because psychotherapy is incompatible with the problem-solving strategies utilized by most people (Heitler, 1976), it is reasonable to assume that directly teaching prospective patients how psychotherapy works would enhance the alliance as well as communicate respect and concern to the patient. Toward this end, several procedures have been developed to facilitate involvement in the therapy process. Although the available evidence is far from conclusive, a variety of these preparatory techniques have demonstrated usefulness for facilitating a therapeutic alliance with relatively unsophisticated patients (Heitler, 1973; Orne & Wender,

1968; Strupp & Bloxom, 1973; Warren & Rice, 1972). It remains to be examined whether or not the therapist, by paying particular attention to the working alliance in early sessions, would equal the effects of extra-therapeutic preparation procedures.

Bordin (1974) pointed to premature termination as the most obvious consequence of poor therapeutic alliance. This assertion, along with Garfield's (1978) finding that most therapy terminates after a few sessions without mutual agreement, indicates that much could be learned about therapeutic relationships by examining the factors associated with premature termination. Most of the existing studies have focused on the patient's perceptions of the therapist and the duration of therapy. Patients who dropped out of therapy have complained of the inexperience or incompetence of the therapist, failure to understand their problems, or inability to help them with their difficulties (Kline, Adrian, & Spevak, 1974; Saltzman, Luetgert, Roth, Creaser, & Howard, 1976). On the other hand, perceptions of the therapist as warm, close, involved, and caring were positively related to duration of therapy (Fiester, 1977; Fiester & Rudesham, 1975; Saltzman et al., 1976).

The complexities of the therapeutic alliance obviously pose great challenges to the investigator who wishes to quantify its salient aspects. In the pioneering effort made by Luborsky (1976), patient communications were scored, and dichotomous judgments were made of the presence or absence of an alliance. Thus, an alliance was rated as existing if patients stated explicitly that they felt better, therapy was helping them, or that they felt understood by the therapist. He demonstrated the ability of this measure of alliance to predict improvement in psychotherapy.

A multidimensional study of early therapeutic relationship and outcome by Saltzman et al. (1976), although not directly addressing the concept of therapeutic alliance, is also highly relevant. They examined 10 client and 11 therapist process variables, using forms completed by the therapists and clients immediately following the sessions. The dimensions that predicted staying in therapy—high anxiety in the client, involvement of the therapist, perception of the therapist as competent and committed, active participation and acceptance of responsibility on the part of the client, mutual respect, and a sense of continuity—are closely related to the alliance as it is conceptualized in the present study. Interestingly, these process variables predicted evaluations of outcome by the therapist but not by the client.

Edward Bordin has been working toward a general theory of psychotherapy in which the working alliance furnishes the power for change in all helping relationships (Bordin, 1974, 1975). Originally, he spoke of the alliance as a necessary but not sufficient condition for psychotherapy. Later, he advanced the idea that the differential effectiveness of therapies resides not in the kinds or styles of interventions but in the *strength* of the working alliance. Although many varieties of alliance exist and may form the basis for distinguishing among therapies, they all potentially produce comparable results. It is "the strength of the working alliance (that) is the key to change in any situation where one person or group of persons turns to others as change agents [Bordin, 1976, p. 1]." Further, failures to produce change in such situations can best be understood as failures of alliance. These provocative statements served as the primary ideas to be explored in this study.

THE STUDY

As the preceding review indicates, research into the nature of the therapeutic relationship is clearly in the earliest stages of exploration, and the implications for the conduct of psychotherapy need further crystallization. The present study was designed to (1) investigate the relationship between strength of the therapeutic alliance and outcome in brief individual psychotherapy; (2) examine differences in the strength and patterning of the therapeutic alliance across time within therapy dyads defined as good outcome cases, poor outcome cases, or premature terminations; and (3) further develop and establish the psychometric properties and construct validity of the Vanderbilt Therapeutic Alliance Scale.

Based on the foregoing discussion, the simplest and most frequently reiterated statement is that the strength of the alliance is directly related to the outcome of psychotherapy. Thus it was predicted that the group mean for the strength of alliance in successfully completed cases would be the highest, in prematurely terminated cases it would be the lowest, and for completed but less successful cases it would fall between these two groups. In brief therapy, early establishment and consistent maintenance of the alliance is essential. This consideration led to differential predictions for the alliance across time within the three groups. The high outcome group was expected to begin with relatively higher alliance scores and to maintain its advantage over the entire course of therapy. Within the low outcome group, two clusters might be anticipated: Those patients who begin high and then flounder, and those who maintain low to moderate levels of alliance throughout therapy. Thus average scores for this group were expected to be lower in the last half of therapy than in the first half. For cases that terminated prematurely, consistently low scores were predicted.

Background

In the Vanderbilt University Psychotherapy Project comparing the effectiveness of professional psychotherapists with that of untrained college professor/counselors, there were 28 cases that involved a trained therapist. Each of nine experienced male therapists treated one to five patients in individual, time-limited (up to 25 sessions), twice-a-week psychotherapy, utilizing whatever techniques they would choose in their daily practices. The patients were drawn from a reasonably homogeneous population; consisting of male college students at a Southern university. All were single, in the age range of 18 to 25, and suffered from anxiety, depression, and difficulties in relating comfortably to peers, particularly females. Major screening criteria included elevated scores ($T > 60$) on scales Depression, Psychasthenia, and Social Introversion on the Minnesota Multiphasic Personality Inventory (MMPI). Prior to assignment to one of the participating therapists, patients were carefully assessed by independent clinicians with identical assessments repeated at termination and at a follow-up interview one year after intake. A comprehensive battery provided evaluations from the perspectives of the patient, the therapist, and the independent clinician. All sessions were audiotaped, and assessment and selected therapy sessions were videotaped as well. Details of the project and major outcome results have been described elsewhere (Strupp & Hadley, 1979).

For the purposes of this study, the patients were divided into three groups based on their status at the termination of therapy: (1) high outcome; (2) low outcome; and (3) premature terminators. The last group included those patients who attended 5 or fewer therapy sessions of the contracted 25. The first two groups were formed on the basis of their composite score on a number of outcome measures from various perspectives. The student's perspective was represented by his or her global rating of improvement and by gain on the three target scales of the MMPI. The therapist and clinician each completed current status rating forms at intake and termination. From these scales, the global improvement rating and gain scores effectiveness were used. Thus, each of three perspectives, patient, therapist, and observer, was represented by four measures in forming the outcome composite score. The two groups were formed by a median split on this measure.

The Vanderbilt Therapeutic Alliance Scale

The study involved two interlocking aspects: (1) the development of a scale to measure the therapeutic alliance from the perspective of clinician observers listening to taped interviews; and (2) the application of this scale in an investigation of the relationship between the alliance and outcome. Holsti (1969) states that the first essential step in a content analysis study is the careful definition of the variables. Thus, a careful and thorough review of expert opinion, theoretical statements, and previous research was the foundation for the composition of items to be included in the scale. Major sources for the items were Bordin

(1976), Greenson (1967), Langs (1976), and Luborsky (1976). The scale was constructed to take advantage of raters' clinical competence, being sufficiently sensitive to capture the quality of the patient–therapist interaction and yet not requiring such a high level of inference that a reasonable degree of agreement would be precluded.

A pilot study using five members of the Vanderbilt research team as raters established for each item acceptable levels of interrater reliability (average Ebel's $R = .78$) and ability to discriminate successfully completed from prematurely terminated cases. The scale used in the present study comprised 44 items, 18 related to the therapist, 14 to the patient, and 12 to their interaction (see Table 1.1 for a list of the items). Each item was rated on a Likert-type scale ranging from 0 (none at all) to 5 (a great deal).

Procedures of the Study

As with any measure of psychotherapy process, many questions about unit length, sampling across and within sessions, medium of presentation, and the clinical sophistication and training required of raters remain to be answered empirically. For the purposes of this project, several a priori decisions were

TABLE 1.1
Vanderbilt University Therapeutic Alliance Scale

Instructions: Rate each interview segment on all the following items.

A.   *To what extent did the therapist:*

1.   Convey the idea that he is competent to help with patients' problems?
2.   Express hope and encouragement, a belief that the patient is making (or can make) progress?
3.   Commit himself and his skills to help the patient to the fullest extent possible?
4.   Show respect, acceptance, and compassion for the patient and his problems?
5.   Focus consistently on understanding the patient with the goal of resolving his problems?
6.   Acknowledge the validity of the patient's feelings, thought, and behavior?
7.   Make sure that the patient understood the procedures of therapy and their rationale, what was asked of him and why?
8.   Make his interventions in a way that preserved the patient's self-esteem and dignity?
9.   Intrude his own life story, ideas, or values on the patient?
10.   Stimulate the patient's curiosity about himself and his world?
11.   Express his own reactions, assets, and liabilities in appropriate ways?
12.   Explore anxieties, resistances, and disturbances in the therapeutic relationship as necessary in the session?

(continued)

TABLE 1.1 (*continued*)

13. Foster undue dependency?
14. Teach the patient to observe his own behavior?
15. Make irrelevant or uncalled for comments?
16. Build a sense of mutuality by using "we" and "us"?
17. Make too early or too deep interventions?
18. Miss interventions where they appeared needed?

B. *To what extent did the patient:*

19. Express that he feels better since beginning therapy?
20. Indicate that he experiences the therapist as understanding and supporting him?
21. Seem to identify with the therapist's method of working, so that he assumed part of the therapeutic task himself?
22. Expect the therapist to change him without accepting his own responsibility for the session?
23. Make an effort to carry out therapeutic procedures suggested by the therapist and work with the insights that emerged?
24. Acknowledge that he had problems that the therapist could help him deal with?
25. Indicate a strong desire to overcome his problems?
26. Talk freely, openly, and honestly with the therapist about his thoughts, feelings, and behavior?
27. Show a willingness to explore his own contribution to his life situation?
28. Act in a hostile, attacking, or critical manner toward the therapist?
29. Act in a mistrustful or defensive manner toward the therapist?
30. Indicate a willingness to discard old behavior and thought patterns and try out new ones?
31. Become so anxious in the session that it interfered with the therapeutic task?
32. Show evidence that he has missed an appointment, come late to sessions, or hesitates to make the next appointment?

C. *The therapist and patient together:*

33. Show enthusiasm that made the session seem alive and energetic.
34. Work together in a joint effort to deal with the patient's problems.
35. Share a common viewpoint about the definition, possible causes, and potential alleviation of the patient's problems.
36. Relate in a realistic, honest, straightforward way, within the bounds of reasonable human interaction.
37. Agree upon the goals and tasks for the session.
38. Focus on the therapeutic task throughout the session, without excessive superficiality.
39. Seem to be engaged in a power struggle.
40. Express directly or indirectly the possibility of premature termination.
41. Allow the session to become ruminative, empty, or boring, without a clear trend or theme.
42. Accept their different roles and responsibilities as part of their relationship.
43. Refer back to experiences they have been through together.
44. Have awkward silences or pauses in their conversation.

made. The first, middle, and last 5-minute segments from each session were chosen to provide the raters with the best overview of the entire session. In order to sample across time in these cases, the sessions at the quartile points were examined: 0% (the first session), 25%, 50%, 75%, and 100% (the last session). Thus five sessions were used from each complete case. For dropout cases, all sessions were rated.

After the representative cases, sessions, and segments were chosen, master tapes were made by dubbing the appropriate parts of therapy interviews from the original recordings. The sessions were randomly arranged on the master tape with the exception that the same dyad did not reappear within four units. At the end of each session (15 minutes), the raters were instructed to complete a rating form. The raters, who were completely unfamiliar with the overall outcome study, had completed internships and other requirements for the Ph.D. in clinical psychology except their dissertations, and they had extensive training and supervised experience in psychoanalytic psychotherapy.

Before beginning the rating task, the raters completed a training course using tapes published by the American Academy of Psychotherapy. The training procedure called for raters to listen to 15 minutes of an interview and make independent ratings, followed by comparison and discussion of items on which there was disagreement. Both raters and the experimenter participated in these discussions. The purposes of the training procedure were (1) to familiarize the raters with the instructions, the rating instrument, and the procedures of their task; and (2) to reach a criterion of one-step agreement on 80% of the items. Eight sessions were used for training purposes, and the agreement criterion was reached on the sixth session. After the training phase, a procedure developed by Rice (Butler et al., 1962; Rice, 1965; Rice & Wagstaff, 1967) was used to check "rater drift." The raters were instructed to compare their ratings at the end of every fourth tape (after every 32 ratings). The raters subsequently worked together in 1- or 2-hour sessions.

Results

Properties of the Alliance Scale

Two judges made 44 ratings on items related to the therapeutic alliance based on listening to excerpts from each of 124 therapy sessions. Reliability and agreement among judges were assessed in several ways. For all the ratings across all sessions and all items, the product–moment correlation between the two judges was .97. Ebel's (1951) intraclass correlation was used to compute reliabilities for individual raters and for average ratings on each item and on the subscale scores. For the items, these correlations ranged from .49 to .87 for individual ratings, with an average R of .69. These correlations reflect the amount of variance in the ratings attributable to true differences among the sessions. The reliability of averaged ratings, which were actually used for data analyses, ranged from .66 to .93 with an average R of .81. For the total-scale score, the reliability of individual ratings was .87 and that of averaged ratings was .93. The therapist, patient, and interaction subscales had R's for individual ratings equal to .90, .81, and .79, respectively; and for average ratings they were .95, .89, and .88, respectively.

Measures of reliability indicate only the degree to which ratings from different sources tend to covary and may mask important differences between raters in the exact numbers assigned to a particular stimulus as long as they change in relatively the same way. For this reason, the extent of agreement and disagreement between the raters was also assessed. The raters agreed exactly on 49% of the ratings and were discrepant by only one step on an additional 43%. These statistics indicated that interrater reliability and agreement were adequate for testing the hypotheses of the study and that we were justified in combining scores by the two raters into composite measures.

Item analyses for the scale as a whole and for the therapist, patient, and interaction subscales indicated that each scale tapped a unified dimension. For the total-scale score, the *alpha* reliability was .95. For the therapist, patient, and interaction subscales, alpha reliabilities were .92, .89, and .87, respectively.

Principal Components Analysis.   Conceptually, the therapeutic alliance is usually spoken of in terms of the contribution of the patient, the therapist, and the treatment situation. Accordingly, the Vanderbilt Therapeutic Alliance Scale was constructed using this theoretical model as a guiding framework. In order to test this view, a principal-components analysis was conducted, using Bartlett's test to determine the number of significant factors that would be extracted. A brief summary of the items contributing to each of these principal components can be found in Table 2.

The first component is determined primarily by therapist items, but it includes a few patient and interaction items. It seems to reflect an optimal therapeutic climate established by the personal and professional qualities of the therapist and accepted by the patient, and it is called *positive climate*. The second, fourth, and fifth components are primarily determined by patient items, with some interaction items. Factor 2, resistance, is defined by actively negative patient behaviors and attitudes. Factor 4 reflects the patient's motivation for therapy in that he acknowledges and focuses on his problems in the sessions in a task-oriented, productive manner. Factor 5 is composed of items that indicate that the patient accepts responsibility for his own behavior both in creating his problems and in taking an active part to bring about changes. Factor 3 is made up of items

TABLE 1.2
Description of Items Defining the Principal Components

Factor 1 *Positive Climate*	Factor 2 *Patient Resistance*	Factor 3 *Therapist Intrusiveness*	Factor 4 *Patient Motivation*	Factor 5 *Patient Responsibility*	Factor 6 *Patient Anxiety*
Therapist	*Patient*	*Therapist*	*Patient*	*Patient*	*Patient*
Competent	Hostile	Imposes own values	Acknowledge problems	Identifies with therapist	Anxious
Hopeful	Defensive	Fosters dependency	Desire to overcome	Responsible for session	*Interaction*
Committed	Missing or late	Irrelevant comments	*Interaction*	Carries out tasks	Awkward pauses
Acceptance	*Interaction*	Inappropriate interventions	Focus on task	Talks freely	
Understanding	Power struggle		Agree on goals	Own contribution	
Validity of feelings	Discuss discontinuing		Active sessions	Tries new behavior	
Structuring			Accept roles		
Preserve self-esteem					
Stimulate curiosity					
Appropriate expression					
Explores resistance					
Teaching					
Mutuality					
Intervene as needed					
Patient					
Feels better					
Feels support					
Interaction					
Enthusiastic					
Joint effort					
Common view					
Realistic					

indicating intrusive therapist behaviors. Items that load on Factor 6 indicate the presence of anxiety.

Testing the Hypotheses

It was predicted that the three groups in this study—high outcome, low outcome, and premature terminators—would differ significantly in the strength of the therapeutic alliance established and its patterning across time. In order to test this hypothesis, analyses of variance were carried out, using treatment outcome as the independent variable. Both the a priori Patient, Therapist, and Interaction subscales and the principal component-factor scores served as dependent variables.

Analyses Involving Dropouts.   The dropout group was small ($n = 6$), and most patients had left therapy by the third session making it impossible to obtain sufficiently reliable estimates of cell means for this group to compare them with the other two groups at all five points in time. Thus, analyses that included this group were carried out for the first and last sessions only. Table 3 shows the results of least-squares ANOVAs based on scores for the a priori subscales. None of these composite variables differed significantly among the outcome groups. There were, however, differences across sessions. Although only the patient subscale achieved statistical significance, we believe that the small sample size limits the power of the tests and thus permits meaningful study of trends. Mean alliance ratings for the last session on the total scale, patient subscale, and interaction subscale were lower than those for the first. However, inspection of the means in Table 4 reveals an interesting pattern. The decline in the overall mean of the total-scale score is attributable to the two groups which continued in treatment. The mean alliance rating for the dropout group actually *increased*. For

TABLE 1.3
F Values for Outcome Group x Session Analyses of Variance
for First and Last Sessions Using Subscale Scores

Source	df	Total	Therapist Subscale	Patient Subscale	Interaction Subscale
Group (A)	2	.32	1.36	.32	.31
Session (B)	1	2.78*	.58	4.36**	3.58*
A x B	2	1.16	2.25	.26	.27

Note: Degrees of freedom for between- and within-groups error = 25.
   *.05 $<p<$ .10
**$p<$ .05

TABLE 1.4
Means and Standard Deviations on Subscale
Scores for First and Last Sessions

Variable	High Outcome[a]		Low Outcome[a]		Dropout[b]	
	First	Last	First	Last	First	Last
Total						
M	112.8	95.5	111.3	96.1	111.3	115.3
SD	23.9	34.8	30.1	31.7	25.6	20.6
Therapist Subscale						
M	45.2	37.1[c]	44.5	38.6[d]	46.7	54.1[c d]
SD	13.1	16.2	15.2	13.5	11.3	12.7
Patient Subscale						
M	36.9	32.4	35.0	29.6	32.8	30.8
SD	8.1	9.7	8.1	10.8	8.8	11.2
Interaction Subscale						
M	30.7	26.0	31.8	27.8	31.8	30.3
SD	5.1	9.9	9.2	8.5	6.7	9.1

[a] $n = 11$

[b] $n = 6$

[c, d] Differences between means significant ($p < .05$, two-tailed t test for a posteriori comparisons).

the patient and interaction subscales the decrease is consistent across groups (although smaller in the dropout group). Thus, the primary contributor to this overall increase in the alliance score of the dropout group is the therapist subscale score. In fact, for 16 of the 18 therapist items, the mean rating for the dropout group was the highest of the three groups, although the differences were not statistically significant.

A similar analysis was conducted using the sums of the ratings on items composing each of the principal components just discussed as dependent variables. The results are summarized in Tables 5 and 6. Here again the variables did not discriminate among the outcome groups, but there were differences between scores on the first and last sessions on Patient Resistance and Motivation. Examination of the means in Table 6 reveals that ratings for the last session were lower than those for the first session. Although dropout patients were slightly (not significantly) more resistant, they were no less motivated or responsible, nor were they more anxious than patients in the other groups. The effects of therapist

TABLE 1.5

F Values for Outcome Group x Session Analyses of Variance
for First and Last Sessions Using Factor Scores

Source	df	Positive Climate	Therapist Intrusiveness	Patient Resistance	Patient Motivation	Patient Responsibility	Patient Anxiety
Group (A)	1	1.04	.50	.72	.37	.19	1.73
Session (B)	1	.25	1.11	4.86**	6.78**	3.32**	3.31
A x B	2	.89	1.69	.13	.83	.31	.10

Note. Degrees of freedom for between- and within-groups error = 25.

* .05 < p < .10
** p < .05

TABLE 1.6
Means and Standard Deviations on Factor
Scores for First and Last Sessions

Variable	High Outcome[b]		Low Outcome[b]		Dropout[c]	
	First	Last	First	Last	First	Last
Positive Climate						
M	43.4	37.3[d]	46.2	40.7	47.3	53.2[d]
SD	16.1	19.7	17.0	17.2	13.0	9.9
Therapist Intrusiveness[a]						
M	13.2	11.0	11.6	10.4[d]	12.0	13.1[d]
SD	3.5	3.8	4.3	3.6	3.5	4.6
Patient Resistance[a]						
M	17.5	15.2	16.7	13.2	14.9	12.7
SD	3.5	5.4	4.6	6.3	4.9	7.2
Patient Motivation						
M	17.3[d]	13.2[d]	17.2	14.8	17.4	16.4
SD	3.9	5.7	4.5	4.1	3.6	4.4
Patient Responsibility						
M	14.4	12.2	13.4	11.4	12.8	12.3
SD	3.6	3.8	3.1	4.6	5.3	5.1
Patient Anxiety[a]						
M	5.8	4.8	4.8	3.7	5.8	5.2
SD	0.8	2.1	1.8	2.3	1.2	2.1

[a]Item scores were reversed, so that higher numbers indicate a more positive quality. *Lower* scores thus mean *more* intrusiveness, resistance, or anxiety.

[b]$n = 11$

[c]$N = 6$

[d]Differences between means significant ($p < .05$, two-tailed t test for a posteriori comparisons).

behaviors were not significant in the ANOVA, but t tests indicated that in the last session there were significant differences between the dropout group and the high outcome group on positive climate and between the dropouts and the low outcome group on therapist intrusiveness. These are indications that the therapists in the dropout group were more actively dealing with the alliance than those in the other two groups, but in a relatively nondirective way.

Analyses Comparing the Outcome Groups.   In order to compare more close-ly the high outcome and low outcome groups, analyses of variance were con-ducted using ratings from all five of the observed points in therapy (see Table 7). Again, there was more variance within the outcome groups than across groups, so that no significant associations between alliance scores and outcome were found. There were, however, significant ($p = .02$) session effects for the total scale, patient subscale, and interaction subscale, with the effect for the therapist subscale approaching significance ($p = .07$). Examination of the means for the sessions (see Table 8) indicates that for the average of the two groups, there was a consistent peak at the 25% point. This effect is due to a strong peak on each subscale at this point in the high outcome group, which offsets a slight drop at the same point in the low outcome group. Comparisons between groups at this point were conducted, even though no effects for groups were found. Such compari-sons obviously must be interpreted with caution. The comparisons indicated that, for the total scale, therapist subscale, and patient subscale, the differences be-tween the groups at this point were significant. When the means for each item were examined separately, the 25% point was the peak for the high outcome group on 34 of the 44 items. For the low outcome group, the lowest ratings occurred at that point on 23 of those items. Thus, there is evidence that the initial phase of therapy can be used to discriminate between more and less successful therapeutic alliances. Strengthening of the alliance here predicted good outcome, whereas a weakening of the alliance predicted poor outcome.

Analyses were also carried out using summed ratings of items composing each of the principal components as dependent variables. The results are summa-rized in Tables 9 and 10. Differences between the two groups approached signifi-cance on the two, negative patient scales, Resistance and Anxiety. The low-

TABLE 1.7
F Values for Outcome Group x Session Analyses of
Variance for All Sessions Using Subscale Scores

Source	df^a	Total	Therapist Subscale	Patient Subscale	Interaction Subscale
Group (A)	1 (20)	.79	.37	2.41	.14
Session (B)	4 (80)	3.12**	2.21*	3.18**	3.29**
A x B	4 (80)	1.43	1.72	.84	1.03

[a]Numbers in parentheses indicate degrees of freedom for error.
*$p = .07$
**$p = .02$

TABLE 1.8
Means and Standard Deviations on Subscale
Scores for All Sessions

Group (n = 11)	1	25%	Session 50%	75%	100%
			Total Score		
High outcome: M	112.8	130.9*a,b,c	105.1^a	107.8^b	95.5^c
SD	23.9	30.2	16.2	24.8	34.8
Low outcome: M	111.4	106.5*	110.7	93.2	96.1
SD	30.1	23.1	28.1	33.5	32.7
			Therapist Subscale		
High outcome: M	45.2	51.1*a,b	38.7^a	41.4	37.1^b
SD	13.1	12.7	8.3	11.7	16.2
Low outcome: M	44.5	40.7*	44.9	34.4	38.6
SD	15.2	12.2	13.2	15.2	13.5
			Patient Subscale		
High outcome: M	36.9	43.1*a	36.4	37.2	32.4^a
SD	8.1	10.4	6.5	9.2	9.7
Low outcome: M	35.0	34.6*	34.9	32.2	29.6
SD	8.1	5.9	9.5	9.7	10.8
			Interaction Subscale		
High outcome: M	30.7	36.6a,b	29.9	29.2^a	26.0^b
SD	5.1	9.4	6.5	7.5	9.8
Low outcome: M	31.8	31.2	30.9	26.5	27.7
SD	9.2	6.4	9.0	9.8	8.5

$a, b, c_p < .05$, Least Significant Difference Test for Comparison within groups.
*$p < .05$, Least Significant Difference Test for comparison between groups.

outcome patients were somewhat more hostile and defensive across all sessions, although the results did not reach statistical significance at any point. These patients were also more anxious and had more awkward silences than the high-outcome patients, with the difference reaching statistical significance at the 25% point. Another difference between the groups at this point was found on the Responsibility scale, with the high-outcome patients assuming more responsibility for their own problems and their own therapy. Again, on the Positive Climate, Resistance, Motivation, Responsibility, and Anxiety scales, the pattern discussed earlier occurred, that is, a peak at the 25% point for the high-outcome group.

TABLE 1.9
F Values for Outcome Group x Session Analyses of Variance for All Sessions Using Factor Scores

Source	df^a	Positive Climate	Therapist Intrusiveness	Patient Resistance	Patient Motivation	Patient Responsibility	Patient Anxiety
Group							
(A)	1 (20)	.09	.26	3.23*	.02	1.26	3.81*
Session							
(B)	4 (80)	1.96*	.29	3.01**	3.28**	3.31**	3.00**
A x B	4 (80)	1.70	.81	.23	1.29	1.06	.30

a Numbers in parentheses indicate degrees of freedom for error.
*$.05 < p < .10$
**$p = .02$

TABLE 1.10
Means and Standard Deviations on Factor Scores
for All Sessions

Group (n = 11)			Session		
	1	25%	50%	75%	100%
	Positive Therapist				
High outcome: M	43.4	54.5 [b,c]	38.6 [b]	41.0	37.3 [c]
SD	16.2	14.8	11.4	17.1	19.7
Low outcome: M	46.2	42.2	45.8	33.9	40.7
SD	17.0	14.7	16.1	16.9	17.2
	Intrusive Therapist [a]				
High outcome: M	13.2	13.1	12.5	12.9	11.0
SD	3.5	3.1	3.2	3.8	3.8
Low outcome: M	11.6	11.2	12.2	10.7	10.4
SD	4.2	3.0	4.0	4.8	3.6
	Resistant Patient [a]				
High outcome: M	17.5	19.5 [b]	19.3	17.0	15.2 [b]
SD	3.5	3.7	2.0	4.9	5.4
Low outcome: M	16.7	16.8	16.2	15.3	13.2
SD	4.6	3.0	4.7	6.3	6.4
	Motivated Patient				
High outcome: M	17.4 [b]	18.6 [c,d,e]	14.3 [d]	14.7 [e]	13.2 [b,c]
SD	3.9	6.8	5.4	3.3	5.6
Low outcome: M	17.2	15.8	16.3	14.3	14.8
SD	4.5	4.4	3.8	4.7	4.1
	Responsible Patient				
High outcome: M	14.3	17.2 [b,c]	13.1 [b]	14.7	12.3 [c]
SD	3.6	5.8	4.2	3.6	3.8
Low outcome: M	13.5	13.6*	13.5	13.2	11.4
SD	3.1	2.4	4.0	4.2	4.6
	Anxious Patient				
High outcome: M	5.8	6.7 [*b]	5.3	5.8	4.8 [b]
SD	0.8	1.5	1.9	2.2	2.1
Low outcome: M	4.8	5.2*	4.7	4.5	3.9
SD	1.8	1.5	2.1	2.2	2.3

[a] Item scores were reversed, so that higher members indicate a more positive quality. *Lower* scores thus mean *more* intrusiveness, resistance, or anxiety.

[b,c,d,e] $p < .05$, Least Significant Difference test for comparisons between groups.
*$p < .05$, Least Significant Difference test for comparisons within groups.

Discussion

In discussing the results of this investigation it may be useful to differentiate between methodological and clinical implications. With respect to the former, the feasibility of constructing a series of items measuring the therapeutic alliance has been demonstrated. Furthermore, it was possible to achieve satisfactory agreement among clinical raters, with levels of reliability and rater agreement at least as high as those in most studies concerned with measurements of the psychotherapeutic process. The establishment of reliability and internal consistency are of course necessary first steps toward the development of a valid measure of the therapeutic alliance, but wider use of the scale and examination of its relationships with other variables are also necessary. An important feature of the present instrument is its ability to assess aspects of the therapeutic alliance on a continuing and inclusive basis. In other words, systematic and multidimensional assessments are made of each therapy segment as opposed to dichotomous judgments on single variables.

An instrument of the kind used in this investigation is based on the assumption that there are important ingredients in *all* therapeutic alliances, that these ingredients are additive (e.g., by summing items in a scale), and that such summations can provide a valid index of the quality of a given alliance. Conversely, there is no provision for the possibility that particular items included in a scale may be more important in one therapeutic dyad than another. By the same token, it is possible that certain qualities of the alliance should receive disproportionate weighting in different dyads or for the same dyad on different occasions. Thus, one cannot make discriminations between statistical and clinical significance, and one is restricted to the judgment that, say, a higher score on a particular scale indicates a better alliance than a lower score. This problem is of course present in all attempts at quantifying essentially qualitative data. Although we have no solutions to offer, the importance of the issue must be kept in mind since it may have a crucial bearing on the interpretation of statistical results.

A principal-components factor analysis yielded six meaningful composite variables. Two of these factors were defined primarily by therapist behaviors and four by patient behaviors. Thus, the a priori interaction subscale was absorbed by the other two presumed contributors to the alliance, with a few items being associated more with therapist items and the rest more with patient items. The first principal component, which accounts for most of the variance, was made up of items that indicated that the *therapist* established a therapeutic climate by conveying his or her professional competence and personal commitment, by treating the patient with respect and understanding, by structuring the therapy situation, and by enlisting the patient as a partner. The second therapist dimension was defined by the extent to which the therapist introduced his own feelings, values, and opinions into the therapy process rather than encouraging the patient independently to explore his situation and to arrive at his own conclusions (see Factor 3 in Table 2).

The *patient* dimension accounting for the largest segment of the variance was defined by active resistance and negative attitudes toward therapy and the therapist (Factor 2, Resistance). That these items formed a separate dimension from those related to overt anxiety in the therapy sessions (Factor 6, Anxiety) indicates that the structure of the patient's defenses is an important element in the therapeutic alliance. Some patients may become hostile or mistrustful and turn the therapy into a power struggle, whereas in others anxiety emerges more directly. The other two patient factors are interpreted as (1) motivation for treatment; and (2) willingness to accept responsibility for one's own life. These two separate composites indicate that it is one thing for a person to acknowledge that he has problems, seek help, and accept the patient role and another to assume responsibility for work with the therapist, to examine one's own contribution to the problem, and actively to bring about the desired changes. We shall discuss this issue more fully in the following.

Therapeutic Alliance and Outcome.   Turning to substantive results, it will be recalled that high-outcome and low-outcome groups were formed on the basis of a composite measure of success in brief psychotherapy, and their ratings for therapeutic alliance were compared using analyses of variance. Overall, these analyses indicated that there was more variance in alliance within the two groups than between them, and thus no significant differences attributable to outcome group were found. There were, however, differences among the sessions from the selected points in time across the course of therapy. Closer examination of these efforts led to the emergence of a pattern that was not strong enough to reach statistical significance because of small sample sizes but was nonetheless considered substantial because of its consistency among individual items, a priori subscale scores, and factor-scale scores. In the initial phase of the therapy, dyads in the more successful group *increased* their alliance, peaking at the first quartile point, then trailing off again in later sessions. The pattern of scores for the less successful group, on the other hand, was a mirror image of that for the more successful group. Their alliance ratings *fell* from their initial equality with the other group and rose again at the midpoint of therapy. However, they never achieved scores as high as the peak of the more successful group. Thus, in the initial phase of therapy, the more successful group showed a peak in therapeutic alliance, whereas the less successful group showed a trough at the corresponding times. In the later phases there were no substantial differences between groups, and by the end of therapy they once more were essentially equal.

Although no effects for outcome group reached statistical significance, there was a notable trend on the factor-scale variables Resistance and Anxiety. Although therapist behaviors and positive patient behaviors did not differentiate the groups, the less successful patients tended to be more hostile, critical, and mistrustful of the therapist and more anxious and awkward in their therapy sessions. These results are consistent with those obtained by Gomes-Schwartz (1978) based on the same data but obtained across all cases using a different instrument, the Vanderbilt Psychotherapy Process Scale (VPPS). With respect to the present study, in the initial phase of therapy, patients were significantly divergent on both the Responsibility and Anxiety factors. Those patients who went on to achieve better outcomes accepted their own role in bringing about change, and they became more open and less anxious in the sessions.

On the whole, the data suggest, first, that the most important phase of therapy for developing a therapeutic alliance and for predicting outcome is the initial phase. Luborsky (1976) reported a similar pattern, with many more signs of alliance present in the initial phase of therapy than in the later phases. This finding is also congruent with the analytic proposition (Freud, 1912; Greenson, 1967; Langs, 1973, 1974) that the formation of an alliance is crucial at the beginning of therapy because it forms the basis for the more difficult work of the middle phase. Langs suggests that after an alliance has been formed, it recedes into the background of therapy and need not be explicit in the relationship unless there is a disruption. This argument is consistent with the data of this study, because the two groups did not differ late in therapy on observable evidence of the alliance. Horwitz (1974, 1976) noted that important processes of internalization occur throughout therapy and that more positive outcomes are observed when the alliance is stronger. Conceivably, such processes proceed without external manifestations, or the current scale is insufficiently sensitive to register their occurrence. Bordin (1975, 1976), by contrast, predicted greater fluctuations in the alliance across the course of therapy. Thus decreases in alliance scores in the final phase might be of more serious concern, and they might predict poorer outcome. These assertions do not necessarily contradict the present findings. In any case, the question remains to be examined in greater detail.

The extent of patient changes in the Vanderbilt project was relatively modest (Strupp & Hadley, 1979), and the consistent drop in alliance scores is perhaps a reflection of halting progress. Our impression is that the drop in alliance scores may be related to the failure of most therapists to deal straightforwardly with issues of termination. Mann (1973) states that this is the most important task in brief therapy. However, the therapists in the Vanderbilt project were not specifically trained in brief therapy techniques and did not, as a rule, change their ordinary practice to accommodate to the stipulated 25-hour limit. Thus, their failure to deal more directly with the problem of termination may have had adverse effects on the therapeutic alliance as well as outcome.

Interpretations of the results obtained in the course of this investigation are circumscribed by the observation that statistical differences within the patient--therapist pairs included in each group were greater than the differences between groups. This finding, which also applied to many of the overall results of the Vanderbilt project, suggested considerable heterogeneity in patient–therapist dyads. To deal with this issue, Strupp (1980a, 1980b, 1980c) undertook more refined analyses of selected individual patient–therapist pairs. The results of these intensive case studies are congruent with a number of the findings obtained in the present investigation. For example, both sets of analyses point to the overriding importance of *patient* characteristics, behaviors, and attitudes that appeared to predict outcome better than therapist characteristics.

Further confirmation for this conclusion was obtained by Gomes-Schwartz (1976) who compared experiential, analytic, and nonprofessional therapists and by Sloane et al., (1975) who studied behavioral and analytic therapies. In other studies dealing with the initial phases of therapy, such patient variables as initiative, active involvement in self-exploration, and internal focus were likewise good predictors of outcome (Kirtner & Cartwright, 1958; Rice & Wagstaff, 1967; Saltzman et al., 1976). In all of these studies it appears that the therapist more or less "permits" the patient to form a therapeutic alliance by being reasonably competent, warm, understanding, and committed. The effectiveness of the therapy then depends on the patient's expectations and characteristic relationship patterns. Some patients are more able and willing to accept the therapist's offer of relatedness and to carry a large share of the therapeutic task themselves. In short-term dynamic psychotherapy, these patients are able to take advantage of the new relationship and to achieve insights that are registered as positive therapeutic changes.

This finding supports the psychoanalytic assertion that the formation of a successful therapeutic alliance depends heavily on the patient's ego strength, capacity for object relatedness, and defensive structure. In the Vanderbilt Project (Strupp, 1980a, 1980b, 1980c) it was clear that those patients who were able to form a productive therapeutic relationship with the therapist early in therapy were likely to have a good therapeutic outcome; conversely, patients who were hostile, negativistic, and otherwise resistive tended to have poorer therapeutic results. There was no evidence that therapists were able to deal effectively with a patient's initial resistances and to turn such efforts to therapeutic advantage. This might mean that either such resistances are largely insurmountable in time-limited psychotherapy (i.e., the patient's characterological patterns are too deeply engrained to yield to interpretive efforts) or the therapists participating in the study were insufficiently skillful. Current research by the Vanderbilt team investigates these issues.

Therapeutic Alliance and Premature Termination. The prediction that poorer therapeutic alliances would be found in cases that terminated with fewer than five sessions was not supported by the data. In fact, the opposite was found to be the case. Whereas all groups were initially equal, the total alliance score for the dropout group actually *increased;* those for the other groups decreased. Examination of the subscale and factor-scale scores indicated that this difference was attributable to substantial differences in the behavior of the therapists. With dropouts, the positive aspects of the therapist's contribution to the alliance were higher in the last session than in the first session. In contrast to the therapists of patients with low outcomes, the therapists of dropouts appeared to be more willing to encourage independence in their patients. Perhaps some patients in the low-outcome group would have dropped out but were kept in therapy through the therapist's insistence. This result was not expected and at first seems incongruent with other studies of premature termination. However, previous research has focused on the patient's pretherapy characteristics, the patient's in-therapy behavior, or the patient's perception of the therapist rather than on actual therapist behavior in the sessions. Thus, the foregoing may be a unique finding deserving further investigation.

At this time, we can only speculate about what happened clinically in the prematurely terminated cases. Although differences between the groups on the patient measures did not achieve statistically significant levels at any point in the therapy, the patients in the dropout group tended to be slightly less involved in the therapy. In early sessions, they seemed to be as motivated to find help with their problems as other patients, but they were also more highly defensive and less willing to assume responsibility for their own behavior and their own therapy. It is likely that their therapists were sensitive to subtle cues of this lack of involvement and, by way of compensation, increased their own contribution to the relationship. Perhaps these patients, who were reluctant to engage in therapy despite their recognition of problems, felt somewhat overwhelmed when confronted with a therapist who was more active than usual in trying to establish a relationship with them. Because most of the therapists in the dropout cases were analytically oriented, the kind of alliance they offered was apt to be incongruent with the patient's defensive stance and lack of internal attribution. This line of reasoning is consistent with Bordin's (1975, 1976) proposal that the establishment of a sound alliance depends on the patient's capacities to meet the demands of the kind of therapy offered. Clearly, the therapeutic alliances in these cases were deficient despite the high total-scale scores. But we should also remember the common clinical observation that there are causes for premature termination of a therapy relationship other than a disrupted alliance, such as external factors that may prevent a patient from continuing in therapy, true improvement as a result of ventilation and support, "flight into health," and numerous others.

Implications for Research and Practice.   One of the most important goals of research in psychotherapy is to furnish a foundation upon which to base sound clinical practice. The concept of therapeutic alliance and the hypotheses for this research grew out of the clinical experience of many psychotherapists, and the findings have implications for clinical application and indicate directions for further exploration. In particular, they point to (1) the importance of the early phase of therapy in determining its ultimate success; and (2) the difficulties inherent in productively engaging a negativistic, defensive, withdrawn, or anxious patient in the therapeutic process. This would be true especially for short-term therapy of the kind typically practiced today in most mental health facilities.

After many years of attention to the therapist's facilitative behaviors and attitudes, a good deal of recent research has converged on evidence that the patient's capacity and willingness to participate in the therapy interaction are among the most important determinants of the changes that can be achieved. To account for these findings, one might be tempted to fall back on the old notion that there are "good" therapy candidates and "bad" therapy candidates. In many ways, too, the evidence supports the idea that the rich get richer (Luborsky, 1959). Those who are already open to relationships with others, who are introspective and verbal, and who assume their tasks in living with a sense of personal responsibility are also those who benefit most from therapy as well as from any other life experience. On the other hand, the real test of psychotherapy lies in its ability to help those individuals who are deficient in these areas.

For this reason, one of the primary objectives of both research and practice in psychotherapy must be to determine the conditions under which positive involvement with a therapist can be brought about in patients who otherwise would adopt a self-defeating stance. Although this kind of reaction may occur with some frequency as the result of the therapist's negative attitudes, insensitivity, or technical errors, it is more likely to be the result of the patient's characterological patterns (Strupp, 1980a, 1980b, 1980c). Reich's (1949) original suggestions for character analysis and analysis of resistance are invaluable in such cases and deserve close attention from both practicing therapists and researchers. Of necessity, however, these techniques take time. One must first help the patient to become aware of the defensive, yet self-defeating, function served by this kind of behavior. These patterns of relationship were adopted for good reasons and will only gradually be dropped when it can be demonstrated that they no longer serve an adaptive function. Thus, one recommendation is patience and gentle confrontation by the therapist in long-term therapy. Sifneos (1972) uses similar techniques in brief therapy, constantly confronting and interpreting negative transference; but even he is pessimistic about the outcome of such cases with short-term contact.

Another option for maximizing the effectiveness of therapy would be to develop and utilize selection criteria and to select only those patients who display the appropriate characteristics for the kind of therapy being offered. Most brief therapy experts (Malan, 1976; Mann, 1973; Sifneos, 1972) advocate the careful screening of patients, and there is a move toward "prescriptive" psychotherapy from other quarters as well (Goldstein & Stein, 1976). Perhaps the patient characteristics found to be predictive in this study and others are relevant only to expressive psychotherapies. Strupp (1963) suggested that the fact that a particular intervention is applicable only to a minority of patients does not diminish its value. Indeed it is the professional and scientific responsibility of psychotherapists to seek as much information as possible about selection criteria for their particular techniques.

Alternatively, it has been possible to alter some of the patient's expectations for therapy and thus to affect the kind of behavior that prevents successful engagement in the process. Role induction films or interviews have proved useful for demonstrating to patients what is expected of them in therapy and thus improving the performance of lower-class patients in group therapy (Strupp & Bloxom, 1973; Hoehn-Saric, Frank, Imber, Nash, Stone, & Battle, 1964). Similar procedures might profitably be used with other patients who appear to be poor prospects for the available therapies. Knowing in advance that the therapist would not assume major responsibility for effecting change may not change the patient's basic responses, but it may reduce possible disappointment and anger, as well as premature termination.

Bordin (1975, 1976) emphasizes strongly the importance of the therapist's and the patient's capacity and willingness to undertake the tasks demanded of the treatment approach they have chosen. This emphasis is clearly related to the desirability of optimally matching patient, therapist, and therapeutic approach. Undoubtedly, this is the direction in which the field must move, if significant progress is to be made. The practitioners of each modality must explicate what demands are made on the participants in terms of personal characteristics and preparation. When clinical and theoretical hypotheses have been advanced, systematic research can be carried out, and a productive feedback system can be developed. Such research should include multiple outcome measures, close mapping of fluctuations in the therapeutic alliance, and study of the reciprocal interactions between patient and therapist in order to determine the nodal points of productive therapeutic change.

A final comment concerning the therapeutic alliance may be in order. Because the strength of the therapeutic alliance did not predict the outcome of psychotherapy in the cases studied here, many questions remain to be answered. For example: How important is the alliance to outcome? Can a patient fail to benefit from psychotherapy even though a positive alliance has been established? Can substantial increases in self-awareness or changes in behavior occur without the formation of a positive working relationship? Morgan, Luborsky, Curtis, and Solomon (1977) found that a poor alliance almost always predicted a poor outcome but that good outcomes occurred in cases where there were many signs of a working alliance as well as in those where there were few. In the present study, despite the caveats mentioned, the evidence showed that there was much overlap in the distribution of therapeutic alliance scores among good and poor outcome groups. Perhaps it is appropriate to conclude that the therapeutic alliance, like Rogers' (1957) "facilitative conditions," comprises a set of variables that are necessary but not sufficient for explaining therapy outcomes in particular cases.

REFERENCES

Auerbach, A., Luborsky, L., & Johnson, M. Clinicians' predictions of psychotherapy outcome: A trial of a prognostic index. *American Journal of Psychiatry*, 1972, *128*, 830–835.

Bordin, E. S. *Research strategies in psychotherapy.* New York: Wiley, 1974.

Bordin, E. S. *The generalizability of the psychoanalytic concept of working alliance.* Paper presented at the meeting of the Society for Psychotherapy Research, Boston, June 1975.

Bordin, E. S. *The working alliance: Basis for a general theory of psychotherapy.* Paper presented at the meeting of the American Psychological Association, Washington, D.C., September 1976.

Butler, J. M., Rice, L. N., & Wagstaff, A. K. On the naturalistic definition of variables: An analogue of clinical analysis. In H. H. Strupp & L. Luborsky (Eds.), *Research in Psychotherapy* (Vol. 2). Washington, D.C.: American Psychological Association, 1962.

Chessick, R. D. *How psychotherapy heals.* New York: Science House, 1969.

DiLoreto, A. O. *Comparative psychotherapy: An experimental analysis.* Chicago: Aldine-Atherton, 1971.

Ebel, R. L. Estimation of the reliability of ratings. *Psychometrika*, 1951, *16*, 407–424.

Fiester, A. R. Clients' perceptions of therapists with high attrition rates. *Journal of Consulting and Clinical Psychology*, 1977, *45*, 954–955.

Fiester, A. R., & Rudestrum, K. E. A multivariate analysis of the early dropout process. *Journal of Consulting and Clinical Psychology*, 1975, *43*, 528–535.

Fiske, D. W., Cartwright, D. S., & Kirtner, W. L. Are psychotherapeutic changes predictable? *Journal of Abnormal and Social Psychology*, 1964, *69*, 418–426.

Frank, J. D. Therapeutic components of psychotherapy. *Journal of Nervous and Mental Disease*, 1974, *159*, 325–343.

Freud, S. The dynamics of the transference. In J. Strachey (Ed. and Trans.) *Standard edition of the complete works of Sigmund Freud* (Vol. 12). London: Hogarth, 1958 (Originally published, 1912.)

Freud, S. On beginning the treatment: Further recommendations on the technique of psychoanalysis. In J. Strachey (Ed. and Trans.) *Standard edition of the complete works of Sigmund Freud* (Vol. 12). Hogarth, 1958. (Originally published, 1913.)

Freud, S. The technique of psychoanalysis. In J. Strachey (Ed. and Trans.) *Standard edition of the complete works of Sigmund Freud* (Vol. 23). London: Hogarth, 1964. (Originally published, 1940.)

Garfield, S. L. Research on client variables in psychotherapy. In S. L. Garfield & A. E. Bergin (Eds.), *Handbook of psychotherapy and behavior change*. New York: Wiley, 1978.

Garfield, S. L., & Wolpin, M. Expectations regarding psychotherapy. *Journal of Nervous and Mental Disease*, 1963, *137*, 353–362.

Gendlin, E. T. *Experiencing and the creation of meaning*. New York: Free Press of Glencoe, 1962.

Goldfried, M. R., & Davison, G. C. *Clinical behavior therapy*. New York: Holt, Rinehart & Winston, 1976.

Goldstein, A. P., & Stein, N. *Prescriptive psychotherapies*. New York: Pergamon, 1976.

Gomes-Schwartz, B. A. *Effective ingredients in psychotherapy: The roles of exploratory processes, therapist-offered relationship, and patient involvement*. Unpublished doctoral dissertation, Vanderbilt University, 1976.

Gomes-Schwartz, B. Effective ingredients in psychotherapy: Prediction of outcomes from process variables. *Journal of Consulting and Clinical Psychology*, 1978, *46*, 1023–1035.

Greenson, R. R. The working alliance and the transference neurosis. *The Psychoanalytic Quarterly*, 1965, *34*, 155–181.

Greenson, R. R. *The technique and practice of psychoanalysis*. New York: International Universities Press, 1967.

Greenson, R. R., & Wexler, M. The non-transference relationship in the psychoanalytic situation. *International Journal of Psycho-Analysis*, 1969, *50*, 27–40.

Halkides, G. *An investigation of therapeutic success as a function of four therapist variables*. Unpublished doctoral dissertation, University of Chicago, 1958.

Heitler, J. B. Preparation of lower-class patients for expressive group psychotherapy. *Journal of Consulting and Clinical Psychology*, 1973, *41*, 251–260.

Heitler, J. B. Preparatory techniques in initiating expressive psychotherapy with lower-class, unsophisticated patients. *Psychological Bulletin*, 1976, *83*, 339–352.

Hoehn-Saric, R., Frank, J., Imber, S., Nash, E., Stone, A., & Battle, C. Systematic preparation of patients for psychotherapy: I. Effects on therapy behavior and outcome. *Journal of Psychiatric Research*, 1964, *2*, 267–281.

Holsti, O. R. *Content analysis for the social sciences and humanities*. Reading, Mass.: Addison-Wesley, 1969.

Horwitz, L. *Clinical prediction in psychotherapy*. New York: Aronson, 1974.

Horwitz, L. *Internalization as a therapeutic process in psychotherapy and psychoanalysis*. Paper presented at the meeting of the Society for Psychotherapy Research, San Diego, June 1976.

Kirtner, W. L., & Cartwright, D. S. Success and failure in client-centered therapy as a function of initial in-therapy behavior. *Journal of Consulting Psychology*, 1958, *22*, 329–333.

Klein, M. H., Mathieu, P. L., Gendlin, E. T., & Kiesler, D. J. *The experiencing scale: A research and training manual*. Madison: Wisconsin Psychiatric Institute, 1970.

Kline, F., Adrian, A., & Spevak, M. Patients evaluate therapists. *Archives of General Psychiatry*, 1974, *31*, 113–116.

Langs, R. *The technique of psychoanalytic psychotherapy* (Vol. 1). New York: Aronson, 1973.

Langs, R. *The technique of psychoanalytic psychotherapy* (Vol. 2). New York: Aronson, 1974.

Langs, R. *The therapeutic interaction* (Vol. 2). New York: Aronson, 1976.

Lazarus, A. A. Multimodal behavioral treatment of depression. *Behavior Therapy*, 1974, *5*, 549–554.

Lemkau, P. V., & Crocetti, G. M. An urban population's opinion and knowledge about mental illness. *American Journal of Psychiatry*, 1962, *118*, 692–700.

Luborsky, L. Psychotherapy. *Annual review of psychology,* 1959, *10,* 317–344.

Luborsky, L. Helping alliances in psychotherapy. In J. Claghorn (Ed.), *Successful psychotherapy.* New York: Brunner/Mazel, 1976.

Luborsky, L., Singer, B., & Luborsky, L. Comparative studies of psychotherapies: Is it true that "Everyone has won and all must have prizes?" *Archives of General Psychiatry,* 1975, *32,* 995–1008.

Malan, D. H. *The frontier of brief psychotherapy.* New York: Plenum, 1976.

Mann, J. *Time-limited psychotherapy.* Cambridge: Harvard University Press, 1973.

Menninger, K. A., & Holzman, P. S. *Theory of psychoanalytic technique* (2nd ed.). New York: Basic Books, 1973.

Mitchell, K. M., Truax, C. B., Bozarth, J. D., & Krauft, C. C. *Antecedents to psychotherapeutic outcome.* (ARR & TC No. 743). University of Arkansas: Arkansas Rehabilitation Services, 1973.

Morgan, R., Luborsky, L., Curtis, H., & Solomon, J. *Therapeutic alliance, therapist behaviors, insight, and resistance: All predictors of outcome in psychotherapy?* Unpublished manuscript, University of Pennsylvania, 1977.

Myerson, P. G. The establishment and disruption of the psychoanalytic "modus vivendi." *International Journal of Psycho-Analysis,* 1953, *54,* 133–142.

Nunnally, J. C. *Popular conceptions of mental health.* New York: Holt, Rinehart & Winston, 1961.

Orlinsky, D. E., & Howard, K. I. The relation of process to outcome in psychotherapy. In S. L. Garfield and A. E. Bergin (Eds.), *Handbook of psychotherapy and behavior change.* New York: Wiley, 1978.

Orne, M. T., & Wender, P. H. Anticipating socialization for psychotherapy: Method and rationale. *American Journal of Psychiatry,* 1968, *124,* 1202–1212.

Parloff, M. B., Waskow, I. E., & Wolfe, B. E. Research on therapist variables in relationship to process and outcome. In S. L. Garfield & A. E. Bergin (Eds.), *Handbook of psychotherapy and behavior change.* New York: Wiley, 1978.

Reich, W. *Character analysis.* New York: Orgone Institute Press, 1949.

Rice, L. N. Therapists' style of participation and case outcome. *Journal of Consulting Psychology,* 1965, *29,* 155–160.

Rice, L. N., & Wagstaff, A. K. Client voice quality and expressive style as indexes of productive psychotherapy. *Journal of Consulting Psychology,* 1967, *31,* 557–563.

Rogers, C. R. The necessary and sufficient conditions of therapeutic personality change. *Journal of Consulting Psychology,* 1957, *21,* 95–103.

Rogers, C. R., Gendlin, E. T., Kiesler, D. J., & Truax, C. B. *The therapeutic relationship and its impact: A study of psychotherapy with schizophrenics.* Madison: University of Wisconsin Press, 1967.

Saltzman, C., Luetgert, M. J., Roth, C. H., Creaser, J., & Howard, L. Formation of a therapeutic relationship: Experiences during the initial phase of psychotherapy as predictors of treatment duration and outcome. *Journal of Consulting and Clinical Psychology,* 1976, *44,* 546–555.

Sifneos, P. E. *Short-term psychotherapy and emotional crisis.* Cambridge: Harvard University Press, 1972.

Sloane, R. B., Staples, F. R., Cristol, A. H., Yorkston, N. J., & Whipple, K. *Psychotherapy versus behavior therapy.* Cambridge: Harvard University Press, 1975.

Sterba, R. The fate of the ego in analytic therapy. *The International Journal of Psycho-Analysis,* 1934, *15,* 117–126.

Strassberg, D., Roback, H., D'Antonio, M., & Gable, H. Self-disclosure: A critical and selective review of the clinical literature. *Comprehensive Psychiatry,* 1977, *18,* 31–39.

Strupp, H. H. The problem of outcome. *Psychotherapy: Theory, Research and Practice*, 1963, *1*, 1–13.

Strupp, H. H. On the technology of psychotherapy. *Archives of General Psychiatry*, 1972, *26*, 270–278.

Strupp, H. H. Toward reformulation of the psychotherapeutic influence. *International Journal of Psychiatry*, 1973, *11*, 263–265.

Strupp, H. H. On the basic ingredients of psychotherapy. *Psychotherapy and Psychosomatics*, 1974, *24*, 249–260.

Strupp, H. H. Success and failure in time-limited psychotherapy: A systematic comparison of two cases (Comparison 1). *Archives of General Psychiatry*, 1980, *37*, 595–603. (a)

Strupp, H. H. Success and failure in time-limited psychotherapy: A systematic comparison of two cases (Comparison 2). *Archives of General Psychiatry*, 1980, *37*, 708–716. (b)

Strupp, H. H. Success and failure in time-limited psychotherapy further evidence (Comparison 4). *Archives of General Psychiatry*, 1980, *37*, 947–954. (c)

Strupp, H. H., & Bloxom, A. L. Preparing lower-class patients for group psychotherapy: Developments and evaluation of a role-induction film. *Journal of Consulting and Clinical Psychology*, 1973, *41*, 373–384.

Strupp, H. H., & Hadley, S. W. Specific versus nonspecific factors in psychotherapy: A controlled study of outcome. *Archives of General Psychiatry*, 1979, *36*, 1125–1136.

Tarachow, S. *An introduction to psychotherapy*. New York: International Universities Press, 1963.

Truax, C. B., & Carkhuff, R. R. *Toward effective counseling and psychotherapy: Training and practice*. Chicago: Aldine, 1967.

Warren, N., & Rice, L. Structuring and stabilizing of psychotherapy for low-prognosis clients. *Journal of Consulting and Clinical Psychology*, 1972, *39*, 173–181.

Weiner, I. B. *Principles of psychotherapy*. New York: Wiley, 1975.

Wilkins, W. Expectancy of therapeutic gain: An empirical and conceptual critique. *Journal of Consulting and Clinical Psychology*, 1973, *40*, 69–77.

Wilson, G. T., & Evans, I. M. Adult behavior therapy and the therapist-client relationship. In C. M. Franks & G. T. Wilson (Eds.), *Annual review of behavior therapy: Theory and practice* (Vol. 2). New York: Brunner/Mazel, 1976.

Wolberg, L. R. *The technique of psychotherapy* (2nd ed.). New York: Grune & Stratton, 1967.

Zetzel, E. Current concepts of transference. *International Journal of Psycho-Analysis*, 1956, *37*, 369–376.

2 On the Definition and Measurement of Wishes

Hartvig Dahl, M.D.
S.U.N.Y Downstate Medical Center

> *it is not really even clear what it comes to to say that a person*
> wants *to do something. . . . What would be a boon for explanations*
> *of behavior would be sharper psychological concepts.*
> —Quine and Ullian [1970, p. 81]

I. INTRODUCTION

Psychoanalysts are frequently put off by researchers who insist on quantifying what appears to the analyst as ineffably qualitative. What they do not understand is what researchers all know intuitively about the relationship between definition and measurement: All measurement can be reduced to some extrapolation of the count of *one*. The count of one presumes that some entity can be *identified*, that it can be *classified* with some degree of reliability, that it can be *recognized*. If one instance can be counted, then in principle any number of such instances can be counted, and the quantitative enterprise is underway. Operational definitions— the procedures by which we identify whatever it is we're interested in—are fundamental to all measurement and to all determination of truth by correspondence. This is the kind of truth that follows from deducing the consequences of a premise or hypothesis and then assessing whether these consequences do in fact occur. Thus quantitative measurement rests fundamentally on a qualitative issue—the classifiability or definition of the object to be measured. When this object is, say, an item of evidence from a psychoanalytic transcript, then a judgment is involved in assessing the likelihood that the item does in fact constitute evidence. Such judgments are not different in principle from counting

though they may go by other names such as scaling; they are probability estimates that the item belongs to a certain class. All this is taken for granted by
psychologists and those few analysts trained in research methods, but it seems
important to spell out for a readership that may include many not so trained.

II. THE ORIGINS OF A DEFINITION OF A WISH:
FREUD AND HELEN KELLER

The studies I report on in this chapter were not, with one exception, designed
with the idea that wishes were the central object of interest, nor were they
planned as a series of empirical investigations into the same subject matter. Each
set had its own motivations and determinants that overshadowed whatever theme
they shared. It was only recently, when I was asked to write a summary of my
psychoanalytic studies, both empirical and theoretical, that I was able to trace a
common thread through them: a preoccupation with wishes, conscious and unconscious, their definition, and their measurement.

Although wishes abound in psychoanalytic discussions and literature, their
status as a concept is at best informal, commonsensical, and usually undefined.[1]
It was not always thus. In the seventh chapter of *The Interpretation of Dreams,*
Freud (1900/1953) proposed side by side two quite different basic conceptions of
motivation. One, made up of the ideas of psychic energy and cathexes, developed into the theory of instinctual drives and became the centerpiece of psychoanalytic motivational concepts; whereas the other, composed of wishes and
experiences of satisfaction, with potential for a cognitive theory of motivation,
nearly perished from neglect. Holt (1976), in an attempt to rehabilitate the
concept of wish, aptly described the existing state of affairs:

> Its theory of motivation is at once the glory of psychoanalysis and its shame. What
> is loosely known as the theory of instincts includes both a number of Freud's most
> important and lasting insights and some of his most regrettable theoretical failings.
> It badly needs fundamental revision; but the process must be both radical and
> conservative—what is not good must be extirpated at the root, but what is good
> must be retained [p. 158].

---

[1]For instance, in a presentation to the N.Y. Psychoanalytic Society on 11 March 1980, Charles
Brenner offered a major revision of "The Psychoanalytic Theory of the Drives" based on the
proposition that all evidence for drives comes from analysts' knowledge of patients' wishes, conscious and unconscious, and that the classification of and generalizations from these wishes make up
the theory of drives. His use of the concept of wish is essentially commonsensical and the closest he
comes to a definition is, "Everyone knows from simple observation of himself and others that wishes
play an important part in mental life."

The basis for a cognitive, as opposed to an instinctual, model of motivation is found in Freud's (1900/1953) formulation of a prototypical motivational event, a hungry baby screaming or kicking helplessly:

> A change can only come about if in some way or other (in the case of the baby, through outside help) an "experience of satisfaction" can be achieved which puts an end to the internal stimulus. An essential component of this experience of satisfaction is a particular perception (that of nourishment, in our example) the mnemic image of which remains associated thenceforward with the memory trace of the excitation produced by the need. As a result of the link that has thus been established, next time this need arises a psychical impulse will at once emerge which will seek to re-cathect the mnemic image of the perception and to reevoke the perception itself, that is to say, to re-establish the situation of the original satisfaction. An impulse of this kind is what we call a wish; the reappearance of the perception is the fulfillment of the wish. . . . Nothing prevents us from assuming that there was a primitive state of the psychical apparatus in which this path was actually traversed, that is, in which wishing ended in hallucinating. Thus the aim of this first psychical activity was to produce a "perceptual identity"—a repetition of the perception which was linked with the satisfaction of the need [pp. 565–566].

The boldness of this cognitive model may have troubled even Freud, for in 1917 he wrote of the "Fiktion" of hallucinatory gratification. Moreover in 1962 Hilgard concluded that evidence did not exist to support the conjecture that the infant hallucinates in response to its needs. "The truth," he wrote "is probably a metaphorical, one, . . . attributing to the infant what is found in adult dreams . . . and in the hallucinations of deprived adults [p. 481]." My own decision to take such a model seriously was indeed influenced by a personal experience of intense hallucinatory wish fulfillment under conditions of extreme dehydration[2] as well as a long-standing commitment to myself to make sense out of the seventh chapter.

But what most persuaded me was startling evidence that I had encountered quite by accident while reading Helen Keller's (1908) account of the nature of her mental life and experiences before Anne Sullivan taught her language when

---

[2]In 1947, while interning at Gorgas Hospital in the Panama Canal Zone, another intern and I capsized in a small boat about 10 miles offshore in the Bay of Panama during a late afternoon squall. We clung to the hull of our overturned boat the first night as we drifted out to sea. The next morning we were able to right the boat and sit inside, up to our necks in warm salt water with only our heads exposed to the sun. During the second night I lost awareness of my surroundings and instead spent what seemed like many hours standing at the water fountain on my hospital ward drinking the most utterly and vividly delicious ice-cold water and observing the ward activities. We were rescued early the following afternoon by a ship appropriately named the USS Recovery; I didn't regain consciousness for several hours.

she was nearly 7 years old. In a key passage Miss Keller described her "unconscious, yet conscious time of nothingness" prior to acquiring language: "When I wanted anything I liked,—ice cream, for instance, of which I was very fond,—I had a delicious taste on my tongue (which, by the way, I never have now), and in my hand I felt the turning of the freezer. I made the sign, and my mother knew I wanted ice cream (pp. 115–116)." For me, the temptation was irresistible to see this as an example of the hallucination of a previous experience of satisfaction; the case is argued in Dahl (1965).[3] But regardless of whether one takes seriously the possibility of actual hallucinatory thinking in early infancy, Freud's proposal does nonetheless offer a remarkably useful first approximation to a definition of *wish* that goes beyond our usual commonsense understanding: an attempt to achieve "perceptual identity" with a previous "experience of satisfaction." Later we see how this definition needs revision.

III. THE "MEASUREMENT" OF AN UNCONSCIOUS WISH USING MULTIVARIATE STATISTICS AND COMPUTER CONTENT ANALYSIS

Innocent of the eventual outcome, I began these studies (Dahl, 1972, 1974) after gaining access to a large amount of data derived from a tape-recorded psychoanalysis done many years ago. The analyst had identified 58 variables of specific interest in the case and had coded the presence of each of these in abbreviated transcripts of 363 sessions. I eliminated some of the variables that had too few entries to be useful and added a few, including a count of the frequency of the analyst's interventions in each hour. I then factor analyzed two correlation matrices[4] of 53 variables, one using a square root transformation of the frequency of occurrence of each variable, the other using dichotomized data in which the mere presence or absence of a variable was coded. Although the outcomes were quite similar, I decided to continue further analysis using the all-or-none data,[5] which yielded six readily interpretable factors. The variables used to define each factor were as follows:

---

[3]In 1965 I was still so steeped in instinctual drive concepts that my attempt to explain this phenomenon was cast in language I now find somewhat embarassing, laced as it was with cathexes, drive energies, neutralized energy, drive-organized memory, etc. I wrote, "the power of a concept to regulate the flow of excitations and lay down structures is a function of its ability to attract and control the distribution of attention cathexes" (all italicized in the original!). I suppose this means something like: Ideas influence what we pay attention to and what we commit to memory.

[4]All correlations referred to in this chapter are product–moment correlations.

[5]The frequency of analyst interventions was not dichotomized. The method employed was a principal-components solution with varimax rotation of six factors accounting for 73% of the trace variance.

1. RESISTANCE I—frequency of analyst speaking, patient's major speech disturbances, interpretations other than genetic (including transference).

2. FAMILY—mother, father, childhood memories, sister, genetic interpretations.

3. SEXUALITY—heterosexual experiences, having a baby, penis envy and castration, masochistic wishes, positive oedipal feelings.

4. DREAMS—dream report, color in dreams, moving or details of a dwelling, major affect in dream or reality.

5. ANXIETY—anxiety, thoughts of doing violence, anality, patient's reflections on quality of her own associations, fear of hurting children.

6. RESISTANCE II—analyst giving instructions about associations, patient's response to interventions as interactions, involvement–separation theme.

The labels for Factors 2 through 5 and their interpretation seem straightforward; the rationale for labeling Factors 1 and 6 *Resistance* is given in Dahl (1972, p. 245).

Having thus reduced the number of variables and grouped them by factor analysis, it was possible to obtain a score representing the amount of each factor present in each of the 363 hours.[6] The point of these procedures was to examine the changes in the factors over time as well as their relationships to each other. For convenience I obtained averages of the factor scores for each of the 108 weeks (which, when interruptions are included, spanned a period of 2½ years) and plotted them as shown in Fig. 1. Although these separate plots contain many interesting features, my real goal was to devise some overall measure for assessing the course of the analysis. First intuitively and then formally I did what is known as a second-order factor analysis; that is, I reduced these six factors to two by combining the two resistance factors into one (R) and combining the other four factors into one that appeared to represent both content and conflict (C). The concept I was trying to measure was "analytic work," a key to understanding the psychoanalytic process but difficult to capture in a single variable.

My reasoning was somewhat as follows: A patient engaged in what we call *analytic work* will, on the average, tend to talk about certain characteristic topics that include conflicts, anxieties and symptoms, sexual experiences, family and childhood experiences as well as dreams. Although we cannot predict ahead of time the pattern of their occurrence and although talking about such matters may indeed sometimes be in the service of resistance, conflicts, if they are to be resolved, must be talked about and dealt with. Therefore it seemed reasonable to adopt the simplifying assumption that the probability of these topics being dis-

---

[6]These factor scores were estimated by treating the variables chosen to represent each factor as predictors of the factor itself and computing beta weights for a linear combination of the variables.

Factor Scores (all or none data)   108 weeks

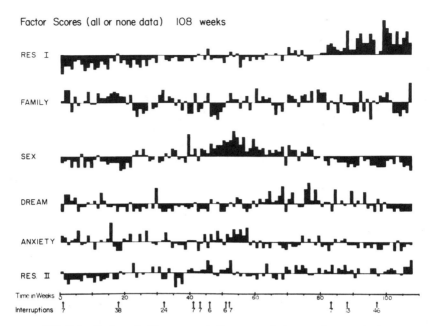

FIG. 2.1.   Each vertical bar represents the average factor score for a week, standardized over the entire 108 weeks. The center line is zero; above the line is a positive score and below is a negative score. The numbers under the arrows at the bottom represent the number of days of an interruption (for various reasons) in the analysis (Dahl, 1972).

cussed would be highest during periods of analytic work and lowest during periods of resistance.[7]

If this reasoning is correct, then the probability of "work" would be greatest when the sum of the four C factors is high and the sum of the two R factors is low; conversely, the probability of work would be lowest when C is low and R is high. Accordingly C minus R ($C - R$) could be used as a rough measure of overall analytic work. The results are plotted in Fig. 2.2 with C, R, and $C - R$ shown separately. The graph of $C - R$ shows dramatically the vicissitudes of analytic work over time. Note that nearly all its values are above the mean until the 38-day interruption of the analysis at the 18th week. Then there is a lot of variability, up and down, until after the 45th week when a rise occurs that peaks at 54 weeks and is followed by a pronounced decline (temporarily reversed by

---

[7]Throughout this discussion the term *analytic work* implies working to overcome the inevitable resistances, whereas the term *resistance* is used in the restricted sense of resistance to doing this analytic work of overcoming resistances.

another positive peak between the 75th and the 80th week) until the end of the period.

Fortunately I had the opportunity to compare the course of the analysis as suggested by the time plot of $C - R$ with the course as described in an independent set of monthly summaries prepared from abbreviated transcripts by an analyst who knew nothing of my measures. The summaries reveal that the patient was a young professional woman who had entered analysis because of difficulties in relationships with men and a wish to change so that she might get married and raise a family. Her analysis had begun with another analyst who fell ill after 102 hours. The analysis was interrupted for several months and then undertaken once again, this time with a woman analyst who happened to be 5 months pregnant at the time. The first 38-day interruption of the analysis occurred when the analyst gave birth. This event corresponds to the sudden shift in the character of the $C - R$ scores. About the 40th week, during a summer when there were a number of short interruptions of the analysis, the patient met a married man, quickly began an affair with him, got pregnant, and during the 53rd week had an abortion with the approval of her lover. At this point the sex factor and the anxiety factor were both high (see Fig. 2.1), but gradually the sexual talk de-

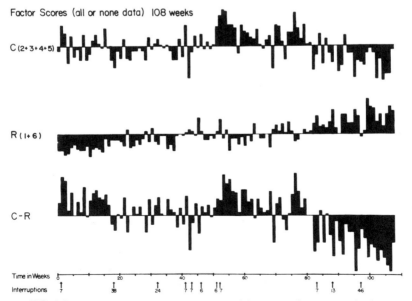

FIG. 2.2.   Each vertical bar represents a sum of the average factor scores for the indicated factors. C is the sum of the factor scores for Factors 2, 3, 4, and 5; R is the sum of Factors 1 and 6; $C - R$ is C minus R. The center line is zero; above the line is a positive score and below is a negative score (Dahl, 1972).

creased, anxiety diminished, and the patient began reporting more dreams. Much of the content of these dreams (corresponding especially to the peak in the $C - R$ score between weeks 75 and 80) is violent and destructive with associations to powerful feelings of jealousy and rage at the birth of a sister when the patient was 2–3 years old. The summary of the case from the 80th week on repeatedly describes the difficult resistance, the stalemate and stagnation in the face of the analyst's increasingly frustrated efforts to deal with the resistance.

In view of the informal success of this first effort to measure analytic work, I decided to use a simple form of computer content analysis further to assess differences in work and resistance sessions. This approach is based on two simplifying assumptions: first, that words, independent of syntax, carry significant information, and, second, that words that occur together are linked in meaning—the principle of association by contiguity widely accepted by analysts. The measuring instrument in this case was the Harvard III Psychosociological Dictionary (Stone, Dunphy, Smith, & Ogilvie, 1966). In this computer dictionary each of about 3200 words is defined by assigning it to one of 55 denotative categories and to one or more of 28 connotative categories; a category, in turn, is defined by the words assigned to it. To obtain characteristic samples of data, factor-score profiles were used to select a group of work hours (high on 2, 3, 4, and 5 and low on 1 and 6), a group of resistance hours (low on 2, 3, 4, and 5 and high on 1 and 6) and a group of "middle" hours with scores near zero on all six factors. Computer programs read the keypunched text of the selected hours and produced a percentage score giving the rate of occurrence of each dictionary category.

The results are shown in graphic form in Fig. 2.3. In 17 categories the scores for 5 work hours were significantly higher than the scores for 5 resistance hours, and the reverse was true in three categories. The 5 middle hours, appropriately, fell nearly on a straight line between the other values. An additional sample of 5 work and 5 resistance sessions replicated the first findings. So it was clear that the dictionary categories were measuring something similar to what the factor scores (derived from the analyst identified variables) had assessed.

What remained, however, was to see if the notions of work and resistance, as measured by multivariate statistics and corroborated by computer content analysis, were in any way akin to the terms as clinicians use them. Would clinicians rate the work hours differently from the resistance hours? Three experienced psychoanalysts were asked to rate 8 (4 work and 4 resistance) hours on a 6-point scale for the amount of analytic work. The reliability of their mean judgments was .90, and the ratings correlated with the $C - R$ overall score .93.[8]

---

[8]Marcia Pollak (1973) did full transcriptions of the same 25 sessions, divided them into minimal idea units (a phrase or sentence) and had raters assess the amount of "perceptual concreteness" expressed in the idea units. The percentage agreement between two judges was 96%, and the ratings

HARVARD DICTIONARY CATEGORIES

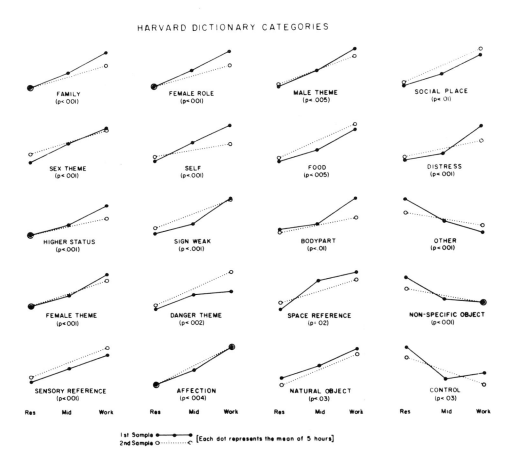

FIG. 2.3.   Scores for 20 Harvard III Psychosociological Dictionary categories for resistance, middle, and work hours. For illustrative purposes, all slopes have been made equivalent and numerical axes omitted. The *p* values, based on linear trend analyses, indicate the significance of the linearity of the relationship between the dictionary category score (plotted vertically) and the three different types of hours (plotted horizontally) (Dahl, 1972).

For the remainder of this section we are concerned with individual words rather than with entire dictionary categories.[9] Many of the words in the Harvard dictionary that might interest us are assigned to both denotative (exclusive) and connotative (overlapping) categories. This fact allows us to ask whether a partic-

---

correlated with $C - R$ .83. Her findings support the notion that the language of "analytic work" is more likely to be close to sensory experience.

[9]Individual words used as data in this section actually represent sets of words sharing a common root (e.g., *anxious–anxiety, ashamed–shame–shamed, guilt–guilty, marry–married–marriage*).

ular word might correlate more highly with the other words in one of its assigned categories than with the words of another category—in other words, to measure the degree to which a word is being used in one sense rather than in another. Table 2.1 shows 13 multiply classified words and their correlations with both denotative and connotative categories. A t test for the significance of the difference between the correlated correlations (McNemar, 1962, p. 140) revealed, for example, that the patient tended to use the word *love* significantly more often in the sense of Affection than Sex Theme and, conversely, that *kiss* occurred in the context of Sex Theme words and almost never with words implying Affection. This method of assessing context of usage seems quite powerful, but to my knowledge it has not been systematically exploited.

Another powerful technique for measuring the context of single-word usage is to look for intelligible patterns of their co-occurrence in the analytic sessions. Because the sample of 25 hours contained several thousand different words, this was quite impossible. It was first necessary to reduce the number of words to a small but meaningful set. The procedure adopted, illustrated in Table 2.2, was to select subsets of words that best reflected each of 15 categories of the Harvard

TABLE 2.1
Words and Categories from the Harvard III Psychosociological Dictionary

WORD [1]	DENOTATIVE CATEGORY [2]	$r_{1,2}$	CONNOTATIVE CATEGORY [3]	$r_{1,3}$	$r_{2,3}$	t	p
LOVE	AFFECTION	.85	SEX THEME	.64	.72	2.51	=.02
KISS	AFFECTION	.19	SEX THEME	.53	.72	-2.66	<.02
MOUTH	BODYPART	.82	SEX THEME	.51	.66	3.09	<.01
VAGINA	BODYPART	.79	FEMALE THEME	.40	.70	4.11	<.001
BREAST	BODYPART	.77	FEMALE THEME	.42	.70	3.44	<.01
ARM	BODYPART	.75	MALE THEME	.59	.85	2.09	<.05
LEG	BODYPART	.41	MALE THEME	.59	.85	-1.95	<.10
PENIS	BODYPART	.92	MALE THEME	.87	.85	1.21	ns
MOTHER	FEMALE ROLE	.71	FAMILY	.82	.90	-2.03	<.06
SISTER	FEMALE ROLE	.52	FAMILY	.67	.90	-2.19	<.05
ANXIOUS	DISTRESS	.57	SIGN WEAK	.36	.83	2.12	<.05
CRY	DISTRESS	.40	SIGN WEAK	.52	.83	-1.13	ns
NAKED	SENSORY REF	.73	SEX THEME	.51	.69	1.92	<.10
			DANGER THEME	.46	.65	2.22	<.05

Adapted from Dahl, 1974.

r_{12} = correlation between the word used by the patient and its denotative dictionary category. r_{13} = correlation between the word and its connotative category. r_{23} = correlation between the denotative and the connotative categories. The t test is for the significance of $r_{12} - r_{13}$. $N = 25$, df $= 22$.

TABLE 2.2
Individual Words from the Sex Theme Category that Were Significantly ($r_{it} \geq .40$)
Correlated with all the Words in the Category

Word [i]	r_{it}	s_i	Index
Love	.64	15.0	10
Sexual	.62	7.4	5
Night	.40	9.6	4
Red	.58	6.7	4
Homosexual	.42	6.9	3
Mouth	.51	6.3	3
Suck	.40	5.0	2
Intercourse	.47	3.7	2
Bed	.44	3.6	2
Kiss	.53	3.2	2
Naked	.51	2.8	1
Animal	.42	3.0	1
Produce	.40	2.8	1

Adapted from Dahl, 1974.

r_{it} = correlation of the word with the category total. s_i = standard deviation. Index ($r_{it}s_i$ rounded to an integer) is used as the criterion for word selection. This index method is equivalent to using item-total covariances as suggested by Nunnally (1967, p. 261).

dictionary that occurred more frequently in work than in resistance sessions. A total score (percent/hour) for the whole category is obtained, and each word in the category is then correlated with the total. The higher this item–total correlation (r_{it}), the better the word represents the category. The standard deviation (s_i) of each word provides a measure of its variability and, other things being equal, the higher the variability, the better the measure. The product of r_{it} and s_i is useful in determining a cutoff point for selecting words for further processing. This procedure permitted a reduction of the set to 47 words.

To determine their co-occurrence patterns, a correlation matrix of these 47 words was factor analyzed.[10] The original factor-loading matrix for 10 rotated factors (Dahl, 1974) shows a very clean *simple structure* with most column loadings either quite high or close to zero with only scattered intermediate values. The first three (largest) factors and Factor 6 seem of special interest. The words with loadings $\geq .60$ on at least one of these four factors are listed in Table 2.3. The intelligibility of the word patterns is partly reflected in our ability to

---

[10]Those readers with some familiarity with factor analysis will perhaps look askance at the ratio of 47 variables correlated over 25 sessions. Normally a ratio of 1 variable to 5 or 10 sessions would be necessary for one to feel free to generalize to the entire population of sessions. We are, however, first and foremost interested in quantitatively *describing* the relationships in *these* 25 sessions, and there is no mathematical reason that prevents doing so.

label the factors as *homosexuality, castration* (symbolically expressed), *incest,* and *loneliness,* respectively. Because factor loadings can be seen as coordinates in an *n*-dimensional space, it is possible to use the loadings of three factors as coordinates in a three-dimensional space such as that represented in Fig. 2.4, where closeness in time has been converted to closeness in space. It is tempting to think of this as the first "literal" psychoanalytic structure!

TABLE 2.3
Factor Loadings on Four Selected Factors for 32 Words that Loaded ≥ .60 on at Least One of the Factors

| | *Factors* | | | |
	1	*2*	*3*	*6*
Afraid	.91*	-.05	-.06	.26
Anxious	.46	-.04	.10	.73*
Ashamed	-.11	-.03	.91*	.06
Baby	-.07	-.05	.66*	-.03
Black	.07	.88*	-.03	-.06
Breast	.96*	-.10	.04	.03
Castrate	.01	.89*	-.06	.09
Close	.28	.73*	-.15	.20
Dress	.60*	.75*	-.02	-.14
Father	.01	.03	.93*	.17
Fear	.60*	.20	-.11	.07
Girl	.49	.10	-.08	.74*
Guilty	-.08	-.11	.89*	-.02
Head	.07	.78*	.24	.18
Homosexual	.64*	-.02	-.10	.23
Intercourse	.24	.17	.71*	-.02
Into	.32	.24	.69*	-.18
Kiss	.90*	.19	.02	-.01
Lonely	-.11	.01	.04	.79*
Marry	.01	.07	.07	.68*
Mouth	.90*	.21	.04	.01
My	.52	.00	.65*	.26
Penis	.93*	.25	.01	.11
Red	.44	.81*	-.03	-.20
Sexual	.75*	.04	.21	-.07
She	.44	.14	.29	.74*
Slightly	.76*	.10	-.05	.04
Tail	.07	.80*	-.03	-.01
Tense	.92*	.00	.00	.14
Up	-.20	.60*	.11	.11
Woman	.61*	.21	.07	.38

Adapted from Dahl, 1974.
High loadings are marked with *. The original matrix included loadings for 47 words derived from a principle-components solution with a varimax rotation of 10 factors.

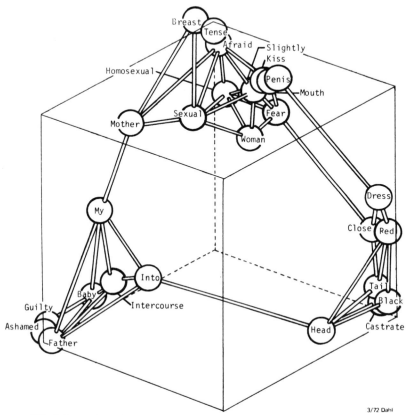

FIG. 2.4. A three-dimensional representation of the three largest factors. Each ball represents a word, and its distance from other words is roughly inversely proportional to its original correlation with that word (Dahl, 1974).

But what is even more striking about these word clusters is that none of them reflect manifest themes in the sessions in which they appear. For example, the seven words with high loadings on Factor 3 (father, ashamed, guilty, intercourse, into, baby, my) all occur in hour 274, but the theme of incest is not manifestly expressed in the text of this hour. I propose instead that this cluster of words is the surface correlate of an unconscious incestuous wish; we might call it the *skeleton of an unconscious wish*. Table 2.4 illustrates the present limits of our ability to represent this word skeleton. And it must be left to the reader to compare the impression given by this skeleton with the impression conveyed in the abbreviated transcript (Dahl, 1974) and judge whether the patient is in fact derivatively expressing an incestuous wish.

TABLE 2.4
Words from Factor 3 (except for *my*) Listed in the Order They Occurred in the
Abbreviated Transcript of Hour 274 Together with the Line Number in Which Each
Was Found

11	Into (A fantasy)				
15		Guilty			
32			Father		
33			Father		
41			Father		
44				Intercourse	
47			Father		
59	Into (An abortion)				
60					Baby
62					Baby
68					Baby
69	Into (Difficulty)				
74			Father		
77						Ashamed
77			Father		
78			Father		
79			Father		
79		Guilty			
87			Father		
97			Father		
98			Father		
100		Guilty			
101	Into (A mess)				
102	Into (A bad situation)				
107		Guilty			
108		Guilty			
111				Intercourse	
115			Father		
120			Father		
122		Guilty			
123			Father		
127	Into (Account)				
128			Father		
129	Into (Trouble)				

Adapted from Dahl, 1974.
Words in parentheses immediately followed each occurrence of *into*.

In any case, the hypothesis that our "measurement" is of an unconscious incestuous wish poses a problem for the definition of a wish proposed in Section I, which calls for achieving "perceptual identity with a previous experience of satisfaction." Even if we imagine, for example, that the previous experience in this case could be a childhood fantasy of incest, nothing the patient reported in hour 274 (not even her taking a married lover and getting pregnant by him) can possibly be construed as achieving perceptual identity with such an earlier fantasy. The best that could be claimed is that some symbolically equivalent behavior might correspond to the earlier fantasy. But this makes it clear that what has been left out of the definition of a wish is some provision for symbolically equivalent expressions and acts. In Section V we see how the definition of a wish must be changed to serve as a fundamental concept in a radically new theory of emotions. In the meantime we return to the problem we left in the hands of the reader: that of judging the presence of unconscious wishes in clinical material.

IV. JUDGMENTS OF EVIDENCE FOR PARTICULAR CLINICAL HYPOTHESES

In the clinical situation we often explain some particular observation by invoking the concept of an unconscious motive. We say that a patient did such and such because of a certain unconscious wish. Moreover, we usually presuppose that such unconscious wishes will persist over time, and therefore our hypothesized motive entails an implicit prediction that the unconscious wish will manifest itself again. What we cannot predict is exactly how or when it will reappear. Rather, we assume that we will be able to recognize the manifestation when we encounter it. Thus the implicit prediction that an unconscious wish will reappear (but in a different form) is actually a prediction not of a single event but of a *class of possible events*. Corroboration or confirmation of our prediction, it follows, entails a judgment of the degree to which a particular clinical observation is a member of the class of possible manifestations of the hypothesized unconscious wish (see Rubinstein, 1980, for an extended discussion). Although psychoanalysts have often been interested in the psychology of such judgments (e.g., the role of empathy, identification, countertransference, and experience in their intuitions), they have not, with occasional exceptions,[11] been interested in the logic of the underlying inferential processes, especially the logic of the relationship between clinical hypotheses involving unconscious wishes and the evidence for them adduced from clinical material.

In 1970 I joined a group of psychoanalysts led by Benjamin Rubinstein at the New York Psychoanalytic Institute to address these issues. We began a 2-year pilot study whose goals were: (1) to develop a scale for clinical judges to use to assess the degree to which a specific item of clinical material supported (constituted evidence for) a specific clinical hypothesis derived from process notes of psychoanalytic sessions; (2) to design a full study that would use verbatim transcripts of sessions from a tape-recorded case; and (3) to provide hypoth-

---

[11]See, for instance, Rubinstein (1973, 1975, 1978, 1980), Edelson (1975, 1977, 1978), and Dahl and Teller (1981).

esis–evidence pairs rated high (good evidence) and low (poor evidence) so that Rubinstein might attempt to transform the statements of the evidence into the statements of the hypothesis and in doing so explicitly note all the auxiliary and ad hoc hypotheses invoked, all the symbolic equivalences necessary, and all the presuppositions required to accomplish the transformation, thereby illuminating the logic and the illogic of the relationship.

Apart from deciding on a 5-point scale (0 to 4) for rating purposes and designing the full study, the main result of the pilot phase was that Rubinstein, using hypothesis–evidence pairs generated from process notes of a single case, was able to produce for two selected pairs, one rated high and the other low, cogent analyses of the steps required to transform the statements of the evidence into the statements of the hypotheses. His results corroborated the clinical ratings (see Appendix in Dahl, Rubinstein, & Teller, 1978).

The full-scale project was implemented using verbatim transcripts of a different recorded case. During the first year a group of analysts jointly and exhaustively examined the first 6 hours of the case and generated over 100 hypotheses about the patient; typical hypotheses postulated unconscious wishes, stated clinical generalizations, made predictions, etc. By consensus the group then selected 25 hypotheses for the second phase. During the second year the same analysts again met to search randomly selected hours (8 hours between sessions 15 and 126) for evidence relevant to the hypotheses. As the group read through a session together, any analyst could stop the reading, identify material in the transcript, and state which hypothesis the material was relevant to. Each analyst then independently rated the degree to which this evidence item supported the hypothesis. In order to obtain a substantial range of evidence ratings, the analysts had specifically agreed that they would not set a threshold level before identifying evidence. They were also enjoined to search particularly for evidence that might contradict or be inconsistent with any of the hypotheses and to identify such items as negative evidence for rating purposes. A record was kept of who identified each item.

Of eight judges one dropped out and took his data with him, and a second dropped out after two rating sessions but left his data. The results summarized here, except for the reliabilities, are based on the ratings of seven judges.[12] A total of 146 evidence items with a mean rating of 2.02 ± .09 were identified as supporting hypotheses. The reliability (alpha coefficient) of these ratings for the five judges for whom there were complete data was .72. Only five evidence items with a mean rating of −1.45 ± .17 were initially identified as negative evidence; the results of their analysis are not included here. Five or more evidence items were found for each of 18 of the hypotheses; the remaining seven

---

[12]The detailed findings in this study are reported in Dahl, Rubinstein, and Wolitzky (in preparation).

received a scattering of 16 supporting items. The judges' ratings divided the hypotheses into three distinct categories with significantly different means:

7 hypotheses with means from 2.34 to 2.61,
5 hypotheses with means from 1.88 to 2.05,
6 hypotheses with means from 1.42 to 1.69.

This trimodal distribution demonstrates the ability of the judges to discriminate the quality of the evidence for different hypotheses. Although roughly equal amounts of evidence were found for the three groups of hypotheses, individual judges differed markedly in the number of items each identified (4 to 42). There was, however, no systematic tendency for any one judge to find evidence for any particular hypothesis or group of hypotheses.

The judges differed significantly from each other in their mean ratings (ranging from 1.42 to 2.40), but they did not differ in the degree to which each agreed with the rest of the group. The mean judge–group correlation, $\bar{r}_{j(T-j)}$, was .54 for seven judges. These preliminary findings suggested that although the judges differed in the average level of their ratings, they were nonetheless able to discriminate among the hypotheses. But there turned out to be a surprise, a serendipitous finding that resulted from recording which judge identified each evidence item.

When the data were reanalyzed to separate the ratings of each judge when he identified an evidence item (the caller) from the ratings of the other judges on the same item, it became immediately obvious that the caller consistently rated the evidence higher than the other judges (means of 2.84 versus 1.86 for seven judges). Moreover, for the three groups of 18 hypotheses, the caller's mean ratings did not differ whereas the significance of the difference for the other judges increased. Also, the mean ratings of all seven judges were higher when they were caller than when they rated an item that another judge called. And when the reliabilities were recomputed with the caller removed, the alpha coefficients increased to an average of .79. Finally, the clearest indication of this caller bias came from comparing the caller–group correlation, $\bar{r}_{c(T-c)} = .31$, with the judge–group correlation when the caller was removed, $\bar{r}_{j(T-j-c)} = .58$, a highly significant difference.

For the psychoanalytic clinical enterprise the results of this study are both reassuring and disturbing. It is reassuring that analysts can make these very complex judgments with reasonable reliability and that they did so in an experimental setting that retained some features characteristic of the actual clinical situation. They used verbatim records, accumulated information about the patient as time went on, generated many different hypotheses about the patient, and then looked for supporting or disconfirming information.

On the other hand, it seems disturbing that the analysts found only a handful of evidence thought to disconfirm any hypothesis, but this may be a problem more apparent than real. For one thing, the lack of correlation between the number of evidence items found for a hypothesis and the mean rating of the hypothesis indicates that the judges found just as much weak evidence as strong evidence. Although there were few negative ratings, there were many weakly positive ratings. Thus the analysts didn't avoid weak evidence. More important, the lack of negative evidence is consistent with the conclusion of Rubinstein (1978), who carefully examined the logic of disconfirmation and cogently demonstrated that the only possible way to refute a proposition of the form ''A has an unconscious wish X'' is to search for and not find good evidence to support it, which is exactly what the analysts appeared to do in the case of the low-rated hypotheses.

More disturbing, and with many implications, is the caller bias in favor of evidence that he himself finds. In the experimental situation we had the judgments of the other analysts to compare the caller with, but in the typical clinical situation there is no check on this predilection to overvalue evidence that one discovers for oneself. It takes little imagination to understand the unhappy consequences of this state of affairs for our confidence in individual clinical reports, much less in the generalized and theoretical accounts derived from them.

One additional result, not discussed previously, was that the logical analyses of the transformation of evidence statements into hypothesis statements turned out to be remarkably and unexpectedly more difficult with this set of hypothesis–evidence pairs than with those from the pilot study. Because of this and because of the serious implications of the finding that we have come to call the ''discovery bias,'' we are now in the process of repeating this study (Dahl et al., 1978) with the main design largely intact but modified to try to solve the logical analysis problem.

V.   A CLASSIFICATION OF EMOTION WORDS AND A REVISED DEFINITION OF A WISH

The motivation for classifying emotion words emerged during the computer content analyses described in Section III from a consideration of the dictionary categories that reflect emotional states. Two emotion categories, distress and affection, were among the Harvard III classes that were higher in work than in resistance sessions. But the word lists that defined these categories seemed overly inclusive. The distress words, for example, although conveying the message quite clearly, subsume nearly all kinds of distress: fear, depression, anxiety, and guilt as well as a variety of physical aches and pains. Furthermore, the factor analysis of 47 significant words had shown that *afraid, tense,* and *fear* loaded highly on Factor 1 (homosexuality), *guilt* and *shame* loaded highly on Factor 3

A 3-DIMENSIONAL CLASSIFICATION TREE

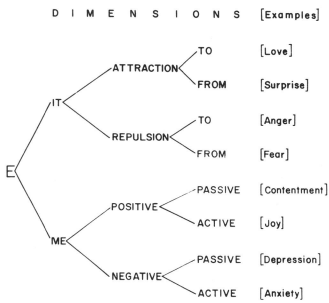

FIG. 2.5. A three-dimensional classificatory tree. An emotion (*E*) is defined by independent decisions on each of the hypothesized dimensions. Included are examples of typical emotions that would result from the eight patterns of choices. All examples except *joy* are taken from the results of the study (Dahl & Stengel, 1978).

(incest) and *anxious* loaded highly on Factor 6 (loneliness). What was demonstrated in this particular case makes general sense—these three forms of distress seem to represent fundamentally different states that are loosely lumped together under the rubric *distress*. Overinclusiveness is a desirable characteristic of the dictionary's connotative (overlapping) categories but not of a denotative (exclusive) category like distress.

A further problem with these categories lay in the absence of any rationale for the way they were constructed, beyond the joint intuitions of Stone, et al. (1978). There was little empirical work demonstrating the reliability of the categories, nor could there be, because a data base sufficiently large and properly designed to make such determinations did not exist.[13]

---

[13]Such a data base now exists in the form of verbatim transcripts on computer tape of 225 psychoanalytic sessions (15 randomly sampled sessions for each of 15 cases). These are the basis for *Word Frequencies of Spoken American English* (Dahl, 1979).

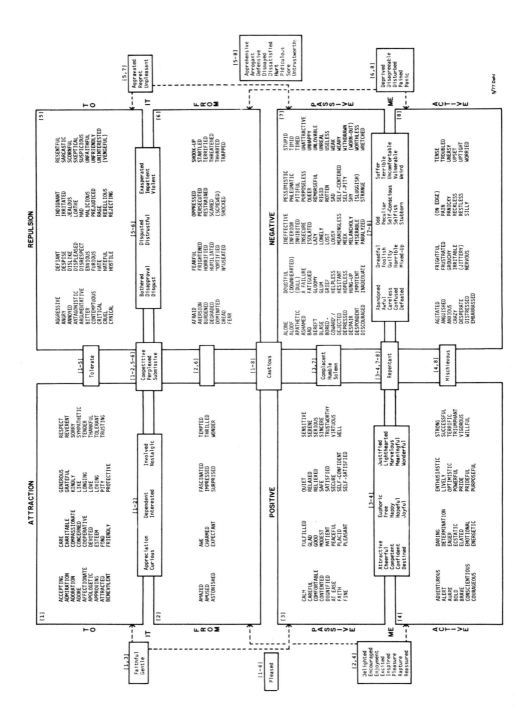

58

Although many classification schemes for emotions have been proposed, almost none of them are accompanied by a classification of a useful number of emotion words. My search for a large list that had been classified according to some clearly describable rationale led to de Rivera (1962) where nearly 200 emotion words were classified according to an abstract six-dimensional scheme. The classification was part of a "decision theory" of emotions, which assumes that a person encountering an object in reality or in fantasy must decide "how to act" toward that object. De Rivera imagined that this "end decision," as he called it, is achieved by some nonconscious cognitive process that makes the equivalent of separate decisions on each of the six hypothetically independent dimensions, culminating in a consciously experienced emotion. One of the appealing features of his scheme was that the first three dimensions closely resembled Freud's (1915/1957) "three polarities" of mental life (subject–object, pleasure–unpleasure, and active–passive). Even more appealing was the ability of 20 judges, using de Rivera's operational definitions, to classify 188 emotion words with agreements far beyond those expected by chance. I decided to modify de Rivera's system and repeat the classifications with more judges and a larger number of words; the methods are detailed in Dahl and Stengel (1978).

After extensive pilot testing, new operational definitions were formulated for the three main dimensions we had decided upon: IT–ME, ATTRAC-TION–REPULSION, and TO–FROM, each assumed to be an independent dimension of a nonconscious cognitive process underlying an emotion. Figure 2.5 illustrates the hypothetical decision tree. A total of 58 judges ranging in age from 18 to 75, all native speakers of American English with at least some college education, classified 371 emotion words on each dimension separately. Among the measures computed for each dimension were alpha-coefficient reliabilities for the 58 judges, r_k, and the percentage of words significantly decided ($p \leq .05$, two-tailed binomial splits). For IT–ME, $r_k = .95$ with 86% decided; for AT-TRACTION–REPULSION, $r_k = .99+$ with 95% decided; and for TO–FROM, $r_k = .97$ with 75% decided. As postulated, the three dimensions were independent, for the correlations among them (between $-.03$ and $-.10$) were insignificant. The results of the classification are shown in Fig. 2.6.

FIG. 2.6.   A graphic summary of the judges' classification of emotion words. The eight main category boxes are numbered 1 through 8 and contain the words (in capital letters) that were decided with a significance of $p \leq .05$, two-tailed, on all three dimensions. The intermediate boxes contain words (initial letter capitalized) that were undecided on one or more dimensions (e.g., *guilty* undecided on PASSIVE–ACTIVE; *pleased* undecided on IT–ME and TO–FROM; and *cautious* undecided on all three). These boxes are numbered to show the alternatives for the partially undecided words: A comma (,) means *and/or*, and a dash (–) means *through*. Thus the words in box 2,4 (e.g., *excited*) could be assigned to box 2 and/or box 4; and the words in box 1–4 (e.g., *pleased*) could be assigned to boxes 1, 2, 3, and/or 4 (Dahl & Stengel, 1978).

Considering the abstractness of the dimensions and the many possible sources of error in the classification process, it seems quite remarkable that, of the 371 original words, the judges agreed significantly ($p \leq .05$, two-tailed) on *all three* dimensions for *259* words; and *153* of these were decided with $p < .001$ (the probability of this occurring on all three dimensions by chance is less than 1 in 1 billion). It is especially interesting to contrast these findings with Brenner's (1974) claims about the uniqueness of emotional experience:

> several hundred words that are listed under the headings of 'affect' or 'emotion' cannot be defined except in approximate terms. They are never precisely the same in any two individuals, and may often be radically different from person to person. . . . Since affects have so often been named on the basis of their conscious aspect alone, it is important to remember that when this is done it may well lead to ambiguity or, worse, to confusion. The same name may be used for very different constellations of pleasure, unpleasure, and ideas in different individuals. Even if those constellations are very similar, moreover, they are never quite the same in any two cases, and the differences are often of considerable practical importance. The reverse is also true. Different names may turn out to refer to very similar affective states. . . . each affect is unique for each individual. Each person's affective life is his own and is never identical with that of another, since each person's wishes, memories, perceptions, fears and expectations are never identical with those of another [pp. 544–545].

Our results flatly contradict Brenner's position. If the differences in our emotional experiences and referents were as substantial as Brenner implies, our judges should have been able to agree only occasionally, perhaps only by chance. The fact is that agreement was neither perfect nor haphazard, and it is hard to see how the data can be explained unless we assume substantially overlapping and intersecting knowledge of specific emotions among the judges. The intrinsic ability of people to communicate their emotions to others successfully must surely rest on this area of shared referents for the labels that they attach to their emotional states.

One of the striking outcomes of this study was the confirmation of a long-standing, almost commonsense distinction between emotions relating to an object (the IT emotions) and feelings relating to oneself (the ME emotions). My attempts to make theoretical sense of this distinction have led to a view of emotions that differs in major respects from other theories (including what passes for a psychoanalytic theory of emotions). This new theory is described at length elsewhere (Dahl, 1978); here I state the main propositions without justification or elaboration.

At the heart of the model lies a revision of the definition of a wish from

Section II—recall that the clue to what was missing was found in Section III. We can now state: *A wish is an attempt to achieve perceptual identity and/or symbolic equivalence with a previous experience of satisfaction.* The implications of the six elements of this definition are as follows:

1. AN ATTEMPT—an active process, otherwise the wish is latent.
2. TO ACHIEVE—a goal is required.
3. PERCEPTUAL IDENTITY—repetition of a perception.
4. AND/OR SYMBOLIC EQUIVALENCE—symbolic expression of goals and alternative or derivative goals.
5. WITH A PREVIOUS—memory is required.
6. EXPERIENCE OF SATISFACTION—initial experiences of satisfaction are phylogenetically adapted, that is, wired in by evolution.[14]

The basic claims of the model focus on the nature of the IT and the ME emotions. The IT emotions are conceived of as a special class of wishes involving objects. These wishes have the essential characteristics of appetites, and the fulfillment of these appetites requires appropriate consummatory acts, just as the fulfillment of the traditional somatic appetites requires suitable consummatory acts. The experience of the emotion is the way we perceive the appetite. The top four boxes of Fig. 2.7 contain the generic name of each IT emotion category (e.g., ATTRACTION TO IT), an example of the class of appropriate consummatory acts (e.g., Take Care of It), and typical emotion words representing the category. According to this conception it can readily be seen that fear is as much of an appetite as thirst or hunger—counterintuitive though it may be—and that satisfaction of the appetite of fear requires a consummatory act of escape from the source or the occasion of fear. In summary, escape from a fear-producing situation is to fear as eating is to hunger. Getting rid of an anger-producing situation is to anger as drinking is to thirst. Tender touching is to feeling tender as

---

[14]Since this definition claims that one can only wish for previous experiences of satisfaction, it is necessary to account for the fact that we nonetheless do acquire and wish for new experiences. Aside from those experiences clearly guaranteed by evolution (e.g., sensory appetites), there are two main ways in which we enlarge our repertoires of satisfying experiences. The first is provided by the IT emotion, ATTRACTION FROM IT, which is the emotional appetite for surprise (see Fig. 2.7), for searching out novelty for its own sake, in short, the emotional aspect of curiosity, which usually guarantees that we will seek out new experiences of satisfaction (Dahl, 1978, pp. 381–383). The second is provided by the ability to represent and express perceptual experience in symbolic form (see element 4 above) and thereby *imagine* what an experience one has never had might be like and to the degree to which this imagining is satisfying; then one would in fact seem to wish for an experience that one has never literally had before.

ATTRACTION TO IT [Take Care of It] *Loving, Tender, Compassionate*	**REPULSION TO IT** [Get Rid of It] *Angry, Contemptuous, Indignant*
ATTRACTION FROM IT [Behold It] *Fascinated, Amused, Surprised*	**REPULSION FROM IT** [Escape from It] *Frightened, Horrified, Startled*
POSITIVE PASSIVE ME ⎡Mission Accomplished (Chein)⎤ ⎣Gratification (Pribram & Melges)⎦ *Contented, Secure, Relaxed*	**NEGATIVE PASSIVE ME** ⎡Mission Failed (Chein)⎤ ⎣Dissatisfaction (Pribram & Melges)⎦ *Depressed, Helpless, Lonely*
─────{ Pleasure — Satisfaction }─────	─────{ Unpleasure — Nonsatisfaction }─────
POSITIVE ACTIVE ME ⎡Mission Going Well (Chein)⎤ ⎣Satisfaction (Pribram & Melges)⎦ *Energetic, Elated, Vigorous*	**NEGATIVE ACTIVE ME** ⎡Mission Not Going Well (Chein)⎤ ⎣Distress (Pribram & Melges)⎦ *Anxious, Distressed, Tense*

FIG. 2.7.   These eight (2^3) generic emotion categories result from the interaction of three orthogonal dimensions adapted from de Rivera (1962). Each category is illustrated by three typical emotion words. The IT emotions are appetites whose satisfaction requires appropriate consummatory acts such as the examples in brackets. The ME emotions are messages (examples in brackets) about the status of satisfaction or nonsatisfaction of appetites and other wishes (Dahl, 1978).

orgasm is to sexual excitement. And who has not planned a vacation to strange and exotic places in anticipation of fulfilling an appetite for novelty, for being surprised and held in fascination?

The ME emotions (usually called affects by psychoanalysts) are conceived of as feedback messages conveying information to oneself about the status of satisfaction (experienced as pleasure) or nonsatisfaction (experienced as unpleasure) of one's appetites and other wishes. The experience of the affect (its *signal*) is the way we perceive the message. And the contents of the messages are classes of *beliefs* about the status of fulfillment of our wishes. The bottom four boxes of Fig. 2.7 contain the generic name of each ME emotion (e.g., POSITIVE PASSIVE ME), two examples of descriptions of the class of message (belief) conveyed, and typical words representing the category. Thus the POSITIVE ME feelings are by definition pleasurable and convey the generic message of satisfaction; they are PASSIVE ME feelings such as contentment when the belief is that our appetites and wishes *have been* satisfied and ACTIVE ME feelings such as enthusiasm when the belief is that we *are being* satisfied and *anticipate* continued or future satisfaction. Correspondingly, the NEGATIVE ME feelings are by definition unpleasurable and convey the generic message of nonsatisfaction; they are PASSIVE ME feelings such as depression when the belief is that one's wishes *cannot be* or *have not been* satisfied and/or *must be given up;* they are ACTIVE ME feelings such as anxiety when the belief is that one's wishes *are not* being satisfied or *are not likely to be* satisfied. The wishes or appetites in question may be either conscious or unconscious, and the range of these includes one's emotional appetites toward other people, one's sensual and erotic appetites, and the entire spectrum of wishes and goals of all kinds that people find to be important and significant to them throughout their lives.

At the beginning of this chapter I emphasized the intimate and necessary relationship between classification and measurement. In a unique single case study designed to pit two psychoanalytic theories of therapy against each other and test their differential predictions of a patient's reaction to an analyst's neutral interventions, Silberschatz (1978) needed a set of dependent variables that would measure both a variety of emotional states and a variety of ways in which the patient might express and convey each state. The theory just outlined implies that consummatory acts and symbolic expressions as well as emotion words themselves should be included in the measurement net. Accordingly, in addition to looking for words from each of the eight categories of emotions, two coders rated sentences for the occurrence of metaphorical expressions of emotion, actions that implied consummation of IT emotions, the indirect expression of the implicit messages of ME emotions, etc. Not only were these ratings done reliably ($\bar{r}_k$ = .83), but these measures also turned out to be decisive in supporting one theory over the other. Moreover, Silberschatz plotted these eight categories over time and found interesting and novel interrelationships in their time courses.

VI.   SOME CLOSING WISHES

In 1978, with Teller, Moss, and Trujillo, I published a paper that presented the *hypothesis* that "certain syntactic properties of a psychoanalyst's interventions communicate countertransference wishes and other warded-off contents." We emphasized the hypothetical nature of our proposal by writing, "What remains for us to determine is whether we have really found what we think we have found." But apparently the 10 examples that we offered were so persuasive that many readers took the case to be already established. A typical comment was, "It seems obvious once you state it." It brought a flood of reprint requests. It was even summarized in Janet Malcolm's *New Yorker* profile on psychoanalysis (1980). And it was used, we were told, to instruct a class for psychotherapists on how not to talk to patients!

We wish the case were proved, for in the meantime we have spent a lot of time collecting 25,000 ratings on 13 scales by 5 judges to assess countertransference and cataloging and cross-referencing over 100 syntactic properties found in 250 individual sentences in 123 analyst interventions. When we're finished, we hope to have found systematic relationships between the countertransference measures and the linguistic variables. We are pitting this hypothesis against the null hypothesis that there is no relationship. But it is well to remember that even if we are able to reject the null hypothesis, we will only have supported, not proved, our original one. Many further studies would be necessary to disentangle the effects of contributing factors such as semantic, phonological, and nonverbal cues. The moral to this is too obvious to need stating.

At this stage of the psychoanalytic research endeavor the truly vital task is not simply empirical studies, but empirical studies that force us to revise our theory, to reformulate our basic propositions, to create statements of theory that will be increasingly accessible to testing. But this is hardly a new idea. In 1972, in a dedication to George Klein after his death, Holt and Peterfreund wrote of the principles that Klein stood for, "the broadening and deepening of the scientific base of psychoanalysis, its enrichment by exchange with other sciences, a commitment to theoretical clarification hand in hand with empirical research [p. 179]."

In practice the job has been difficult. If the reformulation of theoretical propositions is thoroughgoing as, for example, in Rubinstein (1974, 1975) or as proposed by Edelson (1977), then the very unfamiliarity of researchers with the work and the greater ease and accessibility of traditional theoretical propositions makes empirical evaluation of the new ideas unlikely in the near term. But perhaps this strategy has been wrong. Perhaps instead of wholesale revision with its hope of quick revitalization, we should adopt a more modest approach, one in which we take a little piece at a time, revising a bit here, testing the consequences, revising again, etc. Of course, in doing so we run the risk of chaotic theory and thus irrelevant research, and our awareness of this possibility should guide our choices of propositions as candidates for revision.

Undaunted, but modestly, I offer as prototypes for such interaction between theory and empirical work two examples from this chapter. The first is the study reported in Section IV, in which the empirical judgments of evidence for particular clinical hypotheses not only taught us about the clinician's bias in favor of evidence that he himself discovers but also provided the hypothesis–evidence pairs for the critical analyses that explicated the logic, the transformations, and the presuppositions involved in making clinical inferences. It is not unrealistic to hope that such analyses will be helpful in constructing a theory of clinical inference. And because the clinical theory of psychoanalysis consists of generalizations from the claims by individual psychoanalysts about their understanding of the utterances of individual analysands, a theory of the inferential processes underlying these claims would be of enormous value in guiding further research.

The second prototype resides in some empirical implications of the definition of a wish arrived at in Section V—a reformulation that itself followed from an attempt to understand the results of the empirical classification of emotion words. The new definition led initially to a reconception of IT emotions as appetites and the ME emotions as beliefs about the status of satisfaction or nonsatisfaction of wishes in general. In this view, emotions are accorded status as motivations independent of the instinctual drives. There are many practical consequences of such a view that could be empirically examined. A second implication of the definition of a wish lies in its emphasis on the repetitiveness of all behavior, not simply pathological behavior, and it provides a theoretical foundation for this claim. Third, it suggests the importance of asking a kind of question that has seldom been asked, one raised by Premack (1975), about the effects of symbolic behavior on appetitive behavior and vice versa. It does so by making explicit the need for understanding how a symbol can satisfy what previously only a perception could accomplish. Fourth, it makes what is at first a nonobvious prediction that, because memory is postulated as necessary for wishing, persons with severe memory deficits ought to do much less wishing. And finally it points to experiences of satisfaction as an important object for investigation—both into the identification of those that have been provided by evolution and into those that are culturally modified and adapted. Indeed Klein (1972) has done just this in his classification of ''the vital pleasures.''

Whether or not the ''measurement'' of an unconscious wish by objective means, the judging of evidence for clinical hypotheses, the identification of discovery bias, the critical analysis of the bases for clinical inference, the empirical classification of emotion words, the sharpening of the definition of a wish, a new theory of emotions, the measurement of countertransference, and the cataloging of 100 linguistic properties of analyst interventions can in any way be said to be the sort of ''boon'' Quine and Ullian ''want,'' they at least illustrate the intricate interrelatedness of the enterprises of defining, classifying, measuring, and theorizing, which is the point I have been trying to make. Together they provide the matrix for invention and discovery. And I believe that is precisely what most of us engaged in psychoanalytic research want—from time to time just a little perceptual identity or some symbolic equivalence with previous experiences of insight and closure.

ACKNOWLEDGMENTS

Portions of the work reported here were supported by an NIMH Special Research Training Fellowship, a USPHS Research Scientist Development Award (5-K01-MH-23108) and project awards from the Grant Foundation, the New York Psychoanalytic Institute, and the Fund for Psychoanalytic Research. I wish to express my deep appreciation to Dr. Virginia Teller for the many forms of her assistance in the preparation of this manuscript.

REFERENCES

Brenner, C. On the nature and development of affects: A unified theory. *The Psychoanalytic Quarterly,* 1974, *43,* 532–556.

Chein, I. *The science of behavior and the image of man.* New York: Basic Books, 1972.

Dahl, H. Observations on a "natural experiment": Helen Keller. *Journal of the American Psychoanalytic Association,* 1965, *13,* 533–550.

Dahl, H. A quantitative study of a psychoanalysis. *Psychoanalysis and Contemporary Science,* 1972, *1,* 237–257.

Dahl, H. The measurement of meaning in psychoanalysis by computer analysis of verbal contexts. *Journal of the American Psychoanalytic Association,* 1974, *22,* 37–57.

Dahl, H. A new psychoanalytic model of motivation: Emotions as appetites and messages. *Psychoanalysis and Contemporary Thought,* 1978, *1,* 373–408.

Dahl, H. *Word frequencies of spoken American English.* Essex, Conn.: Verbatim, 1979.

Dahl, H., Rubinstein, B., & Teller, V. *A study of psychoanalytic clinical inference as interpretive competence and performance.* Proposal to the Fund for Psychoanalytic Research, 1978.

Dahl, H., Rubinstein, B., & Wolitzky, D. *Judgments of psychoanalytic evidence: Method, reliability, and bias.* In preparation.

Dahl, H., & Stengel, B. A classification of emotion words: A modification and partial test of de Rivera's decision theory of emotions. *Psychoanalysis and Contemporary Thought,* 1978, *1,* 269–312.

Dahl, H., & Teller, V. *The framework for a model of psychoanalytic inference.* Presentation to the Western New England Psychoanalytic Society, New Haven, Conn. March 14, 1981.

Dahl, H., Teller, V., Moss, D., & Trujillo, M. Countertransference examples of the syntactic expression of warded-off contents. *The Psychoanalytic Quarterly,* 1978, *47,* 339–363.

de Rivera, J. A decision theory of emotions (Ph.D. Thesis, Stanford University, 1962) *Dissertation Abstracts International,* 1962, *23,* 296–297 (University Microfilm No. 62-2356).

Edelson, M. *Language and interpretation in psychoanalysis.* New Haven: Yale University Press, 1975.

Edelson, M. Psychoanalysis as science: Its boundary problems, special status, relations to other sciences, and formalization. *Journal of Nervous and Mental Disease,* 1977, *165,* 1–28.

Edelson, M. What is the psychoanalyst talking about? In J. Smith (Ed.), *Psychoanalysis and language.* New Haven: Yale University Press, 1978.

Freud, S. [The interpretation of dreams]. In J. Strachey (Ed. and trans.), *The standard edition of the complete psychological works of Sigmund Freud* (Vol. 5). London: Hogarth, 1953. (Originally published, 1900.)

Freud, S. [Instincts and their vicissitudes]. In J. Strachey (Ed. and trans.), *The standard edition of the* complete psychological works of Sigmund Freud (Vol. 14). London: Hogarth Press, 1957. (Originally published, 1915.)

Freud, S. [A metapsychological supplement to the theory of dreams]. In J. Strachey (Ed. and trans.), The standard edition of the complete psychological works of Sigmund Freud (Vol. 14). London: Hogarth Press, 1957. (Originally published, 1917.)

Hilgard, E. Impulsive versus realistic thinking: An examination of the distinction between primary and secondary processes in thought. Psychological Bulletin, 1962, 59, 481.

Holt, R. Drive or wish? A reconsideration of the psychoanalytic theory of motivation. Psychological Issues, 1976, 9(4), 158–197. (Monograph #36)

Holt, R., & Peterfreund, E. (Eds.). Psychoanalysis and Contemporary Science, 1972, 1, 179.

Keller, H. The world I live in. New York: Century, 1908.

Klein, G. The vital pleasures. Psychoanalysis and Contemporary Science, 1972, 1, 181–205.

Malcolm, J. The impossible profession-II. The New Yorker, December 1, 1980, pp. 79–80.

McNemar, Q. Psychological statistics. New York: Wiley, 1962.

Nunnally, J. Psychometric theory. New York: McGraw-Hill, 1967.

Pollak, M. The function of perceptual concreteness, affect and experiencing in a psychoanalysis. Unpublished doctoral dissertation, New York University, 1973.

Premack, D. Symbols inside and outside of language. In J. Kavanagh & J. Cutting (Eds.), The role of speech in language. Cambridge, Mass.: MIT Press, 1975.

Pribram, K., & Melges, F. Psychophysiological basis of emotion. In P. Vinken & G. Bruyn (Eds.), Handbook of clinical neurology. Amsterdam: North-Holland, 1969.

Quine, W., & Ullian, J. The web of belief. New York: Random House, 1970.

Rubinstein, B. On the logic of explanation in psychoanalysis. Psychoanalysis and Contemporary Science, 1973, 2, 338–358.

Rubinstein, B. On the role of classificatory processes in mental functioning: Aspects of a psychoanalytic theoretical model. Psychoanalysis and Contemporary Science, 1974, 3, 101–185.

Rubinstein, B. On the clinical psychoanalytic theory and its role in the inference and confirmation of particular clinical hypotheses. Psychoanalysis and Contemporary Science, 1975, 4, 3–57.

Rubinstein, B. Psychoanalytic hypotheses and the problem of their confirmation. In K. Irani, L. Horowitz, & G. Myers (Eds.), Pathology and consciousness. New York: Haven, 1978.

Rubinstein, B. The problem of confirmation in clinical psychoanalysis. Journal of the American Psychoanalytic Association, 1980, 28, 397–417.

Silberschatz, G. Effects of the therapist's neutrality on the patient's feelings and behavior in the psychoanalytic situation. Unpublished doctoral dissertation, New York University, 1978.

Stone, P., Dunphy, D., Smith, M., & Ogilvie, D. The general inquirer: A computer approach to content analysis. Cambridge Mass.: MIT Press, 1966.

3

The Subliminal Psychodynamic Activation Method: Overview and Comprehensive Listing of Studies

Lloyd H. Silverman
New York Veterans Administration Regional Office and Research Center for Mental Health, New York University

INTRODUCTION

The "clinical theory" of psychoanalysis is comprised of dynamic and genetic propositions (Hartmann & Kris, 1945). *Genetic propositions* attempt to explain current behavior in terms of earlier events and experiences; *dynamic propositions* address the same behavior from the vantage point of the "here and now" (i.e., the unconscious wishes anxieties, defenses, and fantasies that are motivating the behavior).

Dynamic propositions are, in at least one sense, the most critical to psychoanalysis because clinical practice leans much more heavily on them than on genetic propositions (or on metapsychological propositions that lie outside the realm of clinical observation, Silverman, 1976, pp. 621–622). That is, the great majority of interventions of psychoanalytic therapists consist of interpretations of the currently operative unconscious motives just referred to.

Despite their importance, up until the past 2 decades, there has been relatively little research on dynamic propositions—particularly programmatic research, using experimental methods that have proved capable of relatively easy replication. Thus the claims for the validity of these dynamic propositions have, until recently, rested almost entirely on the reports of psychoanalytic clinicians. As detailed elsewhere (Silverman, 1975; Silverman, Lachmann, & Milich, in press), such reports must be viewed as an unsatisfactory evidential base for a number of reasons, not the least of which is that "clinical data" have rarely if ever allowed controversies *among* psychoanalytic clinicians to be substantively resolved. Thus, it hardly should be surprising that evidence cited from psychoanalytic treatment sessions has not proved useful in resolving controversies *between* psychoanalytic clinicians and clinicians of other persuasions.

I am very grateful to Joseph Masling and Eric Mendelsohn for their many helpful suggestions.

69

The subliminal psychodynamic activation method was developed some 18 years ago as one means by which psychoanalytic dynamic propositions could be subjected to systematic controlled laboratory experimentation. The method involves the observation of behaviors before and after 4-millisecond tachistoscopic exposures of experimental and control stimuli under conditions in which both subject and experimenter are blind to stimulus content. The experimental stimuli consist of verbal messages and/or pictures, with content designed to stimulate the unconscious wishes, anxieties, and fantasies that psychoanalysis views as central motivators of behavior. The control stimuli consist of neutral verbal and pictorial content. In this chapter, I review these studies and comment on the status of the work that has been completed to date. Included is a comprehensive listing of all published articles and dissertations that have used this method.

Subliminal psychodynamic activation experiments can be divided into three types: (1) "laboratory studies" of clinical populations in which the experimental stimuli are intended to either intensify or reduce particular unconscious conflicts and thus exacerbate or diminish the degree of psychopathology manifested within a single laboratory session; (2) laboratory studies of the same kind as those just described, but with nonclinical populations; (3) therapy and educational "adjunct studies" in which subjects are assigned to either an experimental or control group, with each receiving subliminal stimulation over a period of time in an attempt to ascertain if the experimental stimulus can bring about more adaptive behavior.

STUDIES OF CLINICAL POPULATIONS

In these investigations, samples of subjects with a particular kind of psychopathology are seen and stimuli are chosen that on the basis of clinical report and/or theoretical inference would be expected to intensify or diminish the pathology being studied. The subjects in these experiments are seen individually for an experimental session on one day and a control session on another, with their order counterbalanced. The first session begins with the experimenter briefly explaining the purpose of the study and the subject's cooperation is sought. Then the tasks that will be administered (so that the subject's psychopathology can be assessed) are described and the subject is told that several times during these tasks he or she will be asked to view subliminal stimuli that will appear as flickers of light through an eyepiece of a machine (the tachistoscope). The subject is further told that at the end of the experiment he or she will be informed about these stimuli and the purpose that they serve. Then the session proper begins with a "baseline" measure of the subject's propensity for whatever pathological manifestations are being studied. This is followed by the subject being asked to look into the tachistoscope and describe the flickers of light that appear. Four exposures follow of either a stimulus with psychodynamically relevant content (in the experimental session) or one with neutral content (in the control session), each exposure for a 4-millesecond duration. There is then a reassessment of pathology to determine how the subject has been affected by the particular stimulus that has been subliminally exposed.

The procedure for the second session is identical to that just described, except that a different stimulus is exposed between the baseline and reassessment task series. Subjects who were exposed to the stimulus with psychodynamically relevant content in the first session are shown the neutral stimulus in the later session and vice versa. The laboratory arrangement is such that the experimenter who works the tachistoscope and administers the assessment procedures never knows which of the stimuli is being exposed;[1] and other members of the research team who evaluate the material for pathological manifestations are also "blind" to the stimulus conditions.

Studies of Pathology Intensification.   There have been four clinical groups for which pathology intensification has been linked to particular psychodynamic content with three or more samples:

1. Thirteen samples of schizophrenics have shown increases in pathological thinking and/or pathological nonverbal behavior after oral-aggressive content was subliminally introduced (Forest-Letourneau, 1975; Leiter, 1973; Litwack, Wiedemann, & Yager, 1979; Silverman, 1966; Silverman, Bronstein, & Mendelsohn, 1976; Silverman & Candell, 1970; Silverman, Candell, Petit, & Blum, 1971; Silverman & S. E. Silverman, 1967; Silverman & Spiro, 1967; Silverman & Spiro, 1968; Silverman, Spiro, Weissberg, & Candell, 1969; S. E. Silverman, 1969; Spiro & Silverman, 1969).[2]

2. Four samples of depressives have manifested increases in depressive feel-

---

[1]The experimenter inserts the stimulus cards into the tachistoscope according to a code list that another member of the research team has prepared. The cards, which are coded on their backs by the other team member, lie face down and can be inserted without turning them over.

[2]"Pathological thinking" is defined as unrealistic, illogical, or loose thinking and is assessed from psychological tests. A "story recall test" has been used most often, this consisting of the subject's listening to short passages from a cassette tape, for each of which he is asked to "give back as much as you can". The subject's recall is tape-recorded and then scored blindly for "thought disorder" using a manual that is available on request from our laboratory. "Pathological behavior" refers to nonverbal behavior manifested during testing that would be viewed as pathological in the clinical situation. It includes behaviors ranging from psychotic-like (inappropriate laughter, peculiar mannerisms, severe speech blocking, etc.) to anxiety equivalents (nervous tapping of fingers, leg shaking, etc.) and is also scored from a manual from our laboratory that is available on request.

In these experiments, various kinds of oral-aggressive and neutral-control stimuli have been used. They have ranged from pictures of animals (e.g., a lion charging versus a bird flying) to pictures of humans (e.g., a snarling man holding a dagger versus a man holding a newspaper) to verbal messages (e.g., CANNIBAL EATS PERSON versus PEOPLE ARE WALKING). All told, 9 different oral-aggressive stimuli have been used and 11 different neutral stimuli and, for each pairing, it was always the aggressive stimulus that produced more pathology.

ings after the subliminal exposure of oral-aggressive content (Cox, 1974; Miller, 1973; Silverman et al., 1971; Varga, 1973).[3]

3. Three samples of male homosexuals have shown intensifications of their homoerotic orientation after the subliminal exposure of an incest stimulus (Silverman et al., 1976; Silverman, Kwawer, Wolitsky, & Coron, 1973).[4]

4. Three samples of stutterers have manifested intensifications of their speech disorder after the subliminal exposure of an anal stimulus (Silverman et al. 1976; Silverman, Klinger, Lustbader, Farrell, & Martin, 1972).[5]

In addition to those just cited, other psychodynamic formulations have been supported by studies using the subliminal psychodynamic activation method through with fewer than three samples: (1) Hines (1977) found that hospitalized alchoholics manifested an increase in various indices of "ego dysfunction" after the subliminal activation of oral-dependent content.[6] (2) Silverman et al. (1972) found in one sample of stutterers that oral-aggressive content (as well as anal content), when activated subliminally, intensified their speech disturbance.[7]

Whereas in the studies cited up to now it was wish-related content that was subliminally activated, in the next two studies, anxieties that are psycho-analytically understood as reactions to conflictual wishes were activated. (3) Dauber (1979; 1980) found that the stimulus LEAVING MOM IS WRONG, intended to arouse guilt ("superego anxiety"), increased depressive reactions in two samples of depressed college women.[8] (4) Litwack et al. (1979) found that

---

[3]Most often, the measure of depression was the Mood Affect Adjective Check List (Zuckerman & Lubin, 1965). The same oral-aggressive stimuli were used in these experiments as described in Footnote 2.

[4]The measure of "homosexual orientation" consisted of the subjects' ratings of pictures of males and females on a 10-point scale for the degree to which they felt sexually "turned on" by the person in the picture. The higher the ratings for males and the lower the ratings for females, the greater their "homoerotic orientation."

The incest stimulus used was a picture of a nude man and a woman in a sexually suggestive pose, accompanied by the caption FUCK MOMMY.

[5]Stuttering was assessed by having the subjects engage in different speaking tasks with someone in the room blindly noting and rating each instance of stuttering.

The anality stimulus in one study consisted of a picture of a dog defecating (with a picture of a butterfly serving as the control). In a second, it was a picture of a person defecating, accompanied by the caption GO SHIT (with a picture of a person accompanied by the caption MAN THINKING as the control).

[6]"Ego dysfunction" was assessed from Rorschach responses and the story recall test (see Footnote 2).

The "oral-dependent" stimulus was a picture of a woman breast-feeding an infant accompanied by the message MOMMY FEEDS ME.

[7]The oral-aggressive stimulus was a picture of a lion charging with its mouth open and its teeth bared.

[8]Depression was measured by the Mood Affect Adjective Check List (Zuckerman & Lubin, 1965) and a projective TAT scale.

the stimulus I AM LOSING MOMMY, designed to arouse separation anxiety, increased pathological nonverbal behavior in a sample of male schizophrenics.[9] These latter two findings indicate that pathological manifestations can be intensified by activating a link in the psychodynamic "chain" other than wish-related content. (See Silverman, 1977, for data attesting to the pathogenic effects in subliminal psychodynamic activation experiments being transient and a discussion of related ethical issues.)

Can the Results Reported Thus Far Be Understood in Nonpsychoanalytic Terms?

A nonpsychoanalytic alternative and more parsimonious explanation for the findings reported thus far might be that pathology intensified after stimuli were (subliminally) introduced with a negative affective quality. Such an explanation does not have the specificity of the psychoanalytic view that different forms of pathology are related to different unconscious conflicts and that each kind of pathology is viewed as symbolically expressing aspects of one or more particular underlying conflict. Four studies (Lomangino, 1969; Silverman et al., 1976; Silverman & S. E. Silverman, 1967; S. E. Silverman, 1970) make it clear that this more general, nonpsychoanalytic explanation cannot account for all the data. In each of these it was found that just as one kind of negative affective content was intensifying pathology, another kind was not. And, in two of these investigations (Silverman et al., 1976; S. E. Silverman, 1970), there was negative content that did not intensify one kind of pathology but did intensify another. In the Silverman et al. (1976) study, for example, groups of schizophrenics, depressives, homosexuals, and stutterers were seen, each for three (counterbalanced) conditions, in which the following stimuli were subliminally exposed: (1) a wish-related stimulus that the clinical psychoanalytic literature deems as "relevant" for the pathology in question and that had actually intensified this type of pathology in earlier studies: oral-aggressive for the schizophrenics and depressives, incest for the homosexuals, and anal for the stutterers; and (2) a wish-related stimulus that the literature views as "irrelevant" and for which there was no empirical support for a psychodynamic relationship: incest for the schizophrenics and stutterers, aggressive for the homosexuals, and anal for the depressives.[10] The findings for each of these groups were consistent. Whereas further support was obtained for the original "relevant" psychodynamic relationship studied, in *no* instance did the second wish-related condition influence the pathology under

---

[9]The pathology measures in this study were the same as referred to in Footnote 2.

[10]All of these stimuli consisted of pictures of people accompanied by verbal captions such as the incest and anality stimuli described in Footnotes 4 and 5.

consideration; that is, in each case the effect of the irrelevant psychodynamic stimulus did not differ from that of the neutral control condition. Thus, these results are seen as not only consistent with the psychoanalytic position but directly supportive of it.

One other finding that also carries the empirical support for the psychoanalytic proposition under consideration a step further is that the *supraliminal* presentation of psychodynamic content typically does not affect pathology level. In seven studies (Cox, 1974; Lomangino, 1969; Rutstein & Goldberger, 1973; Silverman & Candell, 1970; Silverman & Goldweber, 1966; Silverman et al., 1972; Silverman & Spiro, 1968), in addition to the subliminal psychodynamic-related and control conditions, a third condition was included in which the same stimulus deemed psychodynamically relevant was used again except that the stimulus was shown for 10 seconds rather than for 4 milliseconds. In none of these studies did these supraliminally presented stimuli intensify psychopathology.[11]

Whereas the previous results argue that it is necessary for the psychodynamically relevant stimulus to be out of awareness for pathological reactions to appear, they only indirectly support the proposition that the individual must be unaware of the psychodynamic content itself for the effect to hold. Data bearing more directly on this proposition have emerged from two studies (Rutstein & Goldberger, 1973; Varga, 1973). In both of these studies, the subliminal psychodynamically relevant stimulus contained aggressive content and the dependent variable was depressive feelings as measured by an affect rating scale. Because the same affect list also provided a measure of aggressive feelings, the latter, as a dependent variable, also was examined. In neither study did aggressive feelings intensify; only depressive feelings changed in this way.

---

[11]There were two studies in which a supraliminal condition *did* have an effect. In one of these (Moriarty, 1968), there were losses of cognitive efficiency in schizophrenics after oral-aggressive stimuli were presented supraliminally (as well as subliminally). However, there was no increase in pathological thinking, this being the variable that is viewed as a direct reflection of the schizophrenic process and which *subliminal* aggressive stimulation has proved capable of intensifying.

In the Silverman and Spiro (1968) study, there were two supraliminal conditions, one of which did not yield any pathology intensification, whereas the other did. However, this latter condition not only called for the subjects to view the aggressive (and the neutral control) stimulus supraliminally but also called for their describing what they saw. As detailed elsewhere (Silverman, 1972), the pathology intensification that emerged after the latter condition can be understood as due to the verbalization preventing the subjects from handling the aggressive content adaptively. That is, evidence was cited that under the more usual supraliminal condition (i.e., when the subject views the aggressive stimulus for 10 seconds silently) he or she fantasizes aggressive action, this sparing him the necessity of trying to fend off the activated aggressive ideation with its pathological consequences. If a person is required to describe the stimulus while he is viewing it, however, this apparently interferes with his being able to use the fantasy outlet.

Individual Differences

From a psychoanalytic perspective, one would expect that if account is taken of other characteristics of subjects in a particular pathological sample, in addition to their vulnerability to the pathology that defines the sample, the effects of subliminal psychodynamic activation would emerge more clearly. Or stated otherwise, it has always been part of psychoanalytic thinking to view individual differences as important determiners of the vulnerability of people to the activation of particular unconscious conflicts. Thus failing to consider these differences could be viewed as minimizing the chances of substantial or even statistically significant differences emerging between the effects of experimental and control conditions. Conversely, where individual differences are examined, one would expect stronger results.

This, in fact, has been borne out in three studies (Dauber, 1980; Litwack et al., 1979; Silverman et al., 1976). In the Litwack et al. (1979) study, it was found that for the two experimental stimuli that intensified pathology in the schizophrenic sample—the aggressive stimulus CANNIBAL EATS PERSON and the anxiety-over-separation stimulus I AM LOSING MOMMY—the following two subject variables were relevant to the effectiveness of the experimental conditions: (1) whether the subject tended to defend against aggressive and anxiety-related ideas; and (2) whether the subject's associations to the control stimuli were "neutral."

With regard to the first variable, the overall effects of each of the psychodynamic stimuli were "carried" by those schizophrenics who independently could be characterized as relatively "nondefended".[12] The more "defended" subjects, on the other hand, did not react with increased pathology, presumably because they found more adaptive ways of handling the psychodynamically related contents that were stirred up by the experimental stimuli.

As for the subjects' associations to the control stimulus, as hypothesized, the experimental effects were carried by those subjects whose associations to the control stimulus were indeed neutral. As Litwack et al. (1979) argue: "labeling a stimulus 'neutral' does not make it so, and a subliminal stimulus designed to elicit pathology should not be expected to do so relative to another stimulus which also elicits pathology [p. 87]."

The Silverman et al. (1976) study used a depressive group that was subdivided (post hoc) into one subgroup that used denial against dysphoric affect and another that did not. An increase in dysphoria after subliminal aggressive stimulation only was in evidence for the latter group.

---

[12]"Nondefended" subjects were those whose associations to the aggressive and separation stimuli (after the subliminal part of the experiment was completed) showed no evidence of attempts to mute the impact of what was assumed to be disturbing content.

In the Litwack et al. (1979) and Silverman et al. (1976) studies, the individual differences that were found to bear on the experimental effects emerged in post hoc analyses of the data. Dauber (1980) introduced for the first time an a priori breakdown of his subjects and successfully predicted who would respond to his conflict-intensifying experimental stimuli. His interest, as noted earlier, was in studying depressed college women. In his first study (Dauber, 1979), he found that a sample of these women manifested increased dysphoric reactions after the guilt-inducing stimulus LEAVING MOM IS WRONG. In a follow-up study, Dauber reasoned that only some depressions are guilt-induced and that if he had some way of identifying depressives whose depressions were so based, such a group would clearly be responsive to the guilt-related subliminal message. He thus administered the Depressive Experience Questionnaire (Blatt, D'Affletti, & Quinlan, 1976) that was designed to allow for the distinction between introjective and anaclytic depression (it is the former that is viewed as involving guilt). As he predicted, whereas the latter group showed no response to the LEAVING MOM IS WRONG message, the former group showed a highly significant (p = .001) increase in depression.

Negative Results

Whereas in over 50 clinical samples of various kinds, a subliminal stimulus designed to activate unconscious conflict intensified the pathology under study, in five samples, no such result occurred. Two of these studies involved schizophrenics and three depressives—in each of the five, oral-aggressive stimulation did not intensify the pathology under consideration, as it did in the earlier studies cited with the same two types of populations.

Although no common denominator was found that could account for the two studies of schizophrenics referred to above that produced negative results (Greenberg, 1977;[13] Silverman et al., 1971), such a common factor was noted by Dauber (1979) for the nonreplications with depressives. In finding that his sample of depressed college women did not show intensified depression after the subliminal activation of aggressive wishes (whereas, as noted earlier, they did show such an intensification after the subliminal activation of guilt), he noted the

---

[13]Greenberg actually found a reverse effect—*less* pathology after the aggressive condition. No explanation was offered for this paradoxical result but Greenberg kindly made available to me the Rorschach responses (used as his dependent measure) that he had collected from his subjects. An examination of these suggested that the pathological reduction may have been a function of a general constriction that followed the aggressive condition. Perhaps then, Greenberg's subjects were more resourceful than the schizophrenics seen in the other experiments and were able to maximize their adaptive efforts in the face of threat, this leading to fewer pathological expressions but at the expense of ideational freedom. Obviously, this can be considered as no more than a speculation at this point.

following. In those studies in which subliminal aggressive stimulation *did* intensify depression, the subjects were either psychotics (Cox, 1974; Rutstein & Goldberger, 1973; Silverman et al., 1976) or nonpsychotics who were primed for aggression [14] prior to the aggressive stimulation (Miller, 1973; Varga, 1973). In contrast, in his own sample and two other samples where aggressive stimulation did not intensify depression (Cox, 1974 [who ran both a psychotic and nonpsychotic sample]; Nissenfeld, 1979), the subjects were nonpsychotics who had *not* been primed for aggression. But why should these differences in the samples differentially affect outcome?

A review of some early studies, using the subliminal psychodynamic activation method (Silverman, 1972), allows for the conclusion that in order for the subliminal activation of aggressive wishes to affect behavior, the wishes have to be "pressing" prior to the subliminal stimulation. This state of affairs can be assured either by using psychotic subjects, for the presence of pressing aggressive wishes seems to be part of their psychological state, or by arousing these wishes in nonpsychotics with priming techniques. The findings for depression that Dauber noted were in keeping with this earlier conclusion and the results on which it was based. Further research is very much needed to clarify the relationship between a subject's prior motivational state and his responsiveness to subliminal psychodynamic stimuli. [15]

Studies of Pathology Reduction

I turn now to studies of laboratory effects in clinical populations in which *decreases* in pathological manifestations have been sought. The most frequently used experimental stimulus in these studies has been the verbal message MOMMY AND I ARE ONE, sometimes presented by itself and at other times accompanied by a picture of a man and a woman merged at the shoulders like Siamese twins.

The rationale for the use of this stimulus is as follows. As detailed elsewhere (Silverman 1978; Silverman et al. in press), a number of psychoanalytic clinicians have described the ameliorative effect that symbiotic-like experiences have for some people (i.e., experiences in which there is a merging of representations of the self and representations of the "good mother of infancy" or someone who is unconsciously equated with her). This merging can be gratifying in a number

---

[14]The priming consisted of reading the subjects a passage with a great deal of aggressive imagery with the instructions that they listen carefully and then recall as much of the passage as they could.

[15]The necessity of prior priming for subliminal psychodynamic effects with nonpsychotic subjects only has been found in the case of aggressive stimuli. Stimuli involving content related to incest, anality, and symbiosis have produced psychodynamic effects with nonpsychotic subjects in the absence of priming.

of ways. For example, it can provide a sense of constant oral gratification, or it can imply that loss of the mother cannot take place or that the mother's power and strength are one's own. Presumably, it is because of these many gratifications that merging representations of the self with representations of the good mother leads to more adaptive behavior.

To test this proposition in the laboratory, we attempted to activate an unconscious *fantasy* of symbiotic-like gratification, using the subliminal psychodynamic activation method that had proved successful in earlier studies of pathology intensification. Most of these studies have been conducted with schizophrenics, because it has been through clinical contact with such persons that most of the clinical writings referred to previously (e.g. Searles, 1965) have been based. In 11 studies conducted with male schizophrenics (Bronstein, 1976; Fribourg, 1981; Jackson, 1981; Kaplan, 1976; Kaye, 1975; Leiter, 1973; Mendelsohn, 1981; Silverman & Candell, 1970; Silverman et al., 1971; Silverman et al., 1969; T. Spiro, 1975), there has been a reduction of pathology after the MOMMY AND I ARE ONE stimulus that has not been in evidence after a neutral-control stimulus.[16]

This finding, however, has been subject to the following qualification: It has only been "relatively differentiated" schizophrenics who have responded positively to the "oneness stimulus." That is, in four of the studies cited (Fribourg, 1981; Leiter, 1973; Silverman et al., 1969; T. Spiro, 1975), groups of both relatively differentiated and relatively undifferentiated schizophrenics were seen with the former showing pathology reduction after the experimental stimulus, whereas the latter did not. (In the other eight studies, only relatively differentiated schizophrenics were used.[17])

---

[16]In these studies as well as all others to be cited involving schizophrenics, the same pathology measures were used as were described in Footnote 2. Sometimes one or the other of these measures yielded a significant effect and sometimes both, although it is not yet clear what these variations are due to.

[17]Subjects have been classified on the differentiation variable through the administration of an adjective rating scale (Silverman et al., 1969). Subjects first rate themselves on a 6-point scale for 20 descriptive adjectives. Then, on the same scale, they rate either their own mothers or a picture of a woman intended as a mother figure for the same adjectives. The difference between the self-ratings and the ratings of either the actual mother or the mother figure comprise the differentiation score, with a total of 24 or more qualifying a subject as "relatively differentiated." In various hospital samples, anywhere from 50% to 80% of the patients have been classified as differentiated.

A study by Fribourg (1979) found that 75% of subjects given the Adjective Rating Scale a second time, a month after they were originally tested, retained their classification as either "differentiated" or "nondifferentiated." Thus, the differentiation variable appears to be stable for the majority of schizophrenics. However, because there was a sizable number (25%) for whom this was not the case, it would seem important to administer the adjective rating scale the same day as the experiment proper. This would ensure that the subjects who qualify as "relatively differentiated" would still come under this heading when the subliminal oneness condition is administered.

How has this finding been understood? As detailed elsewhere (Silverman 1978; Silverman et al., in press), we assume that the fantasy of oneness has a dangerous as well as gratifying quality, the former because merging representations of self with representations of someone else can threaten sense of self. Apparently, for the very poorly differentiated schizophrenic, this threat is considerable, so that he cannot take advantage of the gratifying aspects of the oneness fantasy, as the more differentiated schizophrenic can.

That a merging fantasy that threatens sense of self will interfere with, rather than aid, adaptation was more directly supported in another experiment (Silverman, 1970) in which the experimental message was changed from MOMMY AND I ARE ONE to I AM MOMMY. Using a group of relatively differentiated schizophrenics, it was found that the latter message, instead of reducing pathology, increased it, presumably because the new wording connoted a more complete merging of self and object representations and thus threatened sense of self.

A Nonreplication

There has been only one study in which the oneness stimulus has *not* reduced pathology in differentiated male schizophrenics—this reported by Loveland (1978). She gave a group of such patients three subliminal conditions: oneness, control, and aggressive, the last being an attempt to replicate the most frequently reported result on pathology intensification. Loveland replicated the pathology intensification effect for the aggressive stimulus, so that the absence of an effect for her oneness condition could not be attributed to technical problems that sometimes interfere with subliminal registration.[18]

But why then did the oneness stimulus not have the same impact in Loveland's study that it did in the other investigations? The answer, I believe, is that this study was carried out in a psychiatric hospital in Virginia; all the others were conducted in various hospitals in New York. The significance of the different locale was suggested in a telephone conversation that I had with the staff psychologist who supervised Loveland's study. She made the following comment about the use of the MOMMY AND I ARE ONE stimulus. "I think you used the wrong word for mother with our Southern schizophrenics. For most of us down here the word 'mommy' is rather foreign. Southern children typically call their mothers 'mama'".[19]

This remark brought to mind another heretofore puzzling finding. In the results obtained in some of the earlier New York studies, whereas both white and black schizophrenic patients showed the predicted effect, Puerto Rican patients

---

[18]The technical problems relate to illumination level and these are discussed later in the chapter (see page 92).

[19]I am indebted to Mrs. Betty Williams for this observation.

did not. This was the case not only for Puerto Ricans who were bilingual but also for those who for many years spoke only English. Our understanding of this was that for the latter group, as well as the former, the word "mommy" was not used during early childhood, it being this factor that interfered with the MOMMY AND I ARE ONE message "taking." (As a result of this finding, it became part of our research practice some years ago to limit subject selection to native-born Americans.) Loveland's negative results with Southern schizophrenics could be understood in the same way.

Why should it be necessary to use in the oneness stimulus the word for mother that was actually used by the schizophrenic during childhood? One could safely assume that both the Puerto Rican and Southern subjects knew the meaning of "mommy," so that the problem was not that of having used a word that was beyond the participants' comprehension. Rather, we think it was because the word "mommy" for the nonusers did not have the particular connotations that it had for those who have used the word—that of the *good* mother of early childhood. We suppose that in order for a fantasy of oneness with mother to be ameliorative it must be with the mother when she was experienced or fantasized as loving and gratifying. This would be particularly the case with schizophrenics, about whom clinicians generally would agree, mother is most often experienced as ungratifying or in other ways "bad."[20] Oneness experiences with the "bad mother," I assume, would be anything but ameliorative. Consequently, only when the word for mother used in a oneness message specifically stimulates good mother associations is a positive outcome to be expected.

Two implications of this revised formulation can be tested. First, the use of the message MOTHER AND I ARE ONE should not have the same ameliorative effect as MOMMY AND I ARE ONE, because the former word does not refer specifically to the *good* mother. Second, for schizophrenics who used a word other than "mommy" for the good mother, the use of *that* word in the oneness message should produce the same pathology-reducing effect that MOMMY AND I ARE ONE produced in the studies other than Loveland's.

A Sex Difference Among Schizophrenics Emerges

As noted previously, all the studies thus far cited on the ameliorative effects of the MOMMY AND I ARE ONE stimulus used male samples. Cohen's (1977) experiment was the first to use a sample of female (relatively differentiated) schizophrenics. She failed to obtain the experimental effect that had been found for males. Interestingly, however, she did find this effect with a different oneness stimulus—the phrase DADDY AND I ARE ONE (accompanied by the

---

[20]Note that I am writing here of the schizophrenic's *experience* of his mother and not the way she actually was.

picture of the man and woman merged at the shoulders like Siamese twins.) This latter (verbal) stimulus had been used in an earlier experiment by Kaye (1975), who obtained the converse results with a sample of male (differentiated) schizophrenics (i.e., an effect with MOMMY AND I ARE ONE but not with DADDY AND I ARE ONE).[21]

From the studies of Cohen and Kaye it seemed as if male and female schizophrenics respond positively to different kinds of oneness fantasies. However, this conclusion needed confirmation in a single study with schizophrenics of both sexes, in which both MOMMY AND I ARE ONE and DADDY AND I ARE ONE were used. Such a study recently has been completed by Jackson (1981). Male differentiated schizophrenics responded with decreased pathology after MOMMY AND I ARE ONE but not after DADDY AND I ARE ONE, whereas for female differentiated schizophrenics the results were reversed.[22] Thus the sex difference between schizophrenic men and women regarding the type of oneness fantasies that are ameliorative that was suggested by the earlier studies can be viewed as a reliable phenomenon, the theoretical and therapeutic implications of which are discussed elsewhere (Silverman, Lachmann, & Milich, in press).

Laboratory Studies of Pathology Reduction in Nonschizophrenic Clinical Populations

Laboratory studies involving the MOMMY AND I ARE ONE stimulus have been conducted on four nonschizophrenic clinical samples. In each of two groups of homosexual men, this condition resulted in diminished anxiety and defensive-

---

[21]Kaye also found pathology reduction for his sample after the stimulus MY GIRL AND I ARE ONE. Because, as noted previously, Kaye did not obtain the effect with DADDY AND I ARE ONE, he concluded that a fantasy of oneness, in order to be pathology reducing for schizophrenics, cannot involve just *any* significant figure in the schizophrenic's life but must involve a maternal representation; and the stimulus MY GIRL AND I ARE ONE was viewed as referring to such a representation.

It should be added, that in Bronstein's (1976) study (where there was an effect with MOMMY AND I ARE ONE) Kaye's finding with MY GIRL AND I ARE ONE could not be replicated. However, as Bronstein noted, the conditions under which he gave the MY GIRL stimulus were not the same as those of Kaye. Kaye's procedure—but not Bronstein's—included an interview prior to the experiment proper, in which an inquiry was made into each patient's relationships with girlfriends and wives. Bronstein suggests that this may well have served as a priming of ideas related to MY GIRL and that this priming was necessary in order for the experimental stimulus to "take." Further research is needed to test this supposition.

[22]Jackson subdivided his sample and used two kinds of pictures to accompany his MOMMY AND I ARE ONE and DADDY AND I ARE ONE verbal messages. For one subgroup the pictures were of two adults (either a man and a woman, two men, or two women depending on the message and the sex of the subjects) merged at the shoulders like siamese twins. For the other subgroups it was of a mother or a father holding a toddler-age child (either a boy or girl) in her arms with some of the lines of the two figures obliterated so that a merging is suggested. There was no difference between the effects of the two kinds of pictures.

ness (Silverman, Kwawer, Wolitzsky, & Coron, 1973). With depressed women, one positive finding (i.e., diminished depressive reactions following the oneness stimulus) was found by Nissenfeld (1978), but in Dauber's (1980) study, already referred to, in which a guilt-inducing stimulus increased depression, the oneness stimulus failed to be ameliorative.

It is of interest to note that whereas both male samples showed effects, only one of the two female samples did so. Thus, it would seem that as in the case with the schizophrenic samples the MOMMY AND I ARE ONE stimulus is a reliable pathology alleviator for males but not for females. After presenting parallel findings for groups of normal male and female subjects, I further consider this sex difference.

The Specificity of the Oneness Fantasy

After a number of replications of the MOMMY AND I ARE ONE effect were completed, several doctoral students investigated the essentiality of oneness in the pathology-reducing message. Kaplan (1975), in a study of differentiated male schizophrenics, compared the standard message not only with a control but with MOMMY FEEDS ME WELL, MOMMY IS ALWAYS WITH ME, and I CANNOT HURT MOMMY, the latter three being viewed as reassuring messages involving MOMMY but not including the specific element of oneness. Only the oneness stimulus resulted in pathology reduction.

Similarly, Bronstein (1976), with the same kind of population, introduced the new messages MOMMY AND I ARE ALIKE, MOMMY AND I ARE THE SAME, and MOMMY IS INSIDE ME, which he viewed as various ways of fantasizing the internalization of MOMMY other than through oneness. Again, only the oneness stimulus produced ameliorative effects.

On the other hand, in a study by Mendelsohn (1981), the message MOMMY AND I ARE TWO as well as MOMMY AND I ARE ONE was found to ameliorate schizophrenic pathology. (Each of these messages was accompanied by a picture of a man and a woman next to each other—in the former condition, joined at the shoulders; in the latter, simply side by side.) Do these results contradict the conclusion that it is the fantasy of oneness that ameliorates pathology in (differentiated) schizophrenics? I do not think so for the following reason. When Mendelsohn obtained associations to both MOMMY stimuli (i.e., both the messages and the accompanying pictures) from some of his subjects after the experiment was completed, he found that many of the associations to MOMMY AND I ARE TWO had much in common with those to MOMMY AND I ARE ONE. That is, contrary to his expectations, the TWO message, in conjunction with the picture, rather than eliciting associations of alienation or separation, instead stimulated ideas about togetherness and even a figurative oneness.

From this, Mendelsohn argued that the MOMMY AND I ARE TWO stimulus seemed to have activated in his subjects a fantasy involving oneness elements but with greater differentiation from the mothering figure. That is, in keeping with the point made earlier about oneness fantasies being potentially threatening as well as gratifying, the TWO message (at least when accompanied by the picture that has been described)[23] seemed able, at least for certain kinds of subjects, to provide gratifying aspects of oneness while avoiding the mobilization of threat.

Further support for this interpretation emerged from Dauber's (1980) study with depressed college women. As noted earlier, he did not obtain ameliorative effects with the MOMMY AND I ARE ONE stimulus. However, he did obtain such effects with the same MOMMY AND I ARE TWO message–picture combination that Mendelsohn had used. Furthermore, Dauber obtained (from *all* his subjects) associations to MOMMY AND I ARE TWO after the experiment was over. He found that these associations could be classified into two groups—those referring to closeness, togetherness, and a figurative oneness (e.g., sharing the same ideas or being one in spirit) and those related to separation and alienation. The group result of reduced depression after the MOMMY AND I ARE TWO stimulus was found to be carried by the subjects who gave the former kind of associations.

Although further study of the effects of MOMMY AND I ARE TWO with various populations is very much needed, the following formulation seems tenable. With persons for whom oneness poses a particular threat—and both schizophrenics and depressives, particularly college-age depressives can be put under this heading—the TWO stimulus may well provide a safer avenue to symbiotic-like gratifications than the ONE stimulus. This formulation warrants extensive investigation.

LABORATORY STUDIES OF NONCLINICAL POPULATIONS

Several laboratory studies have been carried out with "nonclinical" populations—typically, with unselected college students fulfilling an introductory psy-

---

[23]In the study by Fribourg (1981) noted earlier as one of those in which MOMMY AND I ARE ONE reduced pathology in relatively differentiated schizophrenics, another stimulus also had this effect. This was the message MOMMY GIVES ME EVERYTHING accompanied by a picture of a woman cradling an infant in her arms. Because this effect may have been produced by the picture rather than the words and because, as Fribourg notes, the picture has symbiotic-like connotations, the same type of fantasy may have been activated by this stimulus as by MOMMY AND I ARE ONE. It also is to be noted, however, that whereas this new stimulus only affected the pathological nonverbal behavior measure, MOMMY AND I ARE ONE reduced pathological thinking as well, it being the latter that is linked to "thought disorder," a distinguishing characteristic of schizophrenia.

chology course requirement. Two types of experiments of this kind have undergone replication attempts and it is these that I now review in some detail.

In one of these studies, the effects of oneness fantasies on anxiety level was the point of focus. Florek (1978) initiated this line of investigation by conducting a study at St. John's University with undergraduates, administering the state form of the State-Trait Anxiety Scale and a word-recognition task after a subliminal control and subliminal oneness condition. The latter, however, did not involve the MOMMY AND I ARE ONE stimulus that had been used extensively with clinical populations but instead the message MY LOVER AND I ARE ONE—accompanied by a picture of a man and woman looking lovingly at each other. In keeping with Bergmann's (1971) hypothesis that the experience of being in love involves symbiotic-like experiences (if not memory traces) and the findings of Kaye (1976) with MY GIRL AND I ARE ONE (see Footnote 21), Florek reasoned that college students would respond positively to the message MY LOVER AND I ARE ONE and a pictorial accompaniment.[24]

Florek's results were in keeping with his hypothesis. With a group of undergraduates of both sexes, he found a reduction in anxiety and an increase in word recognition after the oneness stimulus.

In a subsequent study, recently carried out at New York University (Silverman & Grabowski, 1982), the finding on the anxiety measure (though not on word recognition) was replicated.[25] A closer examination of the data from both this experiment and the one conducted by Florek indicated that these group results were carried by female subjects.

---

[24]The picture consisted of a man and a woman looking at each other. For this stimulus as well as MOMMY AND I ARE TWO (Dauber, 1980; Mendelsohn, 1981) and MOMMY GIVES ME EVERYTHING (Fribourg, 1981) it is unclear whether the experimental effects have been produced by the verbal message, the picture, or both in combination. Further experiments are needed to sort out these possibilities. For the MOMMY AND I ARE ONE effect, it is clear from the studies by Bronstein, 1976; Kaplan, 1976; Kaye, 1975; and T. Spiro, 1975, that the verbal message alone reduces pathology in schizophrenics. However, Kaplan (1976) ran two MOMMY AND I ARE ONE groups, one of which was exposed to the picture (of man and woman merged at the shoulders) together with the verbal message. This group produced stronger pathology-reducing effects than the group that was exposed only to the verbal message. No study has yet sought effects for the picture alone.

[25]There also has been one study (Shifren, 1980) that failed to replicate Florek's results. However, in this study a picture was used as an accompaniment to the MY LOVER AND I ARE ONE verbal message that was different from the one employed by Florek (1978) and Silverman and Grabowski (1982). It consisted of a man and woman embracing (instead of looking at each other). It is possible that the new picture activated sexual fantasies and these evoked anxiety in enough subjects so that the anxiety reducing effects of the oneness message were negated. This supposition should, of course, be tested in a single study in which MY LOVER AND I ARE ONE is paired with both pictures. As we have learned in previous experiments, it is hazardous for an experimenter to introduce a new pictorial accompaniment without first pitting its effectiveness against the standard picture.

This sex difference was thus the opposite of the finding noted in the last section for MOMMY AND I ARE ONE, which has been a reliable adaptation-enhancing stimulus for men but not for women. Thus, it was suggested that for (relatively) normal subjects, as well as schizophrenics, a different kind of oneness fantasy may be optimally effective for the two sexes. To test this possibility more rigorously, a further study was conducted in which both male and female college students were given MY LOVER AND I ARE ONE, MOMMY AND I ARE ONE, and a control stimulus, using the same design that has been described. The MY LOVER stimulus significantly reduced anxiety only for the women, whereas the MOMMY stimulus had this ameliorative effect only for the men (Silverman & Grabowski, 1982).

How can we understand this sex difference? Our tentative understanding is that the MY LOVER stimulus was ineffective for the men because it did not have clearly heterosexual connotations. Rather, we surmised, it aroused homosexual threat in some of the sample, thus nullifying the therapeutic ''properties'' of the oneness fantasy.

Conversely, we suspect that MOMMY AND I ARE ONE threatened a portion of this college female sample, as it threatened schizophrenic women (thus the absence of a MOMMY AND I ARE ONE effect in the studies of Cohen (1977) and Jackson (1981) with schizophrenic populations) as well as some women from a nonschizophrenic clinical population. (Whereas the oneness stimulus produced positive results in Nissenfeld's sample of female depressives, it produced no results in Dauber's sample.)

But what makes the MOMMY AND I ARE ONE fantasy threatening for females? Earlier, I proposed that such a fantasy can be threatening to either males or females because it endangers sense of self. Now I would add that this danger is more apt to materialize for females because, as is detailed elsewhere (Silverman et al., in press) females differentiate themselves from their mothers less than males do. Thus, in harboring a symbiotic-like fantasy with mother, it is more likely that a female than a male will feel a threat to sense of self; and consequently a fantasy in which someone other than mother is the ''symbiotic partner'' (e.g., DADDY or MY LOVER) is more apt to be sought by females.[26]

The other type of subliminal psychodynamic activation study that has been conducted with several nonclinical samples has looked at the effects of oedipal stimuli on competitive activity. In a paradigm innovated by Ross (1977), college males, after being primed for competition, particularly in relation to their fathers,

---

[26]As is discussed in Silverman, Lachmann and Milich (in press) it is possible that the DADDY AND I ARE ONE and MY LOVER AND I ARE ONE stimuli triggered post symbiotic fantasies—i.e., fantasies from a later developmental period in which oneness was sought with someone who was *not* a substitute for the ''symbiotic mother''. Further clarifying experiments are very much in order.

throw several series of eight darts, each series being preceded by tachistoscopic stimulation. The oedipal-level stimuli that have been used include one that is intended to sanction surpassing father in competition (BEATING DAD IS OK, accompanied by a picture of an older man looking approvingly at a younger man) and the other, condemning such competition (BEATING DAD IS WRONG, accompanied by a picture of the older man looking disapprovingly). Four experiments were initially conducted in our laboratory (Silverman, Ross, Adler, & Lustig, 1978), with three of them producing positive results. That is, in each of the three, the OK stimulus led to significantly higher dart scores than the WRONG stimulus.[27]

Subsequently, there have been attempts by 11 investigators to replicate this finding. Their results can be categorized under three headings: (1) clear-cut replications; (2) partial replications in which there were the hypothesized effects for the first four dart throws but not for all eight dart throws as there were in the earlier studies; (3) nonreplications. In the first category were experiments reported by Carroll (1979), Glennon (in preparation), Lonski and Palumbo (1978), Palumbo (1979), and Silverstein (1978). Citrin (1979), Shaver (1978), and Swanson (1980) ran experiments that produced results in the second category. In the third category were investigations by Haspel (1979), Heilbrun (1980), Winnett (1981), Shaver (1978) and Swanson (1980), the last two appearing in this category as well as the second because they ran more than one sample.

As to what the negative findings could be due to, Carroll (1979) and Glennon (in preparation) have offered some interesting leads. Each of them independently examined subject variables that correlated with their experimental effects and reached a similar conclusion: The overall group effects obtained were carried by subjects whose defenses could be characterized as relatively "ineffective or unsuccesful" (Carroll, 1979; p. 31).[28]

It is thus possible that the populations in which there have been negative findings using the dart paradigm contained subjects who had stronger defenses than the subjects in the studies that produced positive results. It is also possible that the effectiveness of the subjects' defenses against the oedipal motives that were stimulated varied as a function of other variables (e.g., the varying personalities of the experimenters or subtle differences in procedure). Clearly, further study is called for.

One other finding from the studies using the dart paradigm should be mentioned. In three of the investigations, data emerged arguing for the specificity of

---

[27]The experiment that did not produce positive results is discussed later (p. 92) as an instance in which incorrect lighting conditions produced "bleaching" and precluded subliminal registration.

[28]"Ineffective or unsuccessful defenses" were assessed by Carroll (1979) through an examination of responses on the Defense Mechanism Inventory in relation to performance on a test for hemisphericity.

the oedipal fantasy affecting competitive performance. Lonski and Palumbo (1978) used the messages BEATING MOM IS OK and BEATING MOM IS WRONG as well as BEATING DAD IS OK and BEATING DAD IS WRONG, but they only found their (male) subjects responsive to the DAD messages. Palumbo (1979), while obtaining results for the BEATING DAD stimuli, found his subjects unaffected by the messages BEATING HIM IS OK and BEATING HIM IS WRONG). Thus, experimental effects in these two studies were lost when the sanction and condemnation messages did not specifically involve father.

Silverstein (1978) in one of his experiments approached the issue of specificity differently by presenting an additional pair of stimuli that he hypothesized *would* activate specifically oedipal fantasies. He used the messages WINNING MOM IS OK and WINNING MOM IS WRONG, which he viewed as addressing the libidinal (rather than aggressive) side of the oedipus complex. As a control, he also used the messages WINNING DAD IS OK and WINNING DAD IS WRONG (analogous to Lonski and Palumbo using as controls BEATING MOM IS OK and BEATING MOM IS WRONG). Silverstein found that whereas the WINNING MOM messages affected their subjects, the WINNING DAD messages did not. Taken together, the results from these three experiments argue strongly that oedipal fantasies affect competitive performance in a way that other fantasies—even those that have elements in common with the oedipal fantasies—do not.

Therapy and Educational Adjunct Studies

These investigations were initiated to capitalize on the adaptation-enhancing effects found in the laboratory studies with subliminal oneness stimulation. It was reasoned that because positive effects emerged after the activation of oneness fantasies in single laboratory sessions, their repeated activation over a period of time might well enhance the effectiveness of therapy and educational modalities.

To test this idea, a between-subjects instead of within-subjects design has been used with subjects randomly assigned to an experimental and control group, each of which is given a therapy or educational modality that there is reason to believe is effective in its own right. The modality is accompanied by subliminal stimulation, with the experimental group receiving MOMMY AND I ARE ONE and the control group, a relatively neutral message such as PEOPLE ARE WALKING. Comparisons are then made of the pre- and posttreatment assessments for both groups.

In the studies carried out in our laboratory, this design was used for studying insect phobics who were receiving a variant of systematic desensitization (Silverman, Frank, & Dachinger, 1974); schizophrenics receiving hospital treatment (Silverman, Levinson, Mendelsohn, Ungaro, & Bronstein, 1975); and overweight women receiving behavior modification techniques (Martin, 1975; Silverman, Martin, Ungaro, & Mendelsohn, 1978; Ungaro, 1981). Others have used the technique with other kinds of populations, namely alcoholics receiving counseling (Schurtman, Palmatier, & Martin, in press), cigarette smokers receiving a "rapid smoking" behavior modification intervention (Palmatier & Bornstein, 1980), adolescent "character disorders" with severe learning difficulties being treated in a residential treatment setting (Bryant-Tuckett, 1980), college students in group therapy (Linehan & O'Toole, 1982), and high school and college students being given academic counseling as well as classroom teaching (Ariam, 1979; Zuckerman, 1980; Parker, 1982).

Altogether, 14 studies have been completed in which the MOMMY AND I ARE ONE stimulus has been used as an aid in enhancing adaptation. Of these, 11 have reported positive results (Ariam, 1979; Bryant-Tuckett, 1980; Zuckerman, 1980; Linehan & O'Toole, 1982; Martin, 1975; Palmatier & Bornstein, 1980; Parker, 1982; Schurtman et al., in press; Silverman, et al., 1974; Silverman et al., 1975; Silverman, Martin et al., 1978; Zuckerman, 1980) and 3 have reported negative findings (Condon & Allen, 1980; Emmelkamp & Straatman, 1976; Ungaro, 1981). As detailed elsewhere (Silverman et al., in press) an examination of the results of these studies allows for the following generalizations. Results have been most reliable and strongest when: (1) there have been frequent sessions (i.e., four or five per week); (2) male subjects have been used; (3) subjects have been strongly motivated to change their behavior.

For example, the study by Palmatier and Bornstein (1980) investigating the "staying power" of rapid smoking and other behavioral techniques for helping smokers give up their habit, met all three criteria[29] and produced particularly robust effects. At a 1-month follow-up, 67% of the experimental subjects had remained abstainers, whereas only 12½ of the control subjects could be so classified.

Conversely, in an investigation by Condon and Allen (1980) that attempted to replicate findings from an earlier study (Silverman et al., 1974) on the use of subliminal oneness stimulation accompanying systematic desensitization in the treatment of insect phobias, subliminal stimulation was given only once a week, females were used, and the subjects entered the study to fulfill an introductory psychology class requirement. As noted previously, this was one of the three treatment adjunct studies that produced negative results.[30]

---

[29]Both males and females were used in the Palmatier and Bornstein study, but when a post hoc comparison was made of the results for each of the sexes separately (Palmatier, personal communication), the overall results were found to be "carried" by the males.

[30]In the Silverman et al. (1974) study, although the stimulation was infrequent and females were used, the subjects actively sought treatment for their phobias and thus could be judged to be

TABLE 3.1

Type 1 (Laboratory studies with pathological populations)

1.	Silverman, 1966
2.	Silverman and S. E. Silverman, 1967
3.	Silverman and Spiro, 1967
4.	Silverman and Spiro, 1968
5.	Spiro and Silverman, 1969
6.	Silverman, Spiro, Weissberg and Candell, 1969
7.	Silverman and Candell, 1970
8.	Silverman, Candell, Pettit, and Blum, 1971
9.	Silverman, Klinger, Lustbeder, Farrell, and Martin, 1972
10.	Silverman, Kwawer, Wolitzky, and Coron, 1973
11.	Silverman, Bronstein, and Mendelsohn, 1976

Type 2 (Laboratory studies with normal populations)

12.	Silverman and D. K. Silverman, 1954
13.	Silverman, 1965
14.	Silverman and Foldweber, 1966
15.	Silverman, Ross, Adler, and Lustig, 1978

Type 3 (Treatment adjunct studies)

16.	Silverman, Frank, and Dachinger, 1974
17.	Silverman, Levinson, Mendelsohn, Ungaro, and Bronstein, 1975
18.	Silverman, Martin, Ungaro, and Mendelsohn, 1978

A COMPREHENSIVE LISTING

Tables 3.1 and 3.2, which list all studies involving subliminal psychodynamic activation that have been reported in articles and doctoral dissertations, complete the overview. Table 3.1 cites investigations in which I was one of the investigators, whereas Table 3.2 cites studies of others. The studies in the latter table are categorized under three headings: Clearly Supportive, Clearly Non-supportive, and a middle group that for the various reasons listed, are best seen as requiring some other designation. I have limited Table 3.2 to published articles and doctoral dissertations, because to include other studies would have allowed selectivity to play a role in the listing. That is, since other experimenters—mainly students fulfilling a course requirement—have sometimes told me about their findings and sometimes not, it would have been misleading for the listing to be based on personal report. On the other hand, all articles and dissertations reporting the use

---

considerably more motivated than Condon and Allen's subjects. As is detailed elsewhere (Silverman, 1982), the difference in subject populations would seem to be the most likely reason for the different results found in the two studies.

TABLE 3.2

Clearly Supportive	Mixed Results[a] Non-hypothesized Support Reverse Effects[b]	Clearly Non-supportive
1. Antell, 1969-B	1. Brenner, 1980-A+	1. Condon, 1976-C
2. Ariam, 1979-C	2. Citrin, 1979-B*+	2. Emmelkamp & Straatman,
3. Bronstein, 1976-A+	3. Cohen, 1977-A	1976-C
4. Bryant-Tuckett, 1980-C*	4. Ellman, 1970-B*	3. Gould, 1976-B*
5. Carroll, 1979-B	5. Feldman, 1978-A	4. Heilbrun, 1979-B
6. Cherry, 1977-B	6. Greenberg, 1976-A	5. Raffee, 1979-B
7. Cox, 1974-A	7. Kwawer, 1971-A*	6. Shifren, 1981-B
8. Dauber, 1980-A	8. Milich, 1976-C	7. Ungaro, 1981-C+
9. Forest-Letourneau, 1975-A	9. Moriarty, 1978-A+	8. Winnett, 1981-B
10. Foster, 1981-A	10. Nissenfeld, 1979-A	
11. Fribourg, 1979-A*	11. Ross, 1977-B*+	
12. Fulford, 1980-B	12. Sackeim, 1977-B	
13. Hines, 1977-A	13. Swanson, 1980-B	
14. Jackson, 1981-A*		
15. Kaplan, 1976-A*		
16. Kaye, 1975-A		
17. Leiter, 1973-A*		
18. Linehan, 1979-C		
19. Litwack, 1972-A*		
20. Lodl, 1980-B		
21. Lomangino, 1969-A		
22. Martin, 1975-C*		
23. Mendelsohn, 1979-A		
24. Miller, 1973-A*		
25. Palmatier, 1980-C		
26. Palumbo, 1979-B		
27. Parker, 1977-C*		
28. Rutstein, 1970-A		
29. Schurtman, 1978-C*		
30. S. E. Silverman, 1970-A+		
31. T. Spiro, 1975-A*		
32. Steinberg, 1975-A		
33. Varga, 1973-A*		
34. Zuckerman, 1980-C		

All but two of the studies listed were first carried out as doctoral dissertations and the dates entered are dissertation dates. Whenever a dissertation was later converted into a journal article, a notation to this effect follows the dissertation listing in the References.

a: Two samples were run, with there being significant results for one but not the other.
b: Significant differences between the subliminal experimental and subliminal control condition, but the opposite of what had been hypothesized
A: Type 1 (Laboratory Study with Clinical Population)
B: Type 2 (Laboratory Study with Non-clinical Population)
C: Type 3 (Treatment Adjunct Study)
+: Dissertations for which data were collected in my laboratory
*: Dissertations that I sponsored

of the subliminal psychodynamic activation method are cited in *Psychological Abstracts* and *Dissertation Abstracts;* these reference sources were consulted in the preparation of Table 2.[31]

CONCLUSIONS

What conclusions can be drawn from the overview that has been presented? First, it would seem warranted to maintain that the subliminal psychodynamic activation method has proven capable of demonstrating a number of psychodynamic relationships—relationships between particular unconscious wishes, anxieties, and fantasies and particular behaviors. Over 50 studies have reported results that are clearly positive. Because these studies have been carried out under double-blind conditions, the effects of experimenter bias (Rosenthal, 1966) and subject expectations (Orne, 1962), which so often contaminate the results of psychological experiments, can be judged to be negligible. Moreover, even if one demands evidence for the validity of subliminal psychodynamic activation from outside the laboratory where the method was developed, a large number of studies meet this criterion and the ratio of independent investigations that have been clearly supportive of the phenomenon to those that have been clearly non-supportive is better than 3:1.[32]

None of the above discussion should be taken to justify a complacent attitude regarding either psychoanalytic psychodynamic propositions or the method that has been developed to test them. With regard to the propositions, it can be noted that only a small number of them have been tested and not all of these have received experimental support. The fact that there are many psychodynamic

---

[31]In my comments on the different types of subliminal psychodynamic activation experiments, studies that did not meet this criterion sometimes were brought into the discussion, if they had something special to contribute. It is specifically in Table 3.2, which presents a kind of box score on the outcomes of subliminal psychodynamic activation experiments, that this criterion has been strictly applied.

A few investigations of this activation using auditory stimulation have been carried out; these will warrant a separate report, after more auditory studies have been conducted.

[32]If one simply compares column 1 and column 3 of Table 3.2, the ratio of "Clearly Supportive" to "Clearly Non-supportive" studies is better than 4:1. The "better than 3:1" citation was arrived at after omitting studies from both of these columns in which either I sponsored the doctoral candidate or the data were collected in my laboratory.

In reflecting on the above ratios, the following issue needs to be addressed. Whenever reports of research findings are considered, it is possible that the positive to negative results ratio is artifactually weighted on the former side since positive results studies are more apt to be accepted for publication. However, this would not apply to reports of doctoral dissertations. Once a dissertation study is carried out, it is reported in *Psychological Abstracts* and *Dissertation Abstracts* whether the results are positive or negative; the Table 3.2 listing is almost entirely a listing of studies that were first reported as dissertations.

propositions, about which psychoanalytic clinicians disagree (see Silverman & Wolitzky, 1981) implies that as more hypotheses of different clinicians are put to experimental test, there are bound to be further negative findings.

Of course, it cannot be assumed that simply because an experiment—or even a series of experiments—fails to support a psychoanalytic proposition, the proposition is *necessarily* invalid. The experiment may not do justice to the hypothesis for any number of reasons. Whereas these have been at least implied in my presentation up until now, I think there would be value in explicitly listing the reasons why a subliminal psychodynamic activation experiment might fail to produce positive results even when the hypothesis is valid.

First, the stimulus chosen to ''capture'' the psychodynamic content that is to be activated may have been a bad choice. It is not always easy to judge what verbal and/or pictorial content is appropriate for stirring up a particular unconscious wish, anxiety, or fantasy. A variant of this problem presumably occurred in the Loveland (1977) study already cited, in which the wrong word (''mommy'' instead of ''mama'') was used as the word for the good mother of infancy.

Second, subliminal registration may not take place. For example, this could happen if a subject blinks his eyes during exposure of the stimulus. For this reason it is important that there be several exposures of the stimulus each time a subject looks into the tachistoscope. (We typically expose the stimulus four times, at 10-second interludes.) Also, there are certain lighting conditions that produce ''bleaching'' (Silverman, Ross, Adler, & Lustig, 1978, p. 353) and interfere with subliminal registration: (1) if there is a glare from an overhead incandescent bulb or some other source that falls on a subject's eyes before he looks into the tachistoscope; (2) if there is a marked discrepancy between the illumination of the room (ambient illumination) and the illumination of the blank field that the subject focuses on. In one experiment, for example (Silverman, Ross, Adler, & Lustig, 1978), when the ambient illumination was 15 foot-lamberts and the illumination of the blank field 43 foot-lamberts, there was no evidence of subliminal registration.[33] (3) if the amount of light falling on the stimulus is very high. In another experiment in our laboratory, through an oversight, the blank field was allowed to remain on when the stimulus field came on (as opposed to the blank field being set to go off during the 4 milliseconds when the stimulus field is on as is normally the case). This doubled the amount of illumination that fell on the stimulus and interfered with subliminal registration.[34]

[33]In the other dart experiments in this series, as well as experiments generally in which there have been clear subliminal effects, the illumination of the blank field and the room have been about the same (each ranging from between 8 to 15 foot-lamberts). It also should be noted that the illumination of the stimulus field in these experiments has been between 4 and 10 foot-lamberts, and the ratio of the illumination of the blank field to that of the stimulus field has ranged from 1:1 to 3:1.

[34]This consideration also points to a possible danger that could arise during the treatment adjunct

Third, the hypothesis being tested may have merit but not for the particular sample being studied. For example, in our initial testing of the proposition that oneness fantasies can be ameliorative for schizophrenics, we obtained only a trend in the expected direction (Silverman et al., 1969). In the many follow-up experiments that have been carried out, that have produced significant results, it has become clear that our failure to obtain a significant effect initially was due the initial sample's having contained relatively undifferentiated, as well as relatively differentiated, schizophrenics. Thus, if by chance, the original sample had been comprised of a larger number of undifferentiated schizophrenics, the results would have been negative, a likely consequence of which is that we would have been discouraged from pursuing the hypothesis further.

Another case in point was Dauber's finding from his second study (Dauber, 1980) that the guilt-inducing message LEAVING MOM IS WRONG is only relevant to depressions of college women that are classifiable as "introjective" rather than "anaclitic" types. The group effect he obtained in his first study (Dauber, 1979) although significant was considerably smaller than he obtained for his introjective sample in the second study. That there was a significant effect at all was presumably due to there being a sizable number of introjective depressives in the initial sample. There too, if that sample had been weighted more heavily in the anaclitic direction, he would have obtained no results and could easily have concluded his hypothesis was incorrect.

Fourth, a valid hypothesis may fail to obtain experimental support because the amount of subliminal stimulation provided is insufficient. Whereas the crucial experiments in which "dosage" is varied within a single study have not yet been carried out,[35] there is already suggestive evidence that dosage can affect results. In the therapeutic and educational adjunct studies, the oneness stimulus has very

---

studies. In these, subjects are typically asked to image a tension-producing situation just prior to their looking into the tachistoscope for the subliminal exposures (Silverman, Martin, Ungaro, & Mendelsohn, 1978, p. 435). If the subject closed his eyes during this imaging (which is the inclination of many people), the change in illumination that would take place when he then opens them to focus on the blank field may well produce the kind of bleaching that has been described. Thus, subjects must be instructed to keep their eyes open during the imaging task. For subjects who have difficulty imaging while staring into space, it can be suggested that they project their image onto the blank field of the tachistoscope.

[35]After this was written, a very recent study by Packer (in preparation) met this criterion. She provided behavior assertiveness training accompanied by subliminal stimulation to women volunteers who characterized themselves as inhibited in their interactions with others. All experimental and control subjects were seen for four sessions a week for 3 weeks. All the controls received subliminal neutral stimulation in each of the four sessions, but the experimental subjects were divided into two subgroups. One of these received the experimental stimulus for two of the weekly sessions and the neutral control stimulus for the other two; the other subgroup received the experimental stimulus for all four sessions. The latter subgroup showed stronger experimental effects than the former. Thus, dosage is clearly a crucial variable.

consistently produced positive results when it has been administered four or five times per week but not when it has been administered weekly or biweekly.

Finally, as the dart paradigm results have suggested, particular experimenter characteristics can interfere with psychodynamic effects, at least when oedipal stimuli are used. The results of Citrin (1979) and Silverman, Ross, Adler, & Lustig (1978) indicate that female experimenters do not elicit the same effects with the BEATING DAD stimuli as do male experimenters.[36] The results of Carroll (1979) and Glennon (in preparation), although more clearly suggesting that subject differences can determine whether the oedipal stimuli will affect competitive performance, leave open the possibility that subtle personality characteristics of the experimenter can serve to strengthen or weaken a subject's defenses in the experimental situation and thus influence outcome. This is clearly an area that requires extensive additional study.

The overall implication to be drawn from the previous discussion is that negative results from subliminal psychodynamic experiments can be highly ambiguous. But that is the case in psychology experiments generally (and for that matter in experiments in other fields as well) where the accepted "reading" of negative findings is that they simply disallow rejection of the null hypothesis. It is when positive results issue from these experiments that there is less reason for equivocation than is usually the case. For given the double-blind controls that are in operation and the results of the specificity studies (Silverman et al., 1976, on pathology intensification; Bronstein, 1975, Kaplan, 1975, and Kaye, 1975, on pathology reduction; and Hayden & Silverstein, 1978, Lonski & Palumbo, 1978, and Palumbo, 1979, on changes in competitive performance with normal populations), it would, I believe, be extremely difficult to account for these findings without invoking psychodynamic explanations.

REFERENCES

Antell, M. *The effect of priming and the subliminal presentation of sexual and aggressive stimuli on tests of creativity.* Unpublished doctoral dissertation, New York University, 1969. Also appeared in the following article.

---

[36]I would speculate that when oedipal-level stimuli are used, male experimenters often are perceived as father figures and female experimenters as mother figures. Thus, the sanction implications of the message BEATING DAD IS OK could be enhanced by a male experimenter because by "offering" the stimulus he is, in effect, affirming the message. On the other hand, a female experimenter as "mother" can be unconsciously viewed as a seductress (for stimulating the thought BEATING DAD IS OK), which could intensify rather than alleviate conflict over competition with father. This, in turn, could interfere with the experimental effect. An empirical test of this speculation is in order.

Antell, M. J., & Goldberger, L. The effects of subliminally presented sexual and aggressive stimuli on literary creativity. *Psychological Research Bulletin*, 1978, *18*, (7).

Ariam, S. *The effects of subliminal symbiotic stimuli in Hebrew on academic performance of Israeli high school students*. Unpublished doctoral dissertation, New York University (School of Education), 1979. (An article has just been accepted for publication by the Journal of Abnormal Psychology.)

Bergmann, M. S. On the capacity to love. In J. B. McDevitt & C. S. Settlage (Eds.), *Separation-Individuation: Essays in Honor of Margaret S. Mahler*. New York: International Universities Press, 1971.

Blatt, S. J., D'Afflitti, J. P., & Quinlan, D. M. *Depressive experiences questionnaire*, Yale University School of Medicine, New Haven, Conn., 1976.

Brenner, D. *Specificity of symptom choice in eating disorders*. Unpublished doctoral dissertation, New York University, 1980.

Bronstein, A. *An experimental study of internalization fantasies in schizophrenic men*. Unpublished doctoral dissertation, Yeshiva University, 1976.

Bryant-Tuckett, R. *The effects of subliminal merging stimuli on the academic performance of emotionally handicapped students*. Unpublished doctoral dissertation, New York University, 1980.

Carroll, R. *Neurophysiological and psychological mediators of response to subliminal perception: The influence of hemisphericity and defensive style on susceptibility to subliminally presented conflict-laden stimuli*. Unpublished doctoral dissertation, St. John's University, 1979.

Cherry, E. *On success avoidance in women: A comparative study of psychoanalytic theories*. Unpublished doctoral dissertation, Adelphi University, 1977.

Citrin, M. *The effects of oedipal stimulation on dart throwing competition in college males and females*. Unpublished doctoral dissertation, New York University, 1979.

Cohen, R. *The effects of four subliminally introduced merging stimuli on the psychopathology of schizophrenic women*. Unpublished doctoral dissertation, Columbia University, 1977.

Condon, T. *Systematic desensitization: An evaluation of a psychoanalytic model of its effectiveness*. Unpublished doctoral dissertation, University of Connecticut, 1976. Also appeared in the following article.

Condon, T. J., & Allen, G. J. The role of psychoanalytic merging fantasies in systematic desensitization: A rigorous methodological examination. *Journal of Abnormal Psychology*, 1980, *89*, 437–443.

Cox, L. *Depressive symptoms as affected by aggressive stimuli subliminally and supraliminally presented*. Unpublished doctoral dissertation, Fordham University, 1974.

Dauber, R. *The effects of subliminal stimulation on the affect of depressively prone college students*. Unpublished masters thesis, Loyola University of Chicago, 1979.

Dauber, R. *An investigation of guilt, loss and the separation-individuation process in depression*. Unpublished doctoral dissertation, Loyola University of Chicago, 1980.

Ellman, C. *An experimental study of the female castration complex*. Unpublished doctoral dissertation, New York University, 1970.

Emmelkamp, P. M., & Straatman, H. A psychoanalytic reinterpretation of the effectiveness of systematic desensitization: Fact or fiction? *Behavior Research and Therapy*, 1976, *14*, 245–249.

Feldman, J. B. *The utilization of the subliminal psychodynamic activation method in further examination of conscious and unconscious measures of death anxiety*. Unpublished doctoral dissertation, Case Western Reserve University, 1978.

Florek, W. *Effects of subliminal stimulation of anxiety and cognitive adaptation*. Unpublished manuscript, St. John's University, 1978.

Forest-Letourneau, M. *The effect of subliminal stimulation of aggressive and symbiotic stimulation on the thought processes of chronic schizophrenics.* Unpublished doctoral dissertation, University of Montreal, 1974.

Foster, R. M. *The effects of subliminal tachistoscopic presentation of drive-related stimuli on the cognitive functioning of paranoid and non-paranoid schizophrenics.* Unpublished doctoral dissertation, St. John's University, 1981.

Fribourg, A. *The effect of fantasies of merging with the good mother figure on ego pathology of schizophrenics.* Unpublished doctoral dissertation, New York University, 1979. Also appeared in the following article.

Fribourg, A. Ego pathology in schizophrenia and fantasies of merging with the good mother. *Journal of Nervous and Mental Disease,* 1981, *169,* 337–347.

Fulford, P. F. *The effect of subliminal merging stimuli on test anxiety.* Unpublished doctoral dissertation. St. John's University, 1980.

Glennon, S. *The effect of hemispherity on the subliminal activation of residual oedipal conflicts.* New York University dissertation, in preparation.

Gould, E. *Regression in the service of the ego in relation to audience responsivity to art.* Unpublished doctoral dissertation, New York University, 1976.

Greenberg, N. The effects of subliminal neutral and aggressive stimuli on the thought processes of schizophrenics. *Canadian Journal of Behavioral Science,* 1977, *9,* 187–196.

Hartmann, H., & Kris, E. The genetic approach in psychoanalysis. *Psychoanalytic Study of the Child,* 1945, *1,* 11–30.

Haspel, K. *The effects of priming and subliminal oedipal stimulation on competitive behavior of college males.* Unpublished masters thesis, University of Rhode Island, 1979.

Heilbrun, K. *The effect of subliminally presented oedipal stimuli on competitive performance.* Unpublished doctoral dissertation, University of Texas, 1979. Also appeared in the following article.

Heilbrun, K. Silverman's subliminal psychodynamic activation: A failure to replicate. *Journal of Abnormal Psychology,* 1980, *89,* 560–566.

Hines, K. *Subliminal psychodynamic activation of oral dependency conflicts in a group of hospitalized male alcoholics.* Unpublished doctoral dissertation, Memphis State University, 1977.

Jackson, J. *The effects of fantasies of oneness with mother and father on the ego functioning of male and female schizophrenics.* Unpublished doctoral dissertation, New York University, 1981.

Kaplan, R. *The symbiotic fantasy as a therapeutic agent: An experimental comparison of the effects of three symbiotic elements on manifest pathology in schizophrenics.* Unpublished doctoral dissertation, New York University, 1976.

Kaye, M. *The therapeutic value of three merging stimuli for male schizophrenics.* Unpublished doctoral dissertation, Yeshiva University, 1975.

Kwawer, J. S. *An experimental study of psychoanalytic theories of overt male homosexuality.* Unpublished doctoral dissertation, New York University, 1971. Also one of the studies included in the article by Silverman, L. H., Kwawer, J. S., Wolitzky, C., & Coron, M., 1973, and was summarized in the following article.

Kwawer, J. S. Male homosexual psychodynamics and the Rorschach test. *Journal of Personality Assessment,* 1977, *41,* 10–18.

Leiter, E. *A study of the effects of subliminal activation of merging fantasies in differentiated and non-differentiated schizophrenics.* Unpublished doctoral dissertation, New York University, 1973.

Linehan, E. *A study of the effects of subliminal symbiotic stimulation on self-disclosure during counseling.* Unpublished doctoral dissertation, St. John's University, 1979. Also appeared as the following article.

Linehan, E., & O'Toole, J. The effect of subliminal stimulation of symbiotic fantasy on college students' self-disclosures in group counseling. *Journal of Counseling Psychology,* 1982, *29,* 151–157.

Litwack, T. *A study of certain issues concerning the dynamics of thinking and behavioral pathology in schizophrenics through the use of subliminal stimulation.* Unpublished doctoral dissertation, New York University, 1972. Also appeared as the following article.

Litwack, T. R., Wiedemann, C. F., & Yager, J. The fear of object loss, responsiveness to subliminal stimuli and schizophrenic psycho-pathology. *Journal of Nervous and Mental Disease,* 1979, *167,* 79–90.

Lodl, C. M. *The effects of subliminal stimuli of aggressive content upon the analytic/field-independent cognitive style.* Unpublished doctoral dissertation, Marquette University, 1980.

Lomangino, L. *Depiction of subliminally and supraliminally presented aggressive stimuli and its effects on the cognitive functioning of schizophrenics.* Unpublished doctoral dissertation, Fordham University, 1969.

Lonski, M., & Palumbo, R. *The effects of subliminal stimulation on competitive dart throwing performance.* Unpublished manuscript, Hofstra University, 1978. Available from senior author at Elmhurst Outpatient Department of Creedmore Psychiatric Center, 37–10 114th Street, Corona, N.Y. 11373.

Loveland, L. K. *The effects of subliminal aggressive and symbiotic stimulation of ego functioning in two subtypes of schizophrenics.* Unpublished master's thesis, William and Mary College, 1977.

Martin, A. *The effect of subliminal stimulation of symbiotic fantasies on weight loss in obese women receiving behavioral treatment.* Unpublished doctoral dissertation, New York University, 1975. Also one of the studies included in Silverman, Martin, Ungaro, and Mendelsohn (1978).

Mendelsohn, E. *Responses of schizophrenic men to subliminal psychodynamic stimuli.* Unpublished doctoral dissertation, Yeshiva University, 1979. Also appearing in the following article.

Mendelsohn, E. The effects of stimulating symbiotic fantasies on manifest pathology in schizophrenics: A revised formulation. *Journal of Nervous and Mental Disease,* 1981, *169,* 580–590.

Milich, R. *A study of the effects of symbiotic gratification stimuli and aggressive fantasizing on the psychopathology of chronic hospitalized schizophrenics.* Unpublished doctoral dissertation, Columbia University, 1976.

Miller, J. *The effects of aggressive stimulation upon young adults who have experienced the death of a parent during childhood and adolescence.* Unpublished doctoral dissertation, New York University, 1973.

Moriarty, J. *Cognitive functioning of schizophrenics as affected by aggressive stimuli subliminally and supraliminally presented.* Unpublished doctoral dissertation, Fordham University, 1968.

Nissenfeld, S. *The effects of four types of subliminal stimuli on female depressives.* Unpublished doctoral dissertation, Yeshiva University, 1979. Summarized in article by Slipp and Nissenfeld (1981).

Orne, M. On the social psychology of the psychological experiment. *American Psychologist,* 1962, *17,* 776–783.

Packer, S. *The effects of subliminal psychodynamic activation on behavior assertiveness training in women.* New York University dissertation, in preparation.

Palmatier, J. *The effects of subliminal symbiotic stimulation in the behavioral treatment of smoking.* Unpublished doctoral dissertation, University of Montana, 1980. Also appeared as the following article.

Palmatier, J. R., & Bornstein, P. H. The effects of subliminal stimulation of symbiotic merging fantasies on behavioral treatment of smokers. *Journal of Nervous and Mental Disease,* 1980, *168,* 715–720.

Palmatier, J. R. Personal communication, February, 1981.

Palumbo, R. *The fear of success in adult males: The effects of subliminal messages derived from two theoretical models.* Unpublished doctoral dissertation, Hofstra University, 1979.

Parker, K. A. *The effects of subliminal merging stimuli on the academic performance of college students.* Unpublished doctoral dissertation, New York University, 1977. Also appeared in the following article.

Parker, K. A. The effects of subliminal merging stimuli on the academic performance of college students. *Journal of Counseling Psychology,* 1982, *29,* 19–28.

Raffee, D. *Competitive behavior in women: The influence of unconscious factors.* Unpublished doctoral dissertation, Northwestern University, 1979.

Rosenthal, R. *Experimenter effects in behavioral research.* Englewood Cliffs, N.J.: Prentice-Hall, 1966.

Ross, D. *The effects of subliminal oedipal stimulation on competitive performance in college men.* Unpublished doctoral dissertation, New York University, 1977. Also one of the studies included in the article by Silverman, Ross, Adler, & Lustig (1978).

Rutstein, E. The effects of aggressive stimulation on suicidal patients: An experimental study of the psychoanalytic theory of suicide. Unpublished doctoral dissertation, New York University, 1970. Also appeared as the following article.

Rutstein, E. H., & Goldberger, L. The effects of aggressive stimulation on suicidal patients: An experimental study of the psychoanalytic theory of suicide. In B. Rubinstein (Ed.), *Psychoanalysis and Contemporary Science* (Vol. 2). New York: Macmillan, 1973.

Sackeim, H. *Self-deception: Motivational determinants of the non-awareness of cognition.* Unpublished doctoral dissertation, University of Pennsylvania, 1977.

Schurtman, R. *The effect of psychodynamic activation of symbiotic gratification fantasies on involvement in a treatment program for alcoholics.* Unpublished doctoral dissertation, New York University, 1978. Also appearing as the following article.

Schurtman, R., Palmatier, J. R., & Martin, E. S. On the activation of symbiotic gratification fantasies as an aid in the treatment of alcoholics. *International Journal of Addictions,* in press.

Searles, H. F. *Collected papers on schizophrenia and related subjects.* New York: International Universities Press, 1965.

Shaver, P. A study of dart throwing and oedipal stimulation carried out at New York University. Personal communication, 1978.

Shifren, I. E. *The interaction between hemispheric preference and the perception of subliminal auditory and visual symbiotic gratification stimuli.* Unpublished doctoral dissertation, St. John's University, 1981.

Silverman, L. H. A study of the effects of subliminally presented aggressive stimuli on the production of pathological thinking in a non-psychiatric population. *Journal of Nervous and Mental Disease,* 1966, *141,* 443–455.

Silverman, L. H. A technique for the study of psychodynamic relationships: The effects of subliminally presented aggressive stimuli on the production of pathological thinking in a schizophrenic population. *Journal of Consulting Psychology,* 1966, *30,* 103–111.

Silverman, L. H. Further experimental studies of dynamic propositions in psychoanalysis. *Journal of American Psychoanalytic Association,* 1970, *18,* 102–115.

Silverman, L. H. Drive stimulation and psychopathology: On the conditions under which drive-related external events evoke pathological reactions. In R. R. Holt & E. Peterfreund (Eds.), *Psychoanalysis and Contemporary Science* (Vol. 1). New York: Macmillan, 1972.

Silverman, L. H. On the role of laboratory experiments in the development of the clinical theory of psychoanalysis. *International Review of Psycho-Analysis,* 1975, *2,* 43–64.

Silverman, L. H. Psychoanalytic theory: The reports of my death are greatly exaggerated. *American Psychologist,* 1976, *31,* 621–637.

Silverman, L. H. Unconscious symbiotic fantasy: A ubiquitous therapeutic agent. *International Journal of Psychoanalytic Psychotherapy,* 1978, *7,* 562–585.

Silverman, L. H. A comment on two subliminal psychodynamic activation studies. *Journal of Abnormal Psychology,* 1982, *91,* 126–130.

Silverman, L. H., Bronstein, A., & Mendelsohn, E. The further use of the subliminal psychodynamic activation method for the experimental study of the clinical theory of psychoanalysis. *Psychotherapy: Theory, Research and Practice,* 1976, *13,* 2–16.

Silverman, L. H., & Candell, P. On the relationship between aggressive activation, symbiotic merging intactness of body boundaries and manifest pathology in schizophrenia. *Journal of Nervous and Mental Disease,* 1970, *150,* 387–399.

Silverman, L. H., Candell, P., Pettit, T. F., & Blum, F. A. Further data on effects of aggressive activation and symbiotic merging on ego functioning of schizophrenics. *Perceptual and Motor Skills,* 1971, *32,* 93–94.

Silverman, L. H., Frank, S., & Dachinger, P. Psychoanalytic reinterpretation of the effectiveness of systematic desensitization: Experimental data bearing on the role of merging fantasies. *Journal of Abnormal Psychology,* 1974, *83,* 313–318.

Silverman, L. H., & Goldweber, A. M. A further study of the effects of subliminal aggressive stimulation on thinking. *Journal of Nervous and Mental Disease,* 1966, *143,* 463–472.

Silverman, L. H., & Grabowski, R. *The effects of activating oneness fantasies on the anxiety level of male and female college students.* Unpublished manuscript, Dep't. of Psychology, N.Y.U., 6 Washington Pl., N.Y., N.Y., 1982.

Silverman, L. H., Klinger, H., Lustbader, L., Farrell, J., & Martin, A. The effect of subliminal drive stimulation on the speech of stutterers. *Journal of Nervous and Mental Disease,* 1972, *155,* 14–21.

Silverman, L. H., Kwawer, J. S., Wolitzky, C., & Coron, M. An experimental study of aspects of the psychoanalytic theory of male homosexuality. *Journal of Abnormal Psychology,* 1973, *82,* 178–188.

Silverman, L. H., Lachmann, F., & Milich, R. *The Search for Oneness.* New York: International Universities Press, in press.

Silverman, L. H., Levinson, P., Mendelsohn, E., Ungaro, R., & Bronstein, N. A clinical application of subliminal psychodynamic activation: On the stimulation of symbiotic fantasies as an adjunct in the treatment of hospitalized schizophrenics. *Journal of Nervous and Mental Disease,* 1975, *161,* 379–392.

Silverman, L. H., Martin, A., Ungaro, R., & Mendelsohn, E. Effect of subliminal stimulation of symbiotic fantasies on behavior modification treatment of obesity. *Journal of Consulting and Clinical Psychology,* 1978, *46,* 432–441.

Silverman, L. H., Ross, D., Adler, J., & Lustig, D. A simple research paradigm for demonstrating subliminal psychodynamic activation. *Journal of Abnormal Psychology,* 1978, *87,* 341–357.

Silverman, L. H., & Silverman, D. K. A clinical-experimental approach to the study of subliminal stimulation: The effects of a drive-related stimulus upon Rorschach responses. *Journal of Abnormal and Social Psychology,* 1964, *69,* 158–172.

Silverman, L. H., & Silverman, S. E. The effects of subliminally presented drive stimuli on the cognitive functioning of schizophrenics. *Journal of Projective Techniques,* 1967, *31,* 78–85.

Silverman, L. H., & Spiro, R. H. Some comments and data on the partial cue controversy and other matters relevant to investigations of subliminal phenomena. *Perceptual and Motor Skills,* 1967, *25,* 325–338.

Silverman, L. H., & Spiro, R. H. The effects of subliminal, supraliminal and vocalized aggression on the ego functioning of schizophrenics. *Journal of Nervous and Mental Disease,* 1968, *146,* 50–61.

Silverman, L. H., Spiro, R. H., Weissberg, J. S., & Candell, P. The effects of aggressive activation and the need to merge on pathological thinking in schizophrenia. *Journal of Nervous and Mental Disease,* 1969, *148,* 39–51.

Silverman, L. H., & Wolitzky, C. *The effects of the subliminal stimulation of symbiotic fantasies on the defensiveness of "normal" subjects in telling TAT stories.* Unpublished manuscript, Department of Psychology, New York University, 6 Washington Place, New York, N.Y., 1970.

Silverman, S. E. *The effects of subliminally induced drive derivatives on the ego functioning of schizophrenics.* Unpublished doctoral dissertation, New York University, 1970.

Silverstein, R. *The effects of tachistoscope oedipal stimulation on competitive dart throwing.* Senior honor's thesis, Brown University, 1978.

Slipp, S., & Nissenfeld, S. The experimental study of aspects of the psychoanalytic theory of depression. *Journal of the American Academy of Psychoanalysis,* 1981, *9,* 583–600.

Spiro, R. H., & Silverman, L. H. Effects of body awareness and aggressive activation on ego functioning of schizophrenics. *Perceptual and Motor Skills,* 1969, *28,* 575–585.

Spiro, T. *The effects of laboratory stimulation of symbiotic fantasies and bodily self-awareness on relatively differentiated and non-differentiated schizophrenics.* Unpublished doctoral dissertation, New York University, 1975.

Steinberg, R. *The effects of subliminal mother-need tachistoscopic stimulation on the ego pathology of hospitalized male schizophrenics.* Unpublished doctoral dissertation, Long Island University, 1975.

Swanson, R. *The effects of oedipally related stimuli in the subliminal psychodynamic activation paradigm: A replication and an extension.* Unpublished doctoral dissertation, Loyola University of Chicago, 1980.

Ungaro, R. *The therapeutic effects of subliminal stimulation of symbiotic fantasies on behavior modification treatment of obesity.* Unpublished doctoral dissertation, Adelphi University, 1981.

Varga, M. *An experimental study of aspects of the psychoanalytic study of elation.* Unpublished doctoral dissertation, New York University, 1973.

Winnett, R. L. *The comparative effects of literal and metaphorical subliminal stimulation on the activation of oedipal fantasies in dart-throwing performance and word recall tasks.* Unpublished doctoral dissertation, University of Montana, 1981.

Zuckerman, M. & Lubin, B. *Manual for the Multiple Affect Adjective Checklist.* San Diego: Educational and Industrial Testing Service, 1965.

Zuckerman, S. *The effects of subliminal symbiotic and success-related stimuli on the school performance of high school underachievers.* Unpublished doctoral dissertation, New York University, 1980.

4

Self-Deception, Self-Esteem, and Depression: The Adaptive Value of Lying to Oneself

Harold A. Sackeim, Ph.D.
Department of Psychology
New York University
and
Department of Biological Psychiatry
New York State Psychiatric Institute

The concept of defense forms the heart of psychoanalytic theory. From it is derived the basic claims about the nature of consciousness and the determinants of psychopathology. The aims of this chapter are threefold, each corresponding to a different section. In the first section, a theoretical critique is offered of the psychoanalytic theory of defense. A major claim is that the theory unjustifiably restricts the motives for defense to the avoidance of pain. No allowance is made for self-deception directed toward the pursuit of pleasure. This lacuna is reflected in the theory endowing people with a plethora of defense, but no offense, mechanisms. Acceptance of the possibility of pleasure-directed self-deception, in turn, threatens the psychoanalytic view of the nature of psychopathology. Deception of ourselves need not involve renunciation of wishes but may enhance drive expression and the possibilities of pleasure.

In the second part of this chapter empirical attempts to study and manipulate self-deception are described. A new set of data is presented, addressing the issue that people may deceive themselves in the absence of threat in order to augment self-esteem.

The third part of this chapter raises more general issues about the adaptive value of self-deception. Relations between psychopathology and self-deception are raised and the view is offered that some forms of psychopathology, notably neurotic depressive disorders, may be associated with failure to use self-deceptive strategies. Psychological and neuropsychological evidence is presented in support of this claim. The hypothesis is advanced that defensive or self-deceptive strategies are neuropsychologically represented, adaptive mechanisms by which the brain regulates mood.

THE PSYCHOANALYTIC THEORY OF DEFENSE AND
PSYCHOPATHOLOGY: A CRITIQUE

> Psychoanalysis is a dynamic conception, which reduces mental life to the in-
> terplay of reciprocally urging and checking forces. When it happens that a group of
> ideas remains in the unconscious, psychoanalysis . . . maintains that an active an-
> tagonism of certain groups of ideas has caused the isolation of another group in the
> unconscious. The process which imposes such a fate upon a given group is termed
> by psychoanalysis "repression," and it recognizes in it something analogous to
> reasoned rejection in the sphere of logic. Psychoanalysis can show that such repres-
> sions play an extraordinary part in our mental life, that they may frequently miscar-
> ry in individual cases, and that such miscarriages of repression are the primary
> cause of symptom-formation [Freud, 1910/1963, p.53].

Psychoanalytic theory presents a curiously ambivalent view of man. It is pessimistic in positing that repression is a universal characteristic of the human
condition. The unreasonableness of instinctual urges and the uncompromising
callousness of the exigencies of reality require that we not only fail to recognize
but that we also transfigure and distort our own wishes, thoughts, and feelings.
The nature and content of these distortions determine our character. As Brown
(1959) aptly described the psychoanalytic view, "the essence of the individual is
repression of himself [p. 3]." In this framework, accuracy of self-knowledge or
self-representation is a pretentious, unattainable goal.

One might claim that if we are doomed to continual self-deceit, psychoanalysis compounds the pessimism by further positing that psychopathology is
the natural and expected outcome of self-deception. Failure to acknowledge and
to act on instinctual urges results in tension. Compromise formation may partially relieve tension by permitting distorted expression of impulses. Whether
weighted toward gratification of wishes or toward safety (Fenichel, 1945; Freud,
1923/1960), and as reflected in distortions in our awareness of internal events no
less than in overt behavior, these compromises are viewed in the psychoanalytic
framework as symptoms. Our success at maintaining compromise depends mainly on continuing our failure to recognize the true nature of our intentions. "The
psychoneuroses are substitutive satisfactions of some instinct the presence of
which one is obliged to deny to oneself and others. Their capacity to exist
depends on the distortion and lack of recognition. When the riddle they present is
solved and the solution is accepted by the patient these diseases cease to be able
to exist [Freud, 1910/1957, p. 148]."

The formulation that deception of ourselves necessitates symptomatology
reflects a tacit definition of psychopathology that is absolute. Psychopathology is
the failure to recognize and satisfy fully and directly instinctual demands, regardless of their nature. This definition incorporates a prescription of what the "prop-

er'' or nonpathological relations should be between our conceptions of reality (including our self-perceptions) and reality itself. If our representations of ourselves and of the environment were accurate, we should be in a state of psychological health. That this, in a strict sense, is deemed impossible, guarantees that we are all pathological.

The Meaning of Psychopathology

An objection might be raised to this formulation of traditional psychoanalytic thought. The view of man as psychopathological by necessity rests on but one meaning of the term *psychopathology* and one that derives more from a description of the essential constituents and dynamics of mental life than from the practical problem of discriminating among normal and abnormal phenomena. Certainly, Freud frequently discussed neurosis and normality as if the concepts referred to discrete and discontinuous aspects of behavior. His suggestion that incapacity in love or work is the hallmark of neurosis might be taken as evidence that, in at least one sense, psychopathology was not thought of as a universal characteristic of the human condition. Rather, a relativistic definition of psychopathology is implicit with some, but not all, manifestations of conflict found to be neurotic. This view of psychopathology abolishes the link of necessity between deception of ourselves and pathological behavior.

There are several difficulties in associating a relativistic definition of psychopathology with traditional psychoanalysis. When Freud explicitly addressed the distinction between normality and neurosis (or psychosis), he viewed the concepts as referring to ends of a continuum. Neurotics and so-called normal individuals differ quantitatively, not in kind.

> Neurotics have approximately the same innate dispositions as other people, they have the same experiences and they have the same problems to solve. Why, then, do they live so much worse and with so much greater difficulty and suffer in the process so many more feelings of unpleasure, anxiety, and pain? . . . It is *quantitative disharmonies* that must be held responsible for the inadequacies and sufferings of neurotics [Freud, 1923/1960, p. 81, italics in the original].
>
> Now every normal person is only approximately normal; his ego resembles that of the psychotic in one point or another, in a greater or lesser degree, and its distance from one end of the scale and proximity to the other may provisionally serve as a measure of what we have indefinitely spoken of as ''modification of the ego'' [Freud, 1937/1963, p. 253].

If, indeed, Freud viewed psychopathology as universal, with individuals differing only in degree, what should be made of his suggestions that particular characteristics distinguish the neurotic from the normal? The association of neurosis with incapacity in the areas of work or love was intended more as a description of the characteristics of people who presented themselves for treatment than as an account of the criteria necessary for ascribing psychopathology. Freud recognized that although his comparisons of the neurotic and normal were often normative, his basic theory was not grounded in a fundamentally relativistic view of psychopathology. For instance, in discussing the possibility of complete societies being neurotic, he (1930/1961) wrote, "In an individual neurosis we take as our starting point the contrast that distinguishes the patient from his environment, which is assumed to be 'normal' [p. 91]." Nonetheless, Freud acknowledged that it was possible to "embark upon a pathology of cultural communities [p. 91]" that would require an absolute, nonnormative view of the meaning of psychopathology.

The most telling argument for the claim that classic psychoanalytic theory embodies an absolute view of psychopathology comes from the application of the term *psychopathology* to the apparently "normal" aspects of everyday life. Dreams, jokes, slips of the tongue, and creative acts have regularly been interpreted as neurotic manifestations, instances of pathology. These phenomena may not involve overt incapacity or functional deficit. They may be accompanied by subjective experiences of pleasure, with no attendant anxiety or discomfort. The justification given for viewing these phenomena as instances of pathology is that they are as much a manifestation of repression as behaviors typically thought to be neurotic (e.g., phobias, obsessions, conversion reactions). The same basic processes are believed to underlie both types of phenomena. Sharing of determinants in itself need not entail that differing overt manifestations are all psychopathological, if the criteria for ascribing psychopathology pertain to the surface characteristics that may distinguish the manifestations. In stipulating that the phenomena of everyday life are examples of psychopathology, psychoanalysis makes the claim that, irrespective of their surface features or consequences, the underlying processes are the source of pathology. Regardless of the results, failure to recognize fully and satisfy instinctual demands is psychopathological. Indeed, Freud (1937/1963) openly acknowledged that in psychoanalysis the ascription of psychological health and disorder hinges on a conceptualization of internal processes. "It is impossible to define health except in terms of metapsychology, i.e. of the dynamic relations between those agencies of the psychical apparatus, the existence of which psychoanalysis has discovered, or, if it is preferred, has deduced or conjectured [p. 244]." It is the internalized conflicts, embodied in the notion of repression, that makes us all psychopathological.

It appears that we are left with a basic two-point claim. First, the conflictual nature of instinctual demands and the limitations imposed by the environment require that we inhibit and disguise, from ourselves and others, the nature of our own internal events (wishes, thoughts, and feelings). Second, the act of repression is psychopathological. The universality of repression requires that psycho-pathology is universal.

This would seem to be a dire view of man. Some have developed this theme (Brown, 1959) to argue that the revolution in thought, created by Freud, con-tinued the decentering by science of man's conception of his place in the uni-verse. The contributions of Copernicus, Darwin, and Freud progressively ma-ligned the prominence of man, each attacking at a different level, with the Freudian view mandating that we are not masters in the households of ourselves, that we are irrevocably diseased. Why, then, state at the outset that psycho-analysis assumes an ambivalent posture?

Embedded within traditional psychoanalytic theory is a profound optimism. With respect to each of the two points in the basic formulation, Freud adopted positions that might be described by some as sanguine or "humanistic" and by others as unjustifiably naive. The two issues concern the motives for defense and the relations between rationality and the vicissitudes of psychological health.

Defense Mechanisms: Where Is the Offense?

Following the reformulation presented in *Inhibitions, Symptoms and Anxiety* (Freud, 1926/1959), a basic tenet of psychoanalysis has been the notion that, without exception, the immediate aim of defensive operations is to ward off anxiety. We lie to ourselves in order to forestall or limit psychic pain. The facts that our wishes are conflictual and that reality is often inhospitable and un-changeable provide constant sources of threat. We protect against these threats by renouncing our wishes and distorting our perceptions. We defend.

The defensive operations are the province of the ego. Freud (1937/1963) offered markedly different conceptions of the zest and skill with which the *ego* assumes its role of defender. On the one hand, the ego is portrayed as a reluctant and handicapped protector.

> The psychical apparatus is intolerant of unpleasure and strives to ward it off at all costs and, if perception of reality involves unpleasure, that perception—i.e., the truth—must be sacrificed. For quite a long time flight and an avoidance of a dangerous situation serve as expedients in the face of danger, until the individual is finally strong enough to remove the menace by actively modifying reality. But one cannot flee from oneself and no flight avails against the danger from within; hence the ego's defensive mechanisms are condemned to falsify the inner perception, so that it transmits to us only an imperfect and travestied picture of our id. In its relations with the id the ego is paralysed by its restriction or blinded by its errors, and the result in the sphere of psychical events may be compared to the progress of a poor walker in a country which he does not know [p. 255].

On the other hand, the ego is viewed also as a shark, a schemer, conniving to make the best distortion at the least cost (Freud, 1923/ 1960).

> As a frontier-creature, the ego tries to mediate between the world and the id, to make the id pliable to the world and, by means of its muscular activity, to make the world fall in with the wishes of the id. . . . Whenever possible, it tries to remain on good terms with the id; it clothes the id's *Ucs.* [unconscious] commands with its *Pcs.* [preconscious] rationalizations; it pretends that the id is showing obedience to the admonitions of reality, even when in fact it is remaining obstinate and unyielding; it disguises the id's conflicts with reality and, if possible, its conflicts with the super-ego too. In its position midway between the id and reality, it only too often yields to the temptation to become sycophantic, opportunist and lying, like a politician who sees the truth but wants to keep his place in popular favour [p. 46].

The ambivalence of Freud in describing the ego's degree of acquiescence and chicanery in carrying out its defensive role is not at issue here. What is at issue is the extraordinary restriction placed on the grounds for defensive operations. Whether viewed as a "submissive slave" or as an "opportunist" (Freud, 1923/1960), the ego engages in distortion only to fend off pain or possible loss. Its sole motivation is to avoid unpleasure. The ego never generates self-deceit in the absence of threat, purely to achieve a positive end. Whereas other aspects of behavior are viewed in the Freudian scheme as determined by either the pursuit of pleasure or the avoidance of pain, the mechanisms of defense are geared only in the direction of minimizing unpleasure. Put bluntly, our deceptions of ourselves, achieved exclusively through the use of defense mechanisms, serve just to maintain the status quo. To anthropomorphize, our self-deceptive strategies may be conceived of as members of a sports team never trained in, nor allowed to play, offense.

This restriction on the motives for defense was incorporated consistently in the standard psychoanalytic discussions of the issue. In redefining repression as but a specific instance of a broader class of defensive mechanisms, Freud (1926/ 1959) indicated that all of these deceptive operations served the same purpose, "protection of the ego against instinctual demands" [p. 164]. Fenichel (1945) classified the affects that served as motives of defense as anxiety and the anxiety derivatives, guilt, disgust, and shame. He noted, as well, that the counterforces of the ego, renouncing instinctual impulses, were "governed by a striving to avoid objects" [p. 140]. Likewise, Anna Freud (1966) claimed simply that "defense mechanisms are brought into operation against the instincts" [p. 59]. When conflicts involve the expression of opposing drives, defensive measures come into play in determining which and to what degree drives are manifested. Although expression of drives may produce primary pleasure, they also result secondarily in unpleasure (e.g., guilt feelings or fears or retributions from reality). In such circumstances, Anna Freud claimed "the main purpose [of defense] is to avoid this secondary pain [p. 61]."

The restriction on the motives of defense is also reflected in the more florid, analogical accounts of the ego's role in generating self-deceptions. For instance, in the statement quoted (p. 106), Freud (1923/1960) described the ego as "a politician who sees the truth but wants to *keep his place* in popular favour [p. 46, italics added]." One might ask: Are there not politicians who hide and distort the truth not simply to avoid scandal or to maintain their status but, in addition or instead, to enhance their public position? It would be naive to think otherwise. Even in simile, the goal of defense, as presented in psychoanalysis, is only to prevent loss.

Objection 1: Wish-Fulfilling Distortion. It might be objected that this view of psychoanalytic theory is unfair in that Freud (1940/1949) and others (Fenichel, 1945; Garma, 1932) acknowledged the possibility of wish-fulfilling distortions. At times, the ego may falsify its conception of reality expressly to satisfy an unconscious wish. For instance, Anna Freud (1966) commented that when confronted with a disagreeable event, the child may turn to fantasy and deny the existence of the event. "If the transformation is successful and through the fantasies which the child constructs he becomes insensible of the reality in question, the ego is saved anxiety and has no need to resort to defensive measures against its instinctual impulses and to the formation of neurosis" [p. 80]. This formulation could be broadened so that the instigator of the distortion is not just threat but also the possibility of pleasure.

Wish-fulfilling distortion should then be the road psychoanalysis leaves open by which we may falsify our conceptions of reality and of ourselves in order to achieve some positive end. Psychoanalysis does not provide this option. First, the use of wish-fulfilling distortion is identified, though not exclusively, with psychosis. Freud (1924/1953) once suggested that the primary distinction between the psychotic and neurotic is that, in conflicts between instinctual impulses and associated pain, the neurotic represses the former, obeying the strictures of reality, whereas the psychotic denies the latter and gives expression to the instinct. Anna Freud (1966), likewise, commented that if an adult used fantasy in a manner akin to that acceptable in a child, it would indicate "an advanced stage of mental disease" as would be found in "acute psychotic confusional states" [p. 80]. Distorting one's awareness of self in the service of avoiding unpleasure is viewed as the basis of neurosis. Distorting one's conception of external reality in the service of pleasure or to avoid pain is viewed as most often psychotic.

A second problem in identifying a major role for wish-fulfilling distortion in psychoanalytic theory is that, even in psychosis, psychoanalytic theorists undercut the motivation for such falsification. Anna Freud (1966) emphasized the role of trauma, such as sudden loss of love, as grounds for adults substituting an "agreeable delusion" for an "unbearable reality" [p. 80]. Fenichel (1945) and Garma (1932) claimed that schizophrenic breaks with reality (hallucinatory wish fulfillments) rarely reflect a pursuit of pleasure or an avoidance of a hostile reality but involve instead an avoidance of temptation. "In the majority of cases of schizophrenia, it seems that the break with reality does not serve the purpose of gaining more instinctual pleasure but rather of combating the instinctual drives directed toward objects; reality is repudiated less because of its frustrating effects than because it holds temptations" [Fenichel, 1945, p. 440]. In either case, the role of "wish-fulfilling distortion" is most often seen as defensive; reality is falsified so as not to acknowledge loss or to ward off temptation.

Wish-fulfilling distortion is also conceived of as present in neurosis (Freud, 1940/1949), indicating that it may not be a certain sign of psychosis. As manifested in neurosis, it has not been conceptualized as permitting falsification of our conceptions of ourselves or of the external world in the service of pleasure. Some instances of wish-fulfilling distortions occur when there is a failure of defense. When, for instance, in a slip of the tongue, we blurt out some unconscious impulse, the impulse has been satisfied because it has broken through or overwhelmed the defense. In such cases, the alteration in our behavior occurs despite our attempts to conceal the impulse from ourselves and others. Although such acts may involve wish fulfillment, they do not contain, as a prerequisite for drive expression, distortions in our knowledge of ourselves or of the world. Instead, they are viewed as failures to maintain self-deceptions.

Other instances of neurotic wish-fulfilling distortion may not involve a failure of defense but are interpreted as "wish fulfilling" only in surface characteristics, as in the case of psychosis. The classic example has been fetishism (Fenichel, 1945; Freud, 1940/ 1949), which at first sight would appear to be a neurosis generated in the service of pleasure. On the contrary, the male fetishist is said to be motivated by the avoidance of unpleasure, a fear of castration (Freud, 1940/1949). The unusual sexual behavior is an outcome of unconscious denial of the troublesome perception that the female does not have a penis. Such a formulation takes wish-fulfilling distortion as but a more complex example of falsification directed toward the avoidance of pain. Apparent pleasure-oriented neurotic behavior serves as a screen to ward off threatening impulses or ideas. Whether we turn to neurosis or psychosis, traditional psychoanalytic theory undid its own notion of wish-fulfilling distortion and rejected the possibility that, motivated by the lure of personal profit, people may deceive themselves.

Objection 2: The Development of Ego Psychology.   It might be contended that this is all well and good but that this critique is primarily of historical interest. From within the psychoanalytic community, the charge has been made that the early formulations presented an overly passive view of the ego as an agency reacting to and shaped by the conflicts between instincts and reality. Erikson (1950) claimed that the early formulations presented the ego as a "marionette" manipulated by a "mythical Eros" and presented "human motivation as if libido were the prime substance, individual egos being merely defensive buffers and vulnerable layers between this substance and a vague surrounding "outer world' " [p. 60]. In addition, the criticism was made that the traditional formulations cast individuals' responses to current situations as not only determined by but also as always recapitulating ancient traumas, as if people were only their distant pasts (Rieff, 1959; Shapiro, 1965).

The development of ego psychology altered the psychoanalytic framework. Hartmann (1958) offered the notion that basic psychological structures, such as intelligence, memory, and perception, may develop independent of instinctual conflict. Rapaport and Gill (1959), following Erikson (1950) and Hartmann (1958), distilled an adaptive "point of view" stipulating that any full account of behavior must include an understanding of how the individual and the environment are reciprocally modified. These conceptions in turn led to the formulations that individuals' characteristic modes of adaptation, although grounded in part in early childhood conflict, may become autonomous, active styles of processing information and of interacting with and shaping reality. The notions of cognitive control systems (Gardner, Holzman, Klein, Linton, & Spence, 1959; Klein, 1954) and neurotic styles (Shapiro, 1965) were the outcome of these developments.

In presenting his conception of neurotic styles, Shapiro (1965) emphasized the activeness that was now imparted to the ego. Neurotics were not conceived of as waiting passively for life to stimulate their neuroses. Instead, they were viewed as searching for opportunities to express neurosis. The neurotic is someone whose "make-up and the way he sees things—about which he has no choice—move him to feel, think, and do things that continue the neurotic experience and are indispensable to it" [p. 18]. One would think that these newer formulations, emphasizing the ego's adaptive and active role in relation to the environment, would include the possibility of pleasure-directed distortion.

We noted earlier that Freud presented an ambivalent view of the ego: on the one hand, a slave buffeted by conflicts outside its realm; on the other hand, an opportunist manipulating its own awareness of facts for the sake of protection. The charge that traditional psychoanalytic theory presented a "marionette" view of the ego presumably centered on one side of the ambivalent formulation. We also noted that even when Freud instilled the ego with activity, the motives for defense were restricted, nonetheless, to avoidance of danger and prevention of loss. Likewise, the newer conceptions of ego functioning, at least as represented in Shapiro (1965), did not enlarge on the grounds for distortion.

Shapiro (1965) explicitly addressed the relations between style and defense and the motives for neurotic styles. He argued that the concept of defense needed to be broadened with respect to the processes involved, the mental contents subject to distortions, and the relations between defense and reality. He argued that, as reflected in neurotic styles, defensive operations do not involve specific and isolated "mechanisms" but recruit characteristic and general modes of thinking and feeling. Defensive operations are not brought into play against specific ideas or affects but exclude from consciousness complete classes of private experience. Defensive processes were conceived of as not purely intra-psychic but as part and parcel of how we perceive and communicate with the outside world.

Despite this broadening and the use of new terminology, the grounds for defense remained unchanged. Shapiro (1965) wrote: "A discomforting affect, inconsistent with and intolerable to the existing style, is experienced according to the viewpoint of that style, ... and automatically moves the individual to thoughts and behavior that reduce the tension and lead to a more characteristic frame of mind in which the original affect and its discomfort disappear" [p. 194]. This is but new dressing on the standard position.

What about the increased activity level noted by the newer formulations in describing how individuals participate in their neuroses? The ego is no longer viewed as simply holding the fort but also as searching for opportunities to express neurosis. Is at least some of this search directed toward opportunities to use its well-developed distortive mechanisms so as to experience pleasure? The newer formulations extended the ego's role, so to speak, from perceptual defense to perceptual vigilance, with vigilance restricted to being on the lookout for danger. Shapiro (1965) provided several examples of this vigilance.

> The obsessional person, on close examination, is not simply assailed by doubts and worries; he goes out of his way to find a basis for uncertainty, to find something that will again balance the scales. His attitudes and ways of thinking guarantee that just such a procedure will seem the only prudent and proper one and that the next element of doubt will appear as the obvious next thing to be interested in. Similarly, the paranoid person is not simply visited by apprehensions and defensive suspicions; he searches actively and does not rest until he has located clues to new dangers. The repressive person, not only is subject to forces that oppose clear recollection, but also mistakenly shrinks from facts when they are offered, prefers to move on to the next subject, or sees no reason for being "so serious." And so on [pp. 19–20].

The ego was no longer considered as passively waiting for danger to present itself. Situations were sought out, misconstrued, and falsified so as to appear threatening. Whatever the validity of this formulation, it possesses more than a hint of paradox. The individual is viewed as working hard to distort conceptions of self and of the world in order to be confronted with unpleasure.

Inherent Optimism. I have claimed that this restriction on the motives for defense, represented in newer reformulations of psychoanalytic theory no less than in the traditional model, constitutes a profoundly optimistic view of human motivation. This optimism may be highlighted by comparing the conditions assumed to generate self-deceptive defensive maneuvers and those that fuel other-deception or conscious lying.

The psychoanalytic model of defense mechanisms adopts the philosophical stance that the logic of self-deception may be assimilated with the logic of other-deception (see Fingarette, 1969; Sackeim & Gur, 1978; Sartre, 1958 for discussions of this issue). In both cases, there is a motivated attempt on the part of the deceiver to establish a new belief in the deceived. This new belief contradicts a belief held in actuality by the deceiver and this fact is unknown to the deceived. The contrast between self- and other-deception is that in the former instance the deceiver and the deceived are the same individual, or different aspects of the same "psychical apparatus." Assimilating the logic of self- and other-deception entails, in part, that the self-deceived individual holds two contradictory beliefs and lacks awareness of one of them. This situation has been described by some as paradoxical and has led to debate over the appropriateness of the assimilation (Canfield & Gustafson, 1962; Demos, 1960; Gardiner, 1970; Penelhum, 1966).

Within the context of psychoanalytic theory, there is no tension in positing that individuals may hold contradictory beliefs and lack awareness of one of them. The psychoanalytic restriction on the motives for self-deception does, however, create a new problem in assimilating the logic of the two types of deception. Were the restriction applied to other-deception, we would be forced to claim that people lie to others to protect their backsides, so to speak, but not to obtain pleasure. We could conceptualize people lying so as to escape punishment, to maintain social status, or to alleviate their own suffering; we could not accept the possibility that people lie to others in the absence of possible loss or threat in order to maximize financial gain, to express aggressive or hostile wishes, or to elevate self-esteem, let alone for purely altruistic purposes (e.g., "white" lies). Surely, this would be a curiously naive and optimistic view of the motives for conscious falsehood.

One implication of this restriction on the motives for defense pertains to the clinical situation and the attribution of responsibility for pathological behavior. In accounting for symptomatology, the psychoanalytic model stipulates that compromise formation is instigated because instinctual impulses are dangerous. Defense mechanisms are used to ward off and renounce these impulses so as to avoid pain. Furthermore, this pain is monumental. The anxiety that serves as a signal for defense is only a reminder that, unless wishes are renounced and conceptions of ourselves and the world distorted, we will be overwhelmed with a primary anxiety so basic and intense that it cannot be adequately described (Freud, 1926/1959). The patient whose symptomatology comprises falsifications and distortions that may have been hurtful to self or others comes to understand not simply that the behavior was determined. The behavior was a by-product of an attempt to avoid unimaginable pain and by necessity involved inhibiting and redirecting one's own wishes. If the neurosis were likened to "crimes," the outcome of psychoanalytically oriented therapy may be that patients see themselves like the storekeeper so concerned with honesty and reputation that he frequently errs in counting change in favor of his customers or like the parent who steals food to feed a starving child.

Broadening the motives for defense to include cases of self-deception for the sake of pleasure produces a quite different clinical picture. Individuals may distort their conceptions of themselves and reality to achieve gain. By taking the offensive and seizing suitable opportunities for distortion, they may enhance their self-esteem, augment their financial position, express otherwise objectionable urges, and so on. In the context of therapy directed toward uncovering, patients characterized by such "symptomatology" would also come to understand that their behavior was determined. They may recognize that their distortions were not directed so much as to inhibit wishes but to express them. Their crimes are more like the storekeeper who in counting change continually makes mistakes in his own favor or like the white collar, blueblood, embezzler who steals not out of need but from desire. Casting the distinction in a more extreme way, the traditional psychoanalytic view of the motives for defense makes us all martyrs; the possibility of pleasure-generated distortion suggests that, in at least some cases, the more appropriate model is that of the psychopath.

Objection 3: The Tension-Modulation Model.   Before we conclude that the neglect of self-deception for gain constitutes a theoretical lacuna in psychoanalytic thought, two additional arguments in defense of the theory should be presented. First, according to the economic point of view (Rapaport & Gill, 1959), it makes little difference whether behavior is described as determined by the pursuit of pleasure or the avoidance of pain. Most generally, the psyche is organized by tension-modulating principles. Behavior directed toward positively valued objects (e.g., consumption of food) and away from negatively valued objects (e.g., avoidance of danger) both result in reduction of tension. Because a nonoptimal level of tension is aversive, both pleasure- and avoidance-directed behaviors might be viewed as different ways to minimize unpleasure. For instance, we eat to escape from the aversive state of hunger. Further, the positive feelings or pleasure we experience in reducing the "hunger-generated" tension is a side effect, not a precipitator of the eating behavior. In this sense, all behavior is defensive (i.e., generated to reduce pain). There is no need for psychoanalytic theory to posit pleasure as a motive for self-deception, because pleasure is but a euphemism for the avoidance of pain and/or never an instigator but a consequence of such avoidance.

Full pursuit of this argument would take us far afield. At its base are metapsychological issues about the determinants of behavior (i.e., conceptions of behavior as motivated by drives or as determined by expectations about future consequences and previous reinforcement history). The argument can be simply sidestepped. Even if it were acknowledged that the aim of all behavior is tension modulation, psychoanalytic theory distinguishes between acts directed toward objects and acts directed against or away from objects. As we noted earlier, Fenichel (1945) described the ego's motives for defense as "governed by striving to avoid objects" [p. 140]. Although it may or may not be true that all motivation reduces to an avoidance of aversive tension, psychoanalysis contains a more delineated nosology of motivation, with the pursuit of pleasure and the avoidance of pain as explicit and distinct categorizations (Freud, 1923/1960). The former type is not permitted to serve as a motive for defense.

Objection 4: The Relations Between Wishes and Fears.   The second argument is more troublesome. We have seen that psychoanalytic theory undercut one avenue for positing pleasure-seeking self-deception by interpreting wish-fulfilling distortions as superficial manifestations of more basic fears. The hallucinatory wish fulfillments of the psychotic are, in actuality, attempts to ward off a reality too full of temptation. Unusual sexual proclivities of the neurotic are not generated because they satisfy; they satisfy only because they are symbolic denials of painful ideas. This view can be generalized so that any instance of apparent distortion in the service of pleasure is interpreted fundamentally as an avoidance of threat or pain. In this light, we should reverse the psychoanalytic maxim regarding phobias and claim that, at least in terms of pleasure-directed distortion, behind every wish there is a fear.

Explicit adoption of this position may only be an outward acknowledgment and clarification of how many psychoanalytically oriented clinicians standardly interpret wish-fulfilling distortion. If we are presented with a patient who takes a relatively neutral remark or greeting as a sign of affection, we may wonder whether the patient is troubled by feelings of not being loved or of being unworthy of love. Individuals who have a distorted view of their own importance, power, or abilities may suffer from a narcissistic defect, insecure about their own worth or in conflict about issues surrounding independence, omnipotence, or trust. If one distorts one's awareness of oneself or of external reality to obtain narcissistic supplies or other sources of pleasure, then one must be deficient or in conflict in those areas. If not, why then would individuals secure of their worth exaggerate their importance to self and others? The attempt to use distortion to obtain "false" gratification must also involve a rejection from awareness that one is deficient or in conflict. In the end, apparent pleasure-oriented distortion serves to ward off such painful thoughts.

This argument rests on a purely empirical claim. There is no theoretical restraint in psychoanalysis that entails that apparent pleasure-directed distortions must always be displaced attempts to avoid pain. One can, indeed, conceptualize "offensive mechanisms" by which distortions in awareness of self and reality are executed solely to achieve gain. The previously presented argument is simply that this does not occur. The argument is nefarious in that it stipulates that an unconscious and perhaps undiscoverable fear is behind every wish-fulfilling distortion. If one demonstrates empirically and/or produces clinical evidence that some distortions result in gain, the charge can be made that analysis or under-standing of the distortions is incomplete until there is identification of the hidden motive, the avoidance of mental contents, behind the "screen" motive of gain.

Three considerations weaken the force of this objection. None, taken indi-vidually, is sufficient, but as a group they make the objection less promising and perhaps overturn it. First, we can point out how it is just as plausible for individuals to engage in pleasure-directed self-deception in the absence of threat as in profit-oriented other-deception. Through distortion I may enhance my self-image, not because at heart I am insecure about my worth but because no matter how much I am convinced of my value, believing that I am better is pleasurable. Such self-deceptions may prove to be efficient in constructing or consolidating a solid and perhaps even "healthy" identity. I may misconstrue situations as presenting opportunities for sexual, intellectual, or other advancement, not be-cause those possibilities are dangerous or because I am otherwise warding off drives but because such distortions permit pleasurable drive expression. Like-wise, if I, so to speak, cheat on my income taxes or lie to others to achieve gain, it may not be because I am in financial straits, that I believe "I deserve better from life," or because I am displacing hostile impulses. Rather, it may be that the potential benefits of such other-deception exceed the potential intra- and extrapsychic costs. Indeed, pleasure-directed self-deception may be more "plau-sible" than comparably motivated conscious lying. In self-deception the role of consciously anticipated guilt as a guardian of our integrity should be lessened because the individual is unaware that deception is taking place.

The point of this counterargument is that given (1) that this type of self-deception is readily conceivable, (2) that psychoanalytic theory has endowed individuals with finely tuned self-deceptive strategies (i.e., defense mecha-nisms); and (3) that the theory posits that a pleasure principle directs human motivation, it is implausible that there is an empirical constraint that people only use such strategies in the face of danger and not for profit.

The problem with this response is that it is based only on plausibility. All that is plausible certainly is not true. We may insist that before we acknowledge that the restriction on the motives for defense is unjustified, that it be demonstrated that people do deceive themselves purely for gain.

The second response is that such demonstrations are available. New data from a study examining this issue are described in the second part of this chapter (pp. 122–134). Evidence will be presented that individuals may distort and misidentify objectively innocuous stimuli, lack awareness of such distortion, and yet subsequently manifest enhanced self-esteem. The argument will be made that in the absence of threat these individuals engaged in self-deception, distorting their perceptions of reality, to achieve this gain.

A difficulty with this type of evidence is that the claim can be made that no set of stimuli or no situation is truly innocuous or neutral. We can never guarantee that we have constructed an experimental context where there is ''an absence of threat.'' For instance, it may be that some people are driven to elevate self-esteem, because whatever their tonic level, it is inadequate. Opportunities for self-enhancing distortion must be exploited or these individuals will be in an aversive state. This restatement of the view that behind every apparent wish-directed distortion there is a fear would seem theoretically to undermine empirical attempts to demonstrate the invalidity of the restriction on the motives for defense.

Perhaps this point should not be surrendered so easily. It may also be an empirical matter whether for particular individuals particular experimental contexts are neutral or threatening. For example, experimental situations may be modified to limit the possibility of pleasure-directed self-deception. When self-deceptions typically involve misperceptions of reality, the likelihood of misperception may be lowered by reducing stimulus ambiguity, identifying beforehand relevant stimulus dimensions, and so on. It could be determined whether failure to engage in self-deception following such modifications results in an aversive state. Lack of evidence in this direction should prove embarassing to the view that self-deceptive behavior is always generated to forestall or prevent real or imagined loss.

The third retort is historical. We may ask: Why is it that psychoanalytic theory was (is) characterized by this lacuna, why was such an implausible restriction placed on the motives for defense? If it can be shown that the restriction on the motives for defense was derived from a flawed theoretical perspective, there would be additional grounds for rejecting the restriction.

The Genesis of the Lacuna: Why the Restriction on the Motives For Defense?

At the outset we noted that Freud argued that repression, or self-deception, was an inevitable outcome of conflict between impulses and reality. Reality presented either real traumas or threatened to do so if unconscious impulses were enacted.

Freud, like others at the time (Russell, 1903/1963), viewed the external world as inherently inhospitable. "Life, as we find it, is too hard for us; it brings us too many pains, disappointments and impossible tasks. In order to bear it we cannot dispense with palliative measures" [Freud, 1930/1961, p. 22].

This dire view of man's condition might be the basis, at least in part, for the restriction on the motives for defense. Freud (1930/1961) cast mankind in an irrevocable defensive posture; dealing with misery preempts the pursuit of pleasure.

> It is no wonder if, under the pressure of the possibilities of suffering, men are accustomed to moderate their claims to happiness—just as the pleasure principle itself, indeed, under the influence of the external world, changed into the more modest reality principle—, if a man thinks himself happy merely to have escaped unhappiness or to have survived his suffering, and if in general the task of avoiding suffering pushes that of obtaining pleasure into the background [p. 24].

This view was incorporated in Freud's dictum about the outcome of successful psychoanalysis—a reduction of the level of misery experienced by the neurotic to that of common unhappiness. One ground then for the restriction on the motives for defense may have been the belief that the pursuit of pleasure must be jettisoned to deal with the more pressing business of coping with fear.

If one adopts a more sanguine view of man's possibilities of pain and pleasure, this framework for the restriction on the motives for defense may appear unjustified. Even if one accepts the view that fear of possible suffering is pervasive, the temporal generality of the fearfulness may be questioned. It is incontrovertible that, at times, some, if not all, people experience happiness, and it is possible that some measure of pleasure is obtained through the use of self-deceptive strategies. Indeed, the argument can be turned around. It seems reasonable that if the external world were truly so hostile and uninviting, people would more likely resort to distorting their conceptions of reality and of themselves to achieve positive ends. Although the pessimistic description of man's place in life may help us understand part of the intellectual genesis for restriction on motives of defense, it alone cannot justify it. Were it granted that in relation to the external world we are necessarily in defensive position, we could still ask: Is not an offense at times the best defense?

Freud (1930/1961) recognized that there were several means available by which to cope with the misery. Among them, he described the now standard defensive operations, as well as the possibility of pleasure-directed distortion. After indicating that one method was to isolate oneself and break off relations with the outside world, he wrote:

> But one can do more than that, one can try to re-create the world, to build up in its stead another world in which its most unbearable features are eliminated and

replaced by others that are in conformity with one's own wishes. But whoever, in desperate defiance, sets out upon this path to happiness will as a rule attain nothing. Reality is too strong for him. He becomes a madman, who for the most part finds no one to help him in carrying through his delusion. [p. 28].

Here still Freud casts the attempt to construct a wish-based reality as "desperate" and as oriented to eradicate "unbearable" features. Nonetheless, whether primed by the avoidance of pain or the pursuit of pleasure, Freud undoubtedly viewed wish-based distortion as unlikely to produce gain. He provided two reasons for the unpromising nature of such a strategy. Either reality will be "too strong" for the individual to carry out the delusion or the individual will become mad. Both of these reasons should be examined closely.

Reality and Falsity.   Psychoanalytic theory developed within the context of a positivist philosophical and psychological context. An objectively real world or reality is assumed, and this reality is knowable. Moreover, Freud posited that our representations of reality are veridical; that is, we sense what is there. Associating accurate perceptions of reality with psychoanalytic theory may seem contradictory, given the theory's emphasis on distortion. However, the theory is grounded in the assumption of multiple control or processing systems (Erdelyi, 1974). Ego mechanisms, such as perception or memory, governed by the reality principle, are presumed to be sensitive and "bias-free" processors of information. The decisions or representations based on such processing are accurate. If such representations signal danger, defense mechanisms may be used to deny these representations access to awareness and to construct false representations that will constitute phenomenological experience. At the least, a dual-processing system is proposed, with one system a passive receiver of information that results in veridical representation, and another independent system, an active constructor of representations tuned to motivational concerns.

In claiming that reality is "too strong" for individuals to establish wish-based distortions, Freud was arguing that there are limits to the degree to which the decisions reached by each processing system can diverge. In particular, divergences produced when individuals are faced with threat (distortion of painful representations) are possible, but not those motivated by gain. Before examining the possible justifications for this asymmetry, the viability of the dual-processing model should be addressed.

The notion that at least part of the cognitive apparatus involves passive reception of information and inherently veridical representations is not congruent with current emphases within cognitive psychology. It is accepted by many that cognitive processes are essentially constructive. Neisser (1967), for instance, argued that, "In principle, *all* perceptual phenomena arise from transformations of input information" [p. 140, italics in original] and that "images are indeed constructs, rather than replicas of isolated stimulus patterns [p. 145].'' People are viewed as active processors who transform and integrate sensory input into representations that may or may not be veridical.

Such a formulation does not require the dual stream of processing inherent in the Freudian scheme. A single-decision processor may be subject to distortion, as motivational factors influence (in signal detection terms) the response biases and/or possibly the sensitivity of the processor. Constructions of reality may accommodate fears or wishes. Such a model can account for the manifestations of defensive processes in perception, thought, or memory, without stipulating that simultaneously there is veridical representation of reality.

The contrast between the single-decision model and the dual-processor model highlights another source of inherent optimism in psychoanalytic theory. The dual-processor model requires that at least part of the individual is ''in touch with'' or accurately represents reality. Even when ongoing phenomenological experience is distorted, memories of the unconscious, accurate representations may later be recovered. In the single-processor model, constructions are all that there is, distorted or otherwise, and memory of prior events is but construction based on earlier construction.

If one rejects the dual-processing model and the collateral view that part of the individual is always accurately representing reality, Freud's objection that reality is too strong for wish-based distortion carries less weight. If all we have is our constructions of the world with no opportunity for internal validation, degree of inaccuracy is not at issue. This is not to say that a constructionist model cannot put limitations on the extent to which motivational factors influence sensitivity and response bias parameters. Rather, within the range of possible inaccuracy a single-decision model does not include the conflict between dual representations that Freud emphasized.

This description of the opposing models is not intended as a statement that the dual-processing model is inherently inappropriate. On the contrary, recent research on neodissociation theory with hypnotic analgesia (Hilgard, 1976) and the research reviewed below on self-deception (Gur & Sackeim, 1979; Sackeim & Gur, 1978) support the claim that at times multiple cognitive systems may be dissociated, with one system more accurately reflecting reality than another. Further, revision of the psychoanalytic model is possible such that the system responsible for ''veridical'' representation is not viewed as a passive receiver of information, developing snapshots of the world. The dissociated cognitive systems may be active processors, both based on constructionist principles, with one relatively invariant and the other influenced by motivational factors. It should be noted, however, as discussed in the third part of this chapter, that the dual-processor model is probably more restrictive of the range of possible distortions in perception, thought, or memory. Because it may incorporate a processor likely to be relatively accurate in representation, the degree of distortion permitted in phenomenological experience may be less than in models that do not contain the possibility of internal validation.

We have the sense that the Freudian scheme embodied restraints on the types of distortions that are feasible in nonpsychotic individuals. It appears that wish-directed distortion was thought more likely to conflict with internal representations of reality than fear-directed distortion. The genesis of this view probably derived from Freud's belief that the basic neurotic conflicts are between the demands of the id and those of the external world. In fear-directed distortion, accurate representation of internal events (wishes, thoughts, and feelings) is sacrificed to accommodate a threatening reality. In wish-directed distortion, representations of the external world are made to fit the desires of the individual. In essence, Freud, in claiming that "reality is too strong" to permit wish-based distortion, argued that the reality principle would abide by self-deception in regard to internal but not external events.

This argument is weak on two grounds. First, we should reject as absolute the mapping of wish-directed or fear-directed distortion with misperception of external or internal events, respectively. Certainly wish-directed distortion may involve misreadings of objective, external events, such as how much money we possess and what other people have said to us, but self-deception for gain may also involve subjective, internal events, as in our understanding of our own impulses, fears, abilities, and so on. The same type of perceptions that may be subject to fear-based distortion may be distorted with pleasure as the motive. I may believe that I am more generous, intelligent, or lustful than indeed I am, because I am insecure or threatened (fear-directed distortion). I may likewise hold these beliefs because no matter how much I take pleasure in my qualities, more "good" brings more pleasure.

That the same mental contents may be subject to wish- or fear-directed distortion undoes the argument that the need to represent external reality accurately vitiates all possibility of pleasure-based self-deception. The issue then becomes whether people may use such distortion even in regard to representations of external events.

The second ground for questioning Freud's claim concerns his conceptualization of "external reality." Undoubtedly, many wish-based distortions are likely to involve not simply representations of internal events but also external events. Many things in the world would give us pleasure were they different. Freud's argument may have been that these representations of external events cannot be distorted (by nonpsychotics) because of the power of the reality principle, supported by the verifiability by others of the nature of external reality (e.g., "no one to help us in our delusions").

In regard to some classes of external events, this claim is likely to be true.

Whereas believing one has eaten a fine meal, when none was eaten at all, may be a source of pleasure, such gross distortion of external reality is obviously pathological and not characteristic of "normal" functioning. Some proportion of physical events in the world are so unambiguous and so easily subject to verification by others that their misrepresentation is unlikely in any processing system that is minimally sensitive in discriminating signal from noise (i.e., the presence or absence of the event). However, Freud characteristically discussed representation of external reality as if all events outside the individual were of this type, discrete and unambiguous. This is certainly not the case for a proportion of events in physical reality (what John said to me) or in social reality (what John meant by what he said). Our beliefs about the degree to which others like us, the attractiveness of our spouses, our own productivity, and so on, concern our representations of the external world. They are not easily subject to verification and there is little reason to believe that they are not as easily subject to distortion, wish or fear based, as our representations of our own impulses, feelings, and thoughts.[1]

The foundation for Freud's rejection of the possibility of wish-based distortion (in nonpsychotic individuals) appears to be weak. He identified the likely contents of such self-deceptions as representations of external events. He did not acknowledge that the very same representation of internal events as may be subject to fear-based distortion may be distorted for pleasure. Second, he did not distinguish between classes of external events that may differ in their susceptibility to distortion. By placing all events outside the person on a par with unambiguous and discrete physical events, it appeared that distortions of representation of external reality could only occur with gross malfunctioning and would be nonadaptive. Accepting the possibility that large classes of external events, particularly in the social sphere, may be as or more ambiguous and as difficult to verify as internal events removes the last obstacle.

We have seen that Freud's justifications for denying the possibility and/or viability of wish-based distortion were shaky, at best. Before turning to the

---

[1]This point can be rephrased simply. Some beliefs about external events that could provide pleasure or aid in avoiding pain are so grossly incompatible with reality testing that their maintenance in a self-deceptive system is improbable. From a classic energic point of view, maintaining such repression or denial would consume too much energy and would be too costly. However, not all perceptions or beliefs about external events are so readily subject to reality testing. Further, people may deceive themselves and consciously hold beliefs that are in fact true (see Sackeim & Gur, 1978, for a discussion of this point). Once we allow for varying degrees of confidence in the veracity of our everyday perceptions and beliefs about the external world, Freud's assumption that the representations of external reality cannot be distorted in healthy individuals can be seen as erroneous. This problem in Freud's theory is highlighted by his inconsistency in recognizing slips of memory and of speech while insisting that perception is immaculate.

empirical evidence that pleasure-directed self-deception does occur, the theoretical problems that "offensive mechanisms" offer for psychoanalytic theory of the nature of psychopathology should be raised.

Pleasure, Self-Deception, and Psychopathology

Earlier we noted that psychopathology in the Freudian scheme is viewed as the necessary outcome of defensive processes. Failure to satisfy fully and directly instinctual demands is psychopathological; the act of repression, although universal, is an act of renunciation and pathology.

The theory underlying psychoanalytic treatment incorporates this view. Treatment is geared to undoing self-deceptions and recovering truth. "Finally, we must not forget that the relationship between analyst and patient is based on a love of truth, that is, on the acknowledgment of reality, and that it precludes any kind of sham or deception" [Freud, 1937/1963, p. 266].

Breaking through defensive acts is believed to produce greater possibilities for pleasure. As patients accept that their repression and transformation of impulses have been based on ill-founded fears, more direct and satisfying drive expression becomes possible. Neurotic acts, through the use of self-deception, involve instinctual renunciation; psychoanalysis offers the possibility of greater gratification by promoting self-knowledge.

The claim embodied here is that there is a negative correlation between the extent to which we engage in repression and our prospects for happiness. This claim may make it more understandable why psychopathology is viewed as synonymous with the employment of defensive strategies. Unless the criteria for ascribing psychopathology are morally based (Mowrer, 1960) or are based on the prescription that accurate representations of ourselves and reality is a functional ideal, it is hard to see how the degree to which we lie to ourselves, or to others for that matter, has much to do with psychological health and illness. However, particularly in a model emphasizing the hedonic aspects of human behavior, such as psychoanalysis, the degree to which individuals experience happiness and the ascription of psychopathology may be intimately related. If engaging in self-deception is the process that limits the possibilities of experiencing happiness, then self-deception or repression is a pathological process.

This view is defensible as long as one does not allow for self-deceptive strategies that are pleasure directed. As we have seen, psychoanalytic theory explicitly assumes that all defensive operations involve instinctual renunciation. Impulses in conflict with reality are dangerous and, therefore, repressed and only partially satisfied. The theory does not allow for the possibility that individuals will distort their knowledge of themselves and of the external reality to gratify impulses. If we allow for this possibility, we must accept the notion that self-deception may, at times, result in greater possibilities of happiness than accurate self-representation.

In the short or long run, the view that self-deception may produce greater happiness than its absence contradicts the psychoanalytic presumed negative correlation between extent of utilization of defensive strategies and happiness or psychopathology. Were happiness the single measure of psychological health, individuals capable of maintaining pleasure-oriented self-deceits should be viewed as "healthier" than those less happy but more accurate in self-knowledge. Further, uncovering or working through defenses may be a counterproductive clinical strategy. When self-deceptions are not fear based but only pleasure oriented, their undoing in the course of therapy can only result in a reduction in the possibilities for happiness of the patient. Indeed, stating the converse, it is conceivable that some psychological disorders may result from an inability to use self-deception strategies to promote the experience of pleasure. Effective therapy might entail helping patients acquire self-deceptive strategies so as to maintain an adequate level of self-esteem or mood.

These issues concerning the relations between self-deception and psychopathology are discussed more fully in the third part of this chapter. There, psychological and neuropsychological evidence is presented concerning the adaptive value of self-deceptive strategies. The hypothesis is offered that some forms of neurotic depression are associated with a failure to employ pleasure-directed self-deception and that some forms of treatment for depression may be effective by inadvertently redressing this deficiency. First, however, we turn to empirical work, attempting to demonstrate that pleasure-oriented self-deception does indeed occur.

EMPIRICAL STUDIES OF SELF-DECEPTION

The concept of self-deception has been used by a number of psychologists in accounting for a wide range of behavior. Meehl and Hathaway (1946) and Anastasi (1961) argued that self-deception on the part of respondents contributes more to the lack of validity of self-report personality inventories than does other-deception, or conscious lying. In the area of motivation and personality, Hilgard (1949) claimed that self-deception constitutes a defining characteristic of all defense mechanisms. Murphy (1970, 1975) related the concept of self-deception to possible interpretations of experimental findings on perceptual defense. In the area of problem-solving behavior, Wason and Johnson-Laird (1972) invoked the concept of self-deception as a possible explanation of the persistence of subjects to maintain hypotheses in the face of disconfirmation. Indeed, Mischel (1974), consistent with psychoanalytic theory, viewed all neurotic behavior as instances of self-deceptive acts.

Despite the considerable role given the concept of self-deception in several areas of psychological theorizing, until recently psychologists had not attempted to define what is meant by self-deception and to determine whether specific behaviors of people should be ascribed as self-deceptive. In the philosophical literature it has frequently been remarked that the determination of what is meant by self-deception and the demonstration that people do engage in self-deception have major implications for views concerning the structure of consciousness (Fingarette, 1969; Sartre, 1958). For instance, findings that indicate that people do lie to themselves may also indicate that people can hold beliefs outside of awareness and that the awareness or lack of awareness of particular beliefs is subject to motivational control.

On the basis of a logicolinguistic analysis, we offered four criteria as necessary and sufficient for the ascription of self-deception (Sackeim & Gur, 1978). In our view, attempts to define self-deception that have rejected the assimilation of its logic with that of other-deception have been unsuccessful (Canfield & Gustafson, 1962; Penelhum, 1966). Rather, based on an analysis of the constituents of other-deception, we proposed these four criteria for the ascription of self-deception. For an individual to be self-deceived:

1. The individual must hold two contradictory beliefs (that p and $\sim$ that p).
2. These beliefs must be held simultaneously.
3. One of these beliefs is not subject to awareness.
4. The act that determines which belief is subject to awareness and which belief is not subject to awareness is a motivated act.

The use of the term *self-deception* in everyday life supports the appropriateness of these criteria. Take the examples of the parents who insist that their child is a ''good boy'' despite considerable evidence of delinquency, or the scientist who maintains a cherished hypothesis in the face of repeated disconfirmation. Both sets of individuals sincerely hold their avowed beliefs. However, indirect evidence may be available indicating that they also believe the opposite. When the phone rings at home, the parents may become anxious, expecting the child to be in trouble again. The scientist may appear reluctant to test the hypothesis, postponing analyses, averring that further tests are unnecessary. When at a later time self-deceptions are broken, the parents may remark that ''deep inside'' or ''in their hearts'' they knew all along that the child was a troublemaker, or the scientist may claim that all along he ''sensed'' that the hypothesis was wrong, although neither the parents nor the scientist could ''admit this'' to themselves. Both groups of individuals during the self-deception simultaneously held contradictory beliefs (e.g., the child is good/bad; the hypothesis is right/wrong) but were aware of only one. Further, for such dissociations to be labeled self-deceptive, they cannot come about as a matter of happenstance. At any given moment, we may hold several sets of logically contradictory beliefs that may or may not be subject to conscious attention. In cases of self-deception, the inconsistency and lack of awareness is brought out because the individuals have something to gain. The examples given here of not being aware of the beliefs that the child is rotten or that the hypothesis is wrong are instances where the failure to be aware of a belief may be useful to forestall pain. In the previous section, it is argued that individuals may deceive themselves when the motivation is not to avoid pain but to experience pleasure, as in "delusions of grandiosity."

The term *self-deception* has been used so far interchangeably with the psychoanalytic mechanisms of defense and in particular with the psychoanalytic generic concept of repression. This usage should be qualified. Self-deception is viewed as a supraordinate category subsuming the various psychoanalytic mechanisms of defense. These mechanisms differ among themselves in the manifest form that one belief takes in being incompatible with another. When the individual is unaware of the feelings or belief, "I hate John," the individual may consciously espouse the beliefs, "I have no feelings about John" (repression), "I do not hate John" (denial) "John hates me" (projection), 'I love John' (reaction formation), and so on, all of which are incompatible with the unconscious belief. The various psychoanalytic mechanisms of defense may all be viewed as instances of self-deception.

On the other hand, these mechanisms involve more assumptions about the nature of mental processes than does self-deception, as the latter term is being used here. Freud (1915/1957) noted that the concept of repression predicated not simply that beliefs may not be subject to awareness (i.e., nontransparency in consciousness) but also that such beliefs were stored in an unconscious, fully capable of independent control of behavior (i.e., nonunitarity in consciousness). In the psychoanalytic scheme, wishes, thoughts and feelings not subject to awareness may nonetheless influence or motivate ongoing behavior. To demonstrate self-deception one needs to show that individuals simultaneously hold incompatible beliefs, one of which is not subject to awareness and that this state of affairs is motivationally determined. It is not necessary to demonstrate that beliefs not subject to awareness are stored in an "unconscious," fully capable of independent control of behavior. The demonstration of self-deception is a necessary, but not sufficient, condition for demonstrating repression. Therefore, its scientific investigation would seem to be logically prior.

The experimental phenomenon we have used to examine self-deception concerns people's reactions to listening to their own voice. It has been shown that when subjects are presented with audio- and/or video-tape feedback of self and others, feedback of the self is associated with considerable psychophysiological reactivity (Holzman, Rousey, & Snyder, 1966; Olivos, 1967), changes in affect and constrictions on ideation (Duval & Wicklund, 1972; Holzman & Rousey,

1966; Holzman et al., 1966; Rousey & Holzman, 1967), and changes in self-concepts (Alkire & Brunse, 1974; Boyd & Sisney, 1967; Duval & Wicklund, 1972; Gur & Sackeim, 1978; Storms, 1973). Self-confrontation manipulations have also been shown to influence dream content (Castaldo & Holzman, 1967, 1969) and other behaviors which do not appear to be mediated by conscious awareness (Huntley, 1940; Wolff, 1943). Many people find self-confrontation aversive and the degree to which individuals hold discrepant cognitions about themselves (self-esteem) is related to the aversiveness of self-confrontation (Sackeim & Gur, 1978). Likewise, it has been found that experimental manipulations of self-esteem and cognitive discrepancy influence whether exposure to the self will be experienced as a positive or negative event (Davis & Brock, 1975; Duval, Wicklund, & Fine as cited in Duval & Wicklund, 1972; Gibbons & Wicklund, 1976). It appears that, generally, the less positively individuals feel about themselves, the more aversive they find self-confrontation.

A critical aspect of the voice-confrontation situation is that people frequently make errors in identifying voices as "self" or "other" (Gur & Sackeim, 1979) (Holzman et al., 1966; Olivos, 1967). We hypothesized that many of these errors in identification were instances of self-deception (Gur & Sackeim, 1979; Sackeim & Gur, 1978). Specifically, we argued that people who made false negative (FN) errors by misidentifying the voice of self as that of other (see Table 4.1) found self-confrontation particularly aversive. The FN error was a motivated attempt to avoid the aversiveness of self-confrontation. On the other hand, some people do not find confrontation with the self at all aversive. On the contrary, hearing their own voice, seeing their name in print, or having their photograph taken may be pleasurable experiences. Such individuals may seek out self-confrontation. We hypothesized that the false positive (FP) error (see Table 4.1) was a motivated attempt to hear the "self" when it was not there.

This formulation suggests that the FN error fits the traditional psychoanalytic model of defensive behavior. Distortion of reality (identifying the self as other) occurs so as to avoid pain, the aversiveness of self-confrontation. On the other hand, the FP error appears more consistent with the concept of pleasure-directed self-deception. Voices of strangers are hardly threatening stimuli and we postulated that FP errors involved distortion of reality (identify "other" as self) so as to advance pleasure.

In support of the claim that these errors were instances of self-deception, in one experiment (Gur & Sackeim, 1979) we found that when subjects were incorrect in their self-report identifications of voices, a psychophysiological measure (GSR) indicated that at some level of processing correct discriminations had been made. The voices of self and others resulted in high and low levels of arousal, respectively, regardless of the correctness of the verbal report. The two response systems, verbal report and psychophysiological reactivity, were found

TABLE 4.1
Response Types in Voice Identification Studies as
Determined by Nature of Voice (Self or Other) and Self-Report

Self-Report	Reality (Voice Condition)	
	Self	Other
Self	True positive (TP)	False positive (FP)
Other	False negative (FN)	True negative (TN)

to be independent. In this respect, evidence was provided that when subjects misidentified voices of self or others, they simultaneously held contradictory beliefs (me and ~ me). Obtrusive postexperimental self-reports and unobtrusive indices of awareness were congruent in indicating that virtually all subjects who misidentified the voice of self as other (FN) were not aware of committing these errors, whereas about half of the subjects who made FP errors were unaware of doing so. Therefore, the majority of people who made errors were unaware of holding a correct belief as to the nature of the voice. The first experiment only partially addressed the issue of motivation. It was shown that subjects who made FP errors were low on individual difference measures that predict the aversiveness of self-confrontation; that is, they were high in self-esteem. Furthermore, subjects who misidentified voices of self and others were found to score high on a paper-and-pencil measure of individual differences in tendencies to engage in self-deception, the Self-deception Questionnaire (SDQ; Sackeim & Gur, 1979). These subjects were more likely to deny psychologically threatening statements than subjects who did not commit any errors.

A second study was conducted to examine further the motivational account of misidentifications (Gur & Sackeim, 1979). In this study, the presumed motivational determinants of these errors were experimentally manipulated. Davis and Brock (1975), Duval et al. (as cited in Duval & Wicklund, 1972) and Gibbons and Wicklund (1976) have shown that manipulations that enhance or deflate self-esteem influence the aversiveness of self-confrontation and, accordingly, influence approach or avoidance of selective exposure to the self. Likewise, we found that, subsequent to a voice identification task, subjects who were given a pretreatment of success in their performance on an intelligence task reported less depression, anxiety, and hostility and that they enjoyed hearing their own voices more and found them more pleasant than subjects who were given a failure pretreatment. On the task of identifying voices of self and others, the failure and success groups differed in the speed and certainty of their identifications of voices of self, with the failure group slower and less certain. The two groups did not differ in the speed and certainty of their identifications of voices of others. Most important, the two groups differed in their rates of each type of misidentification. The failure group committed more FN errors than the success group, whereas the success group committed more FP errors than the failure group.

The findings of these two experiments support the contention that FN and FP errors may both be instances of self-deception. Comparison of verbal reports and psychophysiological reactivity indicated that often when subjects' reports were in error, at some level of processing, correct identifications had been made. This indicates that subjects simultaneously held contradictory beliefs, fulfilling the first two criteria for ascribing self-deception. It was also shown that for the most part subjects lacked awareness of having made errors and, therefore, fulfilled the third criterion of establishing that subjects were unaware of holding one of the beliefs.

The evidence for motivation, the fourth criterion, is more circumstantial. In the first study, subjects who made FP errors reported the highest level of self-esteem during pretesting. The presumed motivational determinants of errors were varied in a second study by manipulation of mood and self-esteem. Success and failure groups differed in tendencies to commit either FP or FN errors. This would suggest that decreased self-esteem is associated with the FN error and increased self-esteem with the FP error. Our motivational account was that decreased self-esteem resulted in self-confrontation being more aversive and produced avoidance through the FN error. Increased self-esteem resulted in self-confrontation being pleasurable, a state sought out through the FP error.

There were two shortcomings in the available evidence pertaining to the motivational account of the misidentifications. First, in the experiment that manipulated self-esteem, a failure group was compared to a success group. Although it was established that the motivational manipulation was effective in producing differing behavior and, in particular, differing types of misidentification in the two groups, we do not know whether both or only one of the groups would have differed from a third group that had not received a self-esteem manipulation. Therefore, we cannot conclude that alteration in rates of FN and FP errors was independently produced in both the failure and success group.

The second problem may be of greater theoretical consequence. One can argue that the data presented so far are inadequate in addressing the issue of motivation. These data have addressed the questions: "What characterizes people who make particular types of errors?" and "Do manipulations of presumed determinants influence the types of errors that are committed?" Specifically, the data have not addressed the issue of what people gain by self-deception in this context. If the misidentifications are indeed motivated, the consequences of making particular errors should differ from the consequences of correct identification (Irwin, 1971).

Our motivational account stipulates that the FN error is committed to avoid the aversive consequences of self-confrontation, whereas the FP error is committed to induce a positive state. In the study described next the consequences in regard to self-esteem of correct and incorrect identifications were examined, further testing the motivational account of errors. In so doing, the empirical reality of pleasure-directed self-deception was examined.

Self-confrontation has been found to influence self-evaluation as measured by semantic differential ratings (Coyne & Holzman, 1961; Holzman & Rousey, 1966; Rousey & Holzman, 1968). In particular, following confrontation with the self, the concept MY VOICE was found to be rated as more negative on the evaluation factor and more passive on the activity factor. Given our previous findings relating manipulations of self-esteem to types of errors in identification of self and others (Gur & Sackeim, 1979; Sackeim & Gur, 1978), it was deemed appropriate that in the present investigation semantic differential ratings of the concept MY VOICE be used as dependent measures to examine the consequences of correct and incorrect identifications of self and others.

As in the studies by Holzman and colleagues (Coyne & Holzman, 1966; Holzman & Rousey, 1966; Rousey & Holzman, 1968), in the present investigation subjects were asked to fill out equivalent forms of the semantic differential before, right after, and 5 minutes after listening to voices. A yoked-control design was employed to produce four matched groups of subjects. The groups differed according to whether subjects committed a TP response (correct identification of self), an FN response (misidentification of self), an FP response (misidentification of other), or only TN responses (correct identification of others). Subjects were yoked for the number of voices they identified, the trial on which the classificatory responses were committed, and in postexperimental reports of not being aware of having committed errors in identification.

METHOD

Subjects

The final sample contained 48 undergraduates (28 male, 20 female), selected from a larger pool of 254 subjects (151 male, 103 female) who participated in the study. All subjects were born and lived continuously in the Northeastern United States.

Procedure

When subjects reported to the experiment they were administered a semantic differential (Form A, Coyne & Holzman, 1966) and instructed to rate their present feelings about the concept MY VOICE. After this the voices of all subjects were recorded as they read a standard paragraph, following the procedures described in Gur and Sackeim (1979). They were then taken to another room and administered the instructions for the voice identification task (Gur & Sackeim, 1979). Tapes of same-sex voices were then played to subjects. As explained in the following, for each subject the number of voices on the tape and whether the self appeared on the tape was determined by the yoke and the position within the yoked group that was being filled. Following the identification of the last voice, subjects completed Form B of the semantic differential under the same instructions given for Form A. Subjects were given a 5-minute rest period and then Form C of the semantic differential and the postexperimental questionnaire were administered.

Assignment of Subjects to Yoked Groups.   Master tapes of male and female voices were constructed following the procedures described in Gur and Sackeim (1979). Voices were 4 seconds in duration with a variable silence interval (range = 15–25 seconds, mean = 20 seconds). All voices were reading the same phrase, beginning with the third sentence in the paragraph. The number of voices on master tapes ranged from three to ten. Initial subjects were played tapes that contained 10 voices of others, with the self not appearing on the tapes. When a FP response (misidentification of other as self) was committed the tape was stopped two trials following the response and the subject who committed the FP response was taken as the first member of a potential yoked group. For the next subjects the voice of the self was recorded in the position on the tape in which the FP response was committed. The tapes for these subjects ended two trials of other voices after the voice of self. This procedure was followed until a subject was found who committed a TP response (correct identification of self) and a subject was found who made a FN response (misidentification of self as other) in the appropriate trial. After this, subjects were presented with tapes that did not contain the voice of the self and that were identical to that heard by the subject who committed the FP response. This was continued until a subject was found who correctly identified all the voices of others, a TN subject. This last subject completed the yoked group. In all, the yoked groups were comprised of subjects who except on one critical trial correctly identified all voices of other. On the critical trial, the members of the yoked groups differed in that FP, TP, FN, and TN responses were committed. Because this study was concerned with examining the consequences of self-deception, the motivated selective nonawareness of beliefs, only subjects who were not aware of committing errors were included in the final sample. Any subject who correctly or incorrectly stated on the postexperimental questionnaire that a misidentification had been made was disqualified from inclusion in the final sample. The selection procedure resulted in a sample of 12 yoked groups (7 male, 5 female) or a total of 48 subjects.

RESULTS

For each subject, scores on the evaluation, activity, and potency scales right after (RA) and 5 minutes after (FA) the voice identification task were subtracted from the respective pretask scores (PRE). In order to permit between-scale comparison, z transformations were performed on each set of difference scores. The use of standardized difference scores was justified as there were no differences among the four response groups in pretask ratings on the three semantic differential scales (all F's < 1). A 4 (response group) $\times$ 2 (Sex) $\times$ 3 (semantic differential scale) $\times$ 2 (time of measurement) analysis of variance, with repeated measures on the last two factors, was performed on the standardized scores. A significant interaction was obtained between response group and semantic differential scale, $F(6, 80) = 2.48$, $p < .05$. This indicated that the four response groups differed in their ratings and that this effect should be evaluated separately for each semantic differential scale.

Means of the four response groups on the two standardized scores on each of the three scales are presented in Fig. 4.1. Separate analyses of variance (response group $\times$ sex $\times$ time of measurement) were conducted for scores on each of the three scales. Only the results for the evaluation factor indicated an effect of response group. On this factor, there was a main effect of response group, $F(3, 40) = 3.08$, $p < .05$. As seen in Fig. 1 and confirmed by a priori tests, across the two posttask assessments subjects who made a TP response, that is, correctly identified the self, decreased in self-esteem; this group's change toward greater negative self-evaluation differed from the changes in the other three groups (all p's $< .05$). The group that committed a FP response, that is, wrongly identified a voice as self when it was other, showed an increase in positive self-evaluation. This change differed from that in the other three groups (all p's $< .05$). Subjects who committed FN and TN responses on the critical trial did not differ and showed no change from pretreatment in self-evaluation.

DISCUSSION

Previous investigations had shown that confrontation with the self is frequently aversive and generally results in autonomic arousal, negative self-evaluation, defensive reactions, and constrictions on ideational content. However, the consequences of self-confrontation had not been examined in relation to whether subjects were aware of being confronted with the self and the correctness of such awareness. The results of this study indicated that when subjects were correct in believing that they had heard the voice of self, they demonstrated the negative consequences of self-confrontation. As in the studies by Coyne and Holzman

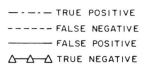

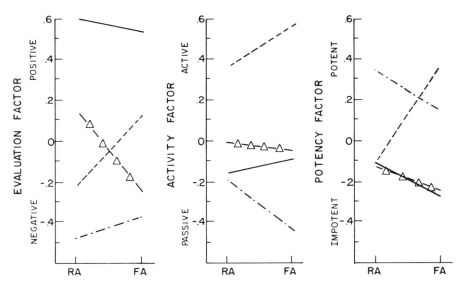

FIG. 1.   Mean standardized differences scores on evaluation, activity, and potency scales from pretask ratings to right after (RA) and to 5 minutes after (FA) voice identifications for subjects who committed true positive, false negative, false positive, and only true negative responses.

(1966) and Holzman and Rousey (1966), in this investigation, after making TP responses subjects rated their voices as more negative on the evaluation scale. Although the results for the activity factor were not significant for these subjects, they were in the same direction as found in the previous studies where confrontation with the self led to increased passive evaluations. On the other hand, as predicted, the negative consequences of self-confrontation were not found in subjects who either misidentified the self (committed FN responses) or in subjects who misidentified others as self (committed FP responses). Subjects who made FN responses showed no change on the evaluation dimension, and subjects who made FP responses evidenced increased positive self-evaluation.

These findings support the claim that errors in identification of self and other are motivated and are instances of self-deceptive behavior. The outcomes of correct and incorrect identifications were found to differ—in this study not engaging in self-deception when confronted with the self resulted in negative consequences. Engaging in self-deception resulted either in positive consequences (FP subjects) or the absence of negative consequences (FN subjects) on measures of self-evaluation.

The findings of this study also bear on the general issue of whether individuals can be unaware of beliefs. An outcome of employing a yoked control design was that subjects who committed TP and FP responses outwardly did not differ in their behavior. Both groups correctly identified the same voices of others. Both groups identified a voice as the self, and these identifications were made on equivalent trials. Both groups reported on the postexperimental questionnaire that they did not make any errors and that the voice of self appeared once on the tape. However, the changes in ratings for these two groups following identifications were quite distinct. These differences between matched groups cannot be accounted for simply by the fact that subjects in the pairs differed as to whether they were actually presented with the voice of self. Subjects who made FN responses were confronted with the self and did not show negative changes in self-evaluation, as did TP subjects. Rather, if engaging in differential behaviors or holding different beliefs resulted in the differences in ratings, then the behaviors or beliefs that distinguished the groups appeared not to be subject to awareness.

Two qualifications should be made in interpreting these findings. First, although the expected effects were obtained in the change scores, the response groups did not differ in pretask ratings. This contrasts with our previous findings (Gur & Sackeim, 1979) that subjects who commit FP responses (misidentify other as self) evidenced heightened self-esteem on self-report inventories completed prior to the voice identification task. Our view has been that these individuals value themselves highly not only as a transient consequence of engaging in this type of self-deception but that they are also typically high in self-esteem as a dispositional quality, making self-confrontation a pleasurable state. The differences among the groups in change scores but not in pretask ratings may have been due to the increased reliability of assessment that accrues with repeated measurement. Another possibility is that evaluation of concept MY VOICE only indirectly taps general self-esteem. Ratings made before the task may have been only weakly related to other aspects of self-concept. The positive mood and increase in general self-esteem that is believed to have occurred in the FP group following the task may have produced a halo effect that would have resulted in increased positive ratings of any aspect of self-concept.

The second issue concerns the evidence that the errors in misidentification are motivated. It has been shown now that the consequences of correct and incorrect identifications differ. As a final technical step in the demonstration that these errors are motivated, it would be necessary to show as well that the errors are made in order to achieve the particular outcomes (Irwin, 1971). For instance, finding that when food is placed in the right-side goal box of a T-maze, a hungry rat runs to the right only partially establishes that the goal box behavior is under motivational control. To rule out alternative explanations, such as position preference, it must be shown that when the contingencies between behavior and outcomes are reversed and food is placed in the left-side goal box, the hungry rat runs to the left. Similarly, to demonstrate conclusively that errors in identification are motivated, it must be shown that when contingencies between behavior and outcomes are changed and misidentifications are followed by negative consequences, the frequencies of such misidentifications decrease. However, although one can easily manipulate contingencies in a T-maze, it is difficult to see how this can be done in regard to the behavior and consequences of identifications of self and others. The outcomes that ensue following such identifications are primarily intrapsychic, as in changes in self-esteem, and are not easily subject to experimenter control.

These problems notwithstanding, the findings of this study support the contention that errors in identification of self and others are instances of self-deception. Further, the study provides empirical support for the contention that the motives for self-deception may pertain to the pursuit of pleasure and not simply the avoidance of pain. As pointed out in the first section, the classic psychoanalytic view is that defensive operations are initiated when people are confronted with threatening stimuli, either internal or external. For instance, Fenichel (1945) in discussing the motives for defense in relation to external reality wrote: "Whenever a stimulus gives rise to painful feelings, a tendency is developed not only to ward off these feelings but also to ward off the stimulus [p. 131]." The motivational account given of FN errors fits this conceptualization. The state engendered by self-confrontation is often threatening or aversive and it is avoided by the commission of these errors. However, one would be hard pressed to argue that FP errors are responses to threatening stimuli. There is no evidence that exposure to voices of others is aversive and the motivational account offered for such errors claims that, by making these misidentifications, individuals are actively distorting reality to engender a preferred state. The results of this study suggest that individuals may distort reality not only in the face of threatening stimuli and not only to protect self-esteem but also in order to enhance actively self-esteem. Labeling both types of behavior as instances of "defensive" phenomena may be a misnomer.

The traditional psychoanalytic view might be rescued by applying the belief that "behind the wish there is a fear." One might be able to undo this demonstration by arguing, for instance, that subjects who made FP responses needed to experience elevated self-esteem or they would have been in an aversive state. One could argue that such individuals, relative to their own standards, are tonically inadequate in self-esteem and they must approach virtually any situation as a potential esteem booster. The analogy might be to that of an individual with a perpetual itch. The itch must be scratched not simply for the sake of pleasure associated with relief but more so because the itch is aversive. Further, no amount of scratching will completely satisfy.

At issue again is the argument that people may distort reality simply to augment pleasure as opposed to the argument that apparent pleasure-directed self-deception occurs only when people are needy and in conflict. It is my view that the available evidence is weighted in favor of the former possibility. There are data indicating that people who make FP responses report tonically high levels of self-esteem and less symptomatology than people who do not make these errors (Gur & Sackeim, 1979; Sackeim & Gur, 1978). Rather than being particularly needy or in conflict, these individuals may, indeed, value themselves highly. They may react to experimental contexts not so much as threats to self-esteem or as requiring self-esteem enhancement but as opportunities to elevate self-evaluation.

As noted in the first section, these alternative accounts might be decided between on empirical grounds. Were it the case that individuals who make FP errors need to do so to avoid a lowering of self-esteem or other aversive consequences, one could conceivably alter the experimental context by making the commission of these errors more difficult (e.g., use stimuli that are unambiguously not the self; announce that the self does not appear on the tape). If in such circumstances there is no evidence that failure to commit the errors results in negative consequences, the "fear behind the wish" argument would be compromised.

There are other empirical grounds for claiming that self-deception may be directed toward the pursuit of pleasure and that, further, lying to oneself may at times be an effective strategy in promoting psychological health. This evidence concerns the adaptive value of self-deception and is reviewed in the next section.

THE ADAPTIVE VALUE OF LYING TO ONESELF

Earlier it was argued that psychoanalytic theory might be characterized as overly optimistic in some of its assumptions about human nature. These assumptions can be summarized as follows:

1. People distort their conceptions of internal and external events only in the face of threat and not to advance pleasure.

2. When people engage in distortion (i.e., use defense mechanisms), they simultaneously represent reality inaccurately and accurately. A two-decision model is assumed, with part of the individual, outside of awareness, processing information about internal and external events in a sensitive and bias-free way.

3. Psychopathology is a result of this falsity with ourselves. Distortions occur in the face of threat, and wishes are inhibited and renounced as a consequence. This renunciation limits the degree or likelihood of experiencing pleasure.

4. The efficacy of psychotherapy and, in particular, psychoanalysis is based on aiding patients to undo distortions and to represent in awareness the accurate perceptions of reality. Conscious acknowledgment and acceptance of the ''truth'' is curative.

In contrast, in this chapter I have argued:

1. People also distort reality (internal and external) for the purpose of advancing pleasure.

2. The two-decision model is reasonable and the empirical evidence for self-deception (Sackeim & Gur, 1978) supports the fact that, at times, such dual processing does occur. However, this does not mean that single-decision distortive processes do not also occur. In such cases, sensitivity and/or criterion biases of processing may be influenced by motivational factors and there is no other level of processing producing more accurate representations.

3. Psychopathology can no longer be identified with the use or consequences of distortive mechanisms. Self-deceptive practices may be efficient strategies by which to promote psychological health and, at least in some circumstances, their use may lead to higher levels of functioning than their absence.

4. In some types of psychopathology, therapy designed to encourage the development and use of self-deceptive strategies may be more ''efficacious'' than therapy directed toward uncovering. There are no necessary relations between the truth or falsity of our representations of ourselves and the world and our possibilities for happiness. At times, encouraging or fostering falsity may be the most effective strategy for promoting psychological health.

In this last section, the relations between self-deception and psychopathology are examined in greater detail. Psychological and neuropsychological evidence is reviewed suggesting that normal functioning is associated with the use of particular distortive strategies and that some forms of depression may be associated with an inability to engage in this type of falsity. Possible applications to various forms of therapy are then discussed.

Self-Deception and Self-Reported Psychopathology

Psychoanalytic theory adopts a rationalist perspective in accounting for psychopathology. As noted, the theory posits a tie between accuracy of representations and psychological health. Psychoanalytic theory is certainly not alone in holding this position. For instance, Rogers (1959) from a phenomenological standpoint viewed psychopathology as a consequence of discrepancy between the individual's understanding of his or her experience and the individual's "actual" organismic experience. Clients are believed to have greater potential for fulfillment when they genuinely accept and integrate organismic experience in self-concept. In the cognitive-behavioral camp, Beck (1967, 1976) has claimed that depression and other types of psychopathology are a result of "bad" thinking. The depressive is characterized by a cognitive triad involving distortion in conceptions of the past, present, and future. Therapy is engineered to teach patients to think in distortion-free ways and to represent reality accurately. Although the theories may differ in their emphases on motivational factors and unconscious determinants, they are harmonious in adopting the rationalist stance that falsity in knowledge of self and the world is connected to psychopathology.

Work on the relations between individual differences in the utilization of self-deception and self-reported psychopathology was, for me, the starting point in questioning the rationalist dictum. Meehl and Hathaway (1946) and Anastasi (1961) had long hypothesized that self-deception influences the results of self-report inventories to a greater extent than does conscious falsehood. This claim seemed to merit empirical attention.

To assess individual differences in tendency to engage in self-deception, a 20-item questionnaire, the SDQ (Sackeim & Gur, 1979), was constructed. Following the classic psychoanalytic theory of defense, items were written so as to be psychologically threatening but universally true if positively endorsed. Content of items concerns mainly themes surrounding sex, aggression, and guilt. Examples are: "Have you ever thought your parents hated you?," "Have you ever enjoyed your bowel movements?," "Have you ever thought of committing suicide in order to get back at somebody?," "Have you ever doubted your sexual adequacy?". Items are responded to on a 7-point Likert scale (not at all–very much so), with total number of denials (responses of 1 and 2) the measure of self-deceptive tendencies. The scale has been shown to have good test–retest reliability in college student samples (Sackeim & Gur, 1979). Regarding the issue of whether the scale genuinely taps self-deception, it was shown that individuals who made errors on the self–other voice identification task score higher on this scale than subjects who made no errors (Gur & Sackeim, 1979).

At issue in designing the scale was whether it could tap self-deceptive tendencies independent of other-deception or conscious lying. The correlation between SDQ scores and scores on traditional lie scales has been found usually to be low to weak (range = 0–.3) (Paulhus, 1980; Sackeim & Gur, 1979; see following). Factor analytic studies of social desirability scales (Damarin & Messick, 1965; Edwards, 1970; Millham, 1974) have found typically two-factor solutions. One interpretation of the solutions is that one factor reflects conscious impression management or lying and the other factor is related to unconscious distortion or self-deception (Damarin & Messick, 1965). Paulhus (1980; cf. Paulhus, in press) recently had a sample of male and female undergraduates complete the Marlowe–Crowne (MC; Crowne & Marlowe, 1964) Need for Approval Scale, the Edwards Social Desirability Scale (SD; Edwards, 1970), the SDQ and the Other-Deception Questionnaire (ODQ: Sackeim & Gur, 1979), the latter constructed explicitly to assess tendencies to engage in conscious falsehood. Scores on the four inventories were factor analyzed and subject to varimax rotation. A two-factor solution was obtained. On the first factor the loadings were: MC = .36, SD = .47, SDQ = .70, and ODQ = .16. On the other factor the loadings were: MC = .60, SD = .20, SDQ = .15, and ODQ = .71. The SDQ and ODQ defined each dimension most strongly and cleanly, with the Marlowe–Crowne confounding the two dimensions and the Edwards Social Desirability Scale loading moderately on the apparent self-deception dimension. It would appear then that individual differences in self-deception can be assessed independently of individual differences in other-deception.

To examine the relations of these dimensions to self-reported psychopathology in one study (Sackeim & Gur, 1979) 250 subjects were administered the Beck Depression Inventory (BDI; Beck, Ward, Mendelsen, Mock, & Erbaugh, 1961), the neuroticism scale of the Eysenck Personality Inventory (EPI-N; Eysenck & Eysenck, 1963), the Manifest Symptom Questionnaire (MSQ; Gur, Sackeim, & Gur, 1976), lie scale of the EPI, the ODQ, and the SDQ. The pattern of intercorrelations for the complete sample is presented in Table 4.2. The three psychopathology scales substantially correlated among themselves, as did the two lie or other-deception scales. The three psychopathology scales were each

TABLE 4.2
Intercorrelations Among Measures of Psychopathology,
Other-Deception, and Self-Deception

	1	2	3	4	5	6
1. BDI	—	.55**	.72**	-.06	-.10	-.34**
2. EPI-N		—	.65**	-.12	-.18**	-.34**
3. MSQ			—	-.16*	-.22**	-.48**
4. EPI-L				—	.57**	.24**
5. ODQ					-	.28**
6. SDQ						—

Note: Correlations are based on a sample of 250 undergraduates (127 male, 123 female), as reported in Sackeim and Gur (1979). BDI = Beck Depression Inventory, EPI-N = Eysenck Personality Inventory Neuroticism Scale, MSQ = Manifest Symptom Questionnaire, EPI-L = Eysenck Personality Inventory, Lie Scale, ODQ = Other-Deception Questionnaire, and SDQ = Self-Deception Questionnaire.
 *p < .05 (two-tailed)
**p < .01 (two-tailed)

negatively correlated with the self-deception score. These negative correlations were all greater than those between the psychopathology and lie measures (all p's $< .001$). Therefore, the greater subjects' tendencies toward self-deception, the less psychopathology they reported. Whereas this pattern also held for other-deception, it was significantly less substantial.

The relations between self-reported psychopathology and SDQ scores have been strong. Indeed, the question could be raised whether the SDQ is not simply a psychopathology measure, with high scores associated with psychological well being. Similarly, it has been pointed out (Sackeim & Gur, 1979) that although the K (Test-Taking Attitude) Scale of the MMPI was offered originally as a general measure of defensiveness (Meehl & Hathaway, 1946), there is evidence that high K scores do not reflect defensiveness or self-deceptive behavior but, rather, psychological health (Heilbrun, 1963). A recent study (Sackeim & Gur, in press), conducted for another purpose, collected data that addressed this issue.

A group of 53 male undergraduates completed the BDI, EPI, MSQ, SDQ, and the Repression–Sensitization Scale (RS; Byrne, 1964) as part of a study on facial asymmetry and psychopathology. The intercorrelations among the scales are presented in Table 4.3. As before, SDQ scores were negatively correlated with the three psychopathology measures (BDI, EPI-N, MSQ). The SDQ correlated negatively with the RS scale that was scored in the direction of sensitization. The lie scale was not significantly associated with any other scale. These results replicated those summarized in Table 4.2.

A factor analysis was performed on the intercorrelations of the six inventories and subjected to varimax rotation. A three-factor solution was obtained, accounting for 87% of the variance. The loadings on each of the three factors are

TABLE 4.3
Intercorrelations Among Measures of Psychopathology,
Other-Deception, and Self-Deception

	1	2	3	4	5	6
1. BDI	—	.57**	.66**	.62**	.06	-.34*
2. EPI-N		—	.72**	.78**	-.20	-.46**
3. MSQ			—	.81**	-.13	-.70**
4. RS				—	-.10	-.52**
5. EPI-L					—	.24
6. SDQ						—

Note: Correlations are based on a sample of 53 male undergraduates. BDI = Beck Depression Inventory, EPI-N = Eysenck Personality Inventory Neuroticism Scale, MSQ = Manifest Symptom Questionnaire, RS = Repression Sensitization Scale, EPI-L = Eysenck Personality Inventory Lie Scale, SDQ = Self-Deception Questionnaire.

*$p < .05$ (two-tailed)
**$p < .001$ (two-tailed)

presented in Table 4.4. The three psychopathology scales and the RS scale all loaded above .7 on the first factor. It is questioned, therefore, whether in normal samples the RS scale is simply another measure of self-reported psychopathology. The second factor was defined by the EPI lie scale, with no other scale loading even moderately. The SDQ had the highest loading on the third factor. This would suggest that a dimension defined by the SDQ is statistically independent of the dimension of self-reported psychopathology (Factor 1). It should be noted that both the MSQ and the RS inventories had moderate negative loadings on the third factor. This would suggest that these two scales also tap some aspects of self-deception. It appears then that, unlike possibly the RS inventory and the K scale, the SDQ may not be a disguised measure of psychopathology.

These findings may be of consequence for the longstanding debate about the relative merits of clinical and actuarial forms of assessment (Holt, 1970; Meehl, 1954). It was noted that a number of theories of clinical phenomena have associated the use of distortion and self-deception with psychopathology. Although there has been no research on this issue, it would not be surprising to learn that as a general rule the more evidence there is of defensive behavior in individuals, the more likely would most clinicians be to attribute psychopathology. On the other hand, the findings indicated that degree of psychopathology as actuarially determined by self-report inventories is negatively associated with degree of self-deceptive behavior. Self-deception may be a moderating variable contributing to the (at times) substantial disagreements between clinical and actuarial forms of assessment.

The findings also raise problems for interpretation. Specifically, one must question why in normal samples individuals who appear to engage in self-

TABLE 4.4
Rotated Factor Loadings of Psychopathology,
Other-Deception, and Self-Deception Measures

	Factor 1 Psychopathology	Factor 2 Other-Deception	Factor 3 Self-Deception
1. BDI	.84	.16	-.09
2. EPI-N	.84	-.22	-.22
3. MSQ	.73	-.04	-.60
4. RS	.83	-.06	-.36
5. EPI-L	-.02	.98	.11
6. SDQ	-.25	.13	.94

Note: Factor analysis with varimax rotation was conducted on the scores of 53 male undergraduates. BDI = Beck Depression Inventory, EPI-N = Eysenck Personality Inventory Neuroticism Scale, MSQ = Manifest Symptom Questionnaire, RS = Repression Sensitization Scale, EPI-L = Eysenck Personality Inventory Lie Scale, SDQ = Self-Deception Questionnaire.

deception the most also frequently report the least psychopathology. We (Sackeim & Gur, 1979) suggested that the most plausible interpretation was that people high in tendencies to engage in self-deception were unlikely to acknowledge psychopathology in themselves. This would suggest that in normal samples "actual" psychopathology is unrelated to or positively associated with degree of self-deception. This claim of plausibility may have been overstated. Given the evidence that has been presented thus far that self-deception may be useful in enhancing self-esteem, we should entertain the view that in at least some populations, or across some range, degree of self-deception and use of other distortive mechanisms (i.e., single-decision models) are positively associated with psychological health.

Studies of Normal Subjects

A large and growing body of findings, mostly within social psychology, points to characteristic distortive mechanisms in normal populations. The phenomena investigated have variously been termed self-serving biases, unrealistic optimism, egocentric attributions, illusions of control, and beneffectance (Greenwald, 1980; Miller & Ross, 1975; Weinstein, 1980). The much corroborated effect is that normal individuals see themselves as contributing more to bringing about positive than negative events, even when objectively there is no difference in control over the two classes of events.

The effect of highlighting the positive and denying the negative pertains not only to normal individuals' evaluations of ongoing behavior but also to memory of the past and to expectancies for the future. The Zeigarnik (1927) effect—people recall interrupted tasks better than completed tasks—may be reversed by associating completion with success and interruption with failure (Glixman, 1949; Rosenzweig, 1943; cf., Greenwald, 1980). Recently, Weinstein (1980) had college students estimate their own chances of experiencing in the future a set of positive and negative events relative to the chances of their classmates experiencing those events. Overall subjects rated their own chances of experiencing positive events as above average and as below average for negative events. For instance, in rating their chances of owning their own home and liking their postgraduation job, six times as many subjects reported that their probabilities were above the average of their peers than below average. In terms of negative events, approximately nine times as many subjects reported that they were less likely than average to have a drinking problem or be divorced after a few years of marriage than those who reported their chances as above average.

Weinstein argued that this unrealistic optimism may have been a consequence of subjects having special access to their own abilities and plans and that they may not have realized that others also had factors working in their favor. In a second study, a group of subjects completed ratings of future events after reading a list of reasons given by other subjects as to the factors that would influence the probabilities of specific events happening to them in the future. Although exposure to this information attenuated somewhat the degree of unrealistic optimism in self-ratings, the basic effect was still maintained strongly.

In sum, there is ample evidence that normal individuals are characterized by biases to affirm or exaggerate positive aspects of their lives and to minimize or deny negative aspects. These biases cut across memory for previous behavior, evaluation of the present, and expectancies for the future. These biases or distortions may or may not be instances of self-deception in the strict sense. As yet, there are no data on whether at some level of processing more accurate representations of reality are made simultaneous with the manifestation of these biases. The distortions may be accounted for by single-decision models that stipulate that normal individuals typically require a good deal more negatively valued information to believe something negative about themselves than positively valued information to endorse something positive (i.e., a criterion-shift explanation). Further, although it would appear that these biases are useful in maintaining or enhancing mood and self-esteem, it is not established whether the biases are motivationally determined, as opposed to being a function of more purely cognitive factors, such as accessibility of information about self and others and probabilistic judgment based on prior history. However, when we consider differences in biases between normal and psychopathological groups, the possibility of a functional, motivationally determined basis for these biases looms larger.

Depression, Cognition, and Reality

Of various forms of psychopathology, depression has received the most discussion and investigation in regard to cognitive representations of self and external reality. In particular, in a series of recent studies (Alloy & Abramson, 1979; Golin, Terrell, Weitz, & Drost, 1979; Lewinsohn, Mischel, Chaplain, & Barton, 1980; Rizley, 1978) causal attributions and accuracy of self-representations have been contrasted in depressed and normal groups.

Some of this work was stimulated by Beck's (1967) model that depression is characterized by marked negativistic distortion. The depressive overgeneralizes from failure experiences, assumes guilt inappropriately, and minimizes experiences of success. In general, the distortions claimed to be symptomatic of depression are the converse of the biases characteristic of normal individuals.

Rizley's (1978) study examined this issue explicitly. Nondepressed students and depressed students, as defined by BDI scores, participated in a number-guessing task. Subjects were told that performance on the task could be influenced by luck, the difficulty of the number pattern, effort, and skill. In actuality the list of numbers to be guessed was random. However, based on number of correct guesses, subjects were told they succeeded or failed at the task. They then completed ratings of the degree to which task difficulty, luck, effort, and ability influenced their performance and the degree to which they had control over and took responsibility for their performance. Rizley interpreted the findings as generally supportive of Beck's model of cognitive distortion in depression. Depressed students attributed failure more to internal factors (skill and effort) relative to nondepressives, whereas the normals attributed success to internal factors more than did depressed subjects. However, these findings should be looked at in another light. The pattern of effects was purely an outcome of normals differing in their ratings as a function of failure and success conditions. In line with the biases just discussed, normals claimed they tried harder and were more skilled when they were told they had succeeded than when they were told they failed. Depressed subjects did not differ in their ratings as a function of success or failure. There was no evidence, consistent with Beck's hypothesis, that depressed subjects were more likely to attribute failure than success to aspects of themselves. Particularly because success and failure were indeed a function of random events, it would appear that the normal controls and not the depressed group evidenced cognitive distortion.

Other lines of evidence support the notion that depressives frequently do not manifest the types of biases, distortions, and/or illusions that characterize nondepressed groups. Golin et al. (1979) replicated the results of a prior investigation with depressed and nondepressed college students (Golin, Terrell, & Johnson, 1977) in a sample of depressed and nondepressed psychiatric patients. In the Golin et al. (1979) study, patients reported their expectancies of success in a dice game, both when they threw the dice and when the dice was thrown by the experimenter (croupier control). Nondepressed psychiatric patients' expectancies of success were higher when they controlled the throws as compared with croupier control. Depressed patients' expectancies did not differ for the two conditions; they did not evidence the normal "illusion of control" (Langer, 1975). Alloy and Abramson (1979), in an intricate set of studies, contrasted depressed and nondepressed students in reports of degree of contingency between their own behavior and certain outcomes. Actual contingencies were manipulated, as was the hedonic value of outcomes (negative, neutral, positive). Generally, depressed students were more accurate than the nondepressed in judging contingencies. In particular, nondepressed subjects underestimated their control over objectively controllable outcomes associated with failure, whereas they overestimated their control over success-related outcomes. Recently, Lewinsohn et al. (1980) found that normal controls and nondepressed psychiatric patients overestimated their degree of social competence relative to observer ratings. The self-ratings of depressed psychiatric patients showed greater concordance with observer ratings.

These lines of investigation converge in indicating that depressive groups do not appear to utilize the cognitive biases and self-deceptive strategies that characterize normals. Surprisingly, the evidence for this claim is stronger, for the most part, than the evidence suggesting that depressives are characterized by a different and perhaps converse set of biases (i.e., to accentuate the negative and minimize or deny the positive). There are some findings (Nelson & Craighead, 1977) suggesting that depressives selectively recall negative events and underestimate in recall the frequency of positive events. However, on the basis of the research to date, one can state with more confidence that depressives often are more accurate than normals in self-perception and do not manifest the possibly "ego-enhancing" biases of normals, than one can claim that depressives manifest possibly "ego-deflating" distortions.

Anosognosia and ECT

It appears then that depressive states are associated with an absence of the cognitive distortions and possibly self-deceptive strategies that typify normal functioning. One way to examine this issue further is to note fluctuations among depressives in the use of these biases as a function of clinical state. Quantitative research of this type was conducted during the 1950s on the construct of anosognosia or denial of illness with psychiatric patients undergoing electroconvulsive therapy (ECT).

Anosognosia was described early in the neurological literature (Babinski, 1914) in relation to hemiplegia. Babinski noted that patients with left hemiplegia frequently denied completely that they were paralyzed. On the basis of work with organic patients, Weinstein and Kahn (1955) developed a test of anosognosia or denial that was used in studies of psychiatric patients. Briefly, patients were administered interviews that among other topics centered on awareness of and attitudes toward illness. They were then administed sufficient amobarbital (sodium amytal) to produce nystagmus and slurred speech. Interviews were then repeated and indications of errors, changes in reference, minimization of symptoms, and displacement were taken as signs of denial and a positive test result.

An intriguing set of findings emerged in studies with patients receiving bilateral ECT (Kahn & Fink, 1958; 1959; Kahn, Fink, & Weinstein, 1956; see Fink, 1979 for a review). On the whole, patients evidenced increasing denial as treatment progressed. Patients who showed marked clinical improvement were most likely to have positive tests early in treatment and to evidence the increasing utilization of denial. Patients who did not respond did not manifest the increase over the course of ECT. In one study (Kahn & Fink, 1959), interviews were conducted with relatives of patients regarding pretreatment disposition to engage in "explicit verbal denial." Those patients rated high in this behavior showed the strongest clinical response to ECT.

These results, lying dormant for some time, invite replication. Further, if supported, it will be important to determine whether similar patterns hold with psychopharmacological and psychotherapeutic forms of intervention. The findings raise the possibility that mood alteration is associated with variation in the use of distortive or self-deceptive strategies, with recovery from depression related to greater utilization of denial.

Toward a Neuropsychology of Defense: Neuropsychodynamics

An area that may be particularly helpful in sorting out the relations between defensive strategies and mood concerns the psychological and psychiatric consequences of damage to the brain. Although it is evident that brain damage may produce marked changes in mood, other psychiatric symptomatology, and shifts in the use of defenses, until recently there has been a notable neglect of these phenomena. Part of this neglect may be attributable to the fact that the phenomena fall at the intersections of neurology, psychology, and psychiatry. As Geschwind (1975) commented, "this common ground unfortunately bears more resemblance to a no-man's-land than to an open border" [p. 1]. Perhaps of greater import than the jurisdictional issue is the bias held by many to view sensorimotor (e.g., paralysis) and cognitive (e.g., aphasia) sequelae as direct consequences of changes in brain functioning produced by brain insult, whereas mood changes are more likely viewed as psychological reactions to other deficits (Goldstein, 1939; Hécaen, 1962; Weinstein & Kahn, 1955). Some recent work has addressed this issue and has suggested that much of the mood change observed following brain insult is directly produced by changes in brain functioning.

Two general classes of mood change have been noted in patients with destructive lesions. A dysphoric reaction has been identified and is characterized by depression, irritability, bouts of tears, and so on. A euphoric and/or indifference reaction has also been identified as characterized by an apathetic or carefree attitude, euphoria, childishness, and/or social disinhibition. Of note, studies contrasting patients with unilateral destructive lesions have consistently found a greater frequency of dysphoric reactions in left-damaged patients and a greater frequency of euphoric-indifference reactions in the right-damaged (Gainotti, 1972; Hécaen, 1962; Hommes, 1965). A similar pattern has been reported in regard to the acute effects of sedation of one side of the brain using the Wada procedure (unilateral intracarotid injection of sodium amytal) (Rossi & Rosadini, 1967; Terzian, 1964). Minutes after barbiturate injection, depending largely upon side of administration, dysphoric or euphoric reactions have been observed (Sackeim & Gur, in preparation).

At issue in interpreting these effects is whether the mood changes are primary effects of brain insult or are secondary reactions. The mood changes may be secondary reactions in either of two senses. First, they may involve psychological reactions to other deficits. For instance, it would not be surprising to find depression in a patient who has lost the capacity to speak. Second, they may be secondary consequences of deficits in the cognitive domain. For instance, a disoriented patient in a confusional state may not be able to recognize the import of his or her medical condition or other events in life and may appear apathetic or carefree.

There are sufficient grounds now to suspect that many of the cases of mood change reflect primary alterations in brain functioning. The fact that with the Wada procedure pronounced mood change is not apparent until sensorimotor and cognitive deficits have disappeared provided a hint in this direction (Rossi & Rosadini, 1967; Sackeim & Gur, in preparation). More critically, the pattern of lateralization effects obtained with acute mood change has been found in a disorder of emotional expression known to be a direct consequence of brain damage. Sackeim, Greenberg, Weiman, Gur, Hungerbuhler, and Geschwind (1982) examined lateralization of insult in neurologic cases of pathological laughing and crying. Patients with the disorder laugh and/or cry uncontrollably, day or night. The outbursts are random and rarely, if ever, can be initiated or stopped voluntarily. Cases have been reported in which the outbursts cease upon the removal of a tumor. Sackeim et al. (1982) found that, like the mood disorders, pathological crying was associated with predominantly left-side destructive lesions and pathological laughing was associated with predominantly right-side destructive lesions. They offered a model of how the two sides of the brain differently subserve positive and negative emotional states.

The mood changes observed in brain-damaged patients are of consequence here because they are associated with characteristic defensive strategies. We noted earlier that Babinski's (1914) original formulation of the concept of anosognosia was based on observation of left hemiplegics. Manifestation of anosognosia or explicit denial of illness is particularly likely in patients with right-side lesions (Cutting, 1978; Hécaen & Albert, 1978) and, furthermore, in patients with destructive lesions exhibiting the euphoric-indifference reaction (Gainotti, 1972). In embarking on a neuropsychology of defense, one might ask, what produces the emergence of anosognosia and how is it related to the positive mood change?

As in the case of mood change, the first problem concerns whether the emergence of the denial is a primary or secondary effect of brain injury. Weinstein and Kahn (1955) viewed anosognosia in psychodynamic terms and argued that the manifestation of gross denial reflected attempts to cope with the trauma of brain damage. Later research demonstrated that the syndrome was more common in right-lesioned than left-lesioned patients. In accommodating these data, Weinstein (Friedland & Weinstein, 1977) argued that right-damaged patients are more likely to have symbolic, language-related skills intact, making it more likely that they would utilize this defense. However, it should be noted that this reformulation does not account for the fact that nonaphasic left-damaged patients, who may have severe deficits in other domains (e.g., sensorimotor) are, nevertheless, less likely to manifest anosognosia than right-damaged patients (Cutting, 1978; Gainotti, 1972).

Others have viewed anosognosia as related to the syndrome of unilateral neglect of one side of space (Heilman, 1978). One could argue that anosognosia is a secondary consequence of a cognitive deficit. Patients may deny left hemiplegia because they are unable to alter body image, to integrate sensory information from one side of space, or because they are so confused they cannot recognize the changes in their functioning. In contrast, it should be noted that anosognosic patients may deny more than that they are paralyzed on one side of the body. They may deny that operations have been performed on them, that they have suffered strokes, that they have memory lapses, that they have urinary incontinence, and so on (Weinstein & Kahn, 1955), symptoms not readily localizable in space. Further, although anosognosia may be associated with disorientation (Cutting, 1978), at least some anosognosics appear to be normally oriented and, except for the gross denial, cognizant of the events around them. Although the evidence is more circumstantial than in the case of mood change, manifestations of anosognosia may well be directly produced by changes in brain functioning that result from insult. A consequence of adopting this view is the position that some type of defensive or self-deceptive strategies must be neurologically represented.

If we entertain the notion that anosognosia is produced as a primary effect of brain damage, the relationship of this syndrome to the euphoric-indifference reaction is at issue. In particular, are these two different expressions of the same syndrome or do the mood changes and defensive manifestations reflect different aspects of neuropsychological functioning? I would suggest that the latter possibility seems more likely. Instances of double dissociation between the syndromes seem to occur.

Patients may manifest euphoric or indifferent mood and not evidence explicit denial of illness (Gainotti, 1972). Indeed, in the same address in which Babinski (1914) offered the term *anosognosia,* he offered the term *anosodiaphoria* to characterize patients who recognized and acknowledged their deficits but seemed inappropriately indifferent or carefree. In the other direction, it appears that with certain types of neuropathology patients may manifest anosognosia while presenting depressed affect. Bear and Fedio (1977) contrasted self- and observer-ratings of the dispositional characteristics of left and right temporal-lobe epileptics. The right temporal epileptics described themselves specifically as less depressed and generally in more positive terms than the left temporal epileptics described themselves. In contrast, oberservers attributed more negative characteristics to the right than left epileptic group. In relation to observer ratings, right temporal epileptics exaggerated positive and minimized negative traits. Left temporal epileptics behaved in an opposite fashion. One interpretation of these findings is that the neuropathology influencing the interictal (between epileptic seizures) behavior of the right epileptics resulted in both greater anosognosia and depressed affect, as would be seen psychiatrically in so-called cases of masked depression. Although they may have acted depressed and exhibited more negative characteristics, their view of themselves, at least as assessed by self-ratings, was anosognosic—highlighting the positive and denying the negative.

The argument being put forth is that both the mood changes and the emergence of gross self-deception may be primary and independent effects of brain damage. The association between anosognosia and euphoric indifference is usually strong, but they are, nonetheless, distinct syndromes. This, of course, would not be unusual. The association between disturbances in the production and comprehension of speech is strong in cases of left-side damage, although the disturbances commonly reflect damage to distinct neural regions subserving different aspects of language.

To make the argument that the defensive attitude represented in anosognosia is a manifestation of release of function produced by brain damage, the issue of the adaptive value of such self-deception should be met head on. Here we can only speculate. However, given the association between anosognosia and positive mood change in cases of destructive lesions, it would not be surprising that such defensive or offensive orientations to a less extreme degree characterize normal functioning and are useful in regulating mood. Certainly the brain must be a mood regulator, as extreme dysphoric or euphoric states are maladaptive. Many of the events in life that influence mood are external and psychological in nature (e.g., losing a spouse, receiving a promotion). One way to regulate mood is to control the interpretations given to those events through the manipulation of distortive defensive or offensive mechanisms. It is a commonplace observation that when normal individuals are told of a major loss (e.g., death of a spouse), the first reaction is often denial. In form, such behavior may differ little from the gross denial exhibited by anosognosic patients. Though differing in whether the instigating factor was primarily psychological (death of spouse) or physical (change in brain functioning), both may reflect the release of a neural mechanism critical to the regulation of mood.

In considering possible neuropsychological bases of self-deceptive phenomena, the focus has been on anosognosia, a strategy that involves denying the negative and possibly exaggerating the positive. In terms of mood regulation, such a strategy would seem geared to protecting or enhancing mood. As just reviewed, it would seem that normal functioning is characterized by this type of bias (Greenwald, 1980; Miller & Ross, 1975; Weinstein, 1980). The usefulness of such a bias would seem transparent. What has been given less attention and may be more troublesome is the possibility that a converse distortive mechanism may also be neurally coded. We should note that left-damaged patients present-ing the dysphoric reaction may not only be depressed in affect, they may be highly self-critical, pessimistic in outlook, and characterized by their own set of cognitive distortions (Gainotti, 1972; Hall, Hall, & Lavoie, 1968). Rossi and Rosadini (1967), in observing dysphoric reactions following unilateral sedation of a hemisphere, commented that some patients claimed that they were going to die, that the future was bleak, and/or that their families would go to ruin. These changes in outlook occurred within minutes of injection and constituted more than simple mood change. Likewise, Bear and Fedio (1977) observed self-observer discrepancies in both the right and left temporal-lobe epileptic groups. The right temporal-lobe group was described previously as anosognosic; the left temporal patients relative to observers minimized the positive about themselves and exaggerated the negative.

It is possible that a distortive mechanism, different from and perhaps opposite to anosognosia, is also neurally represented. Presumably its utility would like-wise be in the area of mood regulation, designed to prevent excessive elevation of mood (e.g., manic states). The existence of such a neurally represented mood regulator is clearly more speculative than even that in the case of a denial mechanism. The fact that, unlike anosognosia, an explicit neurologic syndrome has not been identified in reference to such distortion may not be of much consequence. In cases of anosognosia we are faced with a patient, for example, who after a stroke may be paralyzed and suffering from deficits in a number of domains. It is noteworthy that the patient claims not to be paralyzed and possibly not to have suffered a stroke at all. When a right hemiplegic, also suffering from extensive deficits, appears depressed and moribund and states that life is over and their family is ruined, the behavior may not appear extraordinary.

Implications for Psychopathology and Psychotherapy

In the last section four areas were reviewed relating cognitive distortion to mood. There is considerable evidence that normal functioning is characterized by a set of biases that involve highlighting the positive and minimizing the negative in regard to self-relevant information. Second, it appears that depressed students and psychiatric patients do not manifest these distortions to the same degree or at all. Third, a set of studies on depressed patients receiving ECT suggests that, at least with this form of treatment, relief from depression is associated with greater use of denial and, by implication, with greater use of the types of distortion that characterize normal functioning. Finally, the summary of some of the findings in clinical neuropsychology concerning the effects of brain damage on mood and distortive mechanisms suggests that self-deceptive strategies involved in denial of illness may be neurologically represented. Their association with mood change further suggests that the functional role of these mechanisms may be to regulate mood.

The implications of this view in considering the etiology of forms of psychopathology and, in particular, forms of affective disorders appear to be straightforward. At least some types of depression may not simply be associated with but may be a result of the failure to acquire or to use self-deceptive strategies geared to maintaining or enhancing mood. The grandiosity and euphoria manifested in hypomanic or manic states may be a result of the rigidification and overuse of such mechanisms. These possibilities require investigation, because in none of the areas reviewed has a causal role of cognitive distortions in the genesis of mood disorder been tested explicitly.

It should be noted that although there is substantial evidence that normal and brain-damaged individuals may be characterized by biases by which they accentuate the positive and deny the negative, there are also hints that a different and perhaps opposite type of distortion occurs in depression and in some brain-damaged individuals. For instance, Nelson and Craighead (1977) found that although nondepressed college students underestimated the frequency of negative feedback they had received on a task, depressed students underestimated the frequency of positive feedback. Standard clinical accounts of depressive cognition (Beck, 1967; Freud, 1917/1957) have noted this bias to accentuate the negative and to deny the positive. Without positing this type of distortion, it would be difficult to account for some depressive symptomatology, such as unjustifiable guilt (Abramson & Sackeim, 1977).

Following this formulation, it would be expected that, unlike the classic psychoanalytic position, there are no necessary relations between utilization of defensive and offensive strategies and psychological health. Some distortive strategies, such as those shown in normal individuals, appear useful if not necessary to maintaining and enhancing psychological well being. Their underutilization (depression) or overutilization (mania) may result in psychopathology. Although more hypothetical, there may be a set of distortive mechanisms geared to maintain or deflate mood. Their underutilization (mania) or overutilization (depression) may also be associated with psychopathology.

In this light we might reconsider the data indicating that in normal samples the more individuals engage in self-deception, the less psychopathology they are likely to report. The possibility looms larger that these findings do not reflect simply a report bias. In normal samples, people who typically utilize self-deception to a relatively greater degree actually may be subject to less depressed affect, anxiety, worry, obsessional thoughts, and other symptomatology than others who less typically distort.

In this chapter I have attempted to highlight the adaptive aspects of self-deception and, in particular, its role as an offensive mechanism used to advance pleasure. This position was taken, in part, as a reaction to the rationalist perspective that has informed much of the theorizing about clinical phenomena. It is no news that most people view self-deception as a "bad" thing to do. Pirandello (as cited by Decina, 1978), the Italian playwright, gave vent to these feelings.

> I think that life is a very sad piece of buffoonery because we have in ourselves, without being able to know why, wherefore, or whence, the need to deceive ourselves constantly by creating a reality—one for each and never the same for all—which from time to time is discovered, to be vain and illusory . . . . My art is full of bitter compassion for those who deceive themselves; but this compassion cannot fail to be followed by the ferocious derision of destiny which condemn men to deception.

I have argued here against the Freudian view that it is only the confrontation with pain that forces us into self-deception; rather, the lure of pleasure seems as potent a motive. Further, it may be our biology that is the destiny that "condemns" us to deception. If utilization of self-deceptive strategies is an efficient way to regulate hedonic state, then neural representation of the strategies would seem reasonable.

Whereas psychoanalytic theory presents the notion that failure to be honest with ourselves about our own wishes, thoughts, and feelings is the source of psychopathology, Freud (1917/1957) recognized that, ironically, depressives may be more honest with themselves than other people:

> The patient represents his ego as worthless, incapable of any achievement and morally despicable; he reproaches himself, vilifies himself and expects to be cast out and punished. He abases himself before everyone and commiserates with his own relatives for being connected with anyone so unworthy. . . . It would be equally fruitless from a scientific and a therapeutic point of view to contradict a patient who brings these accusations against his ego. He must surely be right in some way and be describing something that is as it seems to him to be. Indeed, we must at once confirm some of his statements without reservation. He really is as lacking in interest and as incapable of love and achievement as he says. . . . He also seems to us justified in certain other self-accusations; it is merely that he has a keener eye for the truth than other people who are not melancholic. When in his heightened self-criticism he describes himself as petty, egoistic, dishonest, lacking in independence, one whose sole aim has been to hide the weaknesses of his own nature, it may be, so far as we know, that he has come pretty near to understanding

himself; we only wonder why a man has to be ill before he can be accessible to a truth of this kind. (p. 246).

However, to Freud this greater self-knowledge on the part of the depressive was a camouflaged attempt to turn anger inward and castigate the self for unconscious and immoral aggressive wishes.

Regardless of the source of why the depressive fails to deceive themselves in ego-enhancing ways, this failure to use defensive and offensive strategies may be the starting point for effective psychotherapy. The suggestion here is that with at least some patients progress may occur only when they are encouraged to view themselves unrealistically, to exaggerate positive aspects of life, minimize the negative, and in general acquire and utilize the biases and distortions that characterize normal functioning.

Some forms of psychotherapy may inadvertently contain this type of process. Cognitive-behavioral treatment of depressive disorders is believed to be organized around the principle that depressives have characteristic modes of distortion that involve reversal of the normal biases (Beck, 1976). Therapy is designed to correct this type of thought pattern by having patients monitor their thinking, examine the logical relations between ideas, place limits on generalizations, and so on. It may be true that such treatment restricts the possibility of biases to exaggerate the negative and to minimize the positive. I wonder, however, whether such treatment does not inadvertently encourage as well the utilization of ego-enhancing self-deceptive strategies.

Patients are taught to examine the logical flow of ideas. For instance, the thought ''I failed the examination.'' may be followed by ''I feel like a failure.'' It can be pointed out that there is no entailment between failing an exam and feeling like a failure. Certainly, feeling that way about one's complete self is an overgeneralization from a setback in one restricted area. Therefore, if one were rational, one should not feel like a failure after failing an exam. This type of reasoning can be applied to virtually any affect-eliciting situation, positive or negative. To be rational, one should not feel miserable upon losing ones job, spouse, or life. There is no logical entailment, and there cannot be, between events in life and subjective mood states. In some respects, this is the difference between logic and psychologic. Ignoring this distinction may aid patients in acquiring skill in intellectualization, rationalization, and other strategies that may be useful to maintain or enhance mood and self-esteem.

Psychoanalytically oriented psychotherapy and psychoanalysis would seem to be the last place one would search for evidence of curative factors related to the development of self-deceptive strategies. In principle at least, these forms of treatment with neurotics are designed to uncover and not to aid in covering. As Freud (1937/1963) commented, the treatments are based on a ''love of truth'' shared by patient and therapist. We might question whether this love is, at times, the most effective therapeutic strategy. It would seem that there are no clear and absolute relations between degree or depth of utilization of self-deceptive strategies and psychopathology. Particularly given the notion of pleasure-directed self-deception, these strategies may possess important adaptive value in enhancing psychological well being. Clinically, we may be at a crossroads, deciding whether psychotherapy and psychoanalysis should be an educational experience, directed by a search for truth, or whether truth should be jettisoned, with the goal that of relieving suffering. Although fostering self-deception may give us moral qualms, it may also be therapeutic.

ACKNOWLEDGMENTS

I thank my colleagues Paolo Decina, Leo Goldberger, Joseph Masling, and David Wolitzky for stimulating and suggesting a number of the arguments and counterarguments presented here, and Dennis Grega, Ellen Riley, Sara Weber, and Donna M. Zucchi for their comments and forbearance. Most of the empirical research reported on self-deception was conducted in collaboration with Ruben Gur; the new data on self-reported psychopathology and self-deception were collected in collaboration with Andrew Weiman. Preparation of this chapter and some of the research reported herein was supported in part by NIMH Grant MH34404 and MH35636 and by a grant from the Research Challenge Fund of New York University.

REFERENCES

Abramson, L. Y., & Sackeim, H. A. A paradox in depression: Uncontrollability and self-blame. *Psychological Bulletin,* 1977, *84,* 838–851.

Alkire, A. A., & Brunse, A. J. Impact and possible casualty from videotape feedback in marital therapy. *Journal of Consulting and Clinical Psychology,* 1974, *42,* 203–210.

Alloy, L. B., & Abramson, L. Y. Judgment of contingency in depressed and nondepressed students: Sadder but wiser? *Journal of Experimental Psychology: General,* 1979, *108,* 441–485.

Anastasi, A. *Psychological testing.* New York: MacMillan, 1961.

Babinski, J. Contribution à l'étude des troubles mentaux dans l'hémiplégie organique cérébrale (Anosognosie). *Revue Neurologique,* 1914, *27,* 845–848.

Bear, D. M., & Fedio, P. Quantitative analysis of interictal behavior in temporal lobe epilepsy. *Archives of Neurology,* 1977, *34,* 454–467.

Beck, A. T. *Depression: Clinical, experimental, and theoretical aspects.* New York: Harper & Row, 1967.

Beck, A. T. *Cognitive therapy and the emotional disorders.* New York: International Universities Press, 1976.

Beck, A. T., Ward, C. H., Mendelson, M., Mock, J., & Erbaugh, J. An inventory for measuring depression. *Archives of General Psychiatry,* 1961, *4,* 561–571.

Boyd, H., & Sisney, V. Immediate self-image confrontation and changes in self-concept. *Journal of Consulting Psychology*, 1967, *31*, 291–296.

Brown, N. O. *Life against death: The psychoanalytic meaning of history.* New York: Vintage Books, 1959.

Byrne, D. Repression-sensitization as a dimension of personality. In B. A. Maher (Ed.), *Progress in experimental personality research* (Vol. 1). New York: Academic Press, 1964. A-94

Canfield, J. W., & Gustafson, D. F. Self-deception. *Analysis*, 1962, *23*, 32–36.

Castaldo, V., & Holzman, P. S. The effects of hearing one's own voice on sleep mentations. *Journal of Nervous and Mental Disease*, 1967, *144*, 2–13.

Castaldo, V., & Holzman, P. S. The effects of hearing one's own voice on dream content: A replication. *Journal of Nervous and Mental Disease*, 1969, *148*, 74–82.

Coyne, L., & Holzman, P. S. Three equivalent forms of a semantic differential inventory. *Educational and Psychological Measurement*, 1966, *26*, 665–674.

Crowne, D., & Marlowe, D. *The approval motive.* New York: Wiley, 1964.

Cutting, J. Study of anosognosia. *Journal of Neurology, Neurosurgery, and Psychiatry*, 1978, *41*, 548–555.

Damarin, F. & Messick, S. Response styles as personality variables: A theoretical integration of multivariate research. *Educational Testing Service*, Technical Report #RV–65–10, 1965.

Davis, D., & Brock, T. C. Use of first person pronouns as a function of increased objective self-awareness and performance feedback. *Journal of Experimental and Social Psychology*, 1975, *11*, 381–388.

Decina, P. Henry IV by Luigi Pirandello—A psychiatric comment. *Journal of the American Academy of Psychoanalysis*, 1978, *6*, 79–87.

Demos, R. Lying to oneself. *Journal of Philosophy*, 1960, *57*, 588–595.

Duval, S., & Wicklund, R. A. *A theory of objective self-awareness.* New York: Academic Press, 1972.

Edwards, A. L. *The measurement of personality traits by scales and inventories.* New York: Holt, Rinehart & Winston, 1970.

Erdelyi, M. H. A new look at the new look: Perceptual defense and vigilance. *Psychological Review*, 1974, *81*, 1–25.

Erikson, E. H. *Childhood and society.* New York: Norton, 1950.

Eysenck, H. J., & Eysenck, S. B. G. *Eysenck personality inventory.* London: University of London Press, 1963.

Fenichel, O. *The psychoanalytic theory of neurosis.* New York: Norton, 1945.

Fingarette, H. *Self-deception.* London: Routledge & Kegan Paul, 1969.

Fink, M. *Convulsive therapy: Theory and practive.* New York: Raven, 1979.

Freud, A. *The ego and the mechanisms of defense.* New York: International Universities Press, 1966.

Freud, S. [The future prospects of psychoanalytic therapy.] In J. Strachey (Ed.), *The standard edition of the complete psychological works of Sigmund Freud* (Vol. 11). London: Hogarth, 1957. (Originally published, 1910.)

Freud, S. [Psychogenic visual disturbance according to psychoanalytic conceptions.] In P. Rieff (Ed.), *Sigmund Freud: Character and culture.* New York: Collier, 1963. (Originally published, 1910.)

Freud, S. [Repression.] In J. Strachey (Ed. and trans.), *The standard edition of the complete psychological works of Sigmund Freud* (Vol. 14). London: Hogarth, 1957. (Originally published, 1915.)

Freud, S. [Mourning and melancholia.] In J. Strachey (Ed. and trans.), *The standard edition of the complete psychological works of Sigmund Freud* (Vol. 14). London: Hogarth Press, 1957. (Originally published, 1917.)

Freud, S. [*The ego and the id*]. J. Strachey (Ed. and trans.), New York: Norton, 1960. (Originally published in 1923.)

Freud, S. [Neurosis and psychosis.] In J. Riviere (Ed. and trans.). *Collected papers* (Vol. 2). London: Hogarth, 1953. (Originally published, 1924.)

Freud, S. [Inhibitions, symptoms, and anxiety.] In J. Strachey (Ed. and trans.), *The standard edition of the complete psychological works of Sigmund Freud* (Vol. 20). London: Hogarth, 1959. (Originally published, 1926.)

Freud, S. [*Civilization and its discontents*]. J. Strachey (Trans.). New York: Norton, 1961. (Originally published, 1930.)

Freud, S. [Analysis terminable and interminable.] In P. Rieff (Ed.), *Therapy and technique*. New York: Collier, 1963. (Originally published, 1937.)

Freud, S. [*An outline of psychoanalysis.*] J. Strachey (Trans.). New York: Norton, 1949. (Originally published, 1938.)

Friedland, R. P., & Weinstein, E. A. Hemi-inattention and hemisphere specialization: Introduction and historical review. In E. A. Weinstein & R. P. Friedland (Eds.), *Hemi-inattention and hemisphere specialization* (*Advances in Neurology* Vol. 18). New York: Raven, 1977.

Gainotti, G. Emotional behavior and hemispheric side of the lesion. *Cortex*, 1972, *8*, 41–55.

Gardiner, P. L. Error, faith and self-deception. *Proceedings of the Aristotelian Society*, 1970, *50*, 221–243.

Gardner, R., Holzman, P. S., Klein, G. S., Linton, H., & Spence, D. P. Cognitive control: A study of individual consistencies in cognitive behavior. *Psychological Issues*, 1959, *1* (1, Whole No. 4).

Garma, A. Realitaet und das Es in der schizophrenie. *Internationale Zeitschrift fuer Psychoanalyse*, 1932, *18*, 183–200.

Geschwind, N. The borderland of neurology and psychiatry: Some common misconceptions. In D. F. Benson & D. Blumer (Eds.), *Psychiatric aspects of neurologic disease*. New York: Grune & Stratton, 1975.

Gibbons, F. X., & Wicklund, R. A. Selective exposure to self. *Journal of Research in Personality*, 1976, *10*, 98–106.

Glixman, A. F. Recall of completed and uncompleted activities under varying degrees of stress. *Journal of Experimental Psychology*, 1949, *39*, 281–296.

Goldstein, K. *The organism: A holistic approach to biology*. New York: American Book Co., 1939.

Golin, S., Terrell, T., & Johnson, B. Depression and the illusion of control. *Journal of Abnormal Psychology*, 1977, *86*, 440–442.

Golin, S., Terrell, T., Weitz, J., & Drost, P. L. The illusion of control among depressed patients. *Journal of Abnormal Psychology*, 1979, *88*, 454–457.

Greenwald, A. G. The totalitarian ego: Fabrication and revision of personal history. *American Psychologist*, 1980, *35*, 603–618.

Gur, R. C., & Sackeim, H. A. Self-confrontation and psychotherapy: A reply to Sanborn, Pyke and Sanborn. *Psychotherapy: Theory, Research and Practice*, 1978, *15*, 258–265.

Gur, R. C., & Sackeim, H. A. Self-deception: A concept in search of a phenomenon. *Journal of Personality and Social Psychology*, 1979, *37*, 147–169.

Gur, R. C., Sackeim, H. A., & Gur, R. E. Classroom seating and psychopathology: Some initial data. *Journal of Abnormal Psychology*, 1976, *85*, 122–124.

Hall, M. M., Hall, G. C., & Lavoie, P. Ideation in patients with unilateral or bilateral midline brain lesions. *Journal of Abnormal Psychology*, 1968, *73*, 526–531.

Hartmann, H. *Ego psychology and the problem of adaptation*. New York: International Universities Press, 1958. (Originally published, 1939.)

Hécaen, H. Clinical symptomatology in right and left hemispheric lesions. In V. B. Mountcastle (Ed.), *Interhemispheric relations and cerebral dominance*. Baltimore: Johns Hopkins Press, 1962.

Hécaen, H., & Albert, M. L. *Human neuropsychology*. New York: Wiley, 1978.

Heilbrun, A. B. Revision of the MMPI K correction procedure for improved detection of maladjustment in a normal college population. *Journal of Consulting Psychology*, 1963, *27*, 161–165.

Heilman, K. M. Neglect and related disorders. In K. M. Heilman & E. Valenstein (Eds.), *Clinical neuropsychology*. New York: Oxford University Press, 1978.

Hilgard, E. R. Human motives and the concept of the self. *American Psychologist*, 1949, *4*, 374–382.

Hilgard, E. R. Neodissociation theory of multiple cognitive control systems. In G. E. Schwartz & D. Shapiro (Eds.), *Consciousness and self-regulation, Advances in research and theory* (Vol. 1). New York: Plenum, 1976.

Holt, R. R. Yet another look at clinical and statistical prediction: Or, is clinical psychology worthwhile? *American Psychologist*, 1970, *25*, 337–349.

Holzman, P. S., & Rousey, C. The voice as a percept. *Journal of Personality and Social Psychology*, 1966, *4*, 79–86.

Holzman, P. S., Rousey, C., & Snyder, C. On listening to one's own voice: Effects on psychophysiological responses and free associations. *Journal of Personality and Social Psychology*, 1966, *4*, 432–441.

Hommes, O. R. Stemming sanomaliën als neurologisch symptoom. *Nederlands Tijdschrift voor Geneeskunde*, 1965, *109*, 588–589.

Huntley, C. W. Judgments of self based upon records of expressive behavior. *Journal of Abnormal and Social Psychology*, 1940, *35*, 398–427.

Irwin, F. W. *Intentional behavior and motivation: A cognitive theory*. Philadelphia: Lippincott, 1971.

Kahn, R. L., & Fink, M. Changes in language during electroshock therapy. In P. Hoch & J. Zubin (Eds.), *Psychopathology of communication*. New York: Grune & Stratton, 1958.

Kahn, R. L., & Fink, M. Personality factors in behavioral response to electroshock therapy. *Journal of Neuropsychiatry*, 1959, *1*, 45–49.

Kahn, R. L., Fink, M., & Weinstein, E. Relation of amobarbital test to clinical improvement in electroshock. *Archives of Neurology and Psychiatry*, 1956, *76*, 23–29.

Klein, G. S. Need and regulation. In M. R. Jones (Ed.), *Nebraska Symposium on Motivation* (Vol. 2). Lincoln: University of Nebraska Press, 1954.

Langer, E. J. The illusion of control. *Journal of Personality and Social Psychology*, 1975, *32*, 311–329.

Lewinsohn, P. M., Mischel, W., Chaplain, W., & Barton, R. Social competence and depression: The role of illusory self-perceptions? *Journal of Abnormal Psychology*, 1980, *89*, 203–212.

Meehl, P. E. *Clinical versus statistical prediction: A theoretical analysis and a review of the evidence*. Minneapolis: University of Minnesota Press, 1954.

Meehl, P. E., & Hathaway, S. R. The K factor as a suppressor variable in the Minnesota Multiphasic Personality Inventory. *Journal of Applied Psychology*, 1946, *30*, 525–564.

Miller, D. T., & Ross, M. Self-serving biases in the attribution of causality: Fact or fiction? *Psychological Bulletin*, 1975, *82*, 213–225.

Millham, J. Two components of need for approval and their relationship to cheating following failure. *Journal of Research in Personality*, 1974, *8*, 378–392.

Mischel, T. Understanding neurotic behavior: From "mechanism" to "intentionality." In T. Mischel (Ed.). *Understanding other persons*. Totowa, N.J.: Rowman & Littlefield, 1974.

Mowrer, O. H. Sin: The lesser of two evils. *American Psychologist*, 1960, *15*, 301–304.

Murphy, G. Experiments in overcoming self-deception. *Psychophysiology*, 1970, *6*, 790–799.

Murphy, G. *Outgrowing self-deception*. New York: Basic Books, 1975.

Neisser, U. *Cognitive psychology*. New York: Appleton-Century-Crofts, 1967.

Nelson, R. E., & Craighead, W. E. Selective recall of positive and negative feedback, self-control behaviors, and depression. *Journal of Abnormal Psychology*, 1977, *86*, 379–388.

Olivos, G. Response delay, psychophysiologic activation and recognition of one's own voice. *Psychosomatic Medicine*, 1967, *29*, 433–440.

Paulhus, D. L. *Varieties of forced compliance: An assay of the contributions of impression management, self-perception and cognitive dissonance*. Unpublished doctoral thesis, Columbia University, 1980.

Paulhus, D. L. Individual differences, impression management and cognitive dissonance: Their concurrent operation in forced compliance. *Journal of Personality and Social Psychology*, in press.

Penelhum, T. Pleasure and falsity. In S. Hampshire (Ed.), *Philosophy of mind*. New York: Harper & Row, 1966.

Rapaport, D., & Gill, M. M. The points of view and assumptions of metapsychology. *International Journal of Psycho-Analysis*, 1959, *40*, 153–162.

Rieff, P. *Freud: The mind of the moralist*. New York: Viking Press, 1959.

Rizley, R. Depression and distortion in the attribution of causality. *Journal of Abnormal Psychology*, 1978, *87*, 32–48.

Rogers, C. R. A theory of therapy, personality and interpersonal relationships, as developed in the client-centered framework. In S. Koch (Ed.). *Psychology: A study of a science* (Vol. 3). New York: McGraw-Hill, 1959.

Rosenzweig, S. An experimental study of "repression" with special reference to need-persistive and ego-defensive reactions to frustration. *Journal of Experimental Psychology*, 1943, *32*, 64–74.

Rossi, C. F., & Rosadini, G. Experimental analysis of cerebral dominance in man. In C. H. Millikan & F. L. Darley (Eds.), *Brain mechanisms underlying speech and language*. New York: Grune & Stratton, 1967.

Rousey, C., & Holzman, P. S. Recognition of one's own voice. *Journal of Personality and Social Psychology*, 1967, *6*, 464–466.

Rousey, C., & Holzman, P. S. Some effects of listening to one's voice systematically distorted. *Perceptual and Motor Skills*, 1968, *27*, 1303–1313.

Russell, B. A free man's worship. In B. Russell (Ed.), *Mysticism and logic*. London: George Allen & Unwin, 1963. (Originally published, 1903.)

Sackeim, H. A., & Gur, R. C. Self-deception, self-confrontation, and consciousness. In G. E. Schwartz & D. Shapiro (Eds.), *Consciousness and self-regulation, advances in research* (Vol. 2). New York: Plenum Press, 1978.

Sackeim, H. A., & Gur, R. C. Self-deception, other-deception, and self-reported psychopathology. *Journal of Consulting and Clinical Psychology*, 1979, *47*, 213–215.

Sackeim, H. A., & Gur, R. C. Facial asymmetry, perceiver biases, and the communication of emotion. In J. T. Cacioppo & R. E. Petty (Eds.). *Social psychophysiology*. New York: Guilford Press, in press.

Sackeim, H. A., & Gur, R. C. *Brain, thought, and emotion: Hemispheric specialization in personality and psychopathology*. New York: McGraw-Hill, in preparation.

Sackeim, H. A., Greenberg, M. S., Weiman, A. L., Gur, R. C., Hungerbuhler, J. P. & Geschwind,

N. Hemispheric asymmetry In the expression of positive and negative emotions: Neurological evidence. *Archives of Neurology*, 1982, *39*, 210–218.

Sartre, J. P. [*Being and nothingness: An essay on phenomenological ontology.*] H. Barnes (Trans.). London: Methuen, 1958.

Shapiro, D. *Neurotic styles*. New York: Basic Books, 1965.

Storms, M. D. Videotape and the attribution process: Reversing actors' and observers' points of view. *Journal of Personality and Social Psychology*, 1973, *27*, 165–175.

Terzian, H. Behavioural and EEG effects of intracarotid sodium amytal injection. *Acta Neurochirurgica*, 1964, *12*, 230–239.

Wason, P. C., & Johnson-Laird, P. N. *Psychology of reasoning: Structure and context*. Cambridge, Mass.: Harvard University Press, 1972.

Weinstein, E. A., & Kahn, R. L. *Denial of illness: Symbolic and physiological aspects*. Springfield, Ill.: Thomas, 1955.

Weinstein, N. D. Unrealistic optimism about future life events. *Journal of Personality and Social Psychology*, 1980, *39*, 806–820.

Wolff, W. *The expression of personality*. New York: Harper, 1943.

Zeigarnik, B. Ueber das Behalten von erledigten und underledigten Handlungen. *Psychologische Forschung*, 1927, *9*, 1–85.

5 Interests as Object Relations

M. Eagle
York University

INTRODUCTION

Broadly speaking, there are at least three main routes by which empirical evidence has been brought to bear in evaluating psychoanalytic hypotheses and formulations. One is the case report, which has the advantage of being close to the clinical psychoanalytic situation and the disadvantages of being nonsystematic, nonrigorous, and possibly biased in data collection and reporting. The second is the experimental study, designed to test specific psychoanalytic hypotheses (the studies reported in Fisher & Greenberg, 1978 are illustrative of this approach), which has the advantage of rigor and the disadvantage of often being unconvincing in the degree to which it is, in fact, relevant to the psychoanalytic proposition it is designed to test. A third route entails drawing on the extant evidence from a variety of different sources (e.g., physiological, experimental, anecdotal, sociological) in explaining a behavior or aspect of personality of particular importance to psychoanalytic theory. This approach is exemplified by Bowlby's (1969, 1973) efforts to explicate the nature of the affectional bond between infant and mother by appealing to clinical, ethological, epidemiological, and other pertinent data; and by attempts to understand dreams and dreaming through an evaluation of data ranging from clinically reported dreams to systematic content analysis of dreams to experimental REM studies.

This third approach is the one taken in this chapter. The particular behaviors it attempts to understand and the particular psychoanalytic formulations it attempts to evaluate are those pertaining to the development of an interest in objects and the psychological significance and functions of such interests. My main negative claim is that neither traditional psychoanalytic theory nor psychoanalytic ego psychology adequately accounts for the development and psychological significance of having interests. My main positive claims are: (1) that both developmentally and in terms of ongoing everyday functioning, interests are best understood as object relational phenomena, indeed as a kind of object relation; and (2) as is the case with more traditionally understood object relations, interests and related phenomena play a central role in maintaining personality intactness and integrity, particularly in extreme circumstances. Neither traditional Freudian instinct theory nor ego psychology does justice to the object relational nature of interests or to the critical role that interests play in personality functioning.

In making these claims, I draw on evidence from a variety of sources: autobiographical accounts, animal investigations, epidemiological studies, clinical impressions, and studies on infant behavior. It seems to me that this evidence, as well as the general study of interests, illustrates the kinds of findings and considerations that traditional psychoanalytic theory must integrate in order to do full justice to object relational phenomena.

I am not using the term *interests* in any specialized sense, but as one uses it when one talks about being interested in music, literature, or tennis, or when one talks about being interested in one's work or the welfare of this or that person. As it is ordinarily used, "interest" conveys the qualities of cognitive and affective involvement with an object, of modulated pleasure, and of the capacity of the object in which one is interested to hold one's attention. One can speak of an individual having a wide versus a narrow range of interests, deep and intense versus shallow and superficial interests.

FREUDIAN CONCEPTION OF INTERESTS

In traditional psychoanalytic theory, when interests are considered at all, they tend to be viewed as essentially derivative. Thus, in sublimation, the concept in psychoanalytic theory most germane to an understanding of the development of interests, interests result from "the instinct directing itself towards an aim other than, and remote from, that of sexual satisfaction" [Freud, 1914/1957, p. 94]. That is, interests are the product of the diversion of sexual aims to "higher" pursuits. According to this view, the capacity to develop cultural interests depends on one's ability to sublimate or "neutralize" sexual energy.

The term *ego-interests* (*Ich interesse*) does appear in some of Freud's writings (1914/1957, p. 82; 1916–1917/1963, p. 414), but its exact meaning is obscure and it ceases to appear in later works. In some of his work, Freud (1911/1958, pp. 73–4; 1916–17/1963, pp. 414–5) distinguishes between ego-interests or ego-cathexes on the one hand and libidinal-cathexes on the other; and between interest emanating from erotic sources and "interest in general" (Freud, 1911/1958, p. 70, Footnote 2). Here Freud is clearly suggesting the possibility of interests deriving from the ego that are independent of libidinal sources. After that point, on the few occasions that the terms "ego-interests" and "ego-cathexes" are employed, they are clearly derived from the "self-preservative instincts" (see Editor's Footnote 2, Freud, 1916–1917/1963, pp. 414–5). Then, in *Beyond the Pleasure Principle* (1920/1955), the dichotomy between self-preservative and libidinal instincts is given up (self-preservative instincts are equated with "narcissistic libido") and the term ego-interests no longer appears. From that point on, the primary psychoanalytic concept invoked to explain interests that seem remote from instinctual aims is sublimation.

I try to show in this chapter that a formulation of interests in terms of the concept of sublimation does not adequately take account of their development and psychological function. I argue that interests are most meaningfully understood as object relations that involve cognitive and affective links to objects in the world and serve some of the same psychological functions served by more traditionally viewed object relations. Let me present some evidence before discussing more theoretical issues.

Some Empirical Evidence on the Psychological Function of Interests

In ordinary wisdom, the critical role of interpersonal, ideological and cognitive-value connections has long been recognized, as expressed, for example, in observations regarding the importance of "having something to live for." Generally, the "something to live for" is another person, as is shown, for example, by recent epidemiological studies supporting the informal observation that the survivor in a long relationship in which one of the partners has recently died is more susceptible to death (Parkes, Benjamin, & Fitzgerald, 1969) and to illness (Clayton, 1974) than others of his or her age group. The "something to live for" sustaining role can also, however, be played by other objects as well as by abiding interests and values. Thus, it has been shown that among the factors that make for survival among prisoners of war are not only psychological links to others (e.g., one's family or countrymen), but interests of one kind or another. Strassman, Thaler, and Schein (1956), in writing about United States prisoners of war repatriated by the Chinese and North Koreans in 1953, note that: "two things seemed to save the men close to 'apathy' death: getting him on his feet doing something, no matter how trivial, and getting him interested in some current or future problem" [p. 99]. (Nardini [1952] reports similar findings.)

A common theme in autobiographical accounts of people under the dire conditions of imprisonment and concentration camps is the role of interests and values in increasing the liklihood of survival and in maintaining psychological integrity. This is true of people with as wide a range of backgrounds as Malcolm

X (1964), Victor Frankl (1962), George Jackson (1970), and Bruno Bettleheim (1960). One finds in their autobiographical accounts of physical and psychological survival striking similarities regarding the sustaining role played by connections to people as well as to interests and values. In recent review of Bettleheim's (1979) book entitled *Surviving and Other Essays,* Robinson (1979) notes that: "Bettleheim makes what is perhaps the finest point when he notes that the prisoners who did in fact survive were those who lived not for life's sake but for some ideal—cultural or religious—that transcended them" [p. 7]. A similar account is given by Cohen (1953), a Dutch physician who both describes his own concentration camp experiences and summarizes many other accounts. Cohen poses the question: "What individuals were best fitted to adapt themselves, so that there was at least a possibility of their surviving a concentration camp?" [p. 147]. He answers that "many writers, . . . agree that it was of the greatest importance that a person had some spiritual life" [p. 148]. And he adds that "the conception 'spiritual life' is here used to comprise all spiritual values in their widest sense, such as morality, knowledge, emotion, intellect, character, religion, etc." He cites another writer, DeWind, who observes that: "generally speaking, we see in the camp that anyone in whose life there are certain religious bonds (using the term in its most comprehensive sense, so as to include the devotion to a political system or a humanist view of life), manages the most quickly, after the initial stupor. It is therefore no mere accident that convinced Christians as well as the Communists, who would seem to be their psychological opposites, should have shown the greatest power of resistance in camps, and even managed to set up certain forms of anti-Fascist organization" [p. 148].

I have been struck in clinical work with the degree to which lack of interest is a negative prognostic indicator, even when level of presenting manifest pathology is held relatively constant. One can observe people whose lives are filled with pathology and disturbance and who nevertheless are able somehow to prevail and function, on occasion even creatively. In fact, a creative talent or gift, and the intense interest that can accompany it, often can serve to sustain people with considerable pathology. As Kohut (1977) notes, one can observe severely disturbed people who somehow manage to lead "worthwhile lives and are blessed with a sense of fulfillment and joy" [pp. 281–82] despite the overall severity of their pathology. It is possible, perhaps even likely, that without this center of creative interests, such people would decompensate.[1]

---

[1]I had occasion to come to know quite well a gifted musician and composer who by the usual psychiatric criteria was quite disturbed. He was frequently paranoid, oversuspicious, chronically overvigilant, showed extreme mood swings, had periods of intense anxiety, and reported quasi-hallicinatory experiences. Yet, in the 26 years that I knew him he never became seriously disorganized, never was overtly psychotic. It always seemed to me that without his musical gift and passion, which played a central sustaining role in his life, he would have decompensated.

Why should interests play such a vital role in functioning, particularly when we often delegate interests to the peripheral status conveyed by the term *hobby*— pleasant icing, but certainly not a central aspect of one's life? I will try to show, however, that whether or not, as an adult, one has acquired abiding interests is not a casual or peripheral aspect of an individual's behavior, but a central feature of personality, particularly a feature of the development of self and of object relations. First, some basic points must be made regarding the ultimate basis for an interest in objects.

Basis for an Interest in Objects

In traditional Freudian theory the object in object relations is defined in the context of instincts, specifically as: "the thing in regard of which or through which the instinct is able to achieve its aim" [Freud, 1915/1957, p. 122]. According to this view, were these aims to be achieved without objects, there would be no interest in objects. For example, were one to live in a science fiction world in which wishing would indeed make it so, one would presumably never develop a conception of and interest in external objects in reality. This is seen in Freud's treatment of the development of thought.

Freud (1900/1965) proposes that the infant's initial tendency is to attempt to establish wish fulfillment through hallucinatory activity ("the establishment of a perceptual identity along the short path of regression"). But despite this activity, "satisfaction does not follow; the need persists." This forces the psychic apparatus "to seek out other patterns which lead eventually to the desired perceptual identity being established from the direction of the external world" [p. 605].[2] However, Freud reminds us; "all the complicated thought–activity which is spun out from the mnemic image to the moment at which the perceptual identity is established by the external world—all this activity of thought merely constitutes a roundabout path to wish-fulfillment which has been made necessary by experience . . . thought is after all nothing but a substitute for a hallucinatory wish" [pp. 605–06].

In his later work, Freud continues the theme and makes clear his belief that insofar as objects represent unwanted excitation, one's original relation to them can be described as that of "primal hatred." Thus, Freud (1915/1957) writes: "it is undeniable also that hate originally betokens the relation of the ego to the alien external world with its afflux of stimuli. . . . Thus at the very beginning, the external world, objects and that which was hated are one and the same thing" [p. 79]. Also, in a later section: "The relation of hate to objects is older than that

---

[2]Freud added the following footnote in 1919: "In other words, it becomes evident that there must be a means of 'reality-testing' (i.e., of testing things to see whether they are real or not)" [p. 605].

of love. It is derived from the primal repudiation by the narcissistic ego of the external world whence flows the stream of stimuli'' [p. 82].

In this excitation–discharge model, objects are, so to speak, forced on the growing infant by reality constraints and the developing reality-oriented ego. In this conception, an interest in objects is derived from some presumably more basic and primary drives or tendencies.[3] For example, the infant's attachment to mother is said to be ''anaclitic,'' that is, leaning upon or as a ''secondary'' consequence of the mother's role as gratifier of presumably more basic instinctual drives, such as hunger (A. Freud, 1960). This view is expressed clearly by A. Freud (1946) who writes that under pressure of bodily needs, particularly hunger, the baby ''periodically establishes connections with the environment which are withdrawn again after the needs have been satisfied and the tension is relieved.'' She goes on to note that these occasions of gratification ''establish centers of interest to which libidinal energy becomes attached'' [p. 124].

This model of interest in and attachment to objects as secondary and derived from presumably more basic drives is contradicted by three main related sources of data: (1) the growing evidence that an interest in objects and selective preferences for certain stimulus configurations are autonomous inborn, natural propensities that appear at birth or shortly after birth and are not dependent on the vicissitudes of instinctual drive gratification; (2) the findings indicating that both humans and infrahumans are characterized by an instinctual attachment system that is also relatively independent of drives; and (3) the related finding that the effects of object deprivation, including, of course, the all-important maternal deprivation, are not a secondary function of failures in so-called primary drive gratification.

With regard to the first point, the research evidence has established that very young infants show selective preferences for novel visual and auditory stimuli (Friedman, Bruno, & Vietze, 1974; Kearsley, 1973), for one set of geometric features over another (McCall & Nelson, 1970; Ruff & Birch, 1974); for one set of colors over another (Bornstein, 1975); for stimuli of moderate complexity (Fantz, 1958, 1965; Fantz & Fagan, 1975); and for an optimal level of discrepancy from preexisting stimuli (Kinney & Kagan, 1976). It is to be noted that insofar as these studies deal with selective preferences (as determined, for exam-

---

[3]In *Civilization and its Discontents,* Freud (1930/1961) recognizes that ''no other technique for the conduct of life attaches the individual so firmly to reality as laying emphasis on works [and, by implication, one's values and interests]; for his work at least gives him a secure place in a portion of reality, in the human community'' [p. 80]. But soon introduced into the discussion of work are interpretations of it as: ''the possibility it offers of displacing a large amount of libidinal components'' and the way in which ''it makes possible the use of existing inclinations, of persisting or constitutionally reinforced instinctual impulses'' [p. 80].

ple, by visual fixation) the concept of an *interest* in objects seems particularly appropriate to the phenomena in question.

With regard to the second point, Bowlby (1969, 1973) has amassed considerable evidence that both human and infrahuman infants are characterized by an instinctual attachment system that is relatively independent of other drives. That an infant macaque: "will cling with equal vigor to the body of its mother, or to a towel, a diaper, or a rug" [Mason, Hill, & Thompsen, 1974] can hardly be explained as secondary association with hunger or other so-called primary drives. Such findings provide eloquent support for the inborn "object-seeking" propensity of which Fairbairn (1952) spoke.

In his now classic experiment, Harlow (1958) showed decisively that the infant monkey's attachment to a surrogate mother cannot be explained as a secondary derivative of the latter's role in gratification of so-called primary drives (i.e., hunger, thirst). Rather, such attachment seemed to be based on the autonomous need for what Harlow called "contact comfort." Infant monkeys were taken from their natural mothers at birth and were raised by artificial wire and terry cloth surrogate mothers. Harlow reasoned that if the infant monkey's attachment to its mother were secondarily derived from the association of mother with reduction of "primary" drives, then the infant monkey would become attached to whichever surrogate mother reduced the primary drives of hunger and thirst. Instead the infant monkey developed an attachment to the (terry cloth) surrogate mother providing "contact comfort" even when a different surrogate (wire) mother satisfied its so-called "primary" drives.

It is important to note that the surrogate mothers to whom the infant monkeys became attached did not simply serve the function of dispensing "contact comfort" analogously to the surrogate mothers who dispensed milk, but were also clung to and provided a security base in situations of novelty and experienced danger. In other words, although the infant monkeys would go to the milk-dispensing wire mothers when they were hungry, they showed *a generalized attachment* to the terry cloth mother and clung to "her" when they needed comforting and security.

With regard to the third point—the effects of object deprivation (primarily maternal)—the findings are quite striking. Thus, that infant mortality rate of monkeys is influenced by presence or absence of a piece of cheesecloth in the otherwise bare cage can hardly be accounted for in terms of feeding or nutrition (Harlow, 1958). Also, it has been shown that even if visual, auditory, and olfactory interactions are maintained, the prevention of physical contact between infant and mother leads to abnormal development in monkeys (Harlow & Harlow, 1965; Harlow & Zimmerman, 1959; Hinde & Spencer-Booth, 1971). There is similar evidence in children that despite adequate nutrition and medical care, inadequate maternal attention is associated with abnormal development (Powell,

Brasel, & Hansen, 1967a, 1967b; Silver & Finkelstein, 1967) and a higher mortality rate (Bakwin, 1949; Patton & Gardner, 1963). Chronic maternal deprivation is associated also with permanent decreases in body size, a development referred to as "psychological dwarfism" [Thoman & Arnold, 1968]. In an attempt to develop an animal model of human "psychosocial dwarfism," Schanberg and Kuhn (1980) have presented striking evidence that maternal deprivation is a primary factor rather than secondary to other variables. First, they have shown that maternal deprivation of preweaning rat pups results in a decrease in the activity of brain, heart, and liver ornithine decarboxylase (ODC)—a biochemical index of tissue maturation—and that returning the pups to mother increases ODC activity. That the decline in ODC activity is unrelated to food deprivation was conclusively shown by the *absence* of such a decline when the pups were placed with a lactating female rat whose nipples had been tied off and the *presence* of a decline when deprived pups were fed sustacal through an intragastric cannula and when pups were placed with lactating females whose active maternal behavior had been prevented by the anesthetizing effects of urethane (an intervention that did not affect milk production, ejection, or suckling by the pups).

That the denial of tactile stimulation is a critical aspect in the effects of maternal deprivation is shown by the finding that maternally deprived pups who are stroked vigorously on the back and head for 2 hours with a moist camel's hair brush (which is similar to the mother's grooming) did *not* show the usual decline in ODC activity. Shanberg and Kuhn relate these findings to the report that tactile stimulation of premature babies increased their weight gain significantly over controls (White & La Barba, 1976).

To summarize the main point: All the evidence taken together indicates that an interest in objects as well as the development of affectional bonds is not simply a derivative or outgrowth of libidinal energies and aims or a consequence of gratification of other needs, but is a critical independent aspect of development that expresses inborn propensities to establish cognitive and affective links to objects in the world.[4] Apparently, tactile stimulation (and, as other evidence I

---

[4]One can criticize the claim that the basis for an interest in an attachment to objects is inborn and instinctual by pointing to the danger of arbitrarily proliferating instincts. Given the historical realizations of this danger (as seen, for example, in the work of McDougall (1923), one should demand rigorous justification for any claim regarding the instinctual basis for a particular set of behaviors. The kind of evidence I have cited in the previous pages specifying the early, species-wide and "environmentally stable" (Hinde, 1959) behaviors and effects—including visual fixation, selective perceptual preferences, clinging, and the importance of tactile and kinesthetic stimulation (and other behaviors not referred to in these pages, such as smiling and soothability) constitutes adequate justification for such claims and guards against the arbitrary proliferation of instincts. The failure to demonstrate that a given behavior either emerges early in life or shows a regular sequence, is species-

have not cited suggests, kinesthetic stimulation) is, early on, an especially critical dimension of objects to which the infant responds. The research evidence also supports the clinical intuitions and formulations of Balint (1937/1964), who argued that ''primary object love'' more accurately describes the infant's early propensities than Freud's concept of primary narcissism; and those of Fairbairn (1952), who proposed that ''libido is primarily object-seeking rather than pleasure-seeking.''

Although the potential for forming links to objects is inborn, the vicissitudes and course of this capacity are linked to one's developmental history and personality structure. This will be brought out by reference to Mahler's (1968; Mahler, Pine, & Bergman, 1975) concept of separation–individuation and Winnicott's (1958) ideas on transitional phenomena.

SEPARATION–INDIVIDUATION AND TRANSITIONAL PHENOMENA

In all species above a certain level of complexity, development is marked by growth and differentiation of physical and psychological competencies. Behaviorally, such growth is both expressed in and facilitated by, among other things, increasing time spent in play and increasingly independent exploration of the world. Above a certain level of phylogenetic complexity, all animals show this developmental move from helplessness to increasing competence and independence. Indeed, in all such infrahuman species, physical survival depends on the relatively successful negotiation of this developmental move. In humans, this universal story unfolds not only as overt behaviors expressing and mediating more or less competence and separation, but also along more subtle and complex dimensions such as the cohesiveness of self and the nature and form of object relations established, including the establishment of interests. Further, more than in other animals, this move toward what Mahler (1968) has called separation–individuation is embedded in an affective matrix of mother–child interactions. This affective matrix will play a vital part in the degree and manner in which the universal developmental move toward separation–individuation takes place and also is critical in determining the ''fate'' and style of our inborn propensity to respond to objects. As conceived of here, the acquisition of interests is intimately bound up with and is, indeed, an expression of the separation–individuation process. Hence, the object relational factors that determine the course of separation–individuation will also strongly influence the development of interests. We turn now to a more specific consideration of these issues.

---

wide, and is ''environmentally stable'' would constitute adequate grounds for rejecting the claim that the behavior is inborn and instinctual.

It is generally accepted in most developmental theories, including psycho-analytic theory, that the very young infant has not yet achieved differentiation between self and nonself and, indeed, does not yet have either a concept of object or of self. Hence, it would make little sense to speak of the infant at this stage as having a *relationship* to someone or something outside itself.[5] In the course of normal development, the child becomes increasingly capable of true object relations. From the point of view of Mahler's (1968; Mahler et al., 1975) description of development, one can say that the child gradually leaves the stage of symbiosis and moves toward a state of increasing differentiation in which both concept of self and of other are available and in which a relationship between the two is possible. Accompanying and part of this individuation of self is physical and psychological separation from others, ultimately and optimally culminating

---

[5]It should be recognized that although infants are not yet capable of real object relationships, as noted earlier, they do show selective response to and interest in objects. One must distinguish between being capable of a real relationship to an object and showing selective interest in an object. As infant behavior shows, the latter is possible even before the infant has a conception of a separate object or of separate self. For example, infants exhibit curiosity, interest in novelty, and selective preferences of various kinds long before they develop object permanence.

Freud (1914/1957) conceptualized the early state of the infant as "primary narcissism." Because, in the state of "primary narcissism," libido or "sexual energy [is] attached [only] to the ego itself [p. 209]," the infant was presumably incapable of interest in objects. Indeed, Freud's reasons for believing that adults suffering from "narcissistic neuroses" are (i.e., schizophrenia and other psychoses) untreatable by psychoanalytic therapy were cast in terms of distribution of libido. Because their libido presumably was attached to the ego itself, they were incapable of libidinally cathecting objects—that is, they were incapable of forming an interest in and developing a relationship with an object. Freud consistently highlighted withdrawal of interest in objects as the definitive symptom of psychosis.

These formulations have been disputed in regard to both infants and adult psychosis (as well as to the underlying metapsychological assumption that there is an inverse relationship between ego libido and object libido—see Stolorow, 1975). The former was disputed by Balint's (1937) claim that infants show "primary object love" and by Fairbairn (1952), as expressed in his formulation that "libido is object seeking." With regard to adult psychosis, a number of psychoanalytic writers (Arlow & Brenner, 1964; Modell, 1968) have observed that many adult psychotics *do* show an interest, often intense, in objects. Finally, recent work with borderline conditions and narcissistic personality disorders reveals that what distinguishes healthy from disturbed people is not presence or absence of interest in objects, but the *nature and style of such interests*. Thus, people suffering from narcissistic personality disorders can be interested in and react to others with great intensity, but they will often react to others, not as autonomous and fully differentiated separate others, but as "self-objects" (Kohut, 1977), whose importance lies in their capacity to provide self-cohesiveness and self-aggrandizement.

What this discussion suggests is that there are two somewhat separable dimensions in definitions of narcissism: (1) degree of differentiation between self and other; and (2) an interest in objects. The evidence indicates that relative absence or impairment of self–other differentiation (either in the infant or the adult) does not result in an absence of interest, but in a particular style of interests. Further, clinical evidence suggests that in narcissistic conditions, the failure of self–other differentiation is the critical aspect of the pathology and determines other features such as the particular style of interests and object relations.

in the achievement of autonomy. Broadly speaking, according to Mahler, two interrelated sets of factors will play a critical role in the degree to which autonomy is achieved. One is degree of early symbiotic gratification experienced by the child and the other is the mother's attitude toward the child's naturally increasing separation–individuation.

According to theorists like Mahler and Winnicott, it becomes difficult for the child to move successfully toward autonomy and individuation without certain prior basic experiences. In Mahler's terminology, these basic experiences are concerned with symbiotic gratification and in Winnicott's (1965) language they involve ''good enough mothering'' and the introjection of the ''ego-supportive environment.'' An important later aspect of the processes of differentiation and individuation is the child's participation in what Mahler (1968) aptly calls the ''hatching'' process, a process in which the child directs interest and attention to the outside world.

The empirical evidence provides striking support for the formulations of Mahler and Winnicott. The young child whose early experiences result in what Bowlby (1969) calls secure attachment is able to wander away from mother and home to explore new situations for increasing periods of time and with decreasing discomfort (Ainsworth, 1963, 1964, 1967; Bell & Ainsworth, 1972). During the transitional period in which such moves are being tentatively tested, the child will show behavior that Furer (in Mahler, 1968) evocatively calls emotional ''refueling.'' That is, the child will return periodically to home base as if to make certain of mother's presence and to receive emotional ''refueling'' from her.

The concept of emotional ''refueling'' and the general relationship between a safe base and exploration has received strong empirical support among a wide range of species, including birds (Hogan & Abel, 1971; Wilson & Rajecki, 1974); monkeys (Harlow & Harlow, 1965, 1972; Kaufman, 1974) and humans (Ainsworth, 1974; Ainsworth, Bell, & Stayton, 1971). Further, there is evidence that stimuli other than mother can serve as safe base. Thus, Candland and Mason (1968) found a lower heart rate for young monkeys in an unfamiliar room when a towel is present as compared with no towel present. And Hill and McCormack (cited in Mason, 1970) reported a lower cortisol level for young monkeys in a strange environment when they have access to a surrogate. In children, it is established that exploratory behavior increases or diminishes as their mother is present or absent (Ainsworth & Wittig, 1969; Cox & Campbell, 1968; Feldman & Ingham, 1975; Rheingold & Eckerman, 1970). But exploratory behavior also varies with *pictures* of mother (Passman & Erck, 1977) and with security blanket for ''blanket-attached'' toddlers, although for ''non-blanket-attached'' toddlers, the blanket does not have this effect (Passman & Weisberg, 1975).

For humans, the evidence supports the idea of a strong relationship between security of attachment and independent exploratory behavior. Those whose relationship to mother can be characterized as indicating anxious attachment are more likely to show disturbances in play, exploratory behavior, and independent and autonomous activity. And conversely, secure attachment is associated with greater freedom in these areas (Ainsworth et al., 1971; Ainsworth & Wittig, 1969).

This leads to an articulation of the second critical factor influencing separation– individuation. As described by Mahler (1968), the mother not only must be physically and emotionally available during the "hatching" process, but must also permit and encourage the moves toward separation and autonomy. In Winnicott's (1958) terms, the mother must be capable of instituting "gradual failure of adaptation." The human mother is not alone in this task. One can also observe in infrahuman species the mother's complex role in both weaning of early attachment through discouraging excessive proximity and alert availability when the infant is in situations of potential danger or may otherwise need her (Hinde, 1975; Marvin, 1977). What has also been observed in both humans (Devore & Konner, 1974) and monkeys (Kaufman, 1974) is the role of peers and older juveniles in the moves toward separation and autonomy. In other words, and this point is particularly critical in a discussion of interests, separation–individuation not only involves a move *away* from mother, but *toward* a new social context of peers and juveniles. It is worth noting, as an aside, that the role of peers in development has been relatively underemphasized. That infant monkeys separated from each other show the same depression–regression pattern as infants separated from mother (Harlow, 1974) cannot be adequately accounted for by an exclusive emphasis on maternal attachment. Also to be noted is that insofar as peers do not satisfy such basic biological drives as hunger, the evidence on intensity and importance of peer attachment serves as further refutation of the secondary drive model of attachment.

Either the extreme of the mother's unavailability or that of failure to let go will interfere with the separation–individuation process. Although apparently at opposite ends of a continuum, not infrequently one sees these behaviors combined in pathogenic situations. Without a "safe anchorage" and the opportunity for checking back with a secure home base, the individuating process, which would optimally culminate in a secure sense of self and in the capacity for independence and autonomy, is disturbed. In short, the early moves toward independent behavior are delicately dependent on the availability of the attachment figure and the possibility of returning to home base. As noted earlier, in both the young child and the young of infrahuman species, interest in the larger outside world and the freedom and range of exploratory behavior varies with the availability of the security-providing attachment figure. In optimal development of individuation, a benevolent positive feedback process is created whereby early "symbiotic gratification" followed by the availability of mother (a "safe base") during the first tentative "hatching" steps toward independence permits sufficient security for "the predominance of pleasure in separate functioning" and the overcoming of "that measure of separation anxiety that *is* entailed by *each new step of separate functioning*" [Mahler, 1968, p. 20]. The pleasure in separate functioning—in exploring the world, in play, and in contact with peers—then provides further encouragment for still greater separate functioning, with the result that the child becomes increasingly capable of and motivated toward autonomy and independence. Under pathogenic conditions, a potentially benevolent process is replaced by a vicious circle. One such pattern is where the unavailability of a "safe anchorage" renders moves toward separation excessively difficult and frightening with the result that separation anxiety is not overcome by the "pleasures of separate functioning."

In the present context, what is to be especially noted is the degree to which the development of play, exploration, and curiosity—that is, the early basis for the development of interests in objects in the wider outside world—is intimately linked to the vicissitudes of the separation–individuation process. Just as a child will have difficulty developing mature object relations without early symbiotic gratification and the experience of a "safe anchorage," so will he or she similarly have difficulty exploring and exercising with comfort his or her curiosity about objects in the world. In somewhat different language, one can say that whereas secure attachment is associated with curiosity, play, and the capacity to explore and become interested in the world, insecure attachment interferes with these activities and capacities. Both mature object relations and autonomous interests require an individuated self relating to and establishing cognitive, affective, and value ties to independent objects in the world.

The relationship between object relations and interests is further elucidated by Winnicott's (1958) discussion of "transitional objects" and their importance during an intermediate stage in the movement toward individuation and autonomy. I have described the child's early moves toward separation and autonomy and the mother's role in facilitating this process. However, as Winnicott has shown (and, as reported above for the "blanket-attached" toddlers), at a certain stage in the child's development, objects other than mother are also called upon to facilitate this process. We are all familiar with the soothing and security-providing properties of the raggedy blanket or teddy bear and the particular role they play in situations of anxiety and psychological danger.[6] Winnicott has directly related these "transitional phenomena" to the establishment of culture

---

[6]There has been considerable controversy in the psychoanalytic literature as to whether transitional objects are normal or pathological and whether they are to be distinguished from childhood fetishism. There is little point in reviewing this controversy here. The position taken in this chapter is in agreement with Dickes (1978), who maintains that the transitional object is pathological and indistinguishable from fetishism when the extreme relationship to such objects involves the supplanting of the parent and when the object is used for discharge of sexual and aggressive tensions. He suggests—and I agree-that the terms transitional phenomenon and transitional object be reserved for use with the large group of children who use inanimate objects to relieve distress caused by separation.

and cultural interests and it would, therefore, be useful to trace and draw upon Winnicott's subtle and complex formulation in this area.

According to Winnicott, transitional phenomena are transitional in a number of senses. One, as noted previously, at the most apparent level, phenomena are transitional because they occur at a transitional stage in which the child is moving from symbiosis to independence. Two, more subtly, transitional phenomena are transitional in a formal and cognitive sense. That is, as a *representation,* a transitional object is not actually taken to be the mother and yet is also not fully an abstract symbolic representation of her. The transitional object, then, is also transitional in the movement from concrete representation to the achievement of a true symbol. The child knows that the blanket or teddy bear is not the mother and yet he or she reacts *affectively* to these objects and derives comfort from them as if they were mother. Giving external objects the capacity to soothe and comfort permits a freer and safer exploration of and interest in the external world.

This suggests still a third important sense in which the transitional object and earlier transitional phenomena are transitional. The child is not called upon to decide whether the meanings experienced in the object are entirely his or her creation or whether they exist in the external world. In this sense, these meanings are intermediate between the subjective and the objective. In Winnicott's (1958) words: "Of the transitional object it can be said that it is a matter of agreement between us and the baby that we will never ask the question, 'Did you conceive of this or was it presented to you from without?' The important point is that no decision on this point is expected. The question is not to be formulated" [pp. 239–40].

In the course of development the transitional objects of childhood are given up and "there is a gradual extension of range of interest" [p. 232]. Although the specific transitional object loses meaning, it becomes "spread out over the whole intermediate territory between 'inner psychic reality' and 'the external world as perceived by two persons in common,' that is to say, over the whole cultural field" [p. 233]. In other words, a process that began with external transitional objects becomes internalized as cultural interests and values.

As Winnicott notes, in such cultural areas as art, religion, and others the question of subjective or objective, of "Is this my creation or is it part of the external world?" is allowed to be deferred. In this sense, cultural phenomena reflect both inner and outer reality. That is, because they are internalized, they are deeply personal and, so to speak, can be carried around. And because they are consentually validated and communally shared, they speak to our need for connections to objects in the world.

Implied in Winnicott's posited link between transitional phenomena and later cultural activities and interests is the idea that a groundwork for cultural interests

is the need to develop symbolic supportive substitutes for early sources of security and safety. In a sense, they represent internalized home bases to which one
must periodically return before setting out again. In a very advanced manner we
do what Harlow's monkeys and young children do when confronted with
strange, complex, and novel situations. This is surely close to what Winnicott
had in mind when he referred to certain cultural activities (e.g., music, poetry) as
periodic therapeutic regressions and as similar to transitional phenomena.[7;8]

Narcissism and Interests

Difficulties in experiencing deep interests in related areas such as the development of values, ambitions, and ideals, and in object relations play a prominent
part in the modal symptomatology reported by patients today. Many patients tend
to report experiencing meaninglessness and emptiness, including lack of mean-

---

[7]It is important to clarify a point here. It is possible to interpret Winnicott's discussion of
transitional objects as suggesting that cultural interests are entirely or primarily derived from the need
to find symbolic substitutes for maternal security and "safe anchorage." Winnicott is not entirely
clear on this matter. My position is that, as argued earlier, the ultimate basis for an interest in objects
is an inborn predisposition. Indeed, it is this inborn predisposition that partly explains why the child
turns to the transitional object for soothing and comforting. I am suggesting further that the unfolding
of this inborn predisposition serves object relational functions. Under optimal conditions the inborn
predisposition to respond to objects unfolds in the development of a wide range of interests. Given
this development, however, such interests come to serve object relational functions. Thus, although
the development of a particular interest may develop somewhat autonomously, it can come to serve
some of the psychological functions normally served by any strong cognitive–affective tie, that is, by
object relations.

[8]Although the general proposition I am suggesting is that autonomous interests are related to early
security of attachment and relative success in separation–individuation, there are likely to be important additional factors. As noted earlier, Kohut has observed that some very disturbed people can be
capable of pursuing, at least during certain periods, gratifying and creative lives. I have also noted in
Footnote 1 the case of a disturbed and very gifted composer whose passion for music, I believe,
played a critical role in maintaining his psychological integrity. It seems to me that certain people,
endowed with certain talents and sensitivities, may be able to develop particular cultural interests that
can then serve as partial symbolic substitutes for early failures in security and safety. In these cases,
interests may serve, at least with partial success, some of the critical psychological functions served
by ordinary object relations. In this sense, they are similar to the "compensatory structures"
described by Kohut (1977).

It is also possible that of two individuals with the same degree of early security of attachment and
of separation–individuation, one may have been fortunate enough to have had the opportunity later in
life to develop abiding interests. For example, he or she may have been exposed to the kinds of
traditions, values, intellectual challenges, and so on that stimulate the development of interests. The
presence of these abiding interests may then serve important object relational functions and generally
contribute to maintenance of personality integrity, particularly in situations of stress. Obviously, the
social context is an important later factor in determining the likelihood that one will develop deep
abiding interests.

ingful interests, ideals, and values, rather than, for example, simply circum-scribed hysterical or phobic symptoms. It is quite possible that the current preoc-cupation with borderline conditions and narcissistic personality disorders reflects not so much the uncovering of new diagnostic categories, but the style of pathol-ogy that is coming increasingly to characterize today's modal patient. These patients appear to present in extreme form issues and difficulties that are more pervasive and widespread. Thus, at the same time that analysts are preoccupied with narcissistic personality disorders, political scientists, literary critics, histo-rians, and writers for popular magazines are writing about the "new narcissism" as a widespread cultural phenomenon.[9]

A critical feature of this narcissistic style, whether described as a widespread social phenomenon or as a pathological clinical condition, is a relative lack of interest in the object per se. Rather, interest is dictated mainly or entirely by the aims of self-enhancement and self-aggrandizement. For example, when one observes that an individual relates to an object (e.g., music) only or mainly for the purpose of self-aggrandizement, the genuineness of the interest in that object can be questioned. To take another example: In ordinary discourse, when some-one very obviously behaves exhibitionistically, he or she is said to be "showing off." It would be interesting to trace the history of this term, but what seems clear is that when someone is said to be "showing off," what is being "shown" is the self or some part of the self. In other words, rather than immersing oneself in the activity and in the interest pursued or presented, the activity or interest is primarily an instrumentality for the self.[10]

---

[9]The question of the reasons for the recent veritable preoccupation with narcissism and the relatively sudden popularity of this diagnosis is important. I strongly suspect that an explanatory framework that goes beyond an appeal mainly to early infant–mother interactions and includes broad social factors will be necessary to clarify this phenomenon. As Morgenthau and Person (1978) point out, psychoanalytic thinkers tend to conceptualize too readily the psychological effects of broad social and historical factors only or primarily in terms of their expression in child-rearing patterns. For example, Kernberg (1975) states: "I do not think that changes in contemporary culture have effects on patterns of object relations, if we define object relations not simply in terms of actual interactions between a person and others, but in terms of the intrapsychic structures that govern such interactions" [p. 223]. He states further his view that social and cultural changes will influence object relational patterns, symptomatology, and character structure "if and when changes in cultural pat-terns affect family structure to such an extent that the earliest development in childhood would be influenced" [p. 223]. For a contrasting view, which does not rest solely on family structure and child-rearing patterns, see Kovel (1976), Lasch (1978), and Maccoby (1976). My opinion is that the perspective that focuses entirely on the role of child-rearing patterns in mediating social and cultural influences will not be at all adequate in accounting for the shifting nature of pathology and character styles.

[10]It is not that very narcissistic people have no interests, but rather that their interest in objects is solely or primarily an instrumentality for self-aggrandizement. Indeed, as such as instrumentality objects can command intense interest. Hence, it is not a question of self-absorption resulting in little

In the case of performances (e.g., acting, musical performances) the performer's mode of presentation is such that the audience remains always excessively conscious of the performer, rather than the content being presented. For example, with regard to acting, for certain performers, whatever part they are portraying it is *they* of whom we are conscious. Because they have not lost themselves in the part, the audience finds it difficult to attend to the part and to lose consciousness of the performer. The performer is always figure, never ground; always intrusive, never unnoticed. Just as is the case generally of narcissistic interests, the relationship between performer and subject matter (or, more broadly, between self and object) is essentially exploitative rather than respectful and caring. The entire meaning and purpose of the object is limited to the personal self-aggrandizement interests it can serve. It is entirely an instrumentality with little or no separate existence of its own.

It is important to note that an essentially instrumental view of the object appears inescapable in traditional instinct theory insofar as it is conceptualized mainly as "the thing in regard of which or through which the instinct is able to achieve its aim." As noted earlier, according to Freudian theory, were the instinct able to achieve its aim without objects, an interest in objects would never develop. Indeed, Freud (1914/1957) consistently held to the view that the narcissistic condition persists throughout one's lifetime and is only grudgingly and partially relinquished. Accordingly, he writes: "Thus, we form a conception of an original libidinal cathexis of the ego, part of which cathexis is later yielded up to objects, but which fundamentally persists and is related to the object–cathexes much as the body of a protoplasmic animalcule is related to the pseudopodia which it puts out" [p. 58].

Given Freud's drive discharge model and its primary postulate that all behavior is generated by the drive for instinctual gratification, a purely instrumental conception of the object is inevitable. This entire picture alters if one accepts, as the evidence strongly suggests, an independent inborn basis for object relations and for an interest in objects. One would no longer need to derive an interest in objects from some presumably more basic and primary drives. Interestingly, such a reconceptualization would reevoke aspects of Freud's short-lived concept of "ego interests" discussed earlier.

INTERESTS AND EGO PSYCHOLOGY

In the foregoing discussion, I have referred only to Freud's instinct theory and have not yet taken into account the more recent formulations that have come to

libido remaining for objects. Rather, self-involvment and self-absorption determine the *nature* of the interest in objects as vehicles or instrumentalities rather than as autonomous objects.

be known as psychoanalytic ego psychology, as expressed particularly in the writings of Hartmann (1964) and Rapaport (1967) on ego autonomy, "conflict-free" spheres of the ego, neutralization, etc. What are the implications of these theoretical developments for an understanding of the acquisition and psychological functions of interests?

It is the case that a main goal of ego psychology has been to argue for the greater autonomy of behavior from instinctual drives. But the primary focus of ego psychology has been on ego structures and apparatuses and their associated functions. As Apfelbaum (1966) points out, in the structural point of view that has come to characterize ego psychology, the ego is viewed primarily as a structure whose main function (along with reality testing) is to control, delay, and domesticate the "ever-seething cauldron" of id drives. In other words, whereas the ego supplies control and structure, the drives alone supply motivational energy and aims. This point of view is most clearly seen in Rapaport's (1960) writings. So committed is he to keeping drives as *the* exclusive motivational domain that he views exploration, curiosity, and novelty as causes rather than motives, and clearly purposive exploratory, curiosity, and novelty behaviors as caused rather than motivated—that is, as nonmotivational. For Rapaport, any behavior that does not show certain traditional drive characteristics—peremptoriness, cyclicity, selectivity, displaceability, for example—is not to be seen as motivated. This restriction forces Rapaport into the peculiar position of deeming a wide range of goal-directed and planned means–ends choice behavior as nonmotivational. This artificial and awkward categorization of behavior is testimony to the persistence of the idea that only drives provide behavior with motivational aims and motives, whereas the ego provides structures and functions to control, modulate, and carry out these aims.

It is important to note about Rapaport's position that one can be quite consistent in positing autonomous ego functions and nevertheless maintain that a primary role of such functions in ongoing behavior is to serve drive gratification. Indeed, the more intact and "conflict-free" the ego functions, the more efficiently will the drive gratification aims be fulfilled. Hence, an ego psychology thus conceived is not inconsistent with the general idea of Freudian instinct theory that all motivated behavior is in the service of drive gratification.

A somewhat different interpretation of ego psychology and of the concept of ego autonomy has been offered recently by Klein (1976) who interprets Hartmann's writings as suggesting the idea that "conflict-free" ego functions can themselves become an independent, nonlibidinal motivational source of behavior. Indeed, as we shall have occasion to see later, Hartmann (1964) does refer to ego aims and "ego-interests." Implicit in Klein's writings are different related sources of nonlibidinal motivation inherent in ego functioning. These include the possibility of pleasure in adaptive, integrative behavior (which parallels White's

[1963] "competence" and "effectance" motives and Hendrick's [1943] "mastery" motive); pleasure in the sheer exercise of ego functions (which parallels the concept in academic psychology of "intrinsic motivation"—see Hunt, 1965); and the rewarding nature of ego functions residing in the fact that such activities provide "stimulus nutriment" (Rapaport, 1967) necessary for optimal cognitive functioning. (This is similar in many regards to Hebb and Thompson's [1954] notion of optimal arousal level.) Despite these motivational possibilities, however, Klein suggests that ego psychology offers neither a dynamic principle nor an explicit theory of nonlibidinal motivation. Rather, a predominantly structural psychology is grafted on to a preexisting drive discharge model of motivation.

As stated earlier, Hartmann (1964) does occasionally refer to Freud's early concept of "ego-interests" and observes that an individual's goals and behaviors reflect not only instinctual drives, but ego and superego aims. That is, in accord with the "principle of multiple function" (Waelder, 1930), he views all behavior as the resultant of different sets of considerations corresponding to id, ego, and superego. In this sense, Hartmann appears to leave room in psychoanalytic theory for the possibility, indeed the ubiquitousness, of nonlibidinal motives and aims. However, this possibility is not developed. Hartmann makes clear that in his use of the term "ego-interests" he is mindful of its origins in Freud's concept of self-preservative tendencies. As Hartmann points out, Freud first identified such self-preservative tendencies with "ego drives," and their associated cathexes he called "interests" in contrast to the libido of the sexual drives. In fact, Hartmann (1950) continues to use "ego-interests" essentially as an extension of self-preservative trends. Thus, he refers to "ego-interests" as a striving for what is "useful," that is, for social status, wealth, etc.," and observes that "their aims center around one's person (self)" [p. 136]. Here is the clearest indication that in Hartmann's conception of "ego-interests," object relational functions, concerned with the establishment of cognitive and effective links to objects, play little or no role. As if in awareness of this fact, following the passage from which the foregoing conception of "ego-interests" is taken, Hartmann adds that: "it might prove practical to include in the concept of ego interests . . . other groups of ego tendencies . . . the aims of which do not center around the self; for instance, those which affect the outer world not only indirectly, . . . but whose aims are centered around other persons or around things" [p. 136]. This theme, however, is not at all developed. If it were, it might have led to a fuller integration of the object relational with the ego psychological perspective and a recognition, specifically, of what Modell (1975) has referred to as "instincts associated with the ego." Instead, what one observes in Hartmann's discussion of "ego-interests" is: (1) their link to the self-preservative tendencies that Freud initially viewed as "ego drives"; and (2) the frequency with which " 'ego-interests' are . . . rooted in id tendencies" [p. 137] or, as expressed at another point, "in narcissistic, exhibitionistic, aggressive, etc. drive tendencies" [p. 176]. There is practically nothing said in Hartmann's writings of that aspect of interests that involves the establishment of cognitive and affective links to objects. Thus, although ego psychology's concern with ego functions and apparatuses is relevant to the capacity to acquire interests, it does not deal with the object relational aspects of interests. Generally, one can say that although autonomous and conflict-free ego functioning makes possible the accurate perception of an object as it is, it does not adequately account for the affective and cognitive links to objects and the critical role such links play in psychological functioning.

The fact is that in its primary emphasis on functions and apparatuses, ego psychology does not explicitly alter the basic conception of traditional instinct theory in which our interest in objects is a function of their role in instinctual gratification.

Many of the recent findings in this area can, as Modell (1975) notes, be seen to point to "instincts belonging to the ego." (The awkward and inelegant procedure of assigning instincts to the ego rather than referring to instinctual behavior in relation to organisms and individuals is made necessary by the traditional ego–id model, in which drives and aims are assigned to the system id and structures and functions to the system ego). These findings are more consistent with Fairbairn's (1952) conceptualization of the ego as a dynamic structure with its own aims. And these aims, Fairbairn consistently claimed are object seeking. That is to say, the seeking of objects has an independent instinctual basis. The "instincts associated with the ego" may have characteristics different from the traditional id instincts (White [1963] refers to the former as "neurogenic" as contrasted with "viscerogenic" instincts), but there is no reason to believe that they are any less basic or primary. Much of the research on and the discussion of "effectance," "competence," and "mastery" motives (Hendrick, 1943; White, 1960, 1963), exploratory, curiosity, and novelty motives and behavior (Barnett, 1958; Berlyne, 1960, 1966; Butler, 1965; Dember 1961; Piaget, 1952; Rheingold, 1963; Welker, 1961), and "intrinsic motivation" (Hunt, 1965) can be seen as data for a systematic theory of motivation appropriate to ego psychology and to "instincts belonging to the ego."

Despite, then, talk of "ego-interests" and ego aims, Hartmann continues to hold to a conception of the ego primarily as a controlling structure needed to harness the "seething cauldron of the id." It is this general *logic* of the id–ego model that provides the framework for ego psychology. As Klein (1976) puts it: "the psychoanalytic conception of drives as 'blind forces' that need to be controlled has trapped the ego concept; the ego is pictured predominantly as a controlling agency, and in the service of the 'reality principle'" [p. 175]. Hartmann makes clear that although he talks about ego aims, drive properties belong only to the id. Thus, in discussing Freud's equation of self-preservative tendencies with "ego drives," Hartmann (1950) observes that "today we no longer speak of 'drives of the ego' in the strict sense since it was realized that all drives were part of the system id" [p. 135]. Also, as Apfelbaum (1966) notes, in order to avoid the reintroduction of "ego drives" Hartmann rendered "the ego as an organ with a *function* rather than as a representation of a *drive* with an *aim* [Apfelbaum's italics]" [p. 457]. But, Apfelbaum continues, in view of the talk of ego aims, urges toward mastery, etc., "how far can the conception of apparatuses causing such behavior be carried before the organ metaphor breaks down and these apparatuses again take on the character of drives? [p. 457]." And Apfelbaum's question remains cogent even if one were to dispense entirely with the notion of drives. For he is essentially inquiring regarding the motivational status of ego aims in a theory that gives primary, perhaps exclusive, motivational force to instinctual drives.

The result of retaining a model in which all drive properties belong to the system id is, as Klein (1976) notes, that "ego psychology has yet to articulate an active principle of development independent of the model of libidinal drive energy. Yet in assuming nonlibidinal motivations, it cries out for a theory of such a dynamic principle" [p. 159]. That is, although there is casual talk of ego aims, mainly in the context of paying homage to the principle of multiple function, ego psychology offers no systematic theory of motivation that is in any way equivalent to the scope of instinct theory.

Hartmann discusses ego functions such as perception, memory, and thinking as if they could be carried out without objects—as if we could perceive, remember, and think without perceiving, remembering, and thinking *something*.[11] In fact, however, most ego functions not only logically entail objects, but psychologically and biologically *require* objects in order to develop and remain intact (the earlier discussion of Rapaport's [1967] concept of "stimulus nutriment" is obviously relevant here). That is, implicit in ego psychology are object relational aspects that need to be articulated and made explicit. The formulation that ego functions develop autonomously in *"an average expectable environment"* [Hartmann, 1958] hides critical object relational variables. The "average expectable environment" necessary for normal ego development includes such factors as the availability of attachment figures and "stimulus nutriment" from objects.

Somewhat ironically, the very emphasis in ego psychology on the autonomous and "neutralized" nature of ego functions, as a reaction against an exces-

---

[11]The nineteenth-century psychologist and philosopher Brentano (1874/1964) claimed that a basic distinction between mental and physical phenomena rests on the intentionality of the former—that is "the reference to a content, a direction upon a content" What Brentano was pointing to in this highly influential distinction is that one cannot want without wanting something, imagine without imagining something, and so on. One might say that in this formulation, Brentano was providing the philosophical basis for the object relational character of mentation.

sive emphasis on their supposed instinctual origins, leads to a failure to place ego functioning in its proper affective and even instinctual context. That is to say, in Freudian instinct theory, ego autonomy means autonomy from sexual and aggressive conflicts and wishes and their associated affects. In that context, to speak of autonomous interests would mean to emphasize their independence from the instinctual, with instinctual defined as sexual and aggressive drives. If, however, one recognizes the existence of what can be properly called object relational instincts (such as attachment—see Bowlby, 1969; Modell, 1975), it becomes clear that interests can be autonomous in Hartmann's sense—that is, independent of sexual and aggressive drives—but not autonomous of all instinctual and related affective sources. In short, as I have tried to show, interests are always embedded in the instinctual–affective matrix of object relations.

Ego autonomy in Hartmann's sense is not itself sufficient to ensure the development of interests, not because all behavior needs to be energized or motivated by instinctual drives, but because interests always involve an affective tie to the object in which one is interested. The core of truth contained in Freud's concept of sublimation is the recognition that interests always involve an affective link. Generally, one can say that although autonomous and conflict-free ego functioning makes possible the accurate perception of an object as it is, it does not account for the affective links to objects and the critical role such links play in psychological functioning.

Finally, one must not assume that the relationship between ego functioning and interests is unidirectional, for the evidence shows a reciprocal relationship between the two. That is, not only does intact ego functioning permit the development of interests, but conversely, interests and related phenomena are critical for the intact or optimal operation of ego functions. I have already referred to instances in which an abiding and central interest may help prevent ego disorganization in disturbed individuals. I have also referred to the fact that under dire circumstances, those able to call on the inner resources of interests and related structures such as values and ideologies are more likely to maintain intact ego functioning. In addition, there is evidence that under conditions of sensory deprivation, isolation, and various forms of stress, activities that contribute "stimulus nutriment" (e.g., composing a poem) help preserve psychic intactness. In their contribution to "stimulus nutriment," interests play an adaptive role in maintaining ego functions under conditions of sensory deprivation.

As noted, Rapaport (1967) proposes that the ego requires "stimulus nutriment" in order to function adequately and cites as evidence for this hypothesis the finding that ego functions are disrupted by sensory deprivation (Bexton, Heron, & Scott, 1954). He proposes further a dual autonomy such that autonomy of the ego from the id is facilitated by "stimulus nutriment" from the environment, and autonomy of the ego from the environment is facilitated by "stimulus nutriment'' from the id (e.g., affective signals). And, indeed, Rapaport's hypothesis is supported by Goldberger and Holt's (1961) finding that subjects capable of ''regression in the service of the ego'' (as expressed, for example, in capacity to engage in reverie and fantasy) are better able to withstand the cutoff of environmental stimuli entailed by the sensory deprivation experience.

Although Rapaport emphasizes drives as the ''ultimate guarantees'' of the autonomy of the ego from the environment, he also discusses the ''proximal guarantees'' deriving from ego and superego structures that would include ideologies, values, and interests. If one can reformulate Rapaport's ideas into nondrive terms, one can say that the presence of a rich inner life facilitates the autonomy of the ego from the environment and that the availability of environmental stimuli, plus an interest in and ability to respond to them, facilitates the autonomy of the ego from inner demands.

Of course, the first half of this statement is precisely what Cohen and other survivors of imprisonment and ordeals have reported—namely, that a rich inner ''spiritual life'' permitted some independence form the harsh and intolerable environment and thereby facilitated survival. Put in Rapaport's language of ''stimulus nutriment,'' one can say that people without ''nutriment'' from inner sources of interests, values, fantasy, etc. are more dependent on environmental stimuli. Hence, they are in greater difficulty when environmental stimulation is either disrupted or intolerable. By contrast, those people who receive ''nutriment'' from inner resources are more independent of environmental vicissitudes.

Why is ''stimulus nutriment'' so crucial for maintenance of ego intactness? Miller's (1962) interpretation of the isolation and stress data is that some kind of ''mental exercise,'' which he describes as ''the very essence of ego-activity,'' is the critical element in preserving ego intactness. This explanation may be appropriate to isolation situations (e.g., sensory deprivation experiments or solitary confinement), where environmental input is severely reduced and inner stimulation can be seen as compensating, strictly quantitatively, for reduced environmental input. It does not, however, seem to apply to other stress situations (e.g., concentration camps) where the issue is not reduced environmental stimulation, but the intolerable quality of the environment. Even in the former case, however, Miller fails to note a critical nonquantitative aspect common to all forms of ''mental exercise'' used in preserving intactness—that all such activity involves a relationship to either objects or mnemic representations of objects in the world. This is true of all the activities mentioned by Miller, ranging from counting pebbles to ''writing'' poetry to becoming attached to spiders and cockroaches. In short, influenced by an ego psychological conception, Miller is led to ignore the object relational aspect of the intactness enhancing ''mental exercises.''

Cohen's 1953) description of the survival-enhancing value of ideologies and cultural life will again be recalled. As Cohen and others have shown, these "cultural interests" permit escape from a harsh and intolerable environment into an inner life (in Rapaport's terms, they permit autonomy of the ego from the environment). But because the very inner life into which one escapes, by its very nature, is characterized by (internalized) cognitive and affective links to others, one's retreat is personal and yet not autistically personal. Although isolated from the current environment, the individual finds sustenance and support from "silent" links to an internalized cultural world. Because interests are structures that have internalized the cultural world, they permit autonomy both from the external environment and from the more idiosyncratic and autistic aspects of one's inner preoccupations.

The predominant formulations of ego psychology entail a separation between ego psychology and object relations. In a certain sense, as concerns object relations, the theoretical developments of ego psychology have been retrogressive. In instinct theory, insofar as the instinct is partly defined in terms of its object, a basic responsiveness of some kind to objects is clearly implied. By contrast, the formulations of ego psychology are concerned mainly with the development and operation of particular functions, without any explicit consideration of the objects involved in these functioning. If Modell (1975) is correct, the set of functions that inform us about reality are intimately involved with "object love." That is, these functions develop in an object relational matrix and are naturally and spontaneously directed toward objects. A poignant piece of evidence provides support for this idea. Dahl (1965) notes that around the same time that Helen Keller first learned the name of an object, she also kissed and hugged her teacher Anne Sullivan for the first time.

CONCLUSION

What needs to be reiterated in concluding this chapter is that an interest in objects is not simply an outgrowth of libidinal energies and aims, nor the expression of the autonomous working of ego apparatuses and functions. Rather, it is a critical feature of the development of object relations, based on the inborn propensity to establish cognitive and affective links to objects in the world. Current evidence in both humans and animals from a wide range of research areas—on "contact comfort," curiosity, exploratory behavior, response to novelty, early stimulus preferences, effects of physical and social stimulation on cognitive development—all argue against the proposition that successful interests necessarily represent a sublimation and channeling of presumably more basic instinctual drives. This evidence suggests that individuals are capable of interest in activities and objects for their own sake—that is, of being intrinsically motivated (see Hunt, 1965). I would add only that although the potential for intrinsic motivation is inborn, the development of this capacity is linked to one's developmental history. The developmental arrest that results in essentially symbiotic or narcissistic object relations and the egocentricity, exploitative, and exhibitionistic attitudes that characterize these modes of functioning is not compatible with intrinsic motivation. In general, it is likely that the quality of adult interests reflects important aspects of the fate of the inborn propensity to establish links to objects.

It is no wonder, then, that the mundane property of whether one is capable of abiding interests plays such a critical psychological role in extreme circumstances. For, in an important sense, this property reveals and, in part, constitutes the depth and strength of one's internalized cognitive and affective links to the world. Particularly in extreme circumstances, the prognosis of those whose links are tenuous will be more pessimistic than those with vital and tenacious ties. In less extreme, ordinary circumstances these differences will be reflected in the richness and depth of the individual's life and in his characteristic ways of relating to animate and inanimate objects in the world.

REFERENCES

Ainsworth, M. D. The development of infant–mother interaction among the Ganda. In B. M. Foss (Ed.), *Determinants of infant behavior (Vol. 2)*. London: Methuen (New York: Wiley), 1963.

Ainsworth, M. D. Patterns of attachment behavior shown by the infant in interaction with his mother. *Merrill-Palmer Quarterly*, 1964, *10*, 51–58.

Ainsworth, M. D. *Infancy in Uganda: Infant care and the growth of attachment*. Baltimore, Md.; The Johns Hopkins Press, 1967.

Ainsworth, M. D. Infant–mother attachment and social development: Socialization as a product of reciprocal responsiveness to signals. In M. P. Richards (Ed.), *The integration of the child into a social world*. Cambridge: Cambridge University Press, 1974.

Ainsworth, M. D., Bell, S. M., & Stayton, D. C. Individual differences in strange-situation behavior of one-year-olds. In H. R. Schaffer (Ed.), *The origins of human social relations*. London & New York: Academic Press, 1971.

Ainsworth, M. D., & Wittig, B. A. Attachment and exploratory behavior of one-year-olds in a strange situation. In B. M. Foss (Ed.), *Determinants of infant behavior* (Vol. 4). London: Methuen, 1969.

Apfelbaum, B. On ego psychology: A critique of the structural approach to psychoanalytic theory. *International Journal of Psycho-Analysis*, 1966, *47*, 451–475.

Arlow, J. A., & Brenner, C. *Psychoanalytic concepts and the structural theory*. New York: International Universities Press, 1964.

Bakwin, H. Psychological aspects of pediatrics. *Journal of Pediatrics*, 1949, *35*, 512–521.

Balint, M. Early developmental states of the ego. Primary object-love. *International Journal of Psycho-Analysis*, 1937, *30*, 265–273. Also reprinted in *Primary love and psychoanalytic technique*, London: Tavistock Publications, 1964 (New York: Liveright, 1965).

Barnett, S. A. Exploratory behavior. *British Journal of Psychology*, 1958, *49*, 289–310.

Bell, S. M., & Ainsworth, M. D. Infant crying and maternal responsiveness. *Child Development*, 1972, *43*, 1171–1190.

Berlyne, D. E. *Conflict, arousal, and curiosity*, New York: McGraw–Hill, 1960.

Berlyne, D.E. Curiosity and exploration. *Science,* 1966, *153,* 25–33.

Bettleheim, B. *The informed heart: Autonomy in a mass age.* New York: Free Press, 1960.

Bettleheim, B. *Surviving and other essays.* New York: Alfred A. Knopf, 1979.

Bexton, W. H., Heron, W., & Scott, T. H. Effects of decreased variation in the sensory environment. *Canadian Journal of Psychology,* 1954, *8,* 70–76.

Bornstein, M. H. Qualities of color vision in infancy. *Journal of Experimental Child Psychology,* 1975, *19,* 407–419.

Bowlby, J. *Attachment.* New York: Basic Books, 1969.

Bowlby, J. *Separation: Anxiety & anger.* New York: Basic Books, 1973.

Brentano, F. [Psychology from an empirical standpoint] (Transl. by D. B. Terrell.) In G. N. A. Visey (Ed.), *Body and mind.* London: George Allen and Urwin Ltd., 1964. (Originally published, 1874.)

Butler, R. A. Investigative behavior. In A. M. Schrier (Ed.), *Behavior of nonhuman privates.* London: Academic Press, 1965.

Candland, D. K., & Mason, W. A. Infant monkey heartrate: Habituation and effects of social substitutes. *Developmental Psychobiology,* 1968, *1,* 254–256.

Clayton, P. Mortality and morbidity in first year of widowhood. *Archives of General Psychiatry,* 1974, *30,* 747–750.

Cohen, E. A. [*Human behavior in the concentration camp*]. (M. H. Braaksma, trans.) New York: Grosset and Dunlap, 1953.

Cox, F. N., & Campbell, D. Young children in a new situation with and without their mothers. *Child Development,* 1968, *39,* 123–131.

Dahl, H. Observations on ''a natural experiment'': Helen Keller. *Journal of American Psychoanalytic Association,* 1965, *13,* 533–550.

Dember, W. N. Alternation behavior. In D. W. Fiske & S. R. Maddi (Eds.), *Functions of varied experience.* Homewood, Ill.: Dorsey, 1961.

Devore, I., & Konner, M. J. Infancy in hunter–gatherer life: An ethological perspective. In N. F. White (Ed.), *Ethology and psychiatry.* Toronto: University of Toronto Press, 1974.

Dickes, R. Parents, transitional objects, and childhood fetishes. In S. Grolnick & L. Barkin (Eds.), *Transitional objects.* New York: Jason Aronson, 1978.

Fairbairn, W. R. D. *Psychoanalytic studies of the personality.* London: Tavistock Publications, 1952.

Fantz, R. L. Pattern vision in young infants. *The Psychological Record,* 1958, *8,* 43–47.

Fantz, R. L. Visual perception from birth as shown by pattern selectivity. *Annals of the New York Academy of Sciences,* 1965, *118,* 793–814.

Fantz, R. L., & Fagan, J. F. Visual attention to size and number of pattern details by term and pre-term infants during the first six months. *Child Development,* 1975, *46,* 3–18.

Feldman, S. S., & Ingham, M. E. Attachment behavior: A validation study in two age groups. *Child Development,* 1975, *46,* 19–30.

Fisher, S., & Greenberg, R. P. *The scientific evaluation of Freud's theory and therapy.* New York: Basic Books, 1978.

Frankl, V. [Man's search for meaning: An introduction to logotherapy]. (Ilse Losch, trans.) Boston: Beacon Press, 1962.

Freud, A. The psychoanalytic study of infantile feeding disturbances. *Psychoanalytic Study of the Child,* 1946, *2,* 119–132.

Freud, A. Discussion of John Bowlby's paper: *Psychoanalytic Study of the Child,* 1960, *15,* 53–62.

Freud, S. *Interpretation of dreams.* New York: Avon Books, 1965. (Originally published, 1900.)

Freud, S. [Psychoanalytic notes on an autobiographical account of a case of paranoia]. In J. Strachey (Ed. and trans.), *The standard edition of the complete psychological works of Sigmund Freud* (Vol. 12). London: Hogarth Press, 1958. (Originally published, 1911.)

Freud, S. [On narcissism; an introduction]. In J. Strachey (Ed. and trans.), *The standard edition of the complete psychological works of Sigmund Freud* (Vol. 14). London: Hogarth Press, 1957. (Originally published, 1914.)

Freud, S. [Instincts and their vicissitudes]. In J. Strachey (Ed. and trans.), *The standard edition of the complete psychological works of Sigmund Freud* (Vol. 14). London: Hogarth Press, 1957. (Originally published, 1915.)

Freud, S. [Introductory lectures on psychoanalysis]. In J. Strachey (Ed. and trans.), *The standard edition of the complete psychological works of Sigmund Freud* (Vol. 16). London: Hogarth Press, 1963. (Originally published, 1916–1917.)

Freud, S. [Beyond the pleasure principle]. In J. Strachey (Ed. and trans.), *The standard edition of the complete psychological works of Sigmund Freud* (Vol. 18). London: Hogarth, 1955. (Originally published, 1920.)

Freud, S. [Civilization and its discontents]. In J. Strachey (Ed. and trans.), *The standard edition of the complete psychological works of Sigmund Freud* (Vol. 21). London: Hogarth, 1961. (Originally published, 1930.)

Friedman, S. Bruno, L. A., & Vietze, T. Newborn habituation to visual stimuli: A sex difference in novelty detection. *Journal of Experimental Child Psychology*, 1974, *18*, 242–251.

Goldberger, L., & Holt, R. R. Experimental interferences with reality contact. Individual differences. In P. Solomon, P. E. Kubzanski, P. H. Leiderman, J. H. Mendelson, R. Trumbull, & D. Wexler (Eds.), *Sensory deprivation*. Cambridge, Mass.: Harvard University Press, 1961.

Harlow, H. F. The nature of love. *American Psychologist*, 1958, *13*, 673–685.

Harlow, H. F. Induction and alleviation of depressive states in monkeys. In N. F. White (Ed.), *Ethology and psychiatry*. Toronto: University of Toronto Press, 1974.

Harlow, H. F. & Harlow, M. K. Effects of various infant–mother relationships on Rhesus monkey behaviors. In B. Foss (Ed.), *Determinants of infant behavior* (Vol. 4). London: Methuen and Co., 1965.

Harlow, H. F., & Zimmerman, R. R. Affectional responses in the infant monkey. *Science*, 1959, *130*, 421–432.

Hartmann, H. *Ego psychology and the problem of adaptation*. New York: International Universities Press, 1958. (Originally published, 1939.)

Hartmann, H. Comments on the psychoanalytic theory of the ego. *Psychoanalytic Study of the Child*, 1950, *5*, 74–96.

Hartmann, H. *Essays on ego psychology: Selected problems in psychoanalytic theory*. New York International University Press 1964

Hendrick, I. The discussion of the "Instinct to Master." *Psychoanalytic Quarterly*, 1943, *12*, 561–565.

Hinde, R. A. Behavior and separation in birds and lower vertebrates. *Biological Review*, 1959, *34*, 85–128.

Hinde, R. A. Mothers' and infants' roles: Distinguishing the questions to be asked. *Ciba Foundation Symposium*, 1975, *33*, 5–13.

Hinde, R. A., & Spencer-Booth, Y. Effects of brief separation from mother on rhesus monkeys, *Science*, 1971, *173*, 111–118.

Hogan, J. A., & Abel, E. I. Effects of social factors in response to unfamiliar environments in Gallus gallus spadiceus. *Animal Behavior*, 1971, *19*, 687–694.

Hunt, J. M. Intrinsic motivation and its role in psychological development. In D. Levine (Ed.), *Nebraska Symposium on Motivation*, (Vol. 13). Lincoln: University of Nebraska Press, 1965.

Jackson, G. *Soledad brothers: The prison letters of George Jackson*. New York: Coward-McCann, 1970.

Kaufman, I. C. Mother–infant relations in monkeys and humans: A reply to Prof. Hinde. In N. F. White (Ed.), *Ethology and psychiatry*. Toronto: University of Toronto Press, 1974.

Kearsley, R. B. The newborn's response to auditory stimulation. *Child Development*, 1973, *44*, 582–590.

Kernberg, O. *Borderline conditions and pathological narcissism*. New York: Jason Bronson, 1975.

Kinney, D. G., & Kagan, J. Infant attention to auditory discrepancy. *Child Development*, 1976, *47*, 155–164.

Klein, G. S. *Psychoanalytic theory*. New York: International Universities Press, 1976.

Kohut, H. *The restoration of the self*. New York: International Universities Press, 1977.

Kovel, J. *A complete guide to therapy*. New York: Pantheon, 1976.

Lasch, C. *The culture of narcissism*. New York: W. W. Norton, 1969.

Maccoby, M. *The gamesman: The new corporate leaders*. New York: Simon & Schuster, 1976.

Mahler, M. S. *On human symbiosis and the vicissitudes of individuation. (Vol. 1): Infantile psychosis*. New York: International Universities Press, 1968.

Mahler, M., Pine, F., & Bergman, A. *The psychological birth of the human infant: Symbiosis and individuation*. New York: Basic Books, 1975.

Malcolm X. *The autobiography of Malcolm X*. New York: Grove Press, 1964.

Marvin, R. S. An ethological cognitive model for the attenuation of mother–child attachment behavior. In T. M. Alloway, L. Kramer, & P. Pliner (Eds.), *Advances in the study of communications and affect*. New York: Plenum, 1977.

Mason, W. A. Motivational factors in psychological development. In W. J. Arnold & M. M. Page (Eds.), *Nebraska Symposium on Motivation* (Vol. 18). Lincoln: University of Nebraska Press, 1970.

Mason, W. A., Hill, S. D., & Thomsen, C. E.. Perceptual aspects of filial attachment in monkeys. In N. F. White (Ed.), *Ethology and psychiatry*. Toronto: University of Toronto Press, 1974.

McCall, R. B., & Nelson, W. H. Complexity, contours, and area as determinants of attention in infants. *Developmental Psychology*, 1970, *3*, 343–349.

McDougall, N. *An Outline of psychology*. London: Methuen, 1923.

Miller, S. C. Ego autonomy in sensory deprivation, isolation, and stress. *International Journal of Psycho-Analysis*, 1962, *43*, 1–20.

Modell, A. H. *Object love and reality*. New York: International Universities Press, 1968.

Modell, A. H. The ego and the id: 50 years later. *International Journal of Psycho-Analysis*, 1975, *56*, 57–68.

Morgenthau, H., & Person, E. The roots of narcissism. *Partisan Review*, 1978, *45*(3), 337–347.

Nardini, J. E. Survival factors in American prisoners of war. *American Journal of Psychiatry*, 1952, *109*, 244.

Parkes, C., Benjamin, B., & Fitzgerald, R. Broken-heart: A statistical study of increased mortality among widowers. *British Medical Journal*, 1969, *1*, 740–743.

Passman, R. H., & Erck, T. W. *Visual presentation of mothers for facilitating play in children: The effects of silent films of mothers*. Presented to the Society for Research in Child Development, New Orleans, March 1977.

Passman, R. H., & Weisberg, P. Mothers and blankets as agents for promoting play and exploration by young children in a novel environment. The effects of social and nonsocial attachment objects. *Developmental Psychology*, 1975, *11*, 170–177.

Patton, R. G., & Gardner, L. I. *Growth failure in maternal deprivation*. Springfield, Ill: Charles Thomas Co., 1963.

Piaget, J. *The origins of intelligence in children*. New York: International Universities Press, 1952.

Powell, G. F., Brasel, J. A., & Hansen, J. D. Emotional deprivation and growth retardation simulating idiopathic hypopituitarism. I. Clinical evaluation of the syndrome. *New England Journal of Medicine,* 1967, *276,* 1271–1278. (a)

Powell, G. F., Brasel, J. A., & Hansen, J. D. Emotional deprivation and growth retardation simulating idiopathic hypopituitarism. II. Endocrinologic evaluation of the syndrome. *New England Journal of Medicine,* 1967, *276,* 1279–1283. (b)

Rapaport, D. On the psychoanalytic theory of motivation. In M. Jones (Ed.), *Nebraska Symposium on Motivation* (Vol. 8). Lincoln: University of Nebraska Press, 1960.

Rapaport, D. The theory of ego autonomy: A generalization. In M. M. Gill (Ed.), *The collected papers of David Rapaport.* New York: Basic Books, 1967.

Rheingold, H. L. Controlling the infant's exploratory behavior. In B. M. Foss (Ed.), *Determinants of infant behavior (Vol. 2).* New York: John Wiley, 1963.

Rheingold, H. L., & Eckerman, C. O. The infant separates himself from his mother. *Science,* 1970, *168,* 78–83.

Robinson, P. Apologist for the superego (Review of B. Bettelheim's "Surviving and other essays). *New York Times Book Review,* 1979, April 29, pp. 7; 63.

Ruff, H. A., & Birch, H. G. Infant visual fixation: The effect of concentricity, curvilinearity and number of directions. *Journal of Experimental Child Psychology,* 1974, *17,* 460–473.

Schanberg, S. M., & Kuhn, C. M. Maternal deprevation: An animal model of psychosocial dwarfism. In E. Usdin, T. L. Sourkes, & M. B. H. Youdin (Eds.), *Enzymes & neurotransmitters in mental disease.* New York: John Wiley, 1980.

Silver, H. K., & Finkelstein, M. Deprivation dwarfism. *Journal of Pediatrics,* 1967, *70,* 317–324.

Stolorow, R. Toward a functional definition of narcissism. *International Journal of Psycho-Analysis,* 1975, *56,* 179–85.

Strassman, H. D., Thaler, M., & Schein, E. H. A prisoner of war syndrome: Apathy as a response to severe stress. *American Journal of Psychiatry,* 1956, *112,* 998–1003.

Thoman, E. B., & Arnold, W. J. Maternal behavior in rats. *Journal of Comparative Physiological Psychology,* 1968, *65,* 441–446.

Waelder, R. The principle of multiple function. *Psychoanalytic Quarterly,* 1930, *5,* 45–62.

Welker, W. I. An analysis of exploratory and play behavior in animals. In D. W. Fiske & S. R. Maddi (Eds.), *Functions of varied experience.* Homewood, Ill: Dorsey, 1961.

White, J. L., & La Barba, R. C. The effects of tactile and kinesthetic stimulation on neonatal development in the premature infant. *Developmental Psychobiology,* 1976, *9*(6), 569–570.

White, R. W. Competence and psychosexual stages of development. In M. R. Jones (Ed.), *Nebraska Symposium on Motivation* (Vol. 8). Lincoln: University of Nebraska Press, 1960.

White, R. W. Ego and reality in psychoanalytic theory. *Psychological Issues,* 1963, *3,* (3, Monograph No. 11).

Wilson, W. R., & Rajecki, D. W. Effects of the presence of familiar objects on the tendency of domestic chicks to peck in a novel situation. *Revue du Comportement Animal,* 1974, *8,* 95–102.

Winnicott, D. W. *Collected papers: Through pediatrics to psychoanalysis.* New York: Basic Books, 1958.

Winnicott, D. W. *The maturational processes and the facilitating environment.* New York: International Universities Press, 1965.

6

Investigations In The Psychoanalytic Theory Of Object Relations and Object Representations

Sidney J. Blatt, Ph.D.
Yale University
Howard Lerner, Ph.D.
University of Michigan

INTRODUCTION

Since its inception as a field of scientific inquiry at the threshold of the twentieth century, psychoanalytic theory has gone through a number of important revisions, elaborations, and extensions. Initial interest in psychoanalysis was directed toward understanding the impact of the drives, especially infantile sexuality, upon the maturation of the psychic apparatus and its role in the development of psychopathology. Subsequent focus in psychoanalysis was upon the modulating or control functions of the ego—the defenses—and their interaction with the drives. This interest in the modulating functions of the ego was later broadened to include the external, reality-oriented, adaptive functions of the ego. Up to this point psychoanalysis had a primary interest in innate biological forces and how these predispositions unfold in normal personality development and how they could result in personality disturbances. Freud also became interested in cultural phenomena, and psychoanalytic theory began to extend beyond its primary interests in the innate biological predispositions of the organism to include interests in the cultural context and how these factors also influence psychological development. Interest in the superego, as the internalization of cultural prohibitions and standards, lead to a fuller appreciation of the family as the mediating force in the transmission of cultural values. There was interest in the role of parents in shaping psychological development. Psychological growth and development were viewed as a consequence of the care-giving patterns of significant people in the child's early environment and their interaction with the child's evolving libidinal and aggressive drives and the modulating and adaptive functions of his ego. The interpersonal interactions with significant, consistent, care-giving figures were now seen as major factors in the formation of cognitive-affective structures, defined primarily in terms of evolving concepts of the self and of others in the object world (Jacobson, 1964). These structures were seen as the result of the complex interaction between the child's biological endowment and predispositions and the interpersonal matrix of the family and culture. Knowledge gained from psychoanalytic work with children and the observation of the normal and disturbed development of infants and children, contributed to the further appreciation and understanding of early developmental sequences and their role in normal personality development and the occurrence of psychopathology throughout the life cycle.

Research on psychoanalytic concepts has paralleled this progressive extension and elaboration of psychoanalytic theory. Early research focused on the vicissitudes of the drives, and later research considered the modulating and control mechanisms used to contain and direct these drive forces. Subsequently, there was an extensive investigation of ego functions not only as defense mechanisms but as factors vital for adaptation (e.g., cognitive styles and cognitive control principles). Most recently, research interest has been directed toward the investigation of various levels of cognitive-affective structures—the schemata of the representation of self and others—in normal as well as impaired psychological development.

Throughout the wide range of research on psychoanalytic concepts, diagnostic psychological tests (especially projective techniques) have had a central and pivotal role. In fact there has been a reciprocal and mutually beneficial relationship between the concepts of psychoanalytic theory and diagnostic psychological testing. The work of David Rapaport is a foremost example of the interrelationship between the development of psychoanalytic theory and of diagnostic psychological testing. Rapaport found that psychoanalytic concepts provided a remarkably broad theoretical base for psychological assessment and that psychological testing in turn served as a source for observations that lead to theoretical innovations and to the systematic testing of a number of psychoanalytic concepts. Rapaport's contributions to psychoanalytic ego psychology and to metapsychology were directly influenced by his extensive experience in diagnostic psychological assessment. Rapaport's careful observations of test responses of a wide variety of patients contributed to his understanding and explication of many central psychoanalytic concepts. Diagnostic psychological procedures also allowed Rapaport and his colleagues to test empirically many hypotheses that had been generated in the intensive psychoanalytic study of individuals and the complexities of their lives.

Rapaport's contributions in the decades from 1940 to 1960 were primarily concerned with the psychoanalytic concepts of his day, a concern with the economic, topographic, and structural models of psychoanalysis and the study of ego functions: impulse–defense configurations, affect modulation and regulation, and the organization of thought processes and other adaptive functions of the ego. But there have been significant revisions and extensions of psychoanalytic theory in the past 20 years since Rapaport's monumental contributions. These recent developments include an attempt to extend psychoanalytic theory by integrating it with concepts of object relations theory (Blatt, 1974; Blatt, Wild, & Ritzler, 1975; Fairbairn, 1952; Guntrip, 1969; Loewald, 1962, 1970, 1979; Winnicott, 1965); with a broadened, psychodynamically based, developmental theory (Blatt & Wild, 1976; Fraiberg, 1969; A. Freud, 1956; Jacobson, 1964; Mahler, 1968; Mahler, Pine & Bergman, 1965); and a systematic psychology of the self (Balint, 1952; Kohut, 1971, 1977; Winnicott, 1971). These recent developments within psychoanalytic theory are an integral part of a movement away from an "experience-distant" metapsychology that utilizes concepts of structures, forces, and energies—concepts based primarily on a model related to the natural sciences, to a more "experience-near" clinical theory primarily concerned with concepts of the self and others in a representational world (Jacobson, 1964; Sandler & Rosenblatt, 1962) as a central psychological process all within a model based primarily on hermeneutics (Home, 1966; G. Klein, 1976; Steele, 1979). Recent developments in research based on diagnostic psychological testing have paralleled these recent developments in psychoanalytic theory. In particular, there have been several recent attempts to study systematically self and object representations—concepts of self and others, and the nature and quality of interpersonal relationships. In psychoanalytic theory the diagnostic psychological assessment there have been attempts to extend beyond an all-exclusive focus on ego structures, such as impulse–defense configurations and cognitive styles, to include a fuller consideration of the experience of individual in an interpersonal matrix through concepts of self and object representation. The purpose of this chapter is to review these recent developments in diagnostic psychological testing to assess cognitive-affective schemata of object and self representations and to examine whether these studies enrich psychoanalytic theory and provide further understanding of personality development, psychopathology, and the therapeutic process.

II. THE ASSESSMENT OF OBJECT REPRESENTATION

A. Theoretical Introduction

Freud (1923/1961, 1938/1964), in his formulations about the development of the superego, discussed the process of internalization and how "a portion of the external world, has, at least partially, been abandoned as an object and has instead, by identification, been taken into the ego and thus become an integral part of the internal world. This new psychical agency continues to carry on the functions which have hitherto been performed by the people (the abandoned objects) in the external world . . . [Freud, 1938/1964, p. 205]." This conceptualization of internalization was subsequently extended beyond superego formation to include all processes in which interactions with the environment are transformed into inner regulators and are assimilated as characteristics of the self (Hartmann, 1939, Hartmann & Loewenstein, 1962; Schafer, 1968, 1970). The internalization of object relations provides one of the primary bases for the development of intrapsychic structures (Blatt, 1974; Blatt et al., 1975; Govin-Decarie, 1965; Fenichel, 1945; A. Freud, 1952; Glover, 1950; Hartmann, 1950; Hartmann, Kris, & Loewenstein, 1949; Hoffer, 1952; Jacobson, 1964; Kernberg, 1966, 1972; Loewald, 1951, 1960, 1973; Mahler, 1968; Parens, 1971; Schafer, 1968; Stierlin, 1970). Object relations, through the processes of internalization, result in the formation of intrapsychic structures (ego functions and cognitive structures such as object and self representations) that regulate and direct behavior. This interest in object relations and the representational world begun by Freud provided psychoanalytic theory and research a conceptual basis for extending beyond the "experience-distant" metapsychology of a more mechanistic natural science model of impersonal structures, forces, topographies, and energies to a more "experience-near" clinical theory primarily concerned with interpersonal relationships and the representational world as a central theoretical focus (Klein, 1968). Emphasis shifted away from a preoccupation with the microanalysis of thought processes toward a consideration of the quality and nature of object relations, from concepts framed in an abstract metapsychological language to a more phenomenologically based interest in dimensions such as self and object, described in a "middle-level," clinically relevant language (Mayman, 1976). Psychoanalytic theory and research progressively focused upon the complex interactions among early formative interpersonal relationships and how these result in the formation of intrapsychic structures that are best understood in terms of the quality of the representational world. The developmental level of the organization of concepts of self and other are psychological structures that are the consequence of the internalization of formative interpersonal interactions with significant figures. These concepts or representations of self and others in turn shape and direct subsequent interpersonal relationships.

Blatt[1] (1974, 1978) discussed how an understanding of the development of the concept of the object (of the self and others) can be greatly facilitated by an

---

[1]It seems somewhat artificial and incongruous to refer to myself in the third person. But this seems stylistically convenient because this chapter is written in collaboration and cites research that often I have conducted in collaboration with a number of different colleagues (S. J. B.).

integration of psychoanalytic theory with the contribution of cognitive developmental psychology, particularly the formulations of Jean Piaget and Heinz Werner. Piaget and Werner trace the development of cognitive schemata through several major developmental phases of the life cycle. They identified four major levels or types of cognitive schemata through which the child comes to know and think about his world in increasingly sophisticated and symbolic form. According to developmental psychological theory, all thinking involves a series of mental operations that are the result of the internalization of action sequences. The development of mental representation begins early in childhood and proceeds through four basic stages to intellectual maturity in adulthood. In early childhood, the child functions primarily at a "sensorimotor" level and gains increased understanding of his own actions and those of objects. The capacities that evolve during the sensorimotor stage are elaborated further on an implicit level as the child's thinking is no longer exclusively linked to actions. Toward the end of an intuitive, preoperational stage, the child is able to contemplate action and is able to take the view and perspective of another. The contemplation of action is eventually expressed in the representation of operations, at first concretely and later with greater abstraction during a stage of formal operations first attained around the ages of 12 and 13. The growing child is then able to begin to deal with the world on symbolic, logical, propositional, and relational terms. Development, for Piaget and Werner, consists of a progressive unfolding of cognitive structures according to innate principles of functioning in which the construction of new cognitive schemata evolves out of earlier cognitive structures. The child's relationships to his reality become increasingly integrated and the child comes to know the world as a product of his actions upon objects and through the relationship of his actions to his symbolic representation of actual and potential actions and interactions.

The formulations of the cognitive developmental psychologists about the child's development of cognitive schemata are based primarily on the study of the child in states of relative quiescence and as the child responds primarily to inanimate objects. Psychoanalytic theorists offer formulation of the child's development of cognitive structures based on the study of the child in states of relative comfort and discomfort within an interpersonal relationship (Wolff, 1967) expressed primarily in terms of concepts of the self and of others. According to Jacobson (1964), Mahler (1975), A. Freud (1965), Fraiberg (1969), and others, the representations of self and of others are initially vague and variable and only develop gradually to become consistent, relatively realistic representations. Based initially on pleasurable and unpleasurable experiences of frustration–gratification, the child begins to build stable representations of the self and of others and to establish enduring investments and affective commitments. At the earliest stage, the self, the object, and interpersonal experiences are all one, undifferentiated, affective, sensorimotor experience of pleasure or unpleasure. As discussed by Mahler, in early autistic and symbiotic stages the infant is in a state of undifferentiated fusion and attachment to the mother. Slowly, the infant begins to perceive need satisfaction as coming from the mother, and there is a corresponding shift from the internal experience of pleasure to an awareness of a need-satisfying object. At first the object is recognized primarily in terms of its need-gratifying functions and actions. Slowly, the child becomes able to differentiate representations of himself and of others. With development, these representations become more stable and constant and begin to coalesce into an increasing sense of identity.

According to psychoanalytic theory, these mental schemata or structures are transmitted to the child in an interpersonal matrix—in the relationship between the child and its caring agents and in the child's relationship to the culture at large (Parsons & Bales, 1955; Vygotsky, 1962). The child initially internalizes the orderly, predictable regularity of the mother–child, caretaking relationship as the basic differentiation of reality. These differentiations are subsequently extended and elaborated in further interpersonal relationships and experiences within the culture. But it is the basic caring relationship that provided the primary experiences in reality that are internalized as the earliest and most fundamental principles of cognitive organization. The relatively predictable sequences of frustration and gratification in the caring relationship provides the child with the foundations for a sense of organization and coherence. The infant's experiences of the mother's love and care are essential for the development of integration and reality adaptation (Winnicott, 1945). The mother's consistent and reliable care provides the infant with a sense of reality that is predictable, structured, and organized. The internalization of the mother's predictability and organization enables the child to tolerate the delay that is externally imposed and, eventually, to develop the capacity for delay within himself. And this capacity for delay is an earlier step in the establishment of psychological structures that permit partial discharge, anticipation, planning, and transformation. It must be stressed, however, that the amount of structure and organization that the environment must provide for these processes to develop will vary from child to child, depending on the child's biological constitution and temperament (Thomas, Chess, & Birch, 1968). What may be an appropriate degree and form of organization for one child may be insufficient or excessive for another. And even further, the degree and nature of the organization and structure provided by the environment must change in response to the child's development progression. But it is the internalization of the mother's organized and structured responses to the infant that provides the basis for the establishment of cognitive structures (Blatt, 1978).

Broadly defined, object representation refers to the conscious and unconscious mental schemata—including cognitive, affective, and experiential components—of objects encountered in reality. Beginning as vague, diffuse, variable, sensorimotor experiences of pleasures and unpleasure, these schemata gradually expand and develop into differentiated, consistent, relatively realistic representations of the self and the object world. Earlier forms of representations are based more on action sequences associated with need gratification; intermediate forms are based on specific perceptual and functional features; and the higher forms are more symbolic and conceptual (Blatt, 1974). There is a constant and reciprocal interaction between past and present interpersonal relations and the development of representations. These schemata evolve from and are intertwined with the internalization of object relations, and new levels of object and self representation provide a revised organization for subsequent interpersonal relationships (Blatt, 1974).

B. Research Studies

1. Introduction

Based on the principle that when a stimulus is consistently ambiguous, its image is shaped by the organizing characteristics of the individual's representational world, considerable empirical research has investigated the structure and content of early memories (Mayman, 1968), manifest dreams (Brenneis, 1971; Krohn, 1972), the human response on the Rorschach (Blatt & Ritzler, 1974; Blatt, Brenneis, Schimek, & Glick, 1976; Blatt, Schimek, & Brenneis, 1980; Krohn, & Mayman, 1974; Mayman, 1967; Urist, 1973), and open-ended descriptions of significant figures (Blatt, Wein, Chevron, & Quinlan, 1979). These various studies have provided important procedures for assessing object representations and their impairment in various forms of psychopathology. Collectively, these studies, utilizing a variety of content and structural analyses, lend impressive support to the construct validity of object representations as a theoretical dimension that provides important information about the developmental level and quality of interpersonal relationships to which an individual is predisposed. Object representations express the structure or template that determine the nature of the experience of the self and the object world.

Two primary research groups have contributed to the widening scope of the theory of object representation and to the development of procedures for assessing this important dimension of personality organization. These two research groups represent different but not mutually exclusive approaches to the study of object representations. Martin Mayman and his colleagues at the University of Michigan have focused on the thematic elements of object representations and have utilized a variety of projective test procedures to assess these elements, including early memories, manifest dreams, written autobiographies, and Rorschach percepts.

The evaluation of object representations from these sources have been studied in relation to levels of psychopathology, types of character structure, independent rating of object relations, and the capacity to profit from psychotherapy. The research group at the University of Michigan has its theoretical roots in the ego psychological theory and test methods of David Rapaport, integrated with the more recent theoretical contributions of Mahler and Kernberg.

Sidney Blatt and his colleagues at Yale University have focused primarily on the structural dimensions of object representation. Their work, also derived from Rapaport, is based on an integration of object relations theory, ego psychology, and the developmental cognitive theories of Jean Piaget and Heinz Werner. Drawing on projective tests data, particularly the Rorschach, but also the TAT, the manifest content of dreams and open-ended descriptions of significant figures, Blatt and his colleagues have developed procedures for the assessment of object representations and have studied the relationships of object representation to normal development as well as to levels and types of pathology especially in schizophrenia and depression. Their conceptualizations and empirical findings have led to the discovery of differentiations within the broad diagnostic categories of depression and schizophrenia. Their findings also demonstrate that the structure of object representations continue to develop throughout the life cycle into early adolescence and adulthood and that the quality of object representations provides insight into psychotic and the depressive experiences that has implications for the therapeutic process.

In this chapter we review the contributions of the research groups in Ann Arbor and New Haven and present a summary of their theoretical orientation, research methodology and empirical findings in order to highlight their contributions to contemporary psychoanalytic research and theory and to point to some directions for future developments in theory and research on object relations and object representations.

These investigations of object representation reviewed in this chapter also provide a focus for a long-standing but relatively nonintegrated body of research in psychological testing that bears directly on issues central to psychoanalysis. There have been, for example, a number of studies of the human response on the Rorschach and its relationships to individual's capacity to establish meaningful and satisfying interpersonal relationships (Rorschach, 1942). The human response on the Rorschach has been found to reflect a capacity to invest in social relationships (Phillips & Smith, 1953; Piotrowski, 1957; Rapaport, Gill, & Schafer, 1945). It has also been found to be related to advanced cognitive development and a maturity in social relations (Ames, 1960, 1966; Ames, Learned, Metraux, & Walker, 1950; Draguns, Haley, & Phillips, 1967; McFate & Orr 1949; Setze, Setze, Baldwin, Doyle, Kobler, & Kobler, 1957; Thetford, Molish, & Beck, 1951) and the capacity for empathy (Klopfer, Ainsworth, Klopfer, &

Holt, 1954; Mayman, 1967, 1977). The human response has been found to be related to social interests (Dörken, 1954; Fernald & Linden, 1966; Rieger, 1949; Roe, 1951) as well as to a motivation for psychotherapy (Affleck & Mednick, 1959; Gibby, Stotsky, Miller, & Hiller, 1953; Jonietz, 1950; Rogers, Knauss, & Hammond, 1951) and positive outcome (Grauer, 1953; Roberts, 1954; Rogers & Hammond, 1953) and prognosis (Goldman, 1960).

The frequency and quality of human responses on the Rorschach have important diagnostic implications. Parker and Piotrowski (1968), for example, report a preponderance of dehumanized and unreal figures in the Rorschach records of schizophrenics (Allison, Blatt, & Zimet, 1968; Blatt & Ritzler, 1974; Blatt & Wild, 1976; Rapaport, Gill, & Schafer, 1945; Weiner, 1966). Pechaux, Girard, and LeMeé (1956) found that depressed patients have few human responses and that the number of human responses increases as there is decrease in the severity of the individual's depression. There are several reports of a relative absence of human responses in antisocial individuals such as adult criminals (Endara, 1957; Geil, 1945; Walters, 1953), murderers (DeBeudoin, Haimonte, Bessing, & Geissman, 1961), juvenile delinquents (Ray, 1963; Richardson; 1963), and pre-adolescent behavior disorders (Robbertse, 1955). Endara (1957) also found an inverse relationship between human responses and the severity and recidivism of antisocial and criminal behavior.

The importance of human movement responses has been frequently noted (Klopfer et al., 1954; Piotrowski, 1950; Rorschach, 1942; Schactel, 1966) as indication of psychological maturity and the capacity for empathy (Ansbacher, 1947; Mueller & Abeles, 1964; Phillips & Smith, 1953). Human movement responses are related to the capacity for delay (Goldman & Herman, 1961; Meltzoff, Singer, & Korchin, 1953; Singer, Meltzoff & Goldman, 1952), time perspective and orientation (Buchwald & Blatt, 1974; Kurz, 1963; Siegman, 1961), and the capacity for planning (King, 1958), cognitive complexity (Bieri & Blacker, 1956; Nickerson, 1969), and fantasy and dream production (Orlinsky, 1966; Lerner, 1967; Schonbar, 1965).

One of the more dramatic demonstration of the importance of human responses on the Rorschach is the study of Hertzman and Pearce (1947). They found that the content of human responses was related to material that emerged subsequently in psychotherapy. They found that the content of 75% of the human percepts had clearly identifiable personal significance for the individuals and that this material eventually emerged in the therapeutic process. Equally impressive was Orr's (1958) early attempt to develop a scale for assessing the humanness of responses and the demonstration that psychotic patients (Orr, 1958) and convicted criminals (Endara, 1957) had uniformly lower number of responses reflecting living, vital human beings. Pruitt and Spilka (1964) also attempted to assess the degree of "humanness" in Rorschach protocols and found that an increase in this dimension was related to independent assessments of improvement in group therapy. Also, the substantiality of human responses with well-defined boundaries, rather than being vulnerable, penetrable, and insubstantial (Fisher & Cleveland, 1958; Landis, 1970) relates to the severity of psychopathology. The lack of firm boundaries and the presence of themes of penetration distinguished psychotic from nonpsychotic groups (Fisher & Cleveland, 1958; Holtzman, Gorham, & Moran, 1964; Landis, 1970; Reitman, 1962).

These early studies of the human response on the Rorschach are a clear demonstration that an assessment of object relations—of concepts of the self and of others—is related to central issues in personality development and organization and to important differentiations among types of psychopathology. These numerous studies of the human responses on the Rorschach remained relatively unintegrated because they were not rooted in a broader and more comprehensive conceptualization of personality development and organization. The development of object relations theory now offers a general framework for integrating these diverse research findings and for pointing out the need to understand more fully the developmental significance of interpersonal relationships and their contribution to the building of the intrapsychic structures. These early studies clearly indicate that the assessment of the quality of the human figure represented on projective procedures can provide data vital to a sophisticated understanding of personality organization.

2. The Contributions of the Research Group at the University of Michigan

The theoretical orientation of the Michigan research group focuses on "psychosexual ego modes" and the "quality of object representations" that are assessed in "clinically based empathic-intuitive" analyses of the content of projective test data. This approach has lead to the development of several new methods and scales for studying object representations in the content of Rorschach responses, the manifest content of dreams, and early memories.

This research has been based on Mayman's (1963, 1966) interest in the need to develop a clinical theory for psychoanalysis instead of an exclusive concern with the metapsychological, economic, and structural models of psychoanalysis. Mayman (1976) is concerned that psychoanalytic theory has paid relatively little attention to developing more experiential and clinically relevant dimensions and concepts. He (1963) consistently stresses the need to develop a theory of psychoanalysis based on a "middle level language" as part of the "complex, multi-leveled theory" of psychoanalysis and to distinguish among what he sees as three coordinated sets of concepts or languages. First, there is the language employed by the therapist in transaction with the patient during the treatment hour, a language more akin to poetry than science, an admixture of feelings, thoughts, and actions. Outside the consultation room the clinician, according to Mayman, employs a "middle language" of "empirical constructs" that helps formulate clinical generalizations about a patient. A third, more abstract language consists of "systematic" or "hypothetical constructs," a system of impersonal concepts utilizing more objective, third-person terms that constitutes psychoanalytic metapsychology. Mayman argues that these three levels of abstraction should not be confused with each other but rather need to be coordinated with constant reference back to the original primary data base, the clinical material.

Mayman (1976) also sees these very same problems in the analysis of psychological test data. Reports are often written in terms of impulse–defense configurations, ego structures, and cognitive styles, but with relatively little attention given to the forms and qualities of self-experiences, the quality and nature of object relationships the person was likely to establish, and other more phenomenological dimensions such as the range of affective experiences that were available to the person. There is a tendency to neglect the use of more empathetic, first-person terms and concepts for the more impersonal third-person terms of metapsychology.

The research on object representation by the Michigan group uses middle-level concepts such as ego nucleus (Glover, 1950), ego state and ego boundary (Federn, 1952), object and self representation (Jacobson, 1964), and ego identity (Erikson, 1954). Mayman (1963, p. 99), predating Kohut (1971, 1977), noted that the development of a middle-level clinical theory of phenomenologically relevant constructs would lead to the emergence of a psychoanalytic theory of the self rather than a theory of the ego and that this theory would have greater relevance for the understanding of the vicissitudes of the therapeutic process. Mayman (1963) attempted to develop a conceptual system—a subjective language of the therapeutic process that would fill the gap between the abstract language of metapsychology and the primary data base of psychoanalysis. Table 6.1 illustrates Mayman's (1963) initial attempts to develop terms and concepts for this middle language of the clinical theory of psychoanalysis.

The research of Mayman and his colleagues on object representation is an integral part of efforts to develop a middle-level, clinical theory for psychoanalysis and to develop a methodology for the systematic study of these clinically relevant concepts much as Rapaport utilized psychological test data to investigate aspects of the economic and structural theory of psychoanalysis. Mayman (1965, 1967), on theoretical and clinical grounds, argued that the content of early memories and Rorschach human responses is much more than just embellished screens that conceal deeper, more profound levels of unconscious meanings. Earlier Erikson (1950) demonstrated the clinical value of the manifest content of dreams. Like Erikson, Mayman assumed that manifest content expresses levels of ego functioning, the capacity for object relations, and the nature of object rela-

TABLE 6.1
Coordinate Terms of the "Middle" and "Meta"
Psychological Concepts of Psychoanalysis

METAPSYCHOLOGICAL TERMS which, as ordinarily employed refer to ego structures viewed "from the outside " (i.e., in essentially third-person terms)	MEDIATING (MIDDLE LANGUAGE) TERMS which designate ego structures in more subjective terms (i.e., more nearly in keeping with the subjective)
Ego structure; ego-organization; ego apparatuses; ego-state (as defined by Gill and Brenman)	The self; the ego-identity; identity; identity fragments; ego boundary; self-feeling; ego-syntonic; ego-alien; depersonalization; ego state (as defined by Federn)
Structural regression; ego disruption; ego disintegration; primary and secondary process thinking; ego weakness	Ego split; ego-id nucleus; partial identification; identity confusions; conflicting identifications; identity diffusion.
The id; the instincts; affect-charge; cathexis; impulse-derivative	Repressed ego states; repressed affect-states; unconscious (split-off) infantile ego—object relationships; love; hate; "urge:: or "drive"; the source, aim object (and subject? of an instinct)
Superego	Hostile (and loving) introjects
Libido (oral; anal; phallic; and genital)	Sensuous or voluptuous sensori-affective feeling state
Object-cathexis	Parental "images"; parental introjects; internalized other; transference paradigms
The system "Ucs"; the system "Pept-Cs"; attention cathexis; hypercathexis; cognitive and perceptual structures	Latent content; unconscious fantasy; repressed thoughts and affects

[a] From Mayman, (1963).

tional strivings. He (1968) regards character structure as organized around pivotal object relational themes and that early memories are not historical truths but reconstructions of "intrusive interpersonal themes which define that person's enduring view of himself and his enduring expectations of others [p. 304]." Object representations are templates, enduring preformed images, or ingrained expectancies of self and others around which the phenomenological world is structured and into which the experiences are assimilated. The investigation of the content of Rorschach responses (1967) and early memories, as expressions or facets of object representation, are based on the following assumption by Mayman (1967):

When a person is asked to spend an hour immersing himself in a field of impressions where amorphousness prevails and where strange or even alien forms may appear, he will set in motion a reparative process, the aim of which is to replace formlessness with reminders of the palpably real world. He primes himself to recall, recapture, reconstitute his world as he knows it, with people, animals, and things which fit most naturally into the ingrained expectancies around which he has learned to structure his phenomenal world. A person's most readily accessible object representations called up under such unstructured conditions tell much about his inner world of objects and about the quality of relationships with these inner objects toward which he is predisposed [p. 17].

Mayman (1967) developed a number of dimensions to assess the content of Rorschach responses in order to answer the following questions:

What kind of world does each person recreate in the ink-blot milieu? What kinds of animate and inanimate objects come most readily to mind? What manner of people and things is he prone to surround himself with? Does he put together, for example, a peopleless world of inanimate objects: If so, which objects have special valence for him? Do they hint at a certain preferred mode of acting upon the world or of being acted upon by it? Are they, for example, tooth-equipped objects? Or phallically-intrusive objects? Decaying or malformed objects? [p. 17].

In addition to the psychosexual level of the image and the degree of humanness in the response, Mayman also considered the extent to which conflict or rage permeate the portrayal of others and the individual's vulnerability to separation and loss because a stable image of good mothering agent has not been internalized. The Rorschach human response is viewed as a vehicle for understanding "important personal meaning" about "a person's capacity to establish empathic contact with another human being."

In an early study, Mayman (1967) selected Rorschach protocols from the Menninger Foundation Psychotherapy Research Project and distilled from each protocol verbatim clusters of "content-fragments" he considered to be self-representations, object representations, and conflict representations. All patients had been evaluated independently on the Health-Sickness Rating Scale (Luborsky, 1962) as well as on a wide range of other clinical variables. Mayman examined the extent to which ratings of psychopathology, based exclusively on representational content gleaned from the Rorschach administered before treatment, corresponded to the clinical ratings of psychopathology. Editing out all references to traditional Rorschach scoring categories, Mayman asked graduate students and psychology interns to "immerse themselves" in each patient's Rorschach responses, to regard the Rorschach images as a sample of the patient's inner object world, and to assign a rating for the degree of psychopathology implicit in the representational content. Relatively inexperienced judges success-fully predicted ratings based on independent psychiatric evaluations. Consensus ratings of five inexperienced judges correlated .81 with the criterion ($p < .001$) whereas the consensus ratings of six more experienced judges correlated .86 with the criterion. Individual correlations range from .68 to .87 ($p < .001$) and interrater reliability ranged from .67 to .90. In addition to demonstrating that an object relations approach to Rorschach content correlates significantly with inde-pendent ratings of psychopathology, Mayman also demonstrated that inexperi-enced as well as clinically trained judges can make important contributions to research. Mayman concluded that the findings demonstrate the epistomological relevance and scientific credibility of a clinical–intuitive approach of the skilled, trained clinician in using projective data in research.

Much of Mayman's research methodology utilizes the clinical intuitive meth-od from which he has developed new sources of data for the assessment of object representation. Mayman developed novel techniques for inquiry into Rorschach and TAT responses as well as a new psychological assessment procedure—the Early Memories Test (Mayman, 1968). Mayman and Ryan (1972) developed a scale for evaluating the quality of object representation in the themes of early memories. This scale evaluates the thematic content of early memories according to a theory of psychosexual and psychosocial development. Each point on the scale represents a constellation of feeling states, interpersonal conflicts, coping patterns, relationship expectations, and self-experience. According to Mayman and Krohn (1975): "The themes which bind together the *dramatis personae* of a person's early memories define nuclear relationship patterns that are likely to recur repetitively in a wide range of other life situations. They intrude projec-tively into the structure and content of his early memories, just as they intrude repetitively into his evolving relations with significant persons in his life" [p. 160]. The scale is essentially a detailed assessment of psychosexual ego modes, ranging from oral, anal, phallic, and oedipal configurations as well as subtle differentiations within each of these basic modes. In addition, the scale also assesses the quality of object relations represented in the early memories, as the templates or preformed images that determine interpersonal interactions. Thus, the scale has a broader theoretical base than just the nature of instinctual or libidinal preoccupation, but rather it assesses "a multiplicity of different ego states, each organized around a distinctive affect and self-experience, and made up of a definite need, a need appropriate object-relationship and self-representation, and phase appropriate conflicts, defenses, and compromise formations, and ego competencies (Mayman, 1968; p. 309)." The object representation dimension in early memories includes assessing the degree to which the self is represented as living in isolation or in close mutual contact with others, the range of relationships and interpersonal positions depicted in the memory, and the degree to which the relationships are described as impersonal, mechanical, imitative, or mutual. Ryan (1973), studying neurotic outpatients, demonstrated a significant and positive relationship between the levels of object representation in early memories and the ability to enter into a psychotherapeutic relationship. The psychosexual and psychosocial scale of interpersonal themes and the qualitative aspects of early memories are presented in Tables 6.2 and 6.3.

These scales reflect an integration of concepts from ego psychology and object relations theory and their application to the manifest content of object representations. The Early Memories Test provides data of diagnostic and prognostic significance—''They [early memories] provide a clue to habitual emotional attitudes which are still operative and so illuminate in advance the therapeutic problem, how these problems will emerge, and how they will have correspondence in the analysand's life and in the transference'' [Saul, Snyder, & Sheppard, 1956, p. 234].

Mayman's emphatic-intuitive approach to clinical data and his interest in the middle-level language of clinical theory led to the development of several object representation scales and a number of construct validational studies. These studies, conducted by Mayman's students, have refined the concepts of object representation and extended the thematic analysis of object representations to the manifest content of dreams (Krohn, 1972), to autobiographical data (Urist, 1973), and to estimates of the capacity to enter into and benefit from insight-oriented psychotherapy (Hatcher & Krohn, 1980; Ryan, 1973). These scales, designed to evaluate levels of object representation as specific points on a developmental continuum, are correlated with each other (Urist, 1973) and with the Health–Sickness Rating Scale of Luborsky (Krohn & Mayman, 1974).

Krohn's (1972) thematic scale for the assessment of object representations in the manifest content of dreams parallels the scale developed by Mayman and Ryan (1972) for the study of early memories. Krohn views the manifest dream as similar to a Rorschach response or an early memory. In a pilot study he reviewed dreams from a variety of sources. He approached the dreams ''without specific preformed hypotheses, a method that is really an application to research of a psychoanalytic mode of listening and forming clinical hypotheses in which the researcher, by immersing himself in the data, begins to find patterns and correlations that endure across subjects.'' Marked differences were found in the humanness, differentiation, and warmth of various patients' dreams. There were striking differences in the richness versus impoverished portrayals of people and environments. More primitive images closely resembled the crude and bizarre percepts seen in Rorschach responses of more disturbed patients, and the more mature dream images seemed, by contrast, similar to well-constructed Rorschach percepts produced by relatively intact patients. These dimensions also paralleled

TABLE 6.2
Prototypical Interpersonal Themes
in Early Memories

I.   "Oral" configurations

   1. Themes of basic mistrust.
   2. Deprivation of insufficient supplies of attention, food, or love; oral pessimism, dissatisfaction, bitter resentment, sense of fulfillment (rather than of despair as in I. 1)
   3. Aggressive reactions to deprivation or frustration: demanding or grasping needed supplies rather than merely yearning for them as in I. 2.
   4. Gratification themes: sense of snugness, security, basic trust, expectation of fulfillment; sense of personal worth; availability of external comforts and supports.
   5. Gratification themes with a reversal of roles so that one becomes the giver rather than the recipient of nurturant care.

II.   "Anal" configurations: Self-differentiating relationship paradigms

   1. Retentiveness: willful stubbornness, defiance, passive-aggressive noncompliance.
   2. Expulsiveness: hurting self or others by dirting them or treating them like dirt.
   3. Sublimation or reaction formations.

III. "Phallic-intrusive" and "phallic-locomotor" configurations: Pleasure in mastery; pleasure in proofs of one's prowess, strength, or competence

   1. Active forms.
   2. Passive forms.
   3. Being the object of a phallic-aggressive assault.

IV.   "Phallic-sexual" configurations: Activities which are frankly sexual or veiled but recognizably sexual in nature

   1. Intrusive forms: moving outward to make contact with sexual object.
   2. Inceptive forms; trying to excite a sexually desired object to make a frank or veiled sexual approach.

V.   "Oedipal" configurations: Competitive striving to win favor with a love-object

   1. Male relationship patterns:
      a. Hostile competitive
      b. Positive harmonious
   2. Female relationship patterns:
      a. Hostile competitive
      b. Positive harmonious

VI.   "Latency" configurations: More sublimated peer-group activities

   1. Productivity and positive self-esteem.
   2. Inferiority.

[a]From Mayman (1968).

Relationship Paradigms

1. To what extent does one represent himself/herself as living in lonely isolation? In close interaction with others? How wide a range of relationships comes spontaneously to mind? To what extent do mother, father, other family members, and friends "people" the patient's intrapsychic world?
2. What forms of relatedness seem most congenial, most ego-syntonic, easiest to maintain?
3. What is the quality and intensity of feeling implicit in these relationships? What is the "level" of relationship—impersonal? anaclitic? imitative? mutual?
4. Is there evidence of particular psychosexual paradigms serving as models for interpersonal relationships? Evidence of preferred psychosexual positions to escape from other more dangerous positions?

Coping Style

5. Does the patient represent himself as active or passive in his relationships? If active, how? compliant? courageous? venturesome? defiant? autonomous? assertive? self-sufficient? If passive, what form of passivity? timid? self-abasing? compliant? limp? "feeling" and "watching" rather than "doing"?

Self-Structure

6. Where is a person's "self-feeling" most fully invested? In which modalities of experience? sensual? kinaesthetic? affective? introspective? extrospective? What forms of activity does the person readily invest himself in and in which can he not invest himself?
7. What kinds of life experiences seem ego-syntonic and which, by exclusion, ego-alien? Which qualities of experience remain split-off from the self? Which threaten to disorganize the sense of self (i.e., are not only estranged but bring on some depersonalization)?

Images

8. What are the principal representations of mother, father, and self? What is the principal representation of the self in relation to others? In what roles are the significant-others cast?
9. Are there traces of multiple or conflicting representations of significant others and of oneself?
10. Which self-representations seem to have been encouraged or fostered by the parents? Which seem to have been incorporated into the ego-idea?

Defense Modes

11. To what extent do "primal" or archaic memories occur?
12. To what extent is there a masochistic fixation upon fears, disappointments, dangers, injuries, pain, or illness?
13. How much repression do we encounter? To what extent does the patient feel himself cut off from his infantile origins (i.e., early sources of pleasure and early object-ties)? How vague or nebulous are the memories? How selective is the memory process?
14. What defenses other than repression appear in the way in which the story is told? isolation? reaction-formation? projection? denial?
15. To what extent are memories phobic? depressive? self-punitive? counterphobic? withdrawn? conflict-avoidant? shallow? self-preoccupied? warm and human?

[a]From Mayman (1968).

differences noted in the object and self-images that emerged on the Early Memories Test. These dimensions seemed crucial to the clinical evaluation of patients. The more "primitive dream imagery occur in patients judged to be borderline, the more mature images in the healthier, neurotic patients" [Hatcher & Krohn, 1980, p. 303].

Based on these pilot data, Krohn developed the Object Representation Scale for Dreams with a view toward assessing increasing levels of an individual's

TABLE 6.4
Object Representation Scale for Dreams

Scale Point (1). The subject's world seems to be completely lifeless, vacant, alien, strange; it is a world essentially without people; he experiences the world as either very stark and static or very fluid and formless; in short, the world for him is an unpredictable, desolate, often strange and bizarre place that he only rarely understands. For example: (a) The dream is virtually devoid of people or humanlike figures; if people are present as dream figures at all, they are unnamed, extremely vague, and incidental to the action of the dream; (b) the dream setting is very fluid or almost frozen or both; (c) as the dream is read, it may impact a distinct otherworldly, unsettling feeling.

Scale Point (2). People are experienced as insubstantial, fluid, more or less interchangeable. Though people do not seem bizarre or aggressive against one another, the subject experiences others in a vague and undefined fashion. The subject cannot really articulate what someone means to him because he has such an undifferentiated concept of what other people want, feel, or do. Such a subject may be unsure of what did what to whom, because his internal representations of other people are so unstable, diminished, and distorted and because his sense of his own boundaries and the boundaries of other people is so poor. For example: (a) A person changes into another person, comes to resemble another, or is a combination of two people; (b) some aspect of a dream character changes in an unreal way in the dream; (c) a dream character is a combination of two innocuous, stereotyped, fictional, or distant public figures—elves, gremlins, actors; (d) an animal metamorphoses in some way; (e) a person is dead or killed, but in nonbizarre ways—usually not in front of the dreamer, usually not including gory details.

Scale Point (4). The subject's experience of people is, to a great extent, fashioned around those of his needs that the other person can directly gratify and/or around those needs of the other person that the subject can directly gratify. In this sense, people are experienced in an incomplete way: Aspects of the other that do not bear directly on the exchange of gratification are only partially perceived and understood. For example: (a) A dream character interacts minimally with the dreamer; and what interaction there is involves the dream character satisfying emotional (instinctual) needs of the dreamer and/or the converse of that situation; (b) people interaction with the dreamer predominantly on a feeling level without much explicit interaction; (c) the dreamer is involved in self-directed activity exclusively—preening, admiring his own body, practicing something—with others either watching or absent.

Scale Point (5). The subject's world is populated by people who are neither fluid

(*continued*)

capacity for interpersonal relatedness. The scale includes at each developmentally graded point a global description of the representational world depicted by that point and two sample dreams. An abbreviated version of the scale, as recently advanced by Hatcher and Krohn (1980), is presented in Table 6.4. This scale assesses the degree to which people are experienced as whole, consistent, alive, complex, and separate entities. The instrument attempts to establish an ordinal scale ranging from the experience of others as absent, unknown, stark,

TABLE 6.4 (*Continued*)

nor massively distorted by poorly integrated affects; yet they have no real identity. The subject seems to experience other people as more or less interchangeable. Either people are seen as shadowy, with motives that are unclear to the dreamer, or else they are experienced in stereotyped ways. People do not really make sense to the subject: For example, he hears other people but is often unsure of exactly how they mean what they are saying; he is either deaf to what is implicit or reads a great deal of implication into what they are saying. There is no real depth, specificity, or uniqueness to the people in the subject's world. His world seems to be populated with passersbys who either differ little from one another or who fall into one of several rigid, superficial categories. For example: (a) If people known to the dreamer appear in the dream, they have no thoughts, feelings, or intentions; they may be doing things but with no sense of intent or goal; there is no explicit interaction with the dreamer; people may even talk to the dreamer or minimally interact with him, but the interaction or conversation is really only part of some action in the dream; (b) all the people in the dream are anonymous or nearly so; (c) much that is said and done by others in the dream seems unclear, vague, nonsensical, implicit to the dreamer, or highly symbolic; (d) people in the dream are described as innocuous stereotypes (e.g., "lazy men" or "lumberjack types").

Scale Point (8). The subject lives in a lively world of fully human objects. There is a sense of rapport with people and a well-developed understanding of their thoughts, feelings, and *conflicts*. There is a well-articulated internal model of people being involved with each other, including an understanding of why they form relationships, what they get out of them, and what interferes with them. Other people's behavior and personal characteristics are considered in perspective and remain open to reinterpretation. There is a good deal of self- and interpersonal awareness—indeed, a psychological-mindedness. Relationships are, for the most part, not neurotically conceived. For example: (a) A reflective comment is made in the dream report about what the dream is saying, or the self in the dreams reflects during the dream on some aspects of his feelings toward another dream character or on some aspect of that character's conflicts. More than reporting the feelings or wishes of a dream character, the subject spells out an awareness of some conflict(s) in the character, himself, or their relationship; (b) there is a creative use of humor in the dream, particularly centering around the human characters in the dream; (c) something particularly distinctive and subtle about a dream character is noted by the object; (d) the dream characters and their interactions seem only minimally directed by neurotic concerns. There is a maturity about the dream characters.

[a]From Hatcher and Krohn (1980).

desolate, and malignant to an alive, empathic sense of a differentiated, whole, complex human being.

In order to establish the reliability and construct validity of object representations as an empirically, researchable personality dimension, Krohn (1972) and Krohn and Mayman (1974) applied the dream scale across a range of projective media generated by patients selected across a broad spectrum of psychopathology. Data were gathered on patients from separate clinical agencies and three pairs of skilled clinical judges independently applied the scale to the manifest content of dreams, early memories, and Rorschach protocols. Krohn then asked the patients' therapist and the therapists' supervisors to: (1) use the scale to rate the patient's overt and manifest level of object relations; and (2) rate the degree of the patient's psychopathology on the Luborsky Health-Sickness Scale.

Interrater reliabilities on the various scales ranged from 58% to 79% exact agreement and from 74% to 89% agreement within one scale point. Significant correlations were found between the object representation scores across the range of projective data—dreams, early memories, and Rorschach responses, and between these object representation scores and criterion ratings made by the therapist and the therapists' supervisors of the manifest level of object relations and the degree of psychopathology. Analyzing the data through partial correlations, the dream and early memory scores emerged as the best predictors of therapist–supervisor ratings of patients' object relations, whereas the Rorschach ratings correlated most significantly with the global health–sickness score as an index of psychpathology. The ratings of the quality of object representations on the Rorschachs were consistently lower (less intact) than the ratings of the patients' object representations on either manifest dreams or early memories. The authors concluded that the rating of the quality of object representation on the Rorschach is a blend of the level of psychopathology and the quality of object relations, whereas the rating of object representation on the manifest content of dreams and early memories seem to provide a pure-measure of the quality of the patient's object relations.

Krohn and Mayman (1974) summarize their findings as follows:

> The fundamental conclusion to be drawn from this study is that level of object representation appears to be a salient, consistent, researchable personality dimension that expresses itself through a relatively diverse set of psychological avenues ranging from a realm as private as dream life to one as interpersonal as psychotherapy. Moreover, it is not a redundant construct synonymous with level of psychopathology or severity of symptomatology [p. 464].

Urist's (1973) study of object representations on the Rorschach initially reviewed the Rorschach protocols of 250 psychiatric inpatients to identify important qualities of object representation that appear in Rorschach responses. He formulated an integrity dimension of object representation—the degree to which objects and the self are experienced as having an enduring, stable, and internally consistent definition. The integrity dimension was assessed by five Rorschach variables: (1) body image; (2) degree of mutuality within relationships; (3) aliveness; (4) formal thinking; and (5) the degree of fusion in the images. A basic conceptual model behind these five scales, especially the mutuality factor, was the developmental progression of separation individuation from symbiosis to object constancy. These five Rorschach variables were correlated with ratings of patients' object representations gathered independently on other instruments.

Patients from several sources, representing a wide range of psychopathology, were given the Rorschach and a modifed TAT, asked to provide autobiographies, and were rated by the clinical staff. These data were rated on the five scales originally defined as part of integrity dimension. These data were factor analyzed and two primary factors emerged: (1) an "object relations" factor that consisted of ratings of object representation on the different instruments including the clinical judgments; and (2) a boundary factor based on tendencies toward fusion merger and thought disorder that reflected an inability to maintain the cognitive–perceptual boundary between self and other and between objects. The identification of a factor of fusion and thought disorder indicating boundary disturbances is consistent with the formulations of Blatt and his colleagues (Blatt, 1970; Blatt & Ritzler, 1974; Blatt & Wild, 1976; Blatt, Wild, & Ritzler, 1975) indicating the importance of identifying levels of thought disorder and boundary difficulties in seriously disturbed patients. In discussing the implications of his study, Urist (1973) notes:

> Particularly within this more severe realm of psychopathology, issues such as the psychosexual development of the impulse life do not seem to be those most relevant to making important diagnostic distinctions. A pure impulse–defense model generally will tend to blur distinctions between what in object relations terms are clearly different clinical phenomena that should be understood and treated differently. . . . Clinically, the important distinctions to be made among these individuals involved assessing regression within the ego and particularly . . . assessing the level of development of object relations. The high intercorrelation among the varous measures speaks to the validity of the gradations drawn by the scales, and points to their ability to make important distinctions in the structural development of self and object representations [pp. 132–133].

In summary, the research findings of Ryan, Krohn, and Urist, based on the theoretical conceptualizations and research methodology articulated by Mayman, provide further support for the importance of assessing object representations in clinical research and practice. Object representations assessed with several instruments (e.g., early memories, dreams, and the Rorschach) have significant relationships with independent assessments of the capacity to enter into and benefit from psychotherapy (Hatcher & Krohn, 1980; Ryan, 1973). Although Hatcher and Krohn (1980) failed to find a significant correlation between a prognostic evaluation for psychotherapy and object representation in the manifest content of dreams of borderline patients, they found that good prognosis for psychotherapy in neurotic patients was consistently associated with: (1) the capacity for introspection and the ability to see the sources of their problems and behavior as internal; (2) the capacity to tolerate the ambiguity and the irrational in themselves; and (3) the capacity to reflect on conflicts rather than translate them into action. It seems clear that the research group at the University of Michigan, led by Mayman, has developed a conceptual model and assessment procedures that have important potential for the study of different forms of psychopathology and for the study of the psychotherapeutic process.

In summarizing the contribution of Mayman and his colleagues at the University of Michigan one is reminded that it was Mayman (1963) who initially suggested the use of projective tests for the investigation of object representation when he called for an extension of the clinical or ''middle-level language'' of psychoanalysis to psychological test data. Mayman emphasized the importance of clarifying levels of language and abstraction and advocated a systematic coordination of ''middle-level'' and ''meta'' psychological concepts. This emphasis, however, was not designed to debunk metapsychology but, rather, to establish conceptual referents between abstract theory and the more subjective language of experience expressed in the treatment hour. Mayman's contributions revolve around an attempt to transpose the middle-level clinical theory of psychoanalysis into clinically meaningful, empirical, test-related, and researchable concepts. His efforts represent an attempt to add a more experiential, phenomenological, and object relational dimension to theory, clinical assessment, and research by systematizing the first-order abstractions of clinical psychoanalysis. Mayman's conceptual perspective is bolstered by his belief in the scientific credibility of an empathic clinical–intuitive approach to projective data and research; this represents a methodological cornerstone of his work. In terms of research, accent is placed on a clinically based methodology, on the development of means for capturing the complexity and unique nature of clinical phenomena, and on a qualitative approach to data collection and analysis. The specific research efforts of Mayman and his colleagues at the University of Michigan reflect a focal interest in thematic content—allowing the data to speak for themselves, a steadfast clinical locus that is experience-near and that is comprehended through empathic–intuitive skills while at the same time achieving psychometrically respectable levels of reliability and validity and, finally, a commitment to investigating variables directly relevant to psychoanalytic theory and the treatment process.

3. The Contributions of the Research Group at Yale University

A. *Introduction.*   Blatt and his colleagues at Yale, like a number of other psychoanalytically oriented investigators, have commented on "the gap between the theoretical superstructure of psychoanalysis—its metapsychology—and clinical psychoanalysis" and noted the need to

> develop a clinical theory based primarily on concepts of object relations . . . [a theory] which could facilitate the exploration and understanding of genetic, dynamic and adaptive aspects of personality organization . . . [a theory which] offers the potential for integrating the study of impairments in cognitive process, interpersonal relationships, and the representation of the self and the object world within a theoretical model which has etiological, as well as therapeutic, implications [Blatt, Wild, & Ritzler, 1975, pp. 235–236, 281].

Blatt (1975) in much of his research has also been concerned about the frequent failure of many research studies to utilize projective techniques in ways that could appropriately test clinical hypotheses. He (1975) discusses the myth that projective techniques provide unreliable and invalid data that have little to contribute to research as primarily a function of the failure of most research studies to use projective procedures in ways that are consistent with their utilization in the clinical context. Also, many studies fail to develop appropriate criteria for the validation of hypotheses derived from clinical experience. In particular, most research studies rely on the prediction of manifest behavior in a complex social context as the primary criterion for an assessment of psychological states. Blatt (1975) stresses that although we may be able to understand and effectively assess psychological variables, we may still not understand the relationships between internal psychological states and manifest behavior, particularly in a complex social matrix. Blatt calls for the utilization of more precise criteria in more restricted contexts that are understood and can be assessed with a high degree of reliability.

Much of the research conducted by Blatt and his colleagues at Yale have been based on the assumption that two basic features are unique to the human condition—the capacity for symbolic activity and our evolution and existence in a complex interpersonal matrix. Object representations—the symbolic expression of interpersonal relationships—are a primary expression of these two factors. The dimensions of the representational world, the content and structure of the concepts of the self and the object world, express man's unique symbolic capacities and aspects of his complex interpersonal experiences.

Although Blatt and Mayman share a commitment to bring into research the subtle differentiations and observations of the experienced clinician, they differ in that Mayman has focused primarily on theme and content, whereas Blatt and his colleagues have primarily assessed the structural or formal dimensions of object representation. Much of Blatt's clinical research has attempted to assess dimensions of structure that are assumed to constitute a substrate of manifest behavior and content. Blatt assumes that structural dimensions can be assessed with acceptable levels of reliability and that they provide valid data that have considerable generality for understanding human functioning because they are less vulnerable to conscious distortion and the impact of the situational context.

The assessment of structure is a central theoretical construct in multiple areas of discourse. In numerous areas of contemporary investigation there has been a search for the identification of inherent principles of organization that define the relationships among elements and their potential transformations in hierarchically organized systems. This interest in underlying structural principles of organization has been a major emphasis in the physical and biological sciences, as well as in the social sciences and the humanities. In all these disciplines there has been increasing recognition of the need to identify and understand the principles of structural organization that define the interrelationships and potential transformations of elements that determine variations of surface phenomena. Despite this emphasis on underlying structure in numerous fields throughout the twentieth century, large segments of psychology and psychiatry still maintain a primary emphasis on manifest behavior and overt symptoms. There have been notable exceptions, of course, and these exceptions have made major contributions to the understanding of some of the principles inherent in human behavior. These include the Gestalt analysis of perception, contemporary approaches to cognitive processes including the work of Piaget, Werner, Bartlett and others, and of course psychoanalytic theory. The recent contributions of developmental psychoanalysts (Fraiberg, 1969; A. Freud, 1965; Gouin-Decarie, 1965; Jacobson, 1964, Mahler, 1968; Wolff, 1967; etc.) and cognitive developmental psychologists (Piaget, 1954; Werner, 1948) have provided a basis for understanding aspects of the complex cognitive and interpersonal factors inherent in the structural organization that underlie much of manifest behavior (Blatt, 1978).

The development of cognitive schemata, especially the representation of self and others, is considered a central process in both psychoanalytic theory and developmental psychology. Progress in the development of representations is the result of increased levels of internalization and the product of each major development phase. Object representations and mental schemata become increasingly differentiated, integrated, and accurate. They proceed from being global to representations that closely correspond to reality and are well-articulated, highly differentiated, and integrated. These representations evolve from images of objects immediately present in the perceptual field, to "symbolic evocation of absent realities" (Piaget, 1954). Recent research (Bell, 1968, 1970; Clarke-

Stewart, 1973; Gouin-Decarie, 1965) indicates that the child's development of the concept of the inanimate object (as studied by developmental psychologists) and the child's development of the concept of self and the object world (as studied by psychoanalytic theorists) are interrelated and are part of the same developmental process. The study of the representational world in both developmental psychology and psychoanalytic theory is the study of the development of cognitive schemata that give organization and direction to manifest behavior and are expressed in all forms of behavior, including interpersonal relationships, perceptual, and cognitive functions, and conceptions of oneself and others. Blatt (1974; Blatt, Wild & Ritzler, 1975) assumes that fuller understanding of the development of these cognitive schemata—the concepts of the self and the object world—throughout the life cycle, will provide further insight into personality development and various forms of psychopathology.

Within this theoretical commitment to the study of the structure of object and self representations based upon an integration of concepts from cognitive developmental psychology and psychoanalytic theory, Blatt and his colleagues have approached the investigation of object representation in several ways. They have studied the differentiation of boundaries between independent objects (self and nonself) and inside and outside (fantasy and reality) as the initial and most fundamental stages in the development of object representation. Blatt (1970), Blatt and Ritzler (1974), and Brenneis (1971) investigated several levels or types of boundary disturbance in psychosis. Blatt and his colleagues have also investigated more advanced levels of object representation in normal development and in various types of psychopathology. They have investigated aspects of the human response on the Rorschach and the structure and content of object representations in spontaneous, open-ended descriptions of significant others. Utilizing concepts from developmental cognitive psychology and psychoanalytic theory, they have sought to examine the validity of differentiations within various types of psychopathology. They also considered the implications of their findings about the basic experiences of individuals with different types of psychopathology and how this may provide further insight into the mutative factors of the psychotherapeutic process.

B. Disturbances of Boundary Representation.   In a review of the theoretical, clinical, and research literature on schizophrenia Blatt and Wild (1976) examined the hpothesis that schizophrenia can best be understood as an impairment in the capacity to represent basic boundary differentiations. Based on psychoanalytic theory and concepts from developmental psychology, they suggested that one of the earliest and most fundamental cognitive structures in psychological development is the articulation of boundaries. Initially, in development, representations of independent objects (including self and nonself) are merged and fused. Subsequently, after a differentiation between independent objects has been established, there may be difficulty distinguishing the internal representation of the object from the actual object. The individual may have difficulty distinguishing between the external object and associations and reactions to the object; that is, between inside and outside, between fantasy and reality. Eventually with repeated experiences with a consistent need-gratifying object, the child develops the capacity to distinguish the actual object from its mental representation. The child comes to know that the idea of the object is inside, whereas the object itself is outside. The differentiations between self and nonself, between inside and outside, and between the object and mental representations of the object are critical steps in the development of representations. Impaired representations in psychotic adolescents and adults seem to evolve from disturbances in the early stages of development of object representations. The importance of disruptions in the differentiation and representations of boundaries in psychotic states has been suggested in many clinical observations and theoretical formulations (Federn, 1952; A. Freud, 1956; Freud, 1936; Lidz, 1973; Lidz & Lidz, 1952; Rosenfeld & Sprince, 1963; Searles, 1965; Tausk, 1919). Numerous clinicians have described the schizophrenic patients' dilemmas concerning intimacy and how they yearn for symbolic union with the mother but become frightened of a complete loss of self and an annihilation of the object as they begin to merge with the symbiotic partner (Fromm-Reichmann, 1959). This dilemma concerning intimacy in the symbiotic relatedness of the schizophrenic has been conceptualized as a "need–fear dilemma" (Burnham, Gladstone, & Gibson, 1969) in which there is "both an inordinate need and an inordinate fear of objects." The schizophrenic's psychological existence is contingent not only on maintaing contact with the object but on feeling fused with and inseparable from it. But this fusion is also threatening to the schizophrenic's tenous sense of differentiation and he becomes fearful of "domination, enslavement, or engulfment," often alternating between "clinging to" and "avoiding" objects. The yearning for symbiotic union and fear of dissolution and annihilation in this relationship can be understood as reflecting, in part, a failure to establish adequate concepts of the self and of the object. Separation is experienced as total and permanent, whereas closeness and intimacy threaten the tentative differentiation between self and object (Rosenfeld & Sprince, 1963). Impaired representations of boundaries are expressed in the multifaceted cognitive and perceptual dysfunctioning observed in schizophrenia. Impaired representations of boundaries interfere with reality testing and create diffuse perception in which there is difficulty in articulating figure from ground and in maintaining perceptual constancy. Attention is disrupted because there is difficulty distinuishing relevant from irrelevant stimuli; and language and concept formation are disordered because of an inability to maintain the separation among independent concepts, thoughts, and images (Blatt & Wild, 1976; Blatt, et al., 1975).

The formulation of schizophrenia as an expression of disturbances in the capacity to represent boundaries also provides a theoretical framework for understanding paranoid psychosis. There is evidence that differentiation is greater in paranoid patients than in nonparanoid patients and even in normals. There are indications that paranoid patients struggle, in exaggerated ways, to preserve a sense of boundaries. Through the use of heightened cognitive control, exaggerated perceptual articulation, and hyperalert attention, the paranoid patient struggles desperately to keep events and experiences separate and distinct and to preserve and solidify boundaries. According to Blatt et al. (1975), "A preoccupation with power, control, and autonomy, excessive suspiciousness, the isolation of affect, and keeping people at a distance because they are dangerous and threatening may also be expressions of attempts to maintain individuation and separation and to defend against the temptation and threat of merging and fusing" (p. 254).

In research utilizing the Rorschach (Blatt, 1970; Blatt & Ritzler, 1974) and the manifest content of dreams (Brenneis, 1971), the degree of impairment of boundary articulation was found to have important implications for understanding levels and severity of psychosis. Based on formulations from developmental psychology (Piaget, 1954; Werner, 1948; Werner & Kaplan, 1963) and psychoanalytic theory (A. Freud, 1961, 1962; Jacobson, 1964; Mahler, 1968; Schafer, 1968), Blatt and Ritzler (1974) define boundary differentiations as including the initial capacity to differentiate between objects including self-nonself and later to differentiate between the actual object and the mental representation and verbal signifier used to designate the object—a differentation between outside and inside. These various difficulties in maintaining boundaries are often expressed in several different types of thought disorder that Rapaport et al. (1945) noted on the Rorschach. As discussed by Blatt and Ritzler (1974), difficulties in maintaining boundaries between independent objects are indicated by the Rorschach contamination response in which there is a merging and fusing of independent percepts and concepts. The boundaries between separate ideas, images, or concepts are lost, and they merge and fuse into a single discordant unit. (An example of contamination is the response "rabbit hand" to the lower detail of Card X. The images of a rabbit and a hand lose their separateness and fuse into a single response.)

Difficulties in maintaining boundary between inside and outside are indicated by the confabulation response on the Rorschach in which there is a loss of the distinction between an external perception and the personal association and reaction to the perception. What initially may have been an accurate perception becomes lost in extensive, unrealistic, personal elaborations and associations. (An example of a confabulation is the response to Card IX "Looks like twins on the bottom. It looks spiritual or something like the beginning of the world. The division line in the middle is the difference between them, heaven or earth or something.") The initially accurate human response to the lower detail of the card is lost in extensive, unrealistic associations.

A third and less severe level of boundary disturbance is expressed in the fabulized combination response in which independent percepts or concepts maintain their definition and separateness but are placed in some illogical combination simply because they are spatially contiguous. Separate images or concepts do not merge and fuse, and there is no intrusion of unrealistic personal associations, but rather independent images are placed in some inappropriate relationship. In fabulized combinations, a spatial relationship is taken as indicating a real relationship between objects even though the relationship is unrealistic. In a fabulized combination, such as the response "praire dogs standing on a butterfly" given to Card VIII, each image maintains its separate definition and integrity, and the boundary disturbance is expressed in the unrealistic relationship between two separate images.

These three types of thought disorder on the Rorschach (contaminations, confabulations, and fabulized combinations) were initially defined by Rapaport et al. (1945) and later elaborated by Holt (1963), who indicated that they can be scored with a high degree of reliability. Blatt and Ritzler (1974) found that the various levels of disruption of boundary articulation, as measured by types of thought disorder, were related to the relative intactness of a variety of ego functions—to the capacity for reality testing, to the quality of interpersonal relations, and to the nature of object representations. Poorly articulated boundaries occurred primarily in more disturbed, chronic patients who have poor or impoverished personal relationships, seriously impaired ego functions, and a lifelong history of estrangement, isolation, and generally poor adjustment. Brenneis (1971) found that there were a significantly greater number of boundary disturbances in the manifest content of dreams of schizophrenic patients than there were in psychiatric patients with diagnoses other than schizophrenia. Thought disorder involving more adequately articulated boundary distinctions occurs primarily in paranoid patients and those with more acute psychological disorders (Blatt et al., 1975). Johnson (1980) recently found a significant negative ($p < .05$) correlation between thought disorder indicating boundary disruption as defined by Blatt and Ritzler (1974) and independent estimates of paranoid pathology. Johnson's findings are consistent with the conclusions of Blatt and Ritzler (1974) that patients with greater boundary articulation seem to be more actively involved in interpersonal relationships, but these interactions are often characterized by intensity, hostility, and acting out. These patients seem to have more acute pathology, are more fragmented, and are more responsive to therapy.

Blatt and Ritzler found that the degree of boundary disturbance in thought disorder is also related to the concept of the object. Patients with less intact boundary differentiation had a significantly greater number of Rorschach responses and dreams that blended human and inanimate features. These blends of human and inanimate features on the Rorschach could be most subtle, such as in responses like "Pinocchio, Chessman, Lincoln masks, a bust of George Washington, or a cut-out paper doll." The greater number of representations with a blend of human and inanimate features in patients with less intact boundary differentiation supports the hypothesis (Jacobson, 1964; Mahler, 1968; Searles, 1965) that failure in basic individuation and separation is accompanied by difficulty in maintaining the distinction between human, animate, and inanimate realms.

Disturbances in boundary articulation seem to occur in schizophrenic patients in response to stress and conflict. These regressions may occur briefly or persist for a considerable time. Disruptions of boundary representations may occur in borderline patients only partially and temporarily and only after considerable stress and conflict; in more seriously disturbed patients, disturbances in boundary representations are more easily provoked and persist for a considerable time. But the data suggest that a vulnerability in the basic stability of boundary representation is a primary dimension in psychosis.

C. The Concept of the Object on the Rorschach.

1. Normal Development of the Concept of the Object

Based on the intriguing finding that the degree of boundary disturbance in various types of thought disorder are related to distorted representations of human figures (human–inanimate blends), Blatt, Brenneis, Schimek, and Glick (1976) conducted a detailed analysis of the human responses on the Rorschach. The human response to the Rorschach is an ideal dimension for studying object representations. The human response provides a vehicle for assessing the content and the level of cognitive organization in the concepts of self and of the object world.

Using the theoretical formulations of Werner (Werner, 1948; Werner & Kaplan, 1963) and clinical experience as points of departure, Blatt et al., (1976) developed an extensive manual for rating Rorschach human responses in three major areas: differentiation, articulation, and integration. Within each of these areas, categories were established along a developmental continuum. Table 6.5 represents a condensed version of the Developmental Analysis of the Concept of the Object Scale.

TABLE 6.5
Developmental Analysis of the Concept of the Object

A.   *Accuracy of the response*

Responses are classified as perceptually accurate or inaccurate as conforming the configuration of the stimulus properties of the card (F+, F±, F∓, F−). F+ or F± responses are classified as accurate and F- responses and F∓ responses are classified as inaccurate (Rapaport, 1945; Allison, Blatt, & Zimet, 1968)

B.   *Differentiation*

Here responses are classified according to types of figures perceived; whether the figure or subject of the action are quasi-human details: (Hd); human details: Hd; full quasi-human figures: (H); and full human figures: H.

1. *Quasi-human details.* Part of a quasi-human figure is specified.
2. *Human details.* Part of a human figure is specified as human.
3. *Quasi-human responses.* Figures that are whole but less than human or not definitely specified as human.
4. *Human responses.* The figure must be whole and clearly human.

C.   *Articulation*

Responses are scored on the basis of types of attributes ascribed to the figures. A total of seven types of attributes are considered. These types of attributes were selected because they seem to provide information about human or quasi-human figures. The analyses are not concerned with the sheer detailing of features, and a distinction is made between appropriate and inappropriate articulation. The analyses are only concerned with articulations that enrich a human or quasi-human response, that enlarge a listener's knowledge about qualities of the figures represented. A response that states that a man has a head, hands, and feet does not enlarge the listener's knowledge about the man. Possession of these features is presupposed by the initial response, "man." An articulation such as "a man with wings" is scored as an inappropriate articulation because it is an elaboration that adds inappropriate specification of the features of the human or quasi-human figure. There are two general types of articulation: the articulation of (1) perceptual and (2) functional attributes.

1. *Perceptual characteristics:*

   a. *Size or physical structure.* Size or structure is only scored as articulated if there is a *qualitative* description of aspects of body parts or the whole body that are more than a simple enumeration of standard part features. Certain aspects of facial expression are scored as articulations of size or structure including "eyes closed" or "mouth open" in which the description of facial expression amounts to something more than just a description of physical appearance.
   b. *Clothing or hairstyle.* There has to be a qualitative description of some aspect of *either* clothing *or* hairstyle that enriches the description of the figure. Simple mention of items of clothing implied by the response does not enrich one's understanding of the figure and is, therefore, not scored as an articulation.

(continued)

TABLE 6.5 (*Continued*)

c. *Posture.* Posture is scored if the description of body posture is separate from the verb describing the activity of the figure or if the description of facial expression goes beyond mere articulation of the physical appearance of features in that it contains a sense of movement or feeling. Posture is *not* scored if body posture is implied in the verb rather than being separately articulated or if it is simply a description of a figure's position in space (e.g., facing outward).

2. *Functional characteristics:*

a. *Sex.* A specific mention of sex of the figure or an assignment to an occupational category that clearly implies a particular sexual identity. If the final sexual identity is not decided but alternatives are precisely considered, sex is scored as articulated. If, however, the indecision is based upon a vague characterization of the figure with an emphasis upon the sexual nature of the figure as a whole, sex is *not* considered articulated.

b. *Age.* Specific reference is made to some age category that the figure belongs.

c. *Role.* When figures are human, a clear reference to the work a figure does (occupation) is scored as an articulation of role. With regard to quasi-human figures, role is scored if the manner in which the figure if represented implies that it would engage in certain activities rather than others. When sexual identity is clearly indicated in a role designation, both sex and role are scored as articulated. Such a situation exists in responses such as "mother," "witch," "priest."

d. *Specific identity.* Here a figure must be named as a specific character in history, literature, etc. To the degree that age, sex, and occupation are clearly indicated in the specific identity, these features are also scored as articulated. Thus, in the response "Charles DeGaulle," sex and occupation are specified. Such is not the case in the response "piglet."

3. *Degree of articulation.* This is the simple enumeration of the total number of types of features articulated in the seven types of attribution (size, clothing or hairstyle, posture, sex, age, role, and specific identity). Thus, for any single Rorschach response, a total of seven types of features could be articulated. The average number of features taken into account in each human or quasi-human response constitutes the score for the degree of articulation of individual figures.

D.   *Motivation of action*

This is a rating of the degree of internality of the motivation of action attributed to the figures (unmotivated, reactive, and intentional). Reactive explanations involve a focus on past events and behavior explained in terms of causal factors; one assumes that, for certain prior reasons, an individual *had* to do a certain thing. By contrast, intentionality is proactive and implies an orientation toward the present or future. The individual *chooses* to do something to attain a certain end or goal. The ability to choose between motives and to undertake an activity

(*continued*)

TABLE 6.5 *(Continued)*

purposively implies greater differentiation between subject and action than is the case when an individual is impelled to take an action because of past occurrences. For this reason, the analysis of action considers whether or not a motive was provided and whether the motivation was reactive (causal) or intentional.

E.   *Object-action integration*

This is a rating of the degree of integration of the object and its action. Four levels of integration of the object with its action are distinguished (fused, incongruent, nonspecific, and congruent).

1. *Fusion of object and action.* Responses in this category involve an amorphous object in which the object and its action are fused. The object possesses no separate qualities of its own and is defined only in terms of its activity. Nothing is known about the object except what it is doing

2. *Incongruent integration of object and action.* Responses in this category involve those in which there is some separate articulation of object and action. Something is known about the object apart from its activity, but (nevertheless) the activity is incongruous and unrelated to the defined nature of the object. The articulation of action detracts from rather than enriches the articulation of the object.

3. *Nonspecific integration of object and action.* In this category there is some separate articulation of object and its action, but the relationship between the object and its action is nonspecific. The figures, as defined, can engage in the activity described but there is no special fit between object and action. Many other kinds of objects could engage in the activity described. Thus, although the articulation of action does not detract from the articulation of the object, neither does it enrich it.

4. *Congruent integration of object and action.* Responses in this category involve a separate articulation of the object and the nature of its action. The action is particularly suited to the defined nature of the object. By way of contrast with the preceding category, not only must the action be something the object might do, it must be something that the object would be especially likely to do. There is an integrated and particularly well-suited relationship between the object and the specified action. The articulation of the action enriches the image of the object. In responses where the role definition of the object is nothing more than a literal restatement of the action, object and action are not considered integrated. Responses like "dancer's dancing," or "singer's singing" are scored as nonspecified (level 3) relationships. However, responses such as "ballerina dancing" or "character from a Rudolph Friml opera singing" are classified as a congruent integration of object and action.

F.   *Content of action*

1. *Malevolent.* The action is aggressive or destructive or the results of the activity implies destruction or harm or fear of harm.

2. *Benevolent.* The activity is not destructive, harmful, or aggressive. It may be neutral or it may reflect a warm, positive quality.

(continued)

TABLE 6.5 (*Continued*)

G.	*Nature of interaction*

This analysis applies to all responses involving at least two human or quasi-human figures or where a second figure is not directly perceived, but its presence is implied by the nature of the action.

1. *Active-passive interaction.* Two figures involved in an interaction in which one figure is acting upon another figure in an active-passive relationship. One figure is active and the other is entirely passive, so while acted upon, it does not respond in any way.
2. *Active-reactive interaction.* In this type of interaction the figures may be unequal. While one figure is definitely the agent of the activity, acting upon another figure, the second figure is reactive or responsive to the action of the other.
3. *Active-active interaction.* In a third type of interaction, both figures contribute equally to the activity, and the interaction is mutual.

---

[a] From Blatt, Brenneis, Schimek, and Glick (1976).

The development of human responses was studied in a longitudinal sample of normal subjects over a 20-year period from early adolescence to young adulthood. Thirty-seven normal subjects had been given the Rorschach at ages 11–12, 13–14, 17–18, and 30, and these protocols were analyzed in a repeated measures design.

Human responses given to the Rorschach show consistent changes with development. In normal development from preadolescence (age 11–12) to adulthood (age 30) there was a marked increase in the number of well-differentiated, highly articulated, and integrated human figures. There was an increase in the attribution of activity that was congruent with important characteristics of the figures. There was also a significant increase in the degree to which the objects were seen in constructive and positive interactions.

2. The Concept of the Object in Psychosis

The human responses of a sample ($N = 48$) of seriously disturbed, borderline and psychotic adolescent and young adults (mean age 23.5) were compared with the human responses of the normal sample at age 18. In comparison to the human responses of the normal sample, the seriously disturbed adolescent and young adult inpatients had a significantly greater number of human responses at lower developmental levels, that is, responses that were more often quasi-human, distorted, unmotivated, incongruent, passive, and malevolent. But what was surprising was that these responses at lower developmental levels in patients occurred primarily on *accurately* perceived responses. What was even more surprising was the fact that patients had a significantly greater number of responses at higher developmental levels than normals on inaccurately perceived responses. That is, patients had a significantly greater number of developmentally more advanced responses, responses that were undistorted,˙ intact, functionally articulated, integrated and benevolent, than did normals, on *inaccurately* perceived responses (Blatt et al., 1976). Ritzler, Zambianco, Harder, & Kaskey, (1980) also studied the concept of the object on 67 psychotic patients and 20 normals and replicated the findings of Blatt et al. (1976). Ritzler et al. also found that psychotic patients have higher developmental levels of articulation and integration on inaccurately perceived (F−) human responses than do normals, but even further they observed that this pattern was more apparent in schizophrenic than in nonschizophrenic psychotic patients.

These findings indicate that patients, as compared to normals, function at lower developmental levels when in contact with conventional reality but that patients function at higher developmental levels than normals when they give idiosyncratic interpretations of reality. In an attempt to understand this phenomenon further, Blatt et al. (1976) examined in detail the human responses of patients that were inaccurately perceived but at developmentally more advanced levels. These responses did not seem to occur on any particular card, but the content of the responses was almost always positive and tended to be grandiose and mythical, such as figures of Napoleon, Lincoln, a soldier from a Friml opera, a princess, the Little King, a martian, and a knight. Many of these responses seemed to be preformed images that were internally determined and elaborated with little contact with the external stimulus. But they were well-articulated, organized, and integrated. They stood in sharp contrast to the accurately perceived responses of patients that were at developmentally lower levels of organization.

The data consistently indicated that the capacity to perceive reality adequately does not aid psychotic patients to organize their experiences more effectively and to function at higher developmental levels. Quite to the contrary, it seems that in psychotic patients contact with reality, at least in the convential sense, brings with it responses that are at lower developmental levels of thinking and contain malevolent content. It is primarily in the inaccurately perceived responses, when idiosyncratic interpretations of reality are given, that the psychotic patients can function at developmentally higher levels and portray a world that is more differentiated, well-articulated, integrated, benevolent, and kind.

Thus, the data seem to suggest that there are at least two dimensions in the psychotic experience. First, when contact with conventional reality is maintained, the psychotic individual functions at a developmentally lower level and perceives and experiences the world as distorted, undifferentiated, fragmented, malevolent, and destructive. The second dimension indicates that psychotic patients have greater proclivity for experiencing the world unrealistically, but within these unrealistic experiences they are able to function at developmentally higher levels and experience the world as kind and benevolent. For psychotic patients, adequate interpretation of reality seems to be a painful and disruptive experience, and they retreat and withdraw to find comfort and peace. Psychotic patients appear more disorganized when they are struggling to deal with and integrate a painful reality and less disorganized when absorbed in unrealistic experineces. It is only in the most seriously disturbed patients, those with severe boundary disturbances, that both accurately and inaccurately perceived responses seem to be at lower developmental levels. The findings that some seriously disturbed patients have a significantly greater number of human responses that are inaccurate but at higher developmental levels than normals raises a number of complex and important issues about the nature of the psychotic experience (Blatt, et al., 1976). In a recent paper, Blatt and his colleagues (Blatt, Schimek, & Brenneis, 1980) have considered the implications of these findings for the therapeutic process with seriously disturbed patients.

3. The Concept of the Object in Various Types of Psychopathology

Blatt and Lerner (1982), utilizing the object representation scoring manual developed by Blatt et al. (1976), examined the quality of object representation in several patients independently selected as prototypic examples of different clinical disorders. In a clinical analysis of the structure, content and sequence of object representations on the Rorschach, Blatt and Lerner found that there were unique qualities of object representation in various forms of psychopathology. In a nonparanoid schizophrenic patient, the representations were both inaccurate and at the lower developmental levels of differentiation—that is, involving quasi-human and part properties rather than full human figures. They were sparsely and sometimes inappropriately articulated and elaborated and were represented as inert or involved in essentially unmotivated action. There was relatively little interaction between figures, and the content was essentially barren, except for possibly an occasional benign theme, which may reflect restitutional fantasies (Blatt, Schimek & Brenneis, 1980). In contrast, representations in a patient independently diagnosed as having an anaclitic depression or infantile character were usually accurately perceived, total human figures, which were minimally and superficially elaborated (articulated). They were seen as either inactive or involved in action that was usually unmotivated. There was some interaction between figures, but this was primarily an active–passive relationship in which one figure was represented as vulnerable in a depriving, rejecting, undependable relationship. There was little trust in these interpersonal interactions, but this lack of trust did not appear to have a paranoid quality. The destructive interactions were not represented as malignant and intentional, but rather, in a more benign way, as just the way things are. People were represented as undependable and frightening.

In a narcissistic borderline patient, there was a gradual deterioration of object representations. Initially intact, accurately represented, full human figures gradually gave way to inaccurate, inappropriately elaborated, quasi-human representations. There seemed to be a superficial intact quality to the initial responses of benevolent and conventional relationships between figures. Although there was a superficially appropriate and reasonable interaction between figures, the action of each individual figure lacked inner definition, direction, and purpose. There was little meaning or purpose attributed to the action of each individual. Those initial representations that indicated a superficially intact, socially appropriate level of functioning soon gave way to responses that indicate a poorly defined structure. There was a gradual deterioration in the quality of the concept of the object as the representations changed from full human figures to quasi-human figures and quasi-human part properties. Eventually, these responses became inaccurately perceived and inappropriately elaborated. Thus, either with time and/or stress there was a steady and progressive deterioration of the object representations from accurate, well-differentiated, appropriately articulated, full human figures to inaccurately perceived, inappropriately articulated, quasi-human figures and part properties.

In a serious suicidal patient with an introjective depression and profound feelings of self-criticism and guilt (Blatt, 1974), there was an alternation between object representations at a high developmental level (full human figures, accurately perceived, and richly elaborated) with seriously impaired representations (quasi-human details, inaccurately perceived, extensively and inappropriately articulated, and elaborated, in which the activity had a high degree of destructive, malevolent intent). The alternation of these extreme responses expressed both the high developmental level of introjective depression as well as the negative hostile introjects that frequently drive this type of patient to suicide (Blatt, 1974; Blatt, Quinlan, Chevron, McDonald, & Zuroff, 1982).

The object representation of a delinquent adolescent, in contrast, was filled with conventional responses of popular, full human figures, but these were poorly articulated and the action lacked purpose and direction. The action was nonspecific and there was a general lack of detail and elaboration of the accurately perceived figures. There was a representation of superficial, socially appropriate action and interaction, but each individual figure had little inner direction and purpose. But, in contrast to the borderline patient, there was no gradual disintegration in the quality and developmental level of the object representation.

In a patient diagnosed as hysteric, the object representations were accurately perceived, full human figures were well articulated and elaborated, but this articulation was primarily in terms of external, physical details rather than internal, more personal attributes. There was an occasional inappropriate articulation and this usually involved sexual details. The figures were seen as engaged in benevolent but unmotivated activity. There was little internality to the motivation of the action of the figures, things seemed simply to occur. But the interaction between figures was represented as mutual and reciprocal (active–active) and the content of this interaction was usually benevolent and pleasant, almost childlike.

Based on the clinical analyses of these prototypic cases, Blatt and Lerner (1982) concluded that these are important, consistent differences in the structure and content of object representations in patients with different types of psychopathology. These clinical data indicate sufficient basis to use these concepts of object representation in a systematic and empirical study of various forms of psychopathology. In fact several empirical studies, primarily dissertations conducted at Yale, have recently utilized the object representation scale and have found significant differences between different diagnostic groups. Spear (1978), using a summation score of the six dimensions of object representation, found significantly ($p < .01$) greater impairment in the developmental level of object representations in schizophrenic patients than in patients independently diagnosed as borderline. Johnson (1980) found that a measure of field independence correlated significantly ($p < .05$) with the degree of perceptual articulation of object representation and with more advanced developmental level of interaction. Field-independent patients represented more interpersonal interactions as mutual and reciprocal (active–active) ($p < .001$). The developmental level of interactions was also significantly inversely correlated ($p < .001$), with severity of thought disorder defined in degree of boundary disturbance (Blatt & Ritzler, 1974).

In studying the quality of object representation in the Rorschach and at role-playing tasks, Johnson (1980) found a significant ($p < .05$) correlation between the congruence of the object and its action on the Rorschach (Blatt, et al., 1976) and the portrayal of congruent human interactions in role playing. Fibel's (1979) study of experiences of depression in a sample of seriously disturbed adolescent and young adult inpatients found significant and positive correlations between measures of object representation on the Rorschach with independent clinical assessment of the quality of interpersonal relations as defined by developmental stages based on the conceptualizations of Mahler (1975).

In a study of therapeutic change in long-term (12–18 months) hospitalization, Spear (1978) and Spear and Schwager (1980) compared changes in object representation in paranoid and nonparanoid schizophrenic patients. Paranoid schizophrenic patients had an increase in the number of Rorschach responses and thought disorder but a decrease in the developmental level of object representations. Nonparanoid (undifferentiated) schizophrenic patients, in contrast, had a decrease in the number of responses and in thought disorder but an increase in F + % and in the developmental level of object representations. Spear and Schwager (1980) concluded that therapeutic change in paranoid patients involves a decrease in the use of rigid, overdifferentiated defenses and an increased openness and flexibility. The therapeutic change in nonparanoid patients, in contrast, is expressed in an increase in control, adaption, and the quality of interpersonal relations. In a detailed study of several cases to elaborate these findings, Spear (1978) found that the object representation of a nonparanoid, undifferentiated, schizophrenic patient showed substantial increase in differentiation (more whole, intact human figures), fuller articulation of both perceptual as well as functional characteristics, and the representation of more congruent and intentional actions. There was also an increase in the accuracy (F + %) of human responses. In a paranoid patient there was an increase in the number of full human figures on the Rorschach that were more fully articulated. There was an increase in the representation of figures involved in more intentional action that was congruent with the specific attributes of the object. In contrast, however, changes in the conventional Rorschach measures in both cases were inconclusive and equivocal. Spear (1978), p. 7) concludes that measures of object representation developed by Blatt et al. ''appear to present a clearer picture of psychological improvement of these (schizophrenic) patients than does a traditional assessment of changes in the formal scoring patterns and thought organization'' on the Rorschach. These findings suggest than an increased capacity for developmentally more advanced object representations on the Rorschach is more indicative of consistent improvement in psychotherapy with schizophrenic patients than improvements in thought disorder or other aspects of thought organization. Improvement in object representations not only may indicate improved interpersonal relationships but can also indicate greater capacity and willingness to enter into the interpersonal process of psychotherapy.

D. The Concept of the Object in Spontaneous Descriptions of Significant Figures. Blatt and his colleagues (Blatt, Wein, Chevron, & Quinlan, 1979) developed another method of asssessing the content and structure of object representation. Based on clinical data and a theoretical model that integrates concepts from cognitive developmental psychology and psychoanalytic theory, they developed a method for analyzing spontaneous, open-end descriptions of individuals, of others, and of the self. The spontaneous description of significant figures, obtained in either written form or recorded verbally, are evaluated for both content and structural organization. Judges are able to rate, with satisfactory reliability, the following characteristics on a 7-point scale: affectionate, ambitious and striving, benevolent, warm, degree of constructive involvement, intellectual, judgmental, positive ideal, nurturant, punitive, successful, and strong. Judges were also able to rate, on a 3-point scale, the degree of ambivalence the subject felt toward the individual. These 13 characteristics, along with an estimate of verbal fluency of the descriptions, were subjected to a primary-components factor analysis with varimax rotation, and three primary factors emerged that were defined as nurturance, striving, and verbal fluency. The nurturance factor accounted for 40% of the variance and contained significant (> .400) loadings for the characteristics of nurturance, positive ideal, benevolence, warmth, constructive involvement, affectionate, strength, and success. The striving factor accounted for 29% of the variance and contained significant loadings for the characteristics of judgmental, ambitious, punitive, intellectual, ambivalence, success, and strength. The third factor, verbal fluency, accounted for 8% of the variance.

In addition, judges were able to rate, with acceptable levels of reliability, the conceptual level of the descriptions. The conceptual level, scored according to formulations based on concepts of the epigenetic levels of object representation derived from an integration of psychoanalytic and cognitive developmental theory (Blatt, 1974), is an assessment of the cognitive structural organization of the descriptions utilizing the following scale:

1. Sensorimotor-Preoperational Level (Score 1)

The individual is described primarily by his/her activities in reference to the gratification or frustration he/she provides. The description has a personal, subjective focus, with little sense of the individual as a separate and independent entity; he/she is defined primarily in terms of the pleasure or pain he/she provides the subject.

2. Concrete Perceptual Level (Score 3)

The individual is described as a separate entity, but the description is primarily in concrete, literal, often physical terms. There is a globality to the description and an emphasis primarily on what the object literally looks like in its external characteristics or physical properties. There is little appreciation of partial attributes or features. Emphasis is often on how the person appears in his/her external characteristics.

3. Iconic Level

A. *External iconic (Score 5).* The individual is described primarily on the basis of his/her functional attributes and the unique activities that exist independent of any direct or explicit reference to the gratification or frustration he/she provides the subject.

B. *Internal iconic (Score 7).* The individual is described by his/her attributes and properties, not in terms of actions or functions but rather in terms of internal dimensions such as values, thoughts, and feelings.

In both the external and internal iconic levels, the descriptions are primarily undimensional. They do not describe a complexity of actions, feelings, or values in which there are various levels (e.g., manifest behavior versus more latent feelings). There is no subtlety, apparent contradiction, complexity, or development over time.

4. Conceptual Level (Score 9)

The individual is described in a way that integrates all the prior levels. There is an appreciation of the internal in its own right as well as in contrast to the external. Also, there may be a time line with an appreciation of changes and variations. There may be a sense of disjunctiveness in which the manifest, literal, and concrete may appear in contradiction to more internal dimensions, but the apparent contradiction is resolved in an integrated, complex synthesis. At this level, there can be comments about the need-gratifying attributes and physical and functional characteristics of the individual, but the description indicates that the individual is experienced in complex, integrated ways and that a number of different attributes and functions are integrated in a cohesive, complex synthesis.

In the initial study utilizing this procedure, college students were asked to write a brief, one page, description of their mother and of their father. They were allowed 5 minutes for each description. The study was designed to investigate the relations between the intensity and type of depressive experiences in a non-clinical sample and the content and cognitive organization of descriptions of parents. To assess the concurrent validity of the parental descriptions, the three factors of the parental descriptions (nurturance, striving, and fluency as well as conceptual level of descriptions of mother and father) were compared with ratings of each of the parents on the semantic differential. There was marked correspondence between the rating of each parent on the semantic differential and the ratings of the open-ended description of each parent. Particularly impressive were the correlations between the nurturance scale of the descriptions of mother and father and the ratings of the parents on all three dimensions of the semantic differential. For both mother and father, the nurturance scale had highly significant ($p < .001$) positive correlations with evaluation, potency, and activity on the semantic differential. The striving scale and conceptual level of the description of father also correlated significantly ($p < .05$) with potency and activity ratings of the father on the semantic differential. There were no significant findings with the number of words in the parental descriptions.

Of the relationships among aspects of object representations and depression, it was primarily the nurturant scale of the parental descriptions that correlated significantly with measures of depression. Descriptions of both mother and father as nurturant were significantly correlated with a positive self-description on the semantic differential and with lower scores of depression as measured on the Zung Depression Scale (Zung, 1971, 1973) and experiences of depression related to self-criticism as reported on the Depressive Experiences Questionnaire (DEQ) (Blatt, D'Afflitti, & Quinlan, 1976). The striving scale of the parental descriptions and the number of words were not significantly related to the various measures of depression.

Regarding conceptual level of the parental descriptions, there was a significant correlation between the conceptual level and measures of depression. Higher conceptual levels of representations in females were significantly ($p < .01$) and negatively correlated with depression as measured on the semantic differential (real-ideal self-discrepancy) and the Zung Depression Scale. In addition, there was a significant ($p < .05$) and progressive increase in conceptual level of representation as a function of the developmental level of depressive concerns. A lower conceptual level of object representation was found in subjects whose depression was primarily related to issues of dependency; an intermediate conceptual level occurred on those subjects whose depression was primarily related to issues of self-criticism; and the highest conceptual level occurred in those subjects who were not depressed. These findings are consistent with theoretical formulations (Blatt, 1974) that distinguished an anaclitic, or dependent, type of depression from a developmentally more advanced introjective type of depression where the concerns are focused around issues of self-criticism and guilt.

In summary, Blatt et al. (1976) found that descriptions of significant others, such as parents, can be scored reliably and that there are significant relations among types of depression and the content and structure of the descriptions of parents in a sample of normal young adults. It is the representation of parents as lacking in nurturance, support, and affection that is related to depression rather than the representation of parents as strong, harsh, and judgmental. In addition to the content of the descriptions of parents, the structural aspects (the conceptual level) also provided important data for understanding aspects of depression. The results indicate that at least in a sample of college students that written descriptions can provide valuable data for assessing aspects of object representation.

Blatt, Wein, Chevron, and Quinlan (1976) considered the implications of these findings for understanding depression. They point out that a central issue discussed in the psychoanalytic formulations of the etiology of depression is the intensely ambivalent relationship with parents in childhood (Abraham, 1911/1927, 1924/1927; Freud, 1917/1957). Ambivalent feelings are expressed in a wish to destroy the parent but at the same time being frightened of losing the dependent relationship. Because of intense ambivalent feelings, the individual is unable to establish and maintain an object representation of the person with feelings of affection, fondness, and respect (Klein, 1934/1948). Freud's original formulations in *Mourning and Melancolia* (1917/1957) emphasized the disturbances of internalization in depression. These disturbances cause the depressed patient's to attempt to preserve contact and retain the love and approval of the object (Nacht & Racamier, 1960). A. Freud (1965) discussed mourning as "the gradual process of detaching libido from an external image [p. 67]." But without adequate internalization of object, without the establishment of adequate levels of object representation, the object cannot be experienced as lost without precipitating a major crises and depression (Blatt, 1974). "It is the failure to establish good relations and adequate levels of internalization of the object that results in vulnerability to depression. Impairments in the cognitive and affective

TABLE 6.6
Nature of Object Representations in Psychosis and Depression

Psychosis[a]	Nature of Experience	Quality of Object Representation	Quality of Interpersonal Relations
Nonparanoid schizophrenia	Profoundly distorted bodily experience. Experiences of fusing and merging. Fear of annihilation. Need-fear dilemma (Burnham et al., 1969). Internal catastrophe. Overwhelmed and flooded by stimulation. Withdrawal of cathexis. Diffuse, inaccurate unarticulated perception and attention. Intense distractibility and disorganization.	Disruption of boundaries. Inability to maintain basic differentiation between self-other, inside-outside. Boundary disruptions expressed in thought disorder such as contaminations and confabulations. Object representations fluid, amphorous, diffuse, tending to merge and fuse. Distorted representation such as human-inanimate blends. Representations often barren and devoid of substantial content.	Intense, inappropriate closeness (fusion) alternating with profound withdrawal and disengagement. Need-fear dilemma. Intense apprehensions and fears of destruction and annihilation.
Paranoid schizophrenia	Exaggerated maintenance of differentiation between self-other to deal with threat of wish to merge and fuse. Preoccupation with power, control, autonomy. Affective isolation and emotional distancing. Excessive suspiciousness. Hostile interactions and delusional systems (e.g., "influencing machine,"	Sharp differentiation of self-other, but inability to maintain boundaries between inside-outside. These boundary disturbances expressed in thought disorder such as confabulations and fabulized combination (but not contaminations). Sense of danger and malevolence in external reality. Representations of	Isolation and distancing, need to maintain control and sense of autonomy. Projection of anger, fear of destructive reality. Sense of safety found in restitutional, delusional fantasies. Struggle for power, need for clarity and certainty to control projected potential of external danger. Exaggerated, misinterpretation of external signs and

Tausk; "internal police state," Shapiro). Focused attention and highly articulated perception.	idyllic delusional fantasies based on pre-formed images that have an internal logic and consistency but that are maintained independent of experiences in reality (restitution fantasies).	events as having personal significance and meaning.
Depression[b]		
Anaclitic depression		
Feelings of helplessness and depletion. Wishes to be cared for, loved, fed, and protected. Fears of abandonment. Oral cravings. Difficulty expressing anger and aggression.	Accurate representations of well-defined objects in reality, but primarily in sensorimotor-preoperational terms around need gratifying (or frustrating) action sequences.	Relationships determined primarily by issues of need gratification. Little capacity for tolerance of frustration or delay. Apprehension about loss of object's need-gratifying functions. Indiscriminate seeking of gratification and satisfaction. Concern about dependability and object's capacity to provide gratification.
Introjective depression		
Feelings of inferiority, worthlessness, and guilt. Intense need to compensate and/or atone. Concern about gaining approval and recognition. Emphasis on performance and accomplishment as compensation for failure, but with little sustained personal satisfaction or meaning.	Realistic representation of well-defined object but primarily on a perceptual and external iconic level around isolated, static, overstated part properties and features. Little resolution of contradictory properties such that there is often much ambivalence.	Concerns about criticism and censure. Apprehensive about loss of acceptance and approval. Overcompensatory strivings for excessive achievement and perfection. Vulnerable to implications of criticism and rejection. Little sustained enduring sense of self, dependent on external support and reactions.

[a] Derived from Blatt & Wild, 1976; Blatt, Wild, & Ritzler, 1975.

[b] Derived from Blatt, 1974; Blatt, D'Afflitti, & Quinlan, 1976.

development of object representations should be considered a central issue in depression [Blatt et al., 1976].'' Actual, apparent, or fantasized object loss is often a major precipitant of depression because impairments in the development of object representation leave the individual vulnerable to object loss and to depressive experience (Blatt, 1974, p. 515). The findings of a relation between type of depression and conceptual level of the mental representations is consistent with clinical experience and suggest that impairments in the development of levels of mental representations is an important issue in depression.

Blatt et al. (1976), in stressing the importance of assessing the representational world, point out that though external observers may agree consistently that a particular parent is cold and unresponsive or highly critical, one cannot simply assume that the child experiences the parent in the same way. There can be considerable variation among children in their thresholds for experiencing deprivation and severe criticism, and these thresholds would interact with the actual behavior of the parent. Although we need objective assessments of parental behavior and family interactions, it is essential to assess the phenomenological world—how individuals experience, remember, and represent their parents and their family interactions. Open-ended descriptions of signficant others, human responses on the Rorschach and other procedures including the analysis of the content and structure of the manifest dream or stories told to T.A.T. cards provide reliable and valid methods for assessing aspects of this phenomenological world of interpersonal experiences and relationships.

The impairments of representation that occur in patients vulnerable to depression are markedly different than the impairments of representation noted in schizophrenic patients. In schizophrenia, evidence (Lidz, 1973; Wynne & Singer, 1963) indicates that the acute disorganization of the parents have resulted in the patient's failure to establish firm developmentally early differentiations involving the basic definition of the object. In contrast, the impairments of object representation in depressed patients involve issues that are beyond basic boundary differentiation, but rather pertain to either lack of nurturance, affection, and concern or the setting of unusual harsh and rigid standards. Table 6.6 presents a summary of the different quality of object representations in psychosis and depression.

Summary

Throughout his research on psychopathology, Blatt has stressed the importance of evaluating impairments in object representation and their potential role in the vulnerability to develop various forms of psychopathology. He also stresses the need to study the changes that occur in qualitative and structural dimensions of representations during normal development and in psychotherapy. Clinical and research evidence suggests that the content and structure of object representation is a central dimension in schizophrenia and depression and that changes in the structure of object representation should parallel changes in the clinical picture. The sequence of these changes in therapy and their relations to changes in cognitive organization more generally needs to be investigated in the psychotherapeutic treatment of various types of psychopathology.

According to Blatt (1974), object representations emerge as enduring cognitive structures (Mahler, 1963, 1965, 1968; Mahler, Pine, & Bergman, 1975; Schafer, 1958) from the evolving complex affective-interpersonal matrix of the child's interaction within the family. This interaction is redefined and experienced in new ways as major developmental changes occur within the child and as the family changes and responds in various ways to the child's emerging needs and strivings. With the recent development of measures of the mental representations of the self and the object world, the developmental constructs of object representation, which are hypothesized to be a major basis for interpersonal phenomena, are now available for systematic observation. The assessment of object representation has required an integration of psychoanalytic theory, including object relation theory, and cognitive developmental psychology. These procedures provide the basis for the empirical investigation of a wide range of theoretical formulations, including aspects of object relations theory and cognitive developmental theory, as well as factors of the environmental and social matrix in which the child evolves. The content and structure of the representations of self and other develop at the intersection of these various forces—cognitive, affective, interpersonal, and social—and therefore can be crucial variables for studying the multitude of factors that influence normal psychological growth as well as growth within the psychotherapeutic process.

III CONCLUSION

The research on the assessment of object relations and object representation presented in this paper are part of a major revision and extension that has taken place in psychoanalytic concepts and theory. The traditional emphasis on the five metapsychological points of view (Rapaport & Gill, 1959) has been extended to include an emphasis upon the internalization of interpersonal experiences as a central factor in personality development. This emphasis on object relations and the development of the concepts of the self and the object world are part of an attempt to build a clinical theory of psychoanalysis. This theory is directly linked to interpersonal experiences and relationships; human functioning is described in terms of aim, motive, meaning, and the quality of interpersonal relationships. This theoretical innovation in contemporary psychoanalysis has been based on observations made in the clinical context of psychoanalysis as well as in the study of developmental processes in infants and young children and on data and concepts from ethology and comparative psychology. In addition to understanding the vicissitudes of the drives and the ego apparatus, it is now clear that the development and management of intrapsychic conflict must take into account significant past, as well as current, interpersonal experiences and their internalization as cognitive-affective structures of the representational world— concepts of the self and of others. A comprehensive assessment of psychological functioning involves an evaluation of issues of psychosexual development, the vicissitudes of libidinal and aggressive drives, and the structures and schemata of cognitive-affective development that can range from early infant–mother symbiosis to the later stages of separation–individuation in childhood, adolescence and adulthood. The growing number of theoretical, clinical, and research reports, from a variety of perspectives including developmental psychology (e.g., Piaget, Werner), psychoanalytic ego psychology (e.g., Jacobson), psychoanalytic object relations theory (e.g., Fairbairn, Guntrip, Winnicott), and developmental psychoanalysis (Mahler), all point to the importance of including in theoretical formulations the developmental level of the complex cognitive-affective structures of the representational world.

Our review of the work of the two primary research groups that have attempted to assess systematically aspects of the representational world illustrates some of the diversity of formulations and theoretical issues currently being investigated in contemporary psychoanalysis. These studies and their findings have important implications for understanding personality development, an individual's vulnerability to psychopathology, and important dimensions of the therapeutic process. This emphasis on the internalization of object relationships as cognitive-affective structures of the representational world is part of the widening scope of psychoanalysis in which there is the recognition that the expression of drives and modes of adaptation always occur in a matrix of object relationships that provides the shape and focus for all psychological experiences.

The research reviewed in the chapter indicates that there are reliable methods and techniques for the assessment of object relations and object representations and that these constructs are enduring dimensions of personality organization that provide important information about the developmental level of personality organization and the quality of interpersonal relationships to which an individual is predisposed. The research groups at Michigan and at Yale, based on detailed clinical observation and experience, have developed procedures for investigating systematically the nature of the representational world (Sandler & Rosenblatt, 1962). Mayman and his colleagues in Ann Arbor, based partly on the theoretical formulations of Federn, Jacobson, and Kernberg, have investigated the affective-thematic dimensions of human experience. Theoretical constructs such as "affect states," "ego states," "experiences of self," and "sense of identity" have been utilized to provide a phenomenological dimension to traditional psycho-analytic psychology. Blatt and his colleagues in New Haven have attempted to integrate psychoanalytic concepts of ego psychology (e.g., Hartmann, Rapa-port), with concepts from object relations theory (e.g., Klein, Fairbairn, Guntrip), developmental psychoanalysis (e.g., A. Freud, Mahler), and cognitive developmental psychology (Piaget, Werner). The different theoretical orienta-tions of these two research groups have lead them to emphasize different dimen-sions of object relations. The contribution of the Michigan group has focused upon the content and affective themes of object representations, whereas the Yale group has focused more on the cognitive dimension—on the structure of object representation.

For Mayman (1968, pp. 309–310), the concept of "ego state," derived from Federn, is based on an integration of object relations theory and the theory of psychosexual development. The stages of psychosexual development define a variety of "ego states," each organized around a distinctive affect and self experience and made up of a definite need, a need-appropriate object-relation-ship and self-representation, and phase-appropriate conflicts, defenses, compro-mise formations, and ego-competencies. Implicit in an ego-state are oral, anal, and phallic impulses, but these impulses become accessible to the individual (and the clinician) not in id terms as raw impulses but by way of ego derivatives, especially the "ego states." These ego states are organized around prototypical interpersonal themes that can be classified in terms of their characteristic psycho-sexual configuration, relationship paradigm, coping style, self structure, and defensive mode. Each ego state reflects particular qualities of object representa-tion, affective tone, and interpersonal relationships that are coordinated as a functional totality. Through the construct of ego states, Mayman has attempted to move away from a structural approach toward a more humanistic direction (Appelbaum, 1976, p. 251).

In their investigation of object representation from an affective, thematic orientation, Mayman and his colleagues have tried to adhere closely to the clinical data and utilize the judgments of skilled clinicians who immerse them-selves in the data and make ratings in an "intuitive and empathic" manner. Mayman and his colleagues seek to identify the contents of human experiences along a clinically based developmental continuum. They have developed several methods for capturing the complexity and unique nature of clinical phenomena (e.g., early memories, manifest dreams, Rorschach and TAT responses), and they have been particularly interested in those methods that lend themselves to a qualitative analysis of clinical data. Mayman (1976, p. 8) does not argue against including quantitative data and methods in clinical research, but he cautions that "We should be careful to employ methods of data collection and data processing which are uniquely appropriate to the clinical data themselves."

The research methodology and theoretical formulations of the Yale group represent a synthesis of clinical experience with a developmental perspective. The Yale group has attempted to develop research methologies that provide quantitative data derived from clinically relevant observations. Based on a developmental model, they have attempted to demonstrate that valid and clinically relevant distinctions can be drawn among a wide range of patients based on a systematic analysis of the structure of their object representation. Their formulations have introduced a cognitive developmental dimension into psychoanalytic concepts and have provided further understanding of clinical phenomena such as depression (Blatt, 1974) and schizophrenia (Blatt, Wild & Ritzler 1975; Blatt & Wild, 1976; Blatt, Schimek & Brenneis, 1980). These formulations have also provided information about the normal development of object representation that lead to the establishment of mature, stable, and enduring representations (Blatt et al., 1976). Although the research contributions of the Yale group have focused primarily on the human response on the Rorschach, procedures have been developed for the analysis of spontaneous descriptions of parents and other significant figures (Blatt et al., 1979) and the TAT (Blatt, Sugarman, & Bloom-Feshbach, 1981). Recent research (Spear & Schwager, 1980) indicates that the developmental analysis of the concept of the object developed by the Yale group can be utilized across a wide variety of projective test data and that it can yield reliable and valid quantitative data for clinical research (Ritzler et al., 1980) as well as valid qualitative distinctions for the study of the individual patient (Blatt & Lerner, 1982).

The contribution of research teams from Michigan and Yale, summarized in Table 6.7, overlap and in large measure support each other. Whereas the Michigan group stresses the subjective and content dimensions, investigators at Yale tend to empahsize the objective and structural dimensions. Both groups are interested in the individual's construction of reality, particularly interpersonal relationships, and the nature of the mental apparatus and the processes that transform experiences into subjective meaning. They both consider object representations as structures that mediate between the drives and specific experiences of reality. The content provides meaning that can be viewed as appetitive. Thus, the content of the individual's experiences are partly a function of the drives that color experience (Mayman, 1968). The structural dimension provides understanding of object representations as a cognitive construction of invariant structures at different developmental levels that can be considered relatively independent of their contents. From a structural vantage point, object representations also mediate between the drives and the understanding of reality. Object representations develop from pivotal, specific interpersonal experiences related to the drives in an epigenetic series in which there are new levels of schemata that provide meaning. The development of these cognitive-affective structures or schemata provide new meaning for experiences and more effective direction for actions and intentions (Blatt, 1974).

The Michigan and Yale approach to the study of object representation have contributed to the further development of a phenomenological, middle-level clinical theory derived directly from clinical data. Their assessments of object representation provide valid qualitative and quantitative data that can have relevance for a variety of disciplines ranging from the psychoanalytic situation to the broad domain of social psychology, all within a theoretical framework that is experiential and focuses on the nature of interpersonal experiences.

Mayman's formulations of ego states as a middle-level language for describing clinical phenomena and Blatt's integration of psychoanalytic theory, object relations theory, and developmental psychology provide new perspectives on clinical phenomena. Mayman, for example, has demonstrated that early memories are an important source of clinical data, and Blatt has provided a way for conceptualizing different types of thought disorder as degrees of boundary disturbance. Both groups have developed scales for the reliable assessment of the representational world through a variety of projective media including the manifest content of dreams, the human object on the Rorschach, early memories, the TAT, autobiographies and spontaneous descriptions of significant figures. The data from the various studies conducted by these two research groups indicate that object representations are enduring structures that provide information about the individual's level of psychological organization and the type of interpersonal relationship to which he is predisposed. Various dimensions of object representation can be assessed reliably. Subsequent research needs to be directed toward studying the relationships between levels of object representation and other dimensions of personality organization such as preferred modes of defenses, libidinal orientation, psychosexual development, affective tone, and the organization of relatively autonomous ego functions. There is a need to understand the specific genetic antecedents of disruptions in the development of the concept of the object and the self and how these disruptions are dynamically expressed in conflict. There is a need to integrate the different formulations and methods of the research groups at Michigan and at Yale and to study the interaction of the content and the structure of object representations. This more comprehensive analysis of object representations may provide the basis for the fuller assessment of different types of psychopathology and provide a basis for a fuller understanding of normal development of the concept of the object and its impairment in psychopathology (Blatt et al., 1976).

In closing we would like to note that the theory of object relations and the methods for its assessment reviewed in this chapter may have important implications for the understanding and study of the therapeutic process. The development of the representational world into a cohesive and integrated sense of reality

TABLE 6.7
The Assessment of Object Representations

Dimensions of Object Representation	Data Source	Scales	Method	Clinical Focus	Theoretical Background
Mayman et al. at the University of Michigan:					
Thematic-affective	Early memories	Self and object representation rating scales for early memories and for dreams	Clinical-intuitive	Neurotics, character disorder	Ego psychology
a. Relationship paradigms	Dreams				Object relations theory
b. Coping style					
c. Images	Rorschach				Gestalt psychology
d. Self structure					
e. Defensive modes	TAT	Psychosexual object representation scale			
Psychosexual stages	Therapist-supervisor ratings	Mutuality of autonomy scale			
Character formation	Autobiographies				

Blatt et al. at Yale University:

			Clinical-quantitative	Depression, psychosis, normal development	
Structural Development	Rorschach	Developmental level of the concept of representation	Clinical-quantitative	Depression, psychosis, normal development	Object relations theory
a. Differentiation					
b. Articulation	TAT				Ego psychology
c. Integration	Parental descriptions				Cognitive developmental psychology
Boundaries	Depressive experiences questionnaire	Conceptual level of object representation			Interpersonal theory
a. Self-other					
b. Inner-outer					
c. Human-inanimate blends	Manifest content of dreams	Thought disorder on Rorschach			
Thought Disorder	Depressive experiences questionnaire				
a. Contaminations					
b. Confabulations					
c. Fabulized combinations					

239

initially occurs within the context of the primary, caretaking, maternal relationship. This maternal matrix eventually extends to include experiences with other significant figures, especially the father. It is the internalization of these significant interpersonal relationships that results in the child's understanding of reality and of constructing the representational world with its sense of self, of others, and of their interactions. These cognitive structures, built around important interpersonal interactions, generalize and provide the structures for also understanding inanimate dimensions of reality. If the representational world and the sense of reality are established through the internalization of significant interpersonal interactions, then these concepts should have relevance for understanding, and possibly assessing, significant dimensions of the therapeutic process. Formulations about therapeutic action in psychoanalysis and psychoanalytic psychotherapy increasingly emphasize the therapeutic matrix as a significant interpersonal relationship in which the therapist is the mediator in the patient's development of increasing levels of organization (Blatt & Erlich, 1981; Wild & Ritzler, 1975; Blatt, Schimek, & Brenneis, 1980; Loewald, 1979; Winnicott, 1965). As noted by Blatt, Wild, & Ritzler, (1975):

> If the internalization of object relations results in the formation of psychic structures during normal development, then the internalization of significant interactions between the patient and the analyst must play an important role in the therapeutic process. According to Loewald (1960, p. 18), the analyst becomes available as a new object by eliminating, step by step, the transference distortions which interfere with the establishment of new object relationships. And it is the internalization of new and relatively undistorted relations with the analyst which leads to therapeutic change. The consideration of psychopathological conditions as disturbances in object relations and representations offers the potential for integrating the study of impairments in cognitive processes, interpersonal relationships, and the representation of the self and the object world within a theoretical model which has etiological, as well as therapeutic, implications [pp. 280–281].

If there are different types of distortions in content and structure of the representational world in various forms of psychopathology, then one might expect the therapeutic process and the nature of the transference and countertransference issues to express these differences. Differences in object representation prior to beginning therapy may offer some understanding about the potential directions that therapy may unfold. Differences in object representation may provide information about the types of transference resistances that may be encountered in the therapy and the type of countertransference issues the therapist may experience. Progress in therapy should be reflected in modifications of the transference and countertransference issues that emerge in therapy and the quality of the individual's representational world as it evolves toward higher developmental levels. And one might expect different types of changes to occur in various types of patients depending on the nature of the disturbances of their representational world. H. Lerner (1981) recently has investigated shifts in the representational world of a single patient over the course of therapy. In analyzing the patient's initial Rorschach protocol through the use of the concept of the Object Scale developed by Blatt et al. (1976), Urist's (1973) Mutuality of Autonomy Scale, and an Object Relations Scale of P. Lerner and H. Lerner (in press) designed to assess defenses, H. Lerner (1981) was able to demonstrate that these assessments provided information about the quality of interpersonal relationships to which the patient was predisposed and which were eventually expressed in a turbulent therapeutic relationship and a stormy hospitalization. Thus, the various scales developed to assess the nature of the representational world may prove to be effective measures of personality change. Mayman and Krohn (1975) have commented on the multidimensional nature of psychotherapeutic change, and that assessment of an ''inner sense of people and . . . a patient's repertoire of internalized relationship paradigms . . . seems to be a legitimate dimension of change . . . [p. 153].'' Subsequent research needs to be directed toward investigating changes in the content and structure of object representations as a function of long-term intensive treatment.

The research reviewed in this chapter suggests that formulations derived from object relations theory, integrated with other concepts from psychoanalysis and from cognitive theory, developmental psychology, and theories of interpersonal interactions may provide a phenomenologically based, experience-near, and clinically relevant theoretical model that may have important contributions for a fuller understanding of dimensions of psychopathology and of the therapeutic process. The research reviewed in this chapter indicates that there are reliable methods for the assessment of significant dimensions of the representational world and that these assessments can make important contributions not only to our understanding of the nature of psychopathology but also to our further understanding of personality development and the mutative factors in the psychotherapeutic process.

REFERENCES

Abraham, K. Notes on the psychoanalytical investigation and treatment of manic-depressive insanity and allied conditions. In D. Bryan & A. Strachey (Eds. and trans.) *Selected Papers of Karl Abraham, M.D.*, 1927, London: Hogarth Press, pp. 137–156. (Originally published, 1911.)

Abraham, K. A short study of the development of the libido. In D. Bryan & A. Strachey (Eds. and trans.) *Selected Papers of Karl Abraham, M.D.*, 1927. London: Hogarth Press, pp. 418–501.

Affleck, D. C., & Mednick, S. A. The use of the Rorschach test in the prediction of the abrupt terminator in individual psychotherapy. *Journal of Consulting Psychology*, 1959, *23*, 125–128.

Allison, J., Blatt, S. J., & Zimet, C. *The interpretation of psychological tests*. New York: Harper & Row, 1968.

Ames, L. B., Learned, J., Metraux, R. W., & Walker, R. A. *Child Rorschach responses: Developmental trends from 2 to 10 years*. New York: Hoeber, 1950.

Ames, L. B. Changes in Rorschach response throughout the human lifespan. *Genetic Psychology Monograph*, 1966, *74*, 89–125.

Ansbacher, H. L. Adler's place today in the psychology of memory. *Individual Psychology Bulletin*, 1947, *6*, 32–40.

Appelbaum, S. A., Rapaport revisited: Practice. *Bulletin of the Menninger Clinic*, 1976, *40*, 229–237.

Balint, M. *Primary love and psycho-analytic technique*. London: Hogarth, 1952.

Bell, S. M. *The relationship of infant-mother attachment to the development of the concept of object permanence*. Doctoral dissertation. Johns Hopkins University, 1968.

Bell, S. M. The development of the concept of object as related to infant-mother attachment. *Child Development*, 1970, *41*, 292–311.

Bieri, J., & Blacker, E. The generality of cognitive complexity in the perception of people and inkblots. *Journal of Abnormal and Social Psychology*, 1956, *53*, 112–117.

Blatt, S. J. *Some order in thought disorder*. Paper presented to a meeting of Psychologists Interested in the Study of Psychoanalysis (PISP) at the meetings of the American Psychological Association, Washington, D.C., Aug. 30, 1970.

Blatt, S. J. Levels of object representation in anaclitic and introjective depression. *Psychoanalytic Study of the Child*, 1974, *29*, 107–157.

Blatt, S. J. The validity of projective techniques and their research and clinical contribution. *Journal of Personality Assessment*, 1975, *39*, 327–343.

Blatt, S. J. *Paradoxical representations and their implications for the treatment of psychosis and borderline states*. Paper presented to the Institute for Psychoanalytic Research and Training, New York City, May 18, 1978 (Also presented at the Austen Riggs Center, Stockbridge, Mass., October 6, 1976.)

Blatt, S. J., Brenneis, B., Schimek, J. G., & Glick, M. Normal development and psychopathological impairment of the concept of the object on the Rorschach. *Journal of Abnormal Psychology*, 1976, *85*, 364–373.

Blatt, S. J., D'Afflitti, J. P., & Quinlan, D. M. Experiences of depression in normal young adults. *Journal of Abnormal Psychology*, 1976, *85*, 383–389. (a)

Blatt, S. J., D'Afflitti, J. P., & Quinlan, D. M. Depressive experiences questionnaire. New Haven: Yale University, 1976. (b)

Blatt, S. J., & Erlich, S. Levels of resistance in the psychotherapeutic process. In P. Wachtel (Ed.), *Resistance in psychodynamic and behavioral therapies*. New York: Plenum, 1981.

Blatt, S. J., & Lerner, H. The psychological assessment of object representations. *Journal of Personality Assessment*, 1982, In press.

Blatt, S. J., Quinlan, D. M., Chevron, E. S., McDonald, C., & Zuroff, D. Dependency and self-criticism: Psychological dimensions of depression. *Journal of Consulting and Clinical Psychology*, 1982, *50*, 113–124.

Blatt, S. J., & Ritzler, B. A. Thought disorder and boundary disturbances in psychosis. *Journal of Consulting Clinical Psychology*, 1974, *42*, 370–381.

Blatt, S. J., Schimek, J. G., & Brenneis, C. B. The nature of the psychotic experience and its implications for the therapeutic process. In J. Strauss et al., eds., *The Psychotherapy of Schizophrenia*. New York: Plenum, 1980.

Blatt, S. J., Sugarman, A., & Bloom-Feshbach, S. A developmental analysis of object representation on the TAT. Unpublished manual, 1981.

Blatt, S. J., Wein, S. J., Chevron, E., & Quinlan, D. Parental representations and depression in normal young adults. *Journal of Abnormal Psychology,* 1979, *78,* 388–397.

Blatt, S. J., & Wild, C. M. *Schizophrenia: A developmental analysis.* New York: Academic Press, 1976.

Blatt, S. J., Wild, C. M., & Ritzler, B. A. Disturbances of object representations in schizophrenia. *Psychoanalysis and Contemporary Science,* 1975, *4,* 235–288.

Brenneis, C. B. Features of the manifest dream in schizophrenia. *Journal of Nervous and Mental Disease,* 1971, *153,* 81–91.

Buchwald, C., & Blatt, S. J. Personality and the experience of time. *Journal of Consulting and Clinical Psychology,* 1974, *42* 639–644.

Burnham, D., Gladstone, A., & Gibson, R. *Schizophrenia and the need fear dilemma.* New York: International Universities Press, 1969.

Clarke-Stewart, K. A. Interactions between mothers and their young children: Characteristics and consequences. *Monograph of Social Research on Child Development,* 1973, *38* (6–7, Serial No. 153).

DeBeaudoin, G., Haimonte, M. T., Bessing, A., & Geissman, P. Etude d'une Population de 97 Meurtriers internes. Etude Medicolegale, Clinique. Psychologique et Electroencephalographique. *Annual of Medical Psychology,* 1961, *119,* 625–686.

Gouin-Decarie, T. B. *Intelligence and affectivity in early childhood.* New York: International Universities Press, 1965.

Dörken, J. A psychometric evaluation of 68 medical interns. *Journal of the Canadian Medical Association,* 1954, *70,* 41–45.

Draguns, J. G., Haley, E. M., & Phillips, L. Studies of Rorschach content: A review of the research literature Part 1: Traditional content categories. *Journal of Projective Techniques and Personality Assessment,* 1967, *31,* 3–32.

Endara, J. Psicodiagnostico de Rorschach y delincuentas la Representacion de la Figura Humana. *Archives of Criminal Neuropsychiatry,* 1957, *5,* 547–574.

Erikson, E. H. *Childhood and society.* New York: Norton, 1950.

Erikson, E. H. The dream specimen of psychoanalysis. *Journal of the American Psychoanalytic Assoication,* 1954, *2,* 5–56.

Fairbairn, W. R. D. *An object relations theory of the personality.* New York: Basic Books, 1952.

Federn, P. *Ego psychology and the psychoses.* New York: Basic Books, 1952.

Fenichel, O. *The psychoanalytic theory of neurosis.* New York: Norton, 1945.

Fernald, P. S., & Linden, J. D. The human content response in the Holtzman inkblot technique. *Journal of Projective Techniques and Personality Assessment,* 1966, *30,* 441–446.

Fibel, B. *Toward a developmental model of depression: Object representation and object loss in adolescent and adult psychiatric patients.* Doctoral dissertation, University of Massachussetts, 1979.

Fisher, S., & Cleveland, S. E. *Body image and personality.* New York: Von Nostrand, 1958.

Fraiberg, S. Libidinal object constancy and mental representation. *Psychoanalytic Study of the Child,* 1969, *24,* 9–47.

Freud, A. The mutual influences in the development of ego and id. *Psychoanalytic Study of the Child,* 1952, *7,* 42–50.

Freud, A. The Assessment of borderline cases. Research at the Hampstead child therapy clinic and other papers: *The writings of Anna Freud,* 1956, *5,* 301–314. New York: International Universities Press, 1969.

Freud, A. Defense mechanisms. *Encyclopedia Britannica.* Chicago, London, Toronto: William Benton, 1961.

Freud, A. Assessment of childhood disturbances. *The Psychoanalytic Study of the Child*, 1962, *17*, 149–158.

Freud, A. *Normality and pathology in childhood*. New York: International Universities Press, 1965. (a)

Freud, A. *Normality and pathology in childhood: Assessments of development (Vol. VI)*. New York: International Universities Press, 1965. (b)

Freud, S. [Mourning and melancholia]. In J. Strachey (Ed. and trans.), *The standard edition of the complete psychological works of Sigmund Freud* (Vol. 14). London: Hogarth Press, 1957. (Originally published, 1917.)

Freud, S. [The ego and the id]. In J. Strachey (Ed. and trans.), *The standard edition of the complete psychological works of Sigmund Freud* (Vol. 19). London: Hogarth, 1961. (Originally published, 1923.)

Freud, S. [Civilization and its discontents]. In J. Strachey (Ed. and trans.), *The standard edition of the complete psychological works of Sigmund Freud* (Vol. 21). London: Hogarth, 1961. (Originally published, 1930.)

Freud, S. [An outline of psychoanalysis]. In J. Strachey (Ed. and trans.), *The standard edition of the complete psychological works of Sigmund Freud* (Vol. 23). London: Hogarth, 1964. (Originally published, 1938.)

Fromm-Reichmann, F. *Psychoanalysis and psychotherapy: Selected papers*. Chicago: University of Chicago Press, 1959.

Geil, G. W. The similarity in Rorschach patterns of adult criminal psychopaths and pre-adolescent boys. *Rorschach Research Exchange*, 1945, *9*, 201–206.

Gibby, R. G., Stotsky, B. A., Miller, D. R. & Hiller, E. W. *Journal of Consulting Psychology*, 1953, *17*, 348–354.

Glover, E. Functional aspects of the mental apparatus. *International Journal of Psycho-Analysis*, 1950, *31*, 125–131.

Goldman, A. E., & Herman, J. L. Studies in vicariousness: The effect of immobilization on Rorschach movement responses. *Journal of Projective Techniques*, 1961, *25*, 164–165.

Goldman, R. Changes in Rorschach performance and clinical improvement in schizophrenia. *Journal of Consulting Psychology*, 1960, *24*, 403–407.

Graver, D. Prognosis in paranoid schizophrenia on the basis of the Rorschach. *Journal of Consulting Psychology*, 1953, *17*, 199–205.

Guntrip, H. *Schizoid phenomena, object relations and the self*. New York: International Universities Press, 1969.

Hartmann, H. *Ego psychology and the problem of adaptation*. New York: International Universities Press, 1958. (Originally published, 1939.)

Hartmann, H. Comments on the psychoanalytic theory of the ego. *The Psychoanalytic Study of the Child*, 1950, *5*, 74–96.

Hartmann, H., Kris, E., & Loewenstein, R. M. Notes on the theory of aggression. *The Psychoanalytic Study of the Child*, 1949, *4*, 9–36.

Hartmann, H., & Loewenstein, R. M. Notes on the superego. *The Psychoanalytic Study of the Child*, 1962, *17*, 42–81.

Hatcher, R., & Krohn, A. Level of object representation and capacity for intense psychotherapy in neurotics and borderlines. In J. Kwawer, H. Lerner, P. Lerner, & A. Sugarman (Eds.), *Borderline Phenomena and the Rorschach Test*, New York: International Universities Press, 1980.

Hertzman, M., & Pearce, J. The personal meaning of the human figure in the Rorschach. *Psychiatry*, 1947, *10*, 413–422.

Hoffer, W. The mutual influences in the development of ego and id: Earliest stages. *The Psychoanalytic Study of the Child*, 1952, *7*, 31–41.

Holt, R. *Manual for the scoring of primary process manifestations in Rorschach responses.* Unpublished 9th draft. New York University Research Center for Mental Health, 1963.

Holtzman, W., Gorham, D., & Moran, L. A factor-analytic study of schizophrenic thought processes. *Journal of Abnormal and Social Psychology,* 1964, *69,* 355–364.

Home, H. The concept of mind. *International Journal of Psycho-Analysis,* 1966, *47,* 43–49.

Jacobson, E. *The self and the object world.* New York: International Universities Press, 1964.

Johnson, D. *Cognitive organization in paranoid and nonparanoid schizophrenia.* Unpublished doctoral dissertation, Yale University, 1980.

Jonietz, A. K. *A study of the phenomenological changes in perception after psychotherapy as exhibited in the content of Rorschach percepts.* Unpublished doctoral dissertation, University of Chicago, 1950.

Kernberg, O. Structural derivatives of object relationships. *International Journal of Psycho-Analysis,* 1966, *47,* 236–253.

Kernberg, O. Early ego integration and object relations. *Annals of the New York Academy of Science,* 1972, *193,* 233–247.

King, G., A theoretical and experimental consideration of the Rorschach human movement response. *Psychological Monograph,* 1958, *72,* No. 458.

Klein, G., *Psychoanalytic Theory.* New York: International Universities Press, 1976.

Klein, M. A contribution to the psychogenesis of manic-depressive states. In S. Ferenczi (Ed.), *Contributions to psychoanalysis.* London: Hogarth Press, 1948, pp. 282–310. (Originally published, 1934.)

Klopfer, B., Ainsworth, M. D., Klopfer, G., & Holt, R. *Developments in the Rorschach technique: Vol. 1. Techniques and Theory.* New York: World Book, 1954.

Kohut, H. *The analysis of the self.* New York: International Universities Press, 1971.

Kohut, H., *The Restoration of the Self.* New York: International Universities Press, 1977.

Krohn, A., & Mayman, M. Object representations in dreams and projective tests: A construct validational study. *Bulletin of the Menninger Clinic,* 1974, *38,* 445–466.

Krohn, A. *Levels of object representations in the manifest dreams and projective tests.* Unpublished doctoral dissertation, University of Michigan, 1972.

Kurz, R. B. Rorschach correlates of time estimation. *Journal of Consulting Psychology,* 1965, *29,* 379–382.

Landis, B. Ego boundaries. *Psychological Issues,* 1970, *6,* 1–172.

Lerner, H., An object representation approach to psychostructural change: A clinical illustration. Submitted for publication, 1981.

Lerner, P., & Lerner, H., (1981) A comparative study of defensive structure in neurotic, borderline, and schizophrenic patients. *Psychoanalysis and Contemporary Thought.* In press.

Lidz, R. W. *The origin and treatment of schizophrenic disorders.* New York: Basic Books, 1973.

Lidz, R. W., & Lidz, T. Therapeutic considerations arising from the intensive symbiotic needs of schizophrenic patients. In E. B. Brady & F. C. Redlich (Eds.), *Psychotherapy with schizophrenics.* New York: International Universities Press, 1952.

Loewald, H., Ego and reality. *International Journal of Psycho-Analysis,* 1951, *32,* 10–18.

Loewald, H., On the therapeutic action of psychoanalysis. *International Journal of Psycho-Analysis,* 1960, *41,* 16–33.

Loewald, H., Internalization, separation, mourning and the superego. *Psychoanalytic Quarterly,* 1962, *31,* 483–504.

Loewald, H., Psychoanalytic theory and the psychoanalytic process. *The Psychoanalytic Study of the Child,* 1970, *25,* 45–68.

Loewald, H., On motivation and instinct theory. *The Psychoanalytic Study of the Child,* 1971, *26,* 91–128.

Loewald, H., On internalization. *International Journal of Psycho-Analysis*, 1973, *54*, 9–17.

Loewald, H., Reflections on the psychoanalytic process and its therapeutic potential. *Psychoanalytic Study of the Child*, 1979, *34*, 155–168.

Luborsky, L. Clinician's judgments of mental health: A proposed scale. *Archives of General Psychiatry*, 1962, *7*, 407–417.

Mahler, M. Thoughts about development and individuation. *Psychoanalytic Study of the Child*, 1963, *18*, 307–314.

Mahler, M. On the significance of the normal separation-individual phase. In M. Schur (Ed.) *Drives, Affects, Behavior*. (Vol. 2). New York: International Universities Press, 1965.

Mahler, M. *On human symbiosis and the vicissitudes of individuation*. (Vol. 1). New York: International Universities Press, 1968.

Mahler, M., Pine, F., & Bergman, A. *The Psychological birth of the human infant: Symbiosis and individuation*. New York: Basic Books, 1975.

Mayman, M. Psychoanalytic study of the self-organization with psychological tests. In B. T. Wigdor (Ed.). *Recent advances in the study of behavior change: Proceedings of the academic assembly on clinical psychology*. Montreal: McGill University Press, 1963.

Mayman, M. *Manual of instructions for the clinical use of Psychological tests*. Unpublished manuscript, University of Michigan, 1966.

Mayman, M. Object representations and object relationships in Rorschach responses. *Journal of Projective Techniques and Personality Assessment*, 1967, *31*, 17–24.

Mayman, M. Early memories and character structure. *Journal of Projective Techniques and Personality Assessment*, 1968, *32*, 303–316.

Mayman, M. Psychoanalytic theory in retrospect and prospect. *Bulletin of the Menninger Clinic*, 1976, *40*, 199–210.

Mayman, M., A multi-dimensional view of the Rorschach movement response. In M. Rickers-Ovsiakina (Ed.). *Rorschach Psychology*. New York: Robert E. Krieger Publishing Company, 1977, pp. 229–250.

Mayman, M., & Krohn, A. Developments in the use of projective tests in psychotherapy outcome research. In I. Waskow & M. Parloff (Eds.), *Psychotherapy change measures*. Washington, D.C.: National Institute of Mental Health, 1975.

Mayman, M., & Ryan, E. *Level and quality of object relationships: A scale applicable to overt behavior and to projective test data*. Unpublished manuscript, University of Michigan, 1972.

McFate, M., & Orr, F. Through adolescence with the Rorschach. *Rorschach Research Exchange*, 1949, *13*, 302–319.

Meltzoff, J., Singer, J. L., & Korchin, S. J. Motor inhibition and Rorschach movement responses: A test of the sensori-tonic theory. *Journal of Personality*, 1953, *21*, 400–410.

Mueller, W. J., & Abeles, N. The components of empathy and their relationship to the projection of human responses. *Journal of Projective Techniques and Personality Assessment*, 1964, *28*, 322–330.

Nacht, S., & Racamier, P. C. Symposium on "depressive illness": Depressive states. *International Journal of Psycho-Analysis*, 1960, *41*, 481–496.

Nickerson, E. T. Some correlates of M. *Journal of Projective Techniques and Personality Assessment*, 1969, *33*, 203–212.

Orlinsky, D. E. Rorschach test correlates of dreaming and ream recall. *Journal of Projective Techniques and Personality Assessment*, 1966, *30*, 250–253.

Orr, M. *Le Test de Rorschach et l'imago maternelle*. Paris: Groupement Francais du Rorschach, 1958.

Parens, H. A contribution of separation-individuation to the development of psychic structures. In J.

B. McDevitt & C. F. Settlage (Eds.), *Separation-individuation: Essays in honor of Margaret S. Mahler.* New York: International Universities Press, 1971.

Parker, R. S., & Piotrowski, Z. A. The significance of varieties of actors of Rorschach human movement responses. *Journal of Projective Technique and Personality Assessment,* 1968, *32,* 33–44.

Parsons, T., & Bales, R. F. *Family socialization and interaction process.* Glencoe, Ill.: Free Press, 1955.

Pechaux, R., Girard, V., & Le-Mee, M. *Evolution du Rorschach au caurs du Syndrome Depressif. Comptes Rondus du congres des Modecins alenistes et Neurologistes.* Bordeaux, L., 1956.

Phillips, L., & Smith, J. G. *Rorschach interpretation: Advanced technique.* New York: Grune & Stratton, 1953.

Piaget, J. *The construction of reality in the child.* New York: Basic Books, 1954.

Piotrowski, Z. A. A Rorschach compendium: Revised and enlarged. *Psychiatric Quarterly,* 1950, *24,* 543–596.

Piotrowski, Z. A. *Perceptanalysis.* New York: MacMillan, 1957.

Pruitt, W. A., & Spilka, B. Rorschach empathy and object relations scale. *Journal of Projective Techniques and Personality Assessment,* 1964, *28,* 331–336.

Rapaport, D., Gill M., The points of view and assumptions of meta-psychology. International Journal of Psycho-analysis, 1959, *40,* 153–162.

Rapaport, D., Gill, M., & Schafer, R. *Diagnostic psychological testing* (Vols. 1 & 2). Chicago: Yearbook Pub., 1945.

Ray, A. B. Juvenile delinquency pattern on Rorschach inkblots. *Psychologia,* 1963, *6,* 190–192.

Reitman, E. E. *Changes in body image following sensory deprivation in schizophrenic and control groups.* Unpublished doctoral dissertation, University of Houston, 1962.

Richardson, H. Rorschachs of adolescent approved school girls, compared with Ames' normal adolescents. *Rorschach Newsletter,* 1963, *8,* 3–8.

Rieger, A. F. The Rorschach test and occupational personalities. *Journal of Applied Psychology,* 1949, *33,* 572–578.

Ritzler, B., Zambianco, D., Harder, D., & Kaskey, M. Psychotic patterns of the concept of the object on the Rorschach test. *Journal of Abnormal Psychology,* 1980, *89,* 46–55.

Roberts, L. K. The failure of some Rorschach indices to predict the outcome of psychotherapy. *Journal of Consulting Psychology,* 1954, *18,* 96–98.

Roberts, P. M. Personality structure of socially adjusted and socially maladjusted children according to the Rorschach test. *Psychological Monograph,* 1955, *69,* (Whole No. 404.)

Roe, A. Psychological tests of research scientists. *Journal of Consulting Psychology,* 1951, *15,* 492–495.

Rogers, L. S., & Hammond, K. R. Predictions of the results of therapy by means of the Rorschach test. *Journal of Consulting Psychology,* 1953, *17,* 8–15.

Rogers, L. S., Knauss, J., & Hammond, K. R. Predicting continuation in therapy by means of the Rorschach test. *Journal of Consulting Psychology, 1951, 15,* 368–371.

Rorschach, H. [*Psychodiagnostics: A diagnostic test based on perception*]. (P. Lemkau & B. Kroneberg, Trans.) New York: Grune & Stratton, 1942.

Rosenfeld, S. K., & Sprince, M. P. An attempt to formulate the meaning of the concept "borderline." *Psychoanalytic Study of the Child,* 1963, *18,* 603–635.

Ryan, E. R. *The capacity of the patient to enter an elementary therapeutic relationship in the initial psychotherapy interview.* Unpublished doctoral dissertation, University of Michigan, 1973.

Sandler, J., & Rosenblatt, B. The concept of the representational world. *Psychoanalytic Study of the Child.* 1962, *17,* 128–145.

Saul, L. J., Snyder, T. R., & Sheppard, E. On earliest memories. *Psychoanalytic Quarterly,* 1963, *25,* 263–270.

Schactel, E. *Experiential foundations of Rorschach test.* New York: Basic Books, 1966.

Schafer, R. Regression in the service of the ego. In G. Lindzey (Ed.), *Assessment of human motives.* New York: Rinehart, 1958.

Schafer, R. *Aspects of internalization.* New York: International Universities Press, 1968.

Schafer, R. An overview of Heinz Hartmann's contributions to psychoanalysis. *International Journal of Psycho-Analysis,* 1970, *51,* 425–446.

Schonbar, R. Differential dream recall frequency as a component of "Life Style". *Journal of Consulting Psychology,* 1965, *29,* 468–474.

Searles, H. *Collected papers on schizophrenia and related subjects.* New York: International Universities Press, 1965.

Setze, L., Setze, K. D., Baldwin, J. C., Doyle, C. I., Kobler, S. J., & Kobler, F. J. A Rorschach experiment with six, seven, and eight-year-old children. *Journal of Projective Techniques,* 1957, *21,* 166–171.

Siegman, A. W. The relationship between future time perspective, time estimation, and impulse control in a group of young offenders and in a control group. *Journal of Consulting Psychology,* 1961, *25,* 470–475.

Singer, J. L., Meltzoff, J., & Goldman, G. D. Rorschach movement responses following motor inhibition and hyperactivity. *Journal of Consulting Psychology,* 1952, *16,* 359–364.

Spear, W. The relationship of clinical diagnosis to structural and thematic aspects of manifest object representations in hospitalized borderline and schizophrenic patients. Unpublished doctoral dissertation, Columbia University, 1978.

Spear, W., & Schwager, E. New perspectives on the use of psychological tests as a measure of change over the cause of intensive inpatient psychotherapy. Paper presented at meetings of Society for Personality Assessment, Tampa, Fla., 1980.

Steele, R. Psychoanalysis and hermeneutics. *International Review of Psycho-Analysis,* 1979, *6,* 389–412.

Stierlin, H. The function of inner objects. *International Journal of Psycho-Analysis,* 1970, *51,* 321–329.

Tausk, V. On the origin of the "influence machine" in schizophrenia. In R. Fliess (Ed.), *The psychoanalytic reader.* New York: International Universities Press, 1948. (Originally published, 1919.)

Thetford, W. N., Molish, H. B., & Beck, S. J. Developmental aspects of personality structure in normal children. *Journal of Projective Techniques,* 1951, *15,* 58–78.

Thomas, R., Chess, S., & Birch, H. *Temperament and behavior disorders in children.* New York: New York University Press, 1968.

Urist, J. *The Rorschach test as a multidimensional measure of object relations.* Unpublished doctoral dissertation, University of Michigan, 1973.

Vygotsky, L. *Thought and Language.* (Translated by E. Hanfmann & G. Vakar.) Cambridge, Mass.: MIT Press, 1962.

Walters, R. H. A preliminary analysis of the Rorschach records of fifty prison inmates. *Journal of Projective Techniques,* 1953, *17,* 436–446.

Weiner, I. *Psychodiagnosis in schizophrenia.* New York: Wiley, 1966.

Werner, H. *Comparative psychology of mental development.* New York: International Universities Press, 1948.

Werner, H., & Kaplan, B. *Symbol formation: An organismic-developmental approach to language and the expression of thought.* New York: Wiley, 1963.

Winnicott, D. W. Primitive emotional development. *International Journal of Psycho-Analysis,* 1945, *26,* 116–128.

Winnicott, D. W. *The maturational processes and the facilitating environment.* London: Hogarth, 1965.

Winnicott, D. W. *Playing and reality.* New York: Basic Books, 1971.

Wolff, P. H. Cognitive considerations for a psychoanalytic theory of language acquisition. In R. Holt (Ed.), *Motives and thought,* [*Psychological Issues* 18/19:299–343]. New York: International Universities Press, 1967.

Wynne, L. C., & Singer, M. T. Thought disorder and family relations of schizophrenics. II. A classification of forms of thinking. *Archives of General Psychiatry,* 1963, *9,* 199–206.

Zung, W. W. Depression in the normal adult population. *Psychosomatics,* 1971, *12,* 164–167.

Zung, W. W. From art to science. *Archives of General Psychiatry,* 1973, *29,* 328–337.

7 Freud and the Female Reproductive Process: Tests and Issues

Roger P. Greenberg, Ph.D.
Seymour Fisher, Ph.D.
Upstate Medical Center, State University of New York, Syracuse

Soon after we completed a massive review of the research evidence bearing on Freud's ideas (Fisher & Greenberg, 1977), we found ourselves intensively discussing areas in Freud's thinking that had not been carefully subjected to empirical scrutiny. Although our review had uncovered a voluminous research literature relevant to psychoanalytic theories, our discussion focused on ideas that might have been debated or argued but not tested. After pursuing a variety of topics, we found ourselves debating Freud's controversial ideas about the meaning of pregnancy for "normal" women. The discussion led to formulating ways of testing aspects of Freud's hypotheses about the reproductive process in women and to the development of a score for phallic imagery that could be used in our investigations. An intriguing array of findings has begun to emerge from the network of data we and others have collected, and it is our intent to present in this chapter a look at some of the findings and issues we have uncovered.

FREUD'S PENIS–BABY THEORY

Freud's (1924/1961, 1925/1961, 1931/1961, 1933/1964) theories of the Oedipal conflict in women and his concept of penis envy served as a basis for his speculations about the dynamic meaning of pregnancy. He felt that little girls, like little boys, start out with mother as the prime object of love and interest. However, when the little girl makes the inevitable "momentus discovery" that the male possesses a penis whereas she does not, she concludes that she has a castrated and, therefore, inferior body. Freud assumed that the little girl develops a deep sense of disappointment and "penis envy" upon her discovery and that she blames her

251

mother for the predicament in which she finds herself. Freud suggested that the girl's disappointment is fueled by previous frustrations encountered in her relationship with mother. He noted that mother's previous offenses might include such things as insufficient feeding, being overly attentive to other family members, and frustrating the little girl's sexual wishes (possibly by punishing masturbation). For Freud, the little girl's discovery that she lacked a penis served as the trigger that alienated her from mother and caused her to turn toward father. The girl was thought to develop fantasies of regaining her "lost organ" by getting father to impregnate her and, thus, provide her with a baby. Within this framework the potential child had important compensatory value because of its unconscious equation with the penis. To have a child by father was to regain a version of the lost penis.

Freud also felt that up to the point of discovery that boys possessed a penis, the girl's main source of erotic pleasure was the clitoris (through masturbation). The vagina was thought to take on a new significance as the girl fantasized about having her father's child. Freud viewed the average woman as shifting from clitoral to vaginal dominance as she gave up her phallic orientation and moved toward a more passive, receptive, traditional feminine attitude. It should be emphasized that Freud considered the transition from a wish for a penis to a wish for a baby to be the "normal" and desirable course to be followed for female development. However, he also proposed two other less desirable lines of development that could result from the girl's discovery that she lacked a penis. The girl could become very sexually inhibited and neurotic or she could begin to exaggerate her own masculinity. Homosexuality was thought to be the extreme outcome of such a "masculinity complex."

Freud often repeated the description of the penis–baby equation in his writings. For instance, in describing female psychosexual development, Freud (1924/1961) wrote:

> Her Oedipus complex culminates in a desire, which is long retained, to receive a baby from her father as a gift—to bear him a child. One has an impression that the Oedipus complex is then gradually given up because this wish is never fulfilled. The two wishes—to possess a penis and a child—remain strongly cathected in the unconscious and help to prepare the female creature for her later sexual role [p. 179].

In discussing the Oedipal situation, Freud (1925/1961) later stated:

> But now the girl's libido slips into a new position along the line—there is no other way of putting it—of the equation 'penis–child.' She gives up her wish for a penis and puts in place of it a wish for a child; and with that purpose in view she takes her

father as a love object. Her mother becomes the object of jealousy. The girl has turned into a little woman [p. 256].

Finally, Freud (1933/1964) wrote:

The wish with which the girl turns to her father is no doubt originally the wish for the penis which her mother has refused her and which she now expects from her father. The feminine situation is only established, however, if the wish for a penis is replaced by one for a baby, if, that is, a baby takes the place of a penis in accordance with an ancient symbolic equivalence [p. 128].

PERSPECTIVE AND BACKGROUND

In this chapter we present some of the work that grew from our consideration of Freud's ideas about the female reproductive process and the penis–baby equation. It should be stated at the outset that we were initially skeptical of finding much support for Freud's ideas in this area. The skepticism grew in large part from our previous comprehensive review of the literature. In that review we found that Freud was rather consistently wrong in his theories concerning the psychology of women (Fisher & Greenberg, 1977). Yet, our review had also revealed that many other aspects of Freud's thinking were impressively supported by research evidence and that Freud's Oedipal theories, as they apply to women, had remained largely untested. Thus, despite some initial skepticism, we decided to pursue the topic further.

We discuss here the evidence we uncovered pertinent to a number of the major aspects of Freud's reproductive theories. We also take a look at some of the initial research in this area that we have conducted. The first topic to be considered is Freud's notion that women have a chronic sense of body inferiority arising from their inability to accept the fact fully that they do not have a penis. In essence, we are asking whether women really do have a sense of body inadequacy as Freud's propositions proclaim. Second, we are interested in evaluating, from an empirical standpoint, Freud's proposed distinction between clitoral and vaginal preferences. As noted earlier, Freud considered it essential for the development of mature femininity that the woman renounce the clitoris as the focus of her sexual gratification in favor of the vagina. Theoretically, if Freud is correct, there should be fewer indications of psychological conflict and a greater acceptance of self in the woman who has shifted her prime erogenous zone from a supposedly active-phallic-clitoris to the passive-receptive-vagina. Our review evaluates whether this propostion squares with what we now know. We shall also examine the question of whether there is any evidence consistent with Freud's ideas concerning penis-envy attitudes in women. Finally, we offer examples of more direct tests of Freud's thoughts about the female reproductive process and the existence of a penis–baby equation.

BODY INFERIORITY

Only in recent years have empirical data become available that would permit a meaningful appraisal of the proposition that women experience their bodies in a particularly inferior or defective fashion. There are several lines of investigation that are pertinent. Let us begin with the question whether women experience more anxiety or disturbance than men do with reference to their bodies. The findings suggest a negative answer. Indeed, it would appear that generally men have more body anxiety than do women. Studies of various samples of children have disclosed that boys are more preoccupied with getting hurt (Pitcher & Prelinger, 1963), more concerned about possible body mutilation and loss of body parts (Friedman, 1952), and more focused on castration imagery when awaiting surgery (Schneider, 1960). In adult samples it has turned out that men produce more themes of "mutilation" and "death" in their spontaneous verbalizations (Gleser, Gottschalk, & Springer, 1961), display more "castration anxiety" when responding to projective stimuli with castration connotations (Blum, 1949), and are more focused on castration themes in their dreams in nonthreatening situations (Hall & Van de Castle, 1965) and also during and after surgery (Lane, 1966).

Such findings have been reinforced by Fisher's (1970) appraisals of sex differences in body boundary articulation. These appraisals have been based on an index, derived from inkblot responses (Barrier score), that measures the degree to which boundary regions of the body are perceived as clearly differentiating self from nonself objects and also providing protection against intrusion from "out there." Numerous studies (Fisher, 1970) have indicated that the Barrier score is positively correlated with feelings of body security and ability to cope with body threats like injury and incapacitation. Quite consistently, girls have obtained higher Barrier scores than boys, and women attain higher scores than men. It is of interest that Fast and Fisher (1971) observed that males react with greater body boundary disturbance to injections of adrenalin than do women. Further, Fisher reported that men react with more body boundary disruption to threatening messages at both liminal (Fisher, 1971) and subliminal (Fisher, 1975) levels. Overall, the research findings convincingly indicate that the male is less secure about his body than is the female.

Another pertinent line of investigation has shown that women are more aware of, and tuned into, their bodies than are men. This difference in body awareness is apparently linked to the female ascribing a more meaningful role to body experiences than men do. Van Lennep (1957) discovered that women exceed men in referring to body themes in stories they create. Secord (1953) observed that women are more bodily aware as defined by the number of body associations they give to homonyms with both body and nonbody meanings. Korchin and Heath (1961) found that women report more body sensations in a variety of situations. Fisher (1970) undertook a series of studies in which body awareness was evaluated by means of a Body Prominence score based on the number of body references elicited when an individual is asked to list "twenty things you are aware of right now." The well-validated Body Prominence Index has clearly shown greater body awareness in women than in men. But perhaps even more important, it has been noted that whereas body awareness in women is linked with a sense of body security, such awareness in men is associated with oral (activity–passivity) conflicts (Fisher, 1970). That is, the woman who is highly body aware is experiencing her body comfortably; but heightened body awareness in men betokens tension and disturbance. Fisher interpreted his findings to mean that women more than men are socialized to be at ease with their bodies and to perceive more direct and meaningful connections between their bodies and their life roles.

There are other diverse studies that could be cited that point to the female being more comfortable and flexible in dealing with her body than is the male. For example, there is Fisher's (1970) report that men become more anxious than women when they see themselves in a mirror and their appearance has been grossly altered as the result of wearing distorted masks. Or one could mention Cohen's (1963) observation that men are relatively more disturbed by watching a movie full of body multilation themes. Or one could refer to Katcher's (1955) conclusion that girls arrive at a realistic awareness of the size properties of their bodies at an earlier age than do boys. The total evidence is quite convincing that, contrary to Freud's view, women do not experience their bodies in more negative, more depreciated terms than do men.[1]

CLITORAL VERSUS VAGINAL RESPONSE

As earlier noted, Freud not only distinguished between clitoral and vaginal sexual arousal, but assumed that the mature mode was to become minimally reactive to clitoral stimulation and relatively highly responsive to vaginal stim-

---

[1]Although the studies do not support Freud's speculations about body inferiority feelings in women, they are consistent with his ideas concerning castration anxiety and fear of bodily harm in men. We have presented a more detailed discussion of this issue elsewhere (Fisher & Greenberg, 1977).

ulation. A mature woman would presumably attain orgasm primarily from penile intromission. This formulation was originally called into question by Kinsey, Pomeroy, Martin, and Gebhard (1953) and Masters and Johnson (1966) who presented eivdence that a large proportion of the physiological arousal contributing to orgasm (even when it is delivered by the penis inserted in the vagina) directly or indirectly involves the clitoris. However, it was clear from both clinical observation and studies by Fisher (1973) that women do have definite preferences for clitoral versus vaginal stimulation. Further, women differ in their ability to attain orgasm from direct clitoral versus direct vaginal stimulation. Fisher (1973) interviewed and tested 300 normal married women to ascertain whether clitoral versus vaginal preferences were linked with a variety of psychological variables. Preferences were measured by women indicating on a 7-point scale their perception of how much clitoral as compared to vaginal stimulation contributed to their reaching orgasm. One surprising result that emerged from the data was the fact that the greater a woman's vaginal preference the higher was her level of anxiety. The vaginally oriented woman was rated as behaving more anxiously in the laboratory situation by observers. She expressed more psychological distress in autobiographical accounts. She had more difficulty in learning threatening words and produced more unpleasant imagery in her inkblot responses. Thus, it was the clitorally rather than vaginally oriented woman who seemed to be most psychologically comfortable. In the same vein, the vaginally oriented woman was particularly inclined to adopt a depersonalized attitude toward her own body. When describing her body sensations and experiences, she was more likely than the clitorally oriented to use words like "foreign" and "strange" and to indicate "I feel distant from my own body." It is also pertinent that the vaginally oriented woman was less likely to use the term "ecstatic" in depicting how she felt during orgasm and more inclined to choose mildly emotional terms like "happy." The shutting out attitude she manifested toward her body experiences was duplicated in an analogous tendency to mute stimuli from "out there." This was primarily revealed in the imaginative (Thematic Apperception) stories she created. Typically, the vaginally oriented woman tried to portray situations as having little tension. When indications of anxiety did arise, they were quickly reduced in a "they lived happily ever after" fashion. Fisher proposed that the vaginally oriented women adopted a muting stance toward both their bodies and the external world as part of a strategy to minimize potentially anxiety arousing input.

Despite all the personality differences between vaginally and clitorally oriented women, Fisher observed no relationships between clitoral–vaginal preference and ability to attain orgasm consistently. However, Latorre (1979) reported that the vaginally oriented in a sample of unmarried women he studied were likely to be more orgasmic "during coitus" than those with a clitoral preference.

He also reported that the former were more feminine, as defined by a question-naire. The generality of these findings may be questioned because Fisher did not detect either of these relationships in six different samples. It should be added that more recently Fisher (1980) cross-validated, in a sample of black women, many of his original findings concerning the correlates of clitoral–vaginal prefer-ences in white women.

It would seem judicious to conclude that the existing pool of scientific infor-mation does not support Freud's hypothesis that vaginally oriented women are more mature or secure than those who prefer clitoral stimulation. If anything, the data imply the opposite may be true.

PENIS ENVY

Several studies have examined the question of whether penis-envy attitudes exist in women. Levin (1966) tried to find out whether a group of career women (not married and in traditionally "masculine" occupations) would show a greater degree of concern about not possessing a penis than a comparable group of homemakers (married, with children, and not employed). The inkblot responses for both groups were scored on an index designed to detect concern about penis loss. Levin found, as she had predicted, that the total female castration complex score was higher in the career group than it was in the homemaker group. Furthermore, a specific subscore concerned with "envious, hostile, and/or fear-ful reactions to the male genitals" was significantly higher in the career group. Also characteristic of the career group were scores indicating higher activity (energy, independence, and self-assertion) and a higher need for achievement (ambition and drive for status). One interpretation of the results was that women who pursue stereotypic masculine social roles (to the exclusion of the traditional feminine roles) have a greater underlying preoccupation with inadequacy and penis loss. Conversely, the results are consistent with the idea that women with babies (at least in the year 1966) evidence fewer phallic concerns than do ex-clusively career-oriented women working in occupations usually viewed as "masculine."

Ellman (1970) tried to find out if the Levin measure of concern about penis loss could be used to distinguish women in other ways. Her findings indicated that women who produced more penis-envy themes also exhibited more depres-sive affect, more general hostility, and more hostility directed specifically to-ward men. Exposure to a passage about menstruation and a subliminal stimulus (the message, "woman menstruating") were designed to stir up fantasies about the female anatomy and reproductive processes. High penis-envy scorers initially responded to the passage with significant depression and feelings of being defective. Their later response to the experimental manipulation was interpreted as one of defensive denial; they showed increased hypomania, decreased depression, decreased hostility, and a tendency to minimize differences between the sexes. This study, like the Levin experiment, indicated that some women are more preoccupied with "phallic" themes than others. It also demonstrated that a stimulus that raises the image of female sexuality and anatomical differences between the sexes has a greater effect on the reactions of women who are more absorbed by phallic concerns.

Lansky, Crandall, Kagan, and Baker (1961) produced a set of findings that are consistent with the "penis-envy concept." They found that adolescent girls who showed inhibition about responding to inkblot areas resembling female genitalia were unusually critical of their mothers, achievement-oriented, and low in guilt about being aggressive toward authority figures. In line with Freud's ideas, this study implies that females who are uncomfortable with the female reproductive organs are more likely to be aggressive and achievement oriented.

One study (Bombard, 1969) failed to support the penis-envy concept. The experiment evaluated the impact of pictures of nude males and females (with genitals explicitly shown) on groups of women who scored high or low on a measure of masculinity (the Franck–Rosen drawing test). Following exposure to the nude pictures, subjects were asked to compose Thematic Apperception Test stories and to draw male and female human figures. None of the various predictions concerning differences between the high and low masculine women was supported. There were no differences between the groups in their production of story themes concerning intrusion, compensation for defect, or fear of being "found out" (i.e., the discovery by others that she lacks a penis). Also at variance with the predictions, high masculine women did not sketch more phallic-looking human figures.

Although there have been a few other research efforts devoted to the question of penis envy (Conn, 1940; Johnson, 1966; Landy, 1967; Levy, 1940), they have been so poorly controlled or minor in their implications that they do not contribute much to an evaluation of Freud's ideas.

In general, the studies we have described are consistent in indicating that there is a link between phallic concerns and behaviors or goals associated with the traditional sex roles. For example, achievement orientation, aggressiveness, and the expression of hostility have been empirically linked with measures of phallic concern. The findings are thus compatible with Freud's notion of a relationship between attitudes toward the genitals and the acceptance or rejection of the stereotypic female sex role. Similarly, there are investigations supportive of Freud's idea that female homosexuals may feel unusually disturbed when encountering a penis. Freud speculated that this was due to an underlying penis-envy problem. Goldberg and Milstein (1965) found that women were more disturbed in response to a picture of a nude male with exposed genitals if they scored high on a measure of "latent" homosexual tendencies (as derived from the Minnesota Multiphasic Personality Inventory). Through the use of a questionnaire measure, Kaye, Berl, Clare, Eleston, Gershwin, Gershwin, Kogan, Torda, and Wilburn (1967) discovered that female homosexuals had more "fear and/or aversion to the penis" than did nonhomosexuals. Again, as in the previous studies, attitudes toward the penis were found to relate to a woman's sex role perspective.

PREGNANCY AND PHALLIC CONCERNS

There have been very few research reports pertinent to the issue of whether pregnancy has the kind of genital connotations that Freud proposed. Tolor and Digrazia (1977) compared the figure drawings obtained from a group of pregnant women with the drawings produced by a group of women with gynecological problems. As Freud's penis–baby theory would predict, the pregnant women emphasized the genitals in their drawings more than the control subjects did. They also distorted the drawn figures more, made drawings smaller in size, and produced more nude drawings.

Ginsparg (1956) published a study that has some relevance in consideration of the penis–baby issue. She was particularly interested in testing a psychoanalytic theory of postpartum psychosis that had been proposed by Zilboorg (1928a, 1928b). The theory suggested that postdelivery breakdown would be most likely in a woman who had incompletely resolved her Oedipal conflicts. It was thought that such a woman would be more unconsciously preoccupied with possessing a penis ("penis envy") and more identified with masculine than feminine goals. Zilboorg felt that pregnancy provided the vulnerable woman with a substitute penis in the form of the fetus contained within her body. The fetus could fulfill the woman's long-standing wish and provide her with an object of extreme value that had to be retained as part of the body. It was thought that the delivery of the child (penis equivalent) would be extremely disorganizing to such a woman because it would mean the loss of the unconsciously sought after penis.

Ginsparg attempted to test this theory by comparing the responses, on a variety of measures, of women who became psychotic postdelivery, women who became psychotic at a time not associated with pregnancy, and normal women who had just delivered. Ginsparg hypothesized that those women who became psychotic postdelivery would show greater indications of Oedipal conflict, psychosexual immaturity, penis envy, and "female masochism" than women in the other groups. Her findings cannot be seen as supporting a penis–baby link. Although results did show that the postdelivery psychotic women differed from the normal postdelivery women in many of the predicted ways, they did not consistently differ from women who became psychotic outside of a pregnancy context. Furthermore, none of the groups differed from the others on the measure of penis envy used. Overall, then, there were no indications that postdelivery psychotic women were characterized by a unique etiology or a different set of personality traits than those found in other psychotic women.

Probably the most direct published tests of Freud's "penis–baby" concept were presented in two studies we conducted as an outgrowth of our concern about the lack of research in this area (Greenberg & Fisher, 1980). We reasoned that if pregnancy serves to some degree as a penis equivalent for the average woman, as Freud assumed, then women should experience pregnancy as a time of heightened phallic feelings. This hypothesis was tested by two investigations focusing on whether the pregnant state or pregnancy fantasies lead women to an increase in phallic imagery.

For the purposes of our work we developed a measure of phallic imagery based on the responses subjects produce to the projective Holtzman Inkblot Test (Holtzman, Thorpe, Swartz, & Herron, 1961). Our measure simply involves scoring each of a subject's 25 responses to Form A or B of the test as phallic or nonphallic according to a set of predetermined criteria. Each person tested can achieve a phallic imagery score of 0–25 on the measure. The scoring system concentrates on subjects' perceptions of protrusions, extensions, projections, and elongations that can be interpreted as having phallic significance. In essence, the system is quite consistent with Freud's (1900/1953) statement that all "elongated objects" can represent the male organ. He mentioned such objects as tree trunks, umbrellas, sticks, long sharp weapons, ties, snakes, and airplanes as representative of phallic imagery. The scoring system proved to be reliable in that two PhD clinical psychologists achieved a 97% agreement in an independent and blind scoring of 26 protocols (650 responses) for phallic imagery (see Appendix, p. 281 for a list of the explicit criteria used). It should be added that different investigators have used measures of sexual symbolism or phallic imagery in making meaningful predictions of sex differences and other variables (Cameron, 1967; Erikson, 1951; Franck & Rosen, 1949; Jones, 1956; Lessler, 1964; Nathan, 1978; Stennett & Thurlow, 1958; Winter & Prescott, 1957).

In our first study using the measure, we compared the projective responses of women when they were pregnant to their responses when they were not pregnant. We also wished to compare the pregnant group's phallic imagery scores to the scores attained by a control group of nonpregnant women. The pregnant sample consisted of 44 pregnant women with an average age of 24.6 years and an average of 15.2 years of education. The nonpregnant group consisted of 43 women who were 27 years old on the average with a mean of 14.8 years of schooling. The expectant mothers had been pregnant for an average of 24 weeks at the time of initial testing. The study proceeded by having each woman write out her responses to Form B of the Holtzman Inkblot Test. One month following delivery, each woman in the pregnancy group also responded to the first 25 cards of Form A of the test.

The findings were consistent with the penis–baby hypothesis. Women had significantly higher phallic scores when they were pregnant than when they were not. Furthermore, the pregnant group's phallic scores were significantly higher than the scores attained by the nonpregnant control group. After delivery there was no difference between the phallic scores of the women from the pregnant and nonpregnant samples. Overall, then, both the change scores and the sample comparisons revealed that the pregnant state was associated with greater phallic imagery than the nonpregnant state.

These results led us to a second study where we posed the question of whether a woman's phallic imagery score could be raised by the fantasy of becoming pregnant (Greenberg & Fisher, 1980). For this investigation, we examined the effects of a subliminally presented message concerning the theme of becoming pregnant. A subliminal message was used because Silverman (1976) had demonstrated in a variety of studies that out-of-awareness stimuli may be of particular value in evading psychological defenses and testing psychoanalytic hypotheses. A considerable literature has affirmed that subliminal stimuli can affect behavior (Bevan, 1964; Fisher, 1975, 1976; Klein & Holt, 1960; Shevrin, Smith, & Fritzler, 1969; Silverman, 1966; Silverman & Candell, 1970).

Two groups of women (median age 20 years old) served as subjects. Both groups first responded in writing to Form B of the Holtzman Blots while seated alone in a room. The two groups were then exposed to priming procedures and taped auditory subliminal messages dealing with either the theme of becoming pregnant or the theme of being penetrated. Throughout the playing of the out-of-awareness messages, subjects responded to Form A of the inkblot test. A variety of checks indicated that the subjects could not detect that they had been exposed to a taped message.

The following are representative excerpts from the pregnancy and penetration tapes:

Pregnancy

"Reproduction. The birth of a child. I should become pregnant. Entering my uterus. Entering my womb. I could become pregnant. To be fertilized. Becoming pregnant. The contraceptive failed. To become pregnant. I could become pregnant."

Penetration

"I feel opened up" (repeated five times). "Things are getting through" (repeated four times). "It gets into me" (repeated seven times). "I am opened up" (repeated 12 times). "Things are getting into me" (repeated twice). "I am sensitive" (repeated six times). "I feel things inside of me" (repeated six times).

Again the results of the study supported the idea of a phallic-pregnancy link. The women who received the pregnancy message increased significantly in their phallic scores whereas the women who received the penetration message did not. There was no between group difference in the baseline phallic scores obtained before the playing of the messages.

The results of the two phallic scoring studies establish a relationship between phallic imagery and pregnancy. They do not, however, tell us whether babies themselves have phallic significance for their mothers. Our data did reveal that the amount of phallic imagery does not change as the fetus develops and becomes a potentially more real child in the thoughts of the expectant mother. There was no relationship between the number of weeks a woman had been pregnant and her phallic score. Freud felt that newborn babies do have phallic connotations and he suggested that the phallicizing process would be increased if the newborn baby is a boy. This idea has never been directly tested. However, Freud's (1933/ 1964) suggestion that boy babies are more satisfying than girl babies (because they gratify phallic needs more adequately) is consistent with some of the findings in the literature. For example, research shows that there is a preference for boy babies, that boys are particularly desired as first-born or only children, and that families with two girls are more likely to have additional children than families with two boys (Leifer, 1980; Oakley, 1980; Williamson, 1976a, 1976b). During first pregnancies, women are more likely to dream about boy babies than girl babies (Gillman, 1968), more likely to imagine the baby will resemble their husbands rather than themselves (Leifer, 1980), and more likely to hope that the baby will have the father's personality characteristics in preference to their own (Leifer, 1980). Also, women giving birth to boys tend to be more pleased (Oakley, 1980), less depressed (Breen, 1975), and less irritable (Oakley, 1980) than women giving birth to girls. Breen (1975) reports, too, that mothers have more anger toward newborn female children than they have toward newborn males.

CONCEPTUALIZING THE PENIS–BABY FINDINGS

Finding evidence consistent with a preganancy-phallic imagery link in two studies left us in a bit of quandary. Why did we obtain positive results even though other groups of investigations had not supported either Freud's assertions about female body perceptions or his claims about clitoral–vaginal preferences in women? One possible explanation, that does fit the findings, resides in what is emphasized in considering the etiology of phallic feelings. Are phallic feelings the natural result of the little girl's envy for something not possessed or are they derived from societal and family pressures concerning sex differences? Does the phallus attain significance through literal envy of the male anatomy or as a result of the differential treatment of boys and girls? Although the former explanation emphasizes anatomy and biology, the latter explanation stresses the cultural aspects of phallic feelings. Theorists have differed in their portrayal of phallic feelings as arising primarily from biological or cultural causes. Accordingly, conceptualizations have tended to see feelings of inferiority as a basic result of an anatomical difference or as the derived result of the power and privilege accorded men.

The findings we have presented, showing that women do not generally view their bodies as inferior, seem to collide rather directly with a biological explanation for phallic imagery. The findings do not, however, clash with a possible cultural explanation. It is quite conceivable for a woman to feel that she is being inequitably treated because she does not have a penis even though she does not see herself as having an inferior body. The phallus could, therefore, come to have primary significance as a symbol of power and achievement by association with the status accorded males. Other writers, in noting the possible cultural sources for phallic feelings, have pointed out that such feelings may represent a realistic wish for social equality rather than the literal wish to have a penis (Horney, 1937, 1939; Thompson, 1942, 1943).

Consistent with this cultural explanation is Nathan's (1978, 1981) finding that the status of women within a particular culture is inversely related to the amount of phallic imagery they produce. By examining dreams within a variety of cultures, Nathan was able to demonstrate that the higher the status of women, the less their fantasies were taken up with penis-envy themes (as measured through phallic imagery). Similarly, a few studies of children's preferences for being male or female have indicated that the choice is influenced by the relative status of men and women in the particular society under consideration. For example, Vogt and Albert (1970) found that where the status of females was relatively poor in a society (Mormons), 23% of the girls but none of the boys indicated they would prefer to be of the opposite sex. Conversely, among the Zunis where the status of females is relatively high, 10% of the boys and none of the girls indicated an opposite sex preference. Thomas (1965) also found that the female role was preferred more by "deprived" black children than by either white children or nondeprived blacks. Presumably women had relatively higher social status within deprived black families, where the father was often absent, than they had in the other groups sampled. An analysis of phallic representations throughout history also points to the phallus as a symbol of power and dominance (Vangaard, 1972).

The link between pregnancy and the possible achievement aspects of phallicizing has been hinted at by Deutsch (1945), who stated: "A woman who has never been successfully pregnant is deprived of an important experience—the joy of anticipation, the pride of achievement, the anxious tension and its mastery" [p. 164]. Deutsch felt that pregnancy could offer a woman an unusual opportunity for fantasizing about her own wishes and aspirations. The expectant mother could project onto her own child the ability to attain things that she felt had eluded her.

We do not, of course, mean to imply that there is only one motivation for pregnancy. The literature clearly indicates that there are a variety of potential motives for becoming pregnant (Fisher, 1973; Flapan, 1969; Pohlman, 1969). However, one of the major motivations is bound up with achievement concerns. This motive is the woman's wish to establish her identity and perpetuate it into the future (Fisher, 1973; Flapan, 1969; Pohlman, 1969). It has been noted, too, that the future representation of the self may be one way of compensating for present feelings of inadequacy (Flapan, 1969).

NEW FINDINGS ON PHALLIC IMAGERY

This section presents three studies of phallic imagery that have not appeared elsewhere. All three investigations grew from a consideration of Freud's thoughts about the reproductive process in women. All three produced results consistent with those speculations.

Study I

Because previous work indicated that being pregnant has a potent effect on the production of phallic images (Greenberg & Fisher, 1980), it seemed reasonable to conjecture that a clear sign of *not* being pregnant—as indicated by menstruation—should also produce effects on the phallic imagery of women. Theoretically, the effects of phallic imagery would be dependent on how invested a woman is in establishing a "traditional feminine" identity through the production of a baby. In general it would be expected that the greater the investment in having a baby, the more menstruation would be experienced as a time of disappointment and impotence. A study was, therefore, designed to explore the relationship between the production of phallic imagery during menstruation and delay in becoming pregnant.

Research has indicated that a woman's views about the female sex role is one determinant of how she experiences menstruation and the meaning she attributes to it. Miller and Smith (1975), for example, found that traditionally oriented women are more likely to view menstruation as consistent with and perhaps necessary for their self-concept as wives and mothers. On the other hand, non-traditionally oriented women were found to have less investment in menstruation as an indicator of their identity as women. Similarly, Rossi and Rossi (1977) have shown that the most extreme reactions to menstruation occur in women for whom the maternal role is especially important. Other pertinent evidence is provided by Erickson (1977) who found that women who feel good at the time of ovulation tend to have negative reactions during menstruation; those who feel bad at the time of ovulation react positively to menstruation. Thus, women who respond more positively during a maximally fertile phase are most upset during their nonfertile periods. Presumably, the "conventional" women would be characterized by such a pattern.

The findings reviewed suggest that women who resolve their Oedipal conflicts in the manner suggested by Freud (i.e., desiring a baby) are highly attuned to and reactive to the occurrence or nonoccurrence of menstruation.[2] Menstruation is a direct challenge to the Oedipal solution proposed by Freud and would be most frustrating to women desiring a baby, as it is a clear sign that the wished for pregnancy has not taken place. Perhaps this is one of the reasons that a number of investigators have demonstrated that menstrual complaints are more likely to arise in women with a traditional view of sex roles than in those who see themselves as less stereotypically feminine (Brattesani & Silverthorne, 1978; Chernovetz, Jones, & Hansson, 1979; Douvan & Adelson, 1966; Kehoe, 1977; Olds & Shaver, 1980; Paige, 1973; Schneider & Schneider-Duker, 1974).

As noted earlier, phallic imagery can be interpreted as a kind of reassuring fantasy of achievement and power. Therefore, those women who are the most desirous of gaining a sense of power and achievement through having a baby should be the least likely to produce phallic images during menstruation. In other words, the greater the desire for a baby, the less the probability of phallic fantasies during menstruation. This idea translated into the following experimental hypothesis: The less phallic imagery a woman displays during menstruation, the less time she will delay in becoming pregnant following marriage.

The hypothesis was tested in two independent samples of married women, ages 21–45, with at least a high school education. The samples consisted of 32

---

[2]It is, of course, true that menstruation may have meanings linked with issues other than pregnancy for many women. Among the possibilities, writers have alluded to concerns about bodily damage, pride in being a woman, fear of soiling, and guilt about masturbation fantasies. An extended discussion of this issue can be found in Fisher (1973).

266 GREENBERG AND FISHER

and 22 women, respectively. The women had been originally recruited for a larger project examining sexual attitudes and behaviors (Fisher, 1973). Research assistants were not aware of the present hypothesis at the time the data were collected. As part of the larger project, each woman was asked to indicate the number of months she had been married before she became pregnant for the first time. Subjects from both samples also wrote their responses to the first 25 cards from Form A of the Holtzman Inkblot Test within 1 to 3 days after the onset of menstrual flow. Subjects responded to the first 25 cards of Form B of the Holtzman Inkblot Test during a time when they were not menstruating. For the first sample, this occurred within a few days after the cessation of flow, whereas the second sample responded to Form B approximately 1 week before the start of a menstrual flow.

Each of the 25 responses obtained from a woman during a test session was scored as being phallic or nonphallic according to the phallic imagery criteria (Appendix, p. 281). Table 7.1 presents the correlations between the number of months of marriage before pregnancy and the phallic scores attained during menstrual and intermenstrual times. As predicted, within both samples, the lower a woman's phallic score during menstruation, the shorter the time of delay to become pregnant following marriage. Obviously, the result for the combined sample was also highly significant ($p < .005$). There was no relationship between phallic scores produced during the intermenstrual time periods and delay in becoming pregnant. One of the samples did reveal a relationship with change scores such that the more a woman's phallic score was lowered during menstruation, relative to a week before menstruation began, the sooner the woman became pregnant after marriage.

TABLE 7.1
Correlations Between Number of Months Married Before
Pregnancy and Phallic Scores During Menstrual and
Intermenstrual Times

Time of Test	Sample I N = 32	Sample II N = 22	Combined Sample N = 54
During Menstruation (A)	.380**	.373*	.354***
Intermenstruation (B)	.261	-.008	.170
Change Score (A − B)	-.013	.423**	.144

Note. Significance values are for a one-tailed test in the predicted direction.
*$p < .05$.
**$p < .025$.
***$p < .005$.

Study II

A second study was conducted to examine the relationship between phallic imagery and menstrual regularity. As previously indicated, a variety of projects have demonstrated a positive relationship between having menstrual problems and having a traditional feminine sex role orientation (Brattesani & Silverthorne, 1978; Chernovetz, et al., 1979; Douvan & Adelson, 1966; Olds & Shaver, 1980; Paige, 1973; Schneider & Schneider-Duker, 1974). Of particular interest is a study by Kehoe (1977) who found that menstrual irregularity tended to be associated with a traditional feminine sex role orientation, higher scores on a femininity scale, greater indications of dependency needs, and a lack of confidence. She also found more direct evidence of a link between irregularity and pregnancy desires. Irregular women were less likely than regulars to use adequate means of birth control. Findings such as those described hint that one of the underlying factors in functional irregularity may be the desire to have a baby. Clinicians have also proposed a relationship between irregularity and the desire for pregnancy in certain cases (Deutsch, 1944; Gill, 1943).

If it is true that irregularity is significantly linked to pregnancy desires, then one would expect the functionally irregular woman to feel more down and impotent when she is having a period than when she is not as it is a confirmation that she is not pregnant. Presumably, the women with a less urgent desire for pregnancy (regular menses) would be less reactive to the occurrence or nonoccurrence of menstruation. The following hypothesis was derived from these theoretical speculations:

> Women with irregular menstrual periods will show a greater increase in their phallic scores from menstrual to nonmenstrual phases than will women with regular menstrual periods.

This proposition was tested by comparing the phallic imagery scores of a group of women with regular menses to the scores attained by a group of women with irregular periods. As in study I, all the women had been recruited for a larger project examining sexual attitudes and behaviors. They were all married, between the ages of 21 and 45, and had at least a high school education. Regularity was determined by having each subject rate her degree of menstrual regularity on a 5-point scale where one equalled always being regular and five indicated always being irregular. The regular group ($N=35$) was comprised of all women who rated themselves as one or two on the scale; the irregular group ($N=16$) was composed of all the women with a self-rating of four or five. Subjects from both groups responded to 25 cards from the Holtzman Form A during a time when they were having a period and 25 cards from Form B at a time when they were not menstruating. Responses were scored for the presence of phallic imagery.

The data were first examined to see if regular and irregular women produced different patterns in their phallic imagery scores. Table 7.2 shows the percentage of women in each group who produced more phallic responses during menstruation and the percentage who produced more phallic responses during nonmenstrual times. It also shows the percentage of women who showed no differences under the two conditions. A chi-square analysis of these results revealed, as predicted, that the groups did indeed display different patterns of phallic imagery ($\chi^2(2)=6.91$, $p<.01$). Women who had regular menstrual periods were more likely to display phallic imagery during the menstrual phase of their cycle, whereas women with irregular periods were more likely to display phallic imagery during the nonmenstrual phase.

The data were also looked at in terms of change scores (i.e., a woman's phallic score when not menstruating minus her score when menstruating). The mean change score for the regular group was $-.77$ ($\sigma=3.20$) and the mean change score for the irregular group was 1.5 ($\sigma=3.06$). A comparison of the change scores again revealed, as expected, that the irregulars tended to increase their phallic scores in moving from the menstrual to nonmenstrual phase whereas regulars tended to move in the opposite direction, $t(49)=2.42$, $p<.02$.

To determine if the source of the difference could be specified more precisely, the data were subjected to a 2 × 2 analysis of variance for repeated measures. The mean phallic scores attained by the two groups under the two different conditions are presented in Table 7.3. The analysis revealed the anticipated significant interaction between menstrual regularity and time of testing (during menstruation versus other time), $F(1, 49)=5.37$, $p<.05$. There were no significant main effects for either the regularity variable or the time of testing variable by themselves. Post hoc comparisons by means of the Duncan's Multiple Range Test showed that the irregulars produced significantly more phallic imagery than regulars during the nonmenstrual phase of the cycle ($p<.05$). This analysis also showed the trend for irregulars to increase the amount of phallic imagery in

TABLE 7.2
Pattern of Phallic Imagery in Women with Regular
and Irregular Menstrual Cycles

Type of Cycle	Percentage With Higher Phallic Scores		Percentage With Equal Phallic Scores
	Menstrual Phase	*Intermenstrual Phase*	*Both Phases*
Regular	60	34	6
Irregular	25	50	25

TABLE 7.3
Mean Phallic Scores Attained During Menstrual Phases
by Women with Regular and Irregular Menses

Type of Cycle	Menstrual Phase	Intermenstrual Phase
Regular	5.54	4.83
Irregular	5.06	6.56

moving from the menstrual to the nonmenstrual phase ($p<.08$). The regulars produced phallic imagery at approximately the same mean level during the menstrual and nonmenstrual phases.

Overall, the analyses seem to indicate that irregular women shift to higher levels of phallic imagery when they are not menstruating. Furthermore, they produce a level of imagery when not menstruating significantly higher than that produced by regular women. Women with regular periods do not show much change in the amount of phallic imagery as a function of their menstrual periods. However, in contrast to women with irregular menses, their predominant pattern indicates a tendency to produce a bit more phallic imagery during menstruation.

Study III

As proposed by Freud, having a baby is the most "normal" solution to the Oedipal problem. Furthermore, those who arrive at this solution are thought to put aside their phallic sexuality and abandon clitoral eroticism. For Freud, one manifestation of making the shift from clitoral to vaginal dominance is the female's relinquishing masturbation (the manipulation of her phallic organ, the clitoris) in favor of childbearing. Theoretically, the more a woman accepts Freud's solution (penis–baby), the less she will masturbate. Conversely, the less the woman satisfies her needs for achievement and power through a pregnancy solution, the more prone she will be to masturbate. For purposes of investigation, we decided to try to identify two groups of women: a group that accepted Freud's penis–baby solution and a group that did not accept it as a means for satisfying phallic needs. If Freud was correct, those who accept the solution should have less of a desire to masturbate, whereas those who reject the solution should have a greater desire to masturbate.

Using Freud's theory, acceptors were defined as those women who produce the most phallic imagery during pregnancy. Rejectors were defined as those who produce the most phallic imagery during menstruation (i.e., a confirmed nonpregnancy).

This chain of reasoning led to the following hypotheses:

1. There is a negative relationship between the frequency of masturbation and the production of phallic imagery during pregnancy.
2. There is a positive relationship between the frequency of masturbation and the production of phallic imagery during menstruation.
3. There is a significant difference between the obtained correlations in the appropriate direction (i.e., the relationship being negative during pregnancy and positive during menstruation).

As in the previous phallic studies, the hypotheses were tested with the use of data secured as part of a large investigation of sexual attitudes and behaviors (Fisher, 1973).

To test hypothesis I, the Holtzman Inkblot responses of 39 married, pregnant women (mean age approximately 24 years) were scored for phallic imagery. Phallic scores were then correlated with the subjects' ratings on a 5-point scale of how frequently they masturbate (1=never, 5=great frequency). The resulting correlation ($r = -.22$) was in the predicted direction but did not reach a statistically significant level. Therefore, hypothesis I could not be confirmed.

To test hypothesis II, the Holtzman Inkblot responses of 80 married women (mean age approximately 26 years) were scored for phallic imagery. All the women were menstruating at the time they responded to the inkblots. Again phallic scores were correlated with self-ratings on the frequency of masturbation scale. The attained correlation ($r = .31$) was in the predicted direction and was highly statistically significant ($p < .005$, one-tailed test). Thus, hypothesis II was confirmed.

A comparison of the difference between the two obtained correlations constituted the test of hypothesis III. As predicted, the two correlations were in the appropriate opposite directions. A test of the difference proved to be statistically significant ($p < .005$, one-tailed test). Hypothesis III was therefore, supported.

Overall, these findings did show modest support for Freud's ideas. The more a woman produced phallic imagery during menstruation (rejects the penis–baby solution), the more likely she was to masturbate. Women who produced the most phallic imagery during pregnancy (acceptors of the penis–baby solution) showed the predicted trend toward less masturbation, although the trend did not reach significance. A comparison of the correlations revealed that masturbation was differentially associated with phallic imagery. The direction of the relationship depended on when the imagery was measured. Producing phallic responses during menstruation was positively associated with self reports of masturbation, whereas the production of such responses during pregnancy was not.

A few comments about these results are in order. First, it is somewhat surprising that the findings showed even modest support for Freud's propositions, because all the women tested were married and therefore could be viewed as relatively traditional in orientation. Consistent with the idea that most of the tested women were traditional is the rather low reported frequency of masturbation in these groups (both groups had mean ratings of less than 2 on the 5-point scale). In short, the nature of the samples probably worked against the finding of significant differences. It is possible that stronger findings could be obtained by testing groups more heterogeneous in their masturbatory behavior and in their acceptance of the traditional female sex role. It is quite striking that two out of the three hypotheses were supported in view of the particular groups examined.

Comment should also be made about Freud's supposition that masturbation is an indication that a female has a preference for clitoral as opposed to vaginal stimulation. Fisher's (1973) investigation of a number of samples of women found no consistent relationship between masturbatory activity and clitoral preferences. Freud's assumption was not supported. One could then ask, if we drop the notion that masturbation is related to a clitoral orientation, how are we to understand the obtained relationships between phallic imagery and masturbation? We think the answer may lie in an understanding of what masturbatory behavior means to a woman. On the basis of a series of empirical findings, Fisher (1973) pointed out that masturbation seems to be one way a woman has of asserting her independence; it can be seen as a declaration of self-sufficiency. Although women who masturbate frequently have not been found deficient in their ability to engage in or enjoy orthodox sexual intercourse, masturbation provides these women with a recurrent opportunity to reassure themselves that they can attain gratification on their own. They retain the option of not relying on another person to meet their needs. In a sense, therefore, women who masturbate can be seen as rejecting a penis–baby equation. They are less likely to feel they have to receive something from a man to meet their needs. Such an explanation fits the fact that women who masturbate produce more phallic imagery during menstruation than women who do not masturbate. We speculate that masturbating women are less likely than nonmasturbators to experience menstruation as a time of disappointment in not receiving something from someone else.

OVERVIEW AND COMMENT

This chapter has reviewed the experimental evidence pertinent to a number of aspects of Freud's theories on the psychology of the reproductive process in women. These theories grew from Freud's discussion of how Oedipal conflicts are resolved by females. As it turns out, research supports some aspects of Freud's models and contradicts others. This pattern, of confirmation and contradiction, is exactly what we discovered in examining the evidence bearing on other areas of Freud's thought (Fisher & Greenberg, 1977). It highlights our contention that psychoanalytic theory is composed of a series of ideas that have differing degrees of validity. The Freudian schema cannot be accepted or rejected as a single package. Freud apparently was right about some things and wrong about others.

In opposition to Freud's reproductive model, there is a convincing array of evidence indicating that the average woman does not perceive her body as deficient or defective. In fact, research suggests that the average woman feels more secure about her body than the average man does about his. She does not see her body in the depreciated way described by Freud.

Also at variance with Freud's proclamations are the findings regarding preferences for clitoral versus vaginal stimulation. Freud emphasized that a preference for vaginal stimulation was a sign of psychological maturity and an indication of the acceptance of the female sex role. In fact, at times he seems to have defined psychological maturity for women in terms of the acceptance of a traditional female sex role. Furthermore, Freud used masturbation as an index of having a clitoral preference.

There are a number of ways in which the proposed clitoral–vaginal distinction fails to be supported. First, the studies we reviewed showed, in a variety of ways, that the clitorally oriented woman is more psychologically comfortable than the vaginally oriented woman. This is a direct contradiction of Freud's hypothesis. Second, despite repeated tests (Fisher, 1973), no association has been found between preference for vaginal stimulation and scoring high on measures of traditional femininity. Third, according to the available evidence, how frequently a woman masturbates is not related to her having a clitoral orientation. There are problems, too, with an assumption that the adoption of a traditional feminine sex role is psychologically beneficial and "mature" for women. Although it is conceivable that such a proposition may have been supportable at the time that Freud hinted at this possiblity, recent research shows a pattern that runs counter to this idea. For example, Jones, Chernovetz, and Hansson (1978) used an assortment of methods to examine the relationship between the characteristics associated with traditional masculinity or femininity and measures of adjustment. They concluded that the more a female possessed characteristics associated with the conventional *male* role, the more adaptive, competent, and secure she was. Opposite sex-typed females also proved to be less shy, more popular with men, and more heterosexually involved than feminine females. Moreover, when given the chance to indicate a desire to change their characteristics, feminine females seemed to be the most unhappy with themselves. They expressed the greatest desire to change, whereas masculine females expressed the least desire to change; those with mixed characteristics (androgynous) fell between the other groups in their desire to change. Basically, feminine females expressed a wish to attain traits that have been traditionally associated with the male role. Similarly, Olds and Shaver (1980) concluded that, in general, masculinity encompasses a more beneficial cluster of traits for *both* males and females than femininity does. A constellation of masculine characteristics was related in both sexes to fewer conflicts about achievement and fewer physical symptoms. Masculinity was positively associated in men and women with measures of work and mastery. On the other hand, femininity seemed to be a detrimental cluster of traits in both sexes for academic performance and health. Benson (1981) also found indications that the possession of masculine personality traits bodes well for a woman's psychological adjustment. In her study, the more a woman attributed socially desirable masculine characteristics to herself, the less likely she was to engage in self-punitive behavior.

Additional studies have also found high feminine identification to be associated with poorer adjustment, higher levels of anxiety, and greater discomfort (Gray, 1957; Heilbrun, 1962, 1968a, 1968b; Heilbrun & Fromme, 1965; Helper, 1955; Rosenberg, Sutton-Smith, & Morgan, 1961; Webb, 1963). Thus, there are repeated indications that any association of psychological maturity with the female's acceptance of a passive receptive role may not be valid today.

To be fair, we should note that there are limitations in the available data linking maladjustment with femininity. For example, much of the femininity-maladjustment research may be distorted by feminine subjects being less defensive about admitting weakness and emotional upset. This possibility is suggested by Douvan and Adelson's (1966) conclusion, based on a large research project, that high-feminine girls have a heightened awareness of anxiety and internal discomfort and a greater sensitivity to their own feelings. A comparable idea is hinted at by the finding that women are more likely than men to admit to certain unpleasurable sensations and feelings (Hammen & Padesky, 1977; Phillips & Segal, 1969). Independent of the level of symptomatology, women also exceed men in their willingness to seek treatment for emotional and physical problems (Fisher & Greenberg, 1979; Gove & Tudor, 1973). Furthermore, women with a traditional sex role orientation seem more open than "liberated" women to revealing physical illness problems and seeking treatment from a physician (Greenberg & Fisher, 1977; Zeldow & Greenberg, 1980).

Much of the work linking maladjustment with femininity has used college students as subjects. It is quite possible, therefore, that the results merely indicate that women with stereotypically feminine characteristics have a more difficult time adjusting to academic or professional settings where a high value is placed on competition and achievement. It could well turn out that traditionally feminine characteristics are *more* adaptive than masculine characteristics in other types of settings. For instance, Freud's writing implies that women with a traditional feminine orientation might have an easier time adjusting to motherhood than those with a more masculine orientation. Early indications suggest, however, that even this hypothesis is questionable. Breen (1975), in a study of 50 first pregnancies, concluded that the most feminine women in her sample encountered the most problems with childbearing. She felt that adjustment to motherhood was easiest for the women who were most differentiated, less "enslaved" by the experience, and most open to looking at themselves. The best adjusted, from Breen's perspective, seemed to be those who did not aspire to be the "selfless mother" and did not experience themselves as the passive cultural stereotype of femininity. By contrast, Rossi (1965) found that traditionally feminine college graduates had high self-esteem during early motherhood, whereas achievement-oriented young women appeared more plagued by feelings of low self-esteem and doubts during their twenties and early thirties. However, Rossi predicted that the family-oriented woman would experience greater depression and a lower sense of self-esteem than the professional woman 10 to 15 years later when confronting the problems of personal identity. This prediction was subsequently supported by Birnbaum's (1975) study of intellectually gifted homemakers and professional career women in their mid-thirties and early forties. Self-esteem was lowest in the traditional homemakers. This group also exhibited the lower sense of personal competence even with regard to social skills and child care.

Integrating the numerous studies, along with their limitations, leads us to conclude that statements linking traditional femininity with adjustment in women are too general. Feminine characteristics clearly appear to be a handicap in certain achievement situations. Whether they are more adaptive in other contexts, as Freud intimated, remains open to question. We should add that Freud was more circumspect in struggling with the issues of femininity than many writers seem to realize. He was aware that there are problems in equating activity with masculinity and passivity with femininity (Freud, 1933/1964). He pointed out that there are many areas in which femininity is associated with significant activity, one of these areas being child rearing. In general, Freud (1933/1964) concluded that the further you move from the narrow sphere of sexual behavior, the less appropriate it is to equate activity with masculinity.

Our presentation shows that some parts of Freud's reproductive theories have received empirical backing. There are studies linking attitudes toward the genitals with the acceptance or nonacceptance of a traditional female sex role. These investigations suggest, too, that some women are more preoccupied with "penis-envy" themes than are others. The preoccupations seem associated with the predicted feelings of inadequacy, depression, hostility, and the need to achieve.

We have described a series of studies demonstrating that Freud's ideas lead to accurate hypotheses about the relationship among phallic imagery, pregnancy, and menstruation. Specifically, in agreement with Freud's speculation that pregnancy has phallic connotations for women, phallic imagery was elevated during the pregnant state and during exposure to a message about becoming pregnant. A vivid sign of not being pregnant—menstruation—also produced effects on phallic imagery in line with derivations from Freud's statements. Women with irregular menses shifted to higher levels of phallic imagery when not menstruating, whereas women with regular menstrual periods tended to display the opposite pattern. Furthermore, in a manner consistent with Freud's ideas, the amount of delay in becoming pregnant following marriage was significantly related to the level of phallic imagery produced during a woman's menstrual period. In two samples, we found that the less phallic imagery a woman displayed during menstruation, the sooner she became pregnant following marriage. Moderate support was also demonstrated for Freud's theory of a relationship between phallic concerns and masturbation in women. During menstruation, phallic imagery was more apt to be produced by women who masturbate. Women who masturbate were also more likely to produce phallic imagery during menstruation than during pregnancy.

To explain the phallic findings, we have emphasized the probable cultural foundations for phallic imagery in women. On the basis of the evidence to date, it appears that the phallus gains primary symbolic significance through its association with the power and status accorded males. Thus, phallic imagery can be interpreted as a sign that an individual is having achievement and power fantasies.[3]

As a result of the research, we have become sensitized to the fact that all persons have degrees of phallic concerns and needs. However, the needs are met in different ways by different individuals. Whereas babies may help to meet these needs for some women, different solutions seem to be chosen by others. Unlike Freud, we do not consider it appropriate at this point to advocate one method of meeting phallic needs over another. A statement that one way of meeting such needs is good and another is bad comes down to a debate about values and, as such, lies outside the domain of this chapter. It is readily apparent, though, that society continually offers distinct pressures concerning the acceptable ways for women and men to meet their phallic requirements. We do, by the way, feel that phallic needs are a real part of the psychological dynamics of men and efforts are underway to collect data bearing on this topic. Interestingly, Nathan (1978), on the basis of her results, has argued that penis envy may be

---

[3]Incidentally, there is little basis for speculating that the production of phallic imagery is heavily influenced by social desirability or a woman's willingness to reveal embarrassing material. Analyses have shown that phallic scores obtained from subjects have had negligible overt sexual or human body part content. The scores have generally been dependent on phallic symbolic representations (Greenberg & Fisher, 1980). Furthermore, phallic scores have been both positively and negatively associated with self-reports of sexual behavior. The frequency of masturbation was positively related to phallic scores obtained during menstruation and negatively related to phallic scores obtained during pregnancy.

even more of a problem for men than it is for women. Men scored higher than women on her measures of penis concern in dreams.

Freud (1925/1961) commented on his reproductive theories:

> I am inclined to set some value on the considerations I have brought forward upon the psychical consequences of the anatomical distinction between the sexes. I am aware, however, that this opinion can only be maintained if my findings, which are based on a handful of cases, turn out to have general validity and to be typical. If not, they would remain no more than a contribution to our knowledge of the different paths along which the sexual life develops [p. 258].[4]

Above all, our research supports Freud's suspicion that the phallus assumes an important symbolic role in the psychological economy of women. Feelings about power, achievement, and sex role do seem to be played out through a woman's experience of the reproductive process. And, these feelings can apparently be monitored by the measurement of phallic imagery during important reproductive events, such as pregnancy and menstruation. Although the issues are controversial, we have been struck, like Freud, by the myriad emotions and conflicts that are condensed into a reaction to a part of the male anatomy.

REFERENCES

Benson, B. A. Personality correlates of self-punitive behavior. *Journal of Abnormal Psychology,* 1981, *90,* 183–185.

Bevan, W. Subliminal stimulation: A pervasive problem for psychology. *Psychological Bulletin,* 1964, *61,* 81–89.

Birnbaum, J. Life patterns and self-esteem in gifted family oriented and career committed women. In M. Mednick, S. Tangri, & L. Hoffman (Eds.), *Women and achievement.* New York: Wiley, 1975.

Blum, G. S. A study of the psychoanalytic theory of psychosexual development. *Genetic Psychology Monographs,* 1949, *39,* 3–99.

Bombard, J. A. *An experimental examination of penis envy.* Unpublished doctoral dissertation, Wayne State University, 1969.

Brattesani, K., & Silverthorne, C. P. Social psychological factors of menstrual distress. *Journal of Social Psychology,* 1978, *106,* 139–140.

---

[4]Even toward the end of his career, Freud continued to espouse a moderate position about the meaning of femininity. In 1933 he stated:

> That is all I had to say to you about femininity. It is certainly incomplete and fragmentary and does not always sound friendly. But do not forget that I have only been describing women in so far as their nature is determined by their sexual function. It is true that the influence extends very far; but we do not overlook the fact that an individual woman may be a human being in other respects as well. If you want to know more about femininity, enquire from your own experiences of life, or turn to the poets, or wait until science can give you deeper and more coherent information [p. 135].

Breen, D. *The birth of a first child*. London: Tavistock, 1975.

Cameron, P. Confirmation of the Freudian psychosexual stages utilizing sexual symbolism. *Psychological Reports*, 1967, *21*, 33–39.

Chernovetz, M. E., Jones, W. H., & Hansson, R. O. Predictability, attentional focus, sex role orientation, and menstrual-related stress. *Psychosomatic Medicine*, 1979, *41*, 383–391.

Cohen, C. P. *Reactions to perceived somatic vulnerability*. Unpublished doctoral dissertation, University of Kansas, 1963.

Conn, J. H. Children's reactions to the discovery of genital differences. *American Journal of Orthopsychiatry*, 1940, *10*, 747–754.

Deutsch, H. *Psychology of women* (2 vols.). New York: Grune & Stratton, 1944–1945.

Douvan, E., & Adelson, J. *The adolescent experience*. New York: Wiley, 1966.

Ellman, C. S. *An experimental study of the female castration complex*. Unpublished doctoral dissertation. New York University, 1970.

Erickson, B. E. D. *An examination of sexual behavior and of differences among women in patterns of emotional, cognitive, and physical change during the menstrual cycle*. Unpublished doctoral dissertation, University of North Carolina at Chapel Hill, 1977.

Erikson, E. H. Sex differences in the play configurations of pre-adolescents. *American Journal of Orthopsychiatry*, 1951, *21*, 667–692.

Fast, G. J., & Fisher, S. The role of body attitudes and acquiescence in epinephrine and placebo effects. *Psychosomatic Medicine*, 1971, *33*, 63–84.

Fisher, S. *Body experience in fantasy and behavior*. New York: Appleton-Century-Crofts, 1970.

Fisher, S. Boundary effects of persistent inputs and messages. *Journal of Abnormal Psychology*, 1971, *77*, 290–295.

Fisher, S. *The female orgasm*. New York: Basic Books, 1973.

Fisher, S. Effects of messages reported to be out of awareness upon the body boundary. *Journal of Nervous and Mental Disease*, 1975, *161*, 90–99.

Fisher, S. Conditions affecting boundary response to messages out of awareness. *Journal of Nervous and Mental Disease*, 1976, *162*, 313–322.

Fisher, S. Personality correlates of sexual behavior in black women. *Archives of Sexual Behavior*, 1980, *9*, 27–35.

Fisher, S., & Greenberg, R. P. *The scientific credibility of Freud's theories and therapy*. New York: Basic Books, 1977.

Fisher, S., & Greenberg, R. P. Masculinity-femininity and response to somatic discomfort. *Sex Roles*, 1979, *5*, 483–493.

Flapan, M. A paradigm for the analysis of childbearing motivations of married women prior to birth of the first child. *American Journal of Orthopsychiatry*, 1969, *39*, 402–417.

Franck, K., & Rosen, E. A projective test of masculinity-femininity. *Journal of Consulting Psychology*, 1949, *13*, 247–256.

Freud, S. [The interpretation of dreams]. In J. Strachey (Ed. and trans.), *The standard edition of the complete psychological works of Sigmund Freud* (Vol. 5). London: Hogarth, 1953. (Originally published, 1900.)

Freud, S. [The dissolution of the Oedipus complex]. In J. Strachey (Ed. and trans.), *The standard edition of the complete psychological works of Sigmund Freud* (Vol. 19). London: Hogarth, 1961. (Originally published, 1924.)

Freud, S. [Some psychical consequences of the anatomical distinction between the sexes]. In J. Strachey (Ed. and trans.), *The standard edition of the complete psychological works of Sigmund Freud* (Vol. 19). London: Hogarth, 1961. (Originally published, 1925.)

Freud, S. [Female sexuality]. In J. Strachey (Ed. and trans.), *The standard edition of the complete psychological works of Sigmund Freud* (Vol. 21). London: Hogarth, 1961. (Originally published, 1931.)

Freud, S. [Femininity]. In J. Strachey (Ed. and trans.), *The standard edition of the complete psychological works of Sigmund Freud* (Vol. 22). London: Hogarth, 1964. (Originally published, 1933.)

Friedman, S. M. An empirical study of the castration and oedipal complexes. *Genetic Psychology Monographs*, 1952, *46*, 61–130.

Gill, M. Functional disturbance of menstruation. *Bulletin of the Menninger Clinic*, 1943, *7*, 6–14.

Gillman, R. D. The dreams of pregnant women and maternal adaptation. *American Journal of Orthopsychiatry*, 1968, *38*, 688–692.

Ginsparg, S. L. *Post-partum psychosis*. Unpublished doctoral dissertation, Washington University, 1956.

Gleser, G. C., Gottschalk, L. A., & Springer, K. J. An anxiety measure applicable to verbal samples. *Archives of General Psychiatry*, 1961, *5*, 593–605.

Goldberg, P. A., & Milstein, J. T. Perceptual investigation of psychoanalytic theory concerning latent homosexuality in women. *Perceptual and Motor Skills*, 1965, *21*, 645–646.

Gove, W., & Tudor, J. Adult sex roles and mental illness. *American Journal of Sociology*, 1973, *78*, 812–835.

Gray, S. W. Masculinity-femininity in relation to anxiety and social acceptance. *Child Development*, 1957, *28*, 203–214.

Greenberg, R. P., & Fisher S. The relationship between willingness to adopt the sick role and attitudes toward women. *Journal of Chronic Diseases*, 1977, *30*, 29–37.

Greenberg, R. P., & Fisher, S. Freud's penis-baby equation: Exploratory tests of a controversial theory. *British Journal of Medical Psychology*, 1980, *53*, 333–342.

Halls, C. S., & Van de Castle, R. L. An empirical investigation of the castration complex in dreams. *Journal of Personality*, 1965, *33*, 20–29.

Hammen, C. L., & Padesky, C. A. Sex differences in the expression of depressive responses on the Beck Depression Inventory. *Journal of Abnormal Psychology*, 1977, *86*, 609–614.

Heilbrun, A. B., Jr. Parent identification and college adjustment. *Psychological Reports*, 1962, *10*, 853–854.

Heilbrun, A. B., Jr. Sex-role identity in adolescent females. A theoretical paradox. *Adolescence*, 1968, *3*, 79–88. (a)

Heilbrun, A. B., Jr. Sex role, instrumental-expressive behavior and psychopathology in females. *Journal of Abnormal Psychology*, 1968, *73*, 131–136. (b)

Heilbrun, A. B., Jr., & Fromme, D. K. Parental identification of late adolescents and level of adjustment: The importance of parent-model attributes, ordinal position, and sex of the child. *Journal of Genetic Psychology*, 1965, *107*, 49–59.

Helper, M. M. Learning theory and the self-concept. *Journal of Abnormal and Social Psychology*, 1955, *51*, 184–194.

Holtzman, W. H., Thorpe, J. S., Swartz, J. D., & Herron, E. W. *Inkblot perception and personality*. Austin: University of Texas Press, 1961.

Horney, K. *The neurotic personality of our times*. New York: Norton, 1937.

Horney, K. Feminine psychology. In K. Horney (Ed.), *New Ways in Psychoanalysis*. New York: Norton, 1939.

Johnson, G. B. Penis-envy? Or pencil-needing? *Psychological Reports*, 1966, *19*, 758.

Jones, A. Sexual symbolism and the variables of sex and personality integration. *Journal of Abnormal and Social Psychology*, 1956, *53*, 187–190.

Jones, W., Chernovetz, M. E., & Hansson, R. O. The enigma of androgyny: Differential implications for males and females? *Journal of Consulting and Clinical Psychology*, 1978, *46*, 298–313.

Katcher, A. The discrimination of sex differences by young children. *Journal of Genetic Psychology*, 1955, *87*, 131–143.

Kaye, H. E., Berl, S., Clare, J., Eleston, M. R., Gershwin, B. S., Gershwin, P., Kogan, L. S.,

Torda, C. & Wilburn, C. B. Homosexuality in women. *Archives of General Psychiatry*, 1967, *17*, 626–634.

Kehoe, P. *Psychological factors in the experience of premenstrual and menstrual symptomatology.* Unpublished doctoral dissertation, University of Texas, Austin, 1977.

Kinsey, A. C., Pomeroy, W., Martin C., & Gebhard, P. *Sexual behavior in the human female.* Philadelphia: Saunders, 1953.

Klein, G. S., & Holt, R. R. Problems and issues in current studies of subliminal stimulation. In J. G. Peatman & E. L. Hartley (Eds.), *Festschrift for Gardner Murphy*. New York: Harper & Row, 1960.

Korchin, S. J., & Heath, H. A. Somatic experience in the anxiety state: Some sex and personality correlates of "automatic feedback." *Journal of Consulting Psychology*, 1961, *25*, 398–404.

Landy, E. E. Sex differences in some aspects of smoking behavior. *Psychological Reports*, 1967, *20*, 575–580.

Lane, R. W. *The effect of preoperative stress on dreams.* Unpublished doctoral dissertation, University of Oregon, 1966.

Lansky, L. M., Crandall, V. J., Kagan, J., & Baker, C. T. Sex differences in aggression and its correlates in middle-class adolescents. *Child Development*, 1961, *32*, 45–58.

Latorre, R. A. Psychological correlates of preferences for clitoral or vaginal stimulation. *American Journal of Psychiatry*, 1979, *136*, 225–226.

Leifer, M. *Psychological effects of motherhood: A study of first pregnancy.* New York: Praeger Pub., 1980.

Lessler, K. Cultural and Freudian dimensions of sexual symbols. *Journal of Consulting Psychology*, 1964, *28*, 46–53.

Levin, R. B. An empirical test of the female castration complex. *Journal of Abnormal Psychology*, 1966, *71*, 181–188.

Levy, D. M. Control-situation studies of children's responses to the differences in genitalia. *American Journal of Orthopsychiatry*, 1940, *10*, 755–762.

Masters, W. H., & Johnson, V. E. *Human sexual response.* Boston: Little, Brown, 1966.

Miller, W. B., & Smith, P. J. Elimination of the menses: Psychosocial aspects. *Journal of Psychiatric Research*, 1975, *12*, 153–166.

Nathan, S. G. *Penis envy in cross-cultural perspective.* Unpublished doctoral dissertation, New York University, 1978.

Nathan, S. G. Cross cultural perspectives on penis envy. *Psychiatry*, 1981, *44*, 39–44.

Oakley, A. *Women confined: Towards a sociology of childbirth.* New York: Schocken Books, 1980.

Olds, D. E., & Shaver, P. Masculinity, femininity, academic performance, and health: Further evidence concerning the androgyny controversy. *Journal of Personality*, 1980, *48*, 323–341.

Paige, K. E. Women learn to sing the menstrual blues. In *The female experience*. Del Mar, Calif.: Communications Research Instruments Inc., 1973.

Phillips, D. L., & Segal, B. E. Sexual status and psychiatric symptoms. *American Sociological Review*, 1969, *34*, 58–72.

Pitcher, E. G., & Prelinger, E.,*Children tell stories—An analysis of fantasy.* New York: International Universities Press, 1963.

Pohlman, E. *The psychology of birth planning.* Cambridge, Mass.: Schenkman Pub., 1969.

Rosenberg, B. G., Sutton-Smith, B., & Morgan, E. The use of opposite sex scales as a measure of psychosexual deviancy. *Journal of Consulting Psychology*, 1961, *25*, 221–225.

Rossi, A. Barriers to the career choice of engineering, medicine or science among American women. In J. A. Mattfield & C. G. Van Aken (Eds.), *Women and the scientific professions*. Cambridge, Mass.: MIT Press, 1965.

Rossi, A. S., & Rossi, P. E. Body time and social time: Mood patterns by menstrual cycle phase and day of the week. *Social Science Research*, 1977, *6*, 273–308.

Schneider, J., & Schneider-Duker, M. Conservative attitudes and reactions to menstruation. *Psychological Reports*, 1974, *35*, 1304.

Schneider, S. C. *Analysis of presurgical anxiety in boys and girls*. Unpublished doctoral dissertation, University of Michigan, 1960.

Secord, P. F. Objectification of word-association procedures by the use of homonyms: A measure of body cathexis. *Journal of Personality*, 1953, *21*, 479–495.

Shevrin, H., Smith, W. H., & Fritzler, D. E. Repressiveness as a factor in the subliminal activation of brain and verbal responses. *Journal of Nervous and Mental Disease*, 1969, *149*, 261–269.

Silverman, L. H. A study of the effects of subliminally presented aggressive stimuli on the production of pathological thinking in a non-psychiatric population. *Journal of Nervous and Mental Disease*, 1966, *141*, 443–455.

Silverman, L. H. Psychoanalytic theory: 'The reports of my death are greatly exaggerated.' *American Psychologist*, 1976, *31*, 621–637.

Silverman, L. H., & Candell, P. On the relationship between aggressive activation, symbiotic merging, intactness of body boundaries, and manifest pathology in schizophrenics. *Journal of Nervous and Mental Disease*, 1970, *150*, 387–399.

Stennett, R. G., & Thurlow, M. Cultural symbolism: The age variable. *Journal of Consulting Psychology*, 1958, *22*, 496.

Thomas, P. J. *Sub-cultural differences in sex-role preference patterns*. Unpublished doctoral dissertation, Western Reserve University, 1965.

Thompson, C. Cultural pressures in the psychology of women. *Psychiatry*, 1942, *5*, 331–339.

Thompson, C. 'Penis envy' in women. *Psychiatry*, 1943, *6*, 123–135.

Tolor, A., & Digrazia, P. V. The body image of pregnant women as reflected in their human figure drawings. *Journal of Clinical Psychology*, 1977, *33*, 566–571.

Vangaard, T. *Phallos: A symbol and its history in the male world*. New York: International Universities Press, 1972.

Van Lennep, D. J. Projection and personality. In H. P. David & E. Von Bracken (Eds.), *Perspectives in personality theory*. New York: Basic Books, 1957. pp. 259–277.

Vogt, E. Z., & Albert, E. M. (Eds.), *People of Rimrock: A study of values in five cultures*. New York: Atheneum, 1970.

Webb, A. P. Sex-role preferences and adjustment in early adolescents. *Child Development*, 1963, *34*, 609–618.

Williamson, N. E. Sex preferences, sex control and the status of women. *Signs: Journal of Women in Culture and Society*, 1976, *1*, 847–862. (a)

Williamson, N. E. *Sons or daughters: A cross cultural survey of parental preferences*. Beverly Hills, Calif.: Sage, 1976. (b)

Winter, W. D., & Prescott, J. W. A cross-validation of Storer's test of cultural symbolism. *Journal of Consulting Psychology*, 1957, *21*, 22.

Zeldow, P. B., & Greenberg, R. P. Who goes where: Sex-role differences in psychological and medical help seeking. *Journal of Personality Assessment*, 1980, *44*, 433–435.

Zilboorg, G. Malignant psychoses related to childbirth. *American Journal of Obstetrics and Gynaecology*, 1928, *15*, 145–158. (a)

Zilboorg, G. The dynamics of schizophrenic reactions related to pregnancy and childbirth. *American Journal of Psychiatry*, 1928, *8*, 733–767. (b)

APPENDIX

Phallic Scoring.   A response was scored as exhibiting phallic imagery if it met any of the following criteria:

1. All elongated objects like arrow, spear, gun, umbrella, cane, knife, pole, cigar or cigarette or pipe, rod, candle, chimney stack, weather vane, masts, ship, tank, rocket, airplane, automobile, missile, motorboat, ski, flute.

2. All *explicit* references to human body protrusions: for example, nose, chin, tongue sticking out, penis, ponytail, extended legs or arms, fingers, but not hands.

3. All explicit references to body attachments with phallic connotations: for example, helmet with horns, artificial nose, spurs, cigarette or cigar or pipe in mouth, snorkel, blowpipe, peashooter, musical instruments in phallic shape.

4. All explicit references to protrusion in insects and animals and plants: for example, horns, antennae, claws, trunk, tail, tentacles, 'long' neck, pointed ears, projection, thumb, finger, branch, top of Christmas tree.

5. Geographical formations with phallic shape: for example, mountain peak, stalagmite, pointed rock.

6. References to "projection" motion or spatial contexts like sticking out, shooting out, sticking up, protruding, towering, soaring, taller than, bigger than, longer than, pointing, shooting.

Name Index

Subject Index